ALTERNATIVE EDUCATION

MARIO D. FANTINI, one of the nation's best-known educational reformers, is a leading spokesman for increasing educational options
for students, parents, and teachers within our public schools. Presently Professor and Dean of Education at the State University of
New York at New Paltz, he was architect of the controversial
school decentralization plan for New York City. As a Ford Foundation officer, Dr. Fantini helped initiate some of the most innovative programs now being implemented throughout the country. He
is an active speaker, author and co-author of many books.

Books by Mario D. Fantini

COMMUNITY CONTROL AND THE URBAN SCHOOL (with Marilyn Gittell
and Richard Magat)

TOWARD HUMANISTIC EDUCATION (with Gerald Weinstein)

DECENTRALIZATION: ACHIEVING REFORM (with Marilyn Gittell)

DISADVANTAGED: CHALLENGE TO EDUCATION (with Gerald Weinstein)

MAKING URBAN SCHOOLS WORK: SOCIAL REALITIES AND THE URBAN
SCHOOL (with Gerald Weinstein)

PUBLIC SCHOOLS OF CHOICE: A PLAN FOR THE REFORM OF AMERICAN
EDUCATION

WHAT'S BEST FOR THE CHILDREN? RESOLVING THE POWER STRUGGLE
BETWEEN PARENTS AND TEACHERS

DESIGNING EDUCATION FOR TOMORROW'S CITIES (with M. A. Young)

ALTERNATIVE EDUCATION: A Source Book for Parents, Teachers, Students, and Administrators

EDITED BY MARIO D. FANTINI

Anchor Books
Doubleday & Company, Inc.
Garden City, New York
1976

Anchor Books Edition: 1976

Library of Congress Cataloging in Publication Data
Main entry under title:

Alternative education.

   Bibliography.
   Includes index.
   1. Educational innovations—United States.
2. Education—United States—1965–
I. Fantini, Mario D.
LA230.A57   371.3
ISBN 0-385-06389-X
Library of Congress Catalog Card Number 73-13104

Acknowledgments

The compilation of a diverse set of papers into an edited manuscript is seldom the work of any one person. That this book has reached final publication is a tribute to the efforts of many thoughtful persons, especially Myra Klahr, Mary Ellen Travis, John Pearce, Sally Abbott, and Loretta Barrett. Further, as editor, I owe an unusual debt of gratitude to the authors who contributed to this volume. Finally, a word to my family, who provided their usual moral support.

This book is dedicated to my family
   Temmy, Steffan, Todd, Brianne, Marc
My parents
   Carolina and Mariano
My sister
   Alma

Contents

Introduction   xv

Section I.
THE ALTERNATIVE MOVEMENT: BACKGROUND,
PHILOSOPHY, AND CRITICISM   EDITOR'S COMMENTS   1

"The What, Why, and Where of the Alternatives Movement"
BY MARIO D. FANTINI   3

"The Traditional School: Keep It Among the Alternatives"
BY GENE I. MAEROFF   16

"Schools Within Schools: Solving the Problem of Differing
Needs" BY MARIO D. FANTINI   22

"Alternative Educational Programs: Promise or Problems?"
BY MARIO D. FANTINI   26

"The Alternative to Schooling" BY IVAN ILLICH   34

"CBE Views the Alternatives" BY MORTIMER SMITH   48

Section II.
FREE AND INDEPENDENT ALTERNATIVE
SCHOOLS: OUTSIDE THE SYSTEM   EDITOR'S
COMMENTS   57

"The Free School Movement—a Perspective" BY LAWRENCE
A. CREMIN   59

"The Free School Movement" BY ALLEN GRAUBARD   66

Selections from " 'I Will Mess Up on My Own': An Analysis
of the First Six Months of Penn Circle Community High
School" BY DAVID ZAREMBKA   87

"The Independent Public Schools" BY SUSAN S. EGAN   93

"Thoreau School Wants to Join Wallkill Central" BY KARL
RODMAN   100

Section III.
ALTERNATIVES WITHIN THE SYSTEM   EDITOR'S
COMMENTS   105

"Matching Teaching-Learning Styles" BY MARIO D. FANTINI   107

"The Mini-School Story: A Plan to End the Drop-out Rate,"
from *Mini School News*   112

"Fourteen New Mini-Schools All Set to Go," from *Mini
School News*   113

"Alternatives in the Public School" BY MARIO D. FANTINI   115

"The Philosophy, the Academic Program, the Main Building,
Selection of Students and Staff" from Metro High School   124

"Education by Choice: A Program of the Quincy Public
Schools" BY DR. BRANDT G. CROCKER, RICHARD F. HAUGH, AND
DONALD A. PRICE   132

"Space for Learning" BY AASE ERIKSEN   153

"The St. Paul Open School" BY WAYNE JENNINGS   160

"Outward Bound Approaches to Alternative Schooling" BY
JOSEPH J. NOLD   164

"We Hope You Like Your School As Much As We Like
Ours, Alternative Schools 1975" BY DONALD R. WALDRIP   171

"The Alternate College of State University College, Brock-
port" BY ARMAND BURKE   186

"Five O'Clock High," letter from Dr. Gary Cameron, Prin-
cipal, Sunset High School, Las Vegas, Nevada   200

Section IV.
IMPLEMENTATION OF PUBLIC SCHOOL
ALTERNATIVES   EDITOR'S COMMENTS   203

"Designing and Implementing Alternative Schools" BY
BRUCE HOWELL   205

"Decision Making in Alternative Schools" BY ALLAN
GLATTHORN   212

Selections from "It Works This Way for Some: Case Studies
of Fifteen Schools" BY MICHAEL BAKALIS   221

"Los Angeles School Superintendent's Memo to Board of
Education Proposing Guidelines for Alternative Schools"
BY WILLIAM J. JOHNSTON   252

"The Alternative High School Program: Draft III" by the
Steering Committee for the Alternative High School Program,
Needham, Massachusetts   256

"How to Choose a Mini-School: A Guidebook for Families,"
from Alum Rock Union Elementary School   267

Section V.
DEVELOPING ALTERNATIVES DISTRICTWIDE:
MINNEAPOLIS STORY   EDITOR'S COMMENTS   271

"2 Board of Education Decisions Affect SEA" BY SALLY
FRENCH   273

"SEA Negotiates 3 Year Three Million Dollar Contract with
NIE" BY SALLY FRENCH   275

Selections from *Southeast Alternatives* 1972–73 BY SALLY
FRENCH   277

"Board Approves Alternative Schools," newspaper report
March 14, 1973 BY GREG PINNEY   296

Section VI.
EVALUATING ALTERNATIVES   EDITOR'S COMMENTS   299

"The Shanti Evaluation: Even Wilbur and Orville Couldn't
Make It Fly" BY GENE MULCAHY   301

"Student Evaluations: Freedom, Responsibility, and Learning"   304

Selections from "Policies and Standards for the Approval of
Optional Schools and Special Function Schools" 308

Selections from "Evaluation of High School in the Commu-
nity," New Haven, Connecticut BY JOHN D. MC CONAHAY, PH.D.,
SHIRLEY FREY-MC CONAHAY, EDISON J. TRICKETT, PH.D., JUDITH
E. GRUBER, AND WILLIS D. HAWLEY   313

"The Alternative School Transcript" from Home Base School 328

"Education by Choice," 1973–74 Evaluation Summary of
Quincy Senior High II Program BY DR. BRANDT G. CROCKER,
RICHARD F. HAUGH, AND DONALD A. PRICE   333

Section VII.
FINANCING ALTERNATIVE SCHOOLS   EDITOR'S
COMMENTS   349

"Fiscal Aspects of Alternative Schools" BY WILLIAM WHITE 351

"Hustling: How to Write a Proposal"   355

"Berkeley: Experimental Schools Proposal Abstract" BY
RICHARD L. FOSTER   364

"External and Internal Education Vouchers" BY MARIO D. FANTINI 367

"A School Voucher Experiment Rates an 'A' in Coast District" BY EVAN JENKINS 377

"Matters of Choice"—A Ford Foundation Report on Alternative Schools 383

California Alternative School Assembly Bill No. 1052 389

Section VIII.
POLITICS EDITOR'S COMMENTS 395

"Politics, Rage and Motivation in the Free Schools" BY JONATHAN KOZOL 397

"Alternatives: 90% Political, 10% Educational, The Political Demise of Markles Flats" BY JONATHAN DAITCH 406

"The Politics of Implementation at 'Any' Alternative School" BY ALAN SUGARMAN 409

"Is a Collision Between Parents and Teachers Inevitable?" BY MARIO D. FANTINI 414

"Students at Metro Play the Political Game" by Students of the Chicago Public High School for Metropolitan Studies 421

"Seattle Public Schools: Planning Process for Alternative Programs" 423

"Conclusions, Feasibility Study for the Design and Implementation of an Education Voucher System in Rochester, New York" BY PHALE HALE, LARRY O. MAYNARD, AND ELEANOR PECK 429

"Rochester TA Digs in for Voucher Battle" 432

"Rochester Voucher Proposal Analyzed by NYSUT Leader" BY DAN SANDERS 433

"Where We Stand: Rochester's Fight Is Our Fight" BY THOMAS HOBART 439

"Voucher Proposal Defeated in Rochester" 442

"Few Using Vouchers to Pay for School" BY ROBERT REINHOLD 444

Section IX.
TEACHER PREPARATION FOR ALTERNATIVE SCHOOLS EDITOR'S COMMENTS 451

"Intern Survival Handbook from Shanti School, Hartford, Connecticut" 453

"Teacher Adaptation to an Informal School" BY AASE ERIK-
SEN AND FREDERICK M. FISKE   462

"Indiana University Alternative School Teacher Education
Program" BY ROBERT D. BARR   470

"National Alternative Schools Program" BY PHIL DE TURK
AND RAY IVEY   474

Index   485

Bibliography   489

INTRODUCTION

Since the latter part of the 1960s, I have been engaged in an attempt to promote educational options and choice within our public school system. During the 1960s, the voice of criticism rang loud and clear concerning our schools. While I consider myself a critic of public education, I also consider myself a reformer. Reformers usually have proposals to make. It is important, I think, to offer constructive plans for solving some of our problems. It does us little good to begin and end with criticism. Moreover, I am a firm believer in public education. It is conceivable that when the final history of the United States is written, the idea that this society could offer a free system of public education to its citizens will have to be recognized as one of its noblest achievements. Consequently, I am not interested in destroying the potential of a free system of public education. Rather, I am constantly searching for ways of reforming and renewing this public framework. Thus, there will be an emphasis in this volume on expanding the boundaries of public education. For me, alternative education presents an important breakthrough in this respect and represents the first phase of a much lengthier process of fundamental reform.

Now that the smoke of the 1960s has cleared, it is fair to say that we have learned some important lessons, especially in the educational arena. For one thing, *we assumed during the 1960s that the problems which were made salient by the increased federal attention to the schools were with the learner, his family and background.* New terms began to surface, "disadvantaged," "culturally deprived," "disruptive," and the like. New public policies resulted in such legislation as the Elementary and Secondary Education Act, which promoted compensatory education—an attempt to isolate the casualties of a public school system and to offer concentrated programs of remediation. In other words, we tried to change the learner to fit the school. This add-on approach to school improvement, while making good sense at the time, has not yielded the gains expected. Continuing a more-of-the-same policy, even in concentrated fashion, does not have pay-off.

It is costly, and has, in part, resulted in a lack of confidence in the ability of school people to solve their problems. Moreover, the glamour of innovation which also characterized the 1960s: new math, new science, team teaching, programmed instruction, TV teaching, etc., has too met with lackluster results. Trying to improve schools by introducing "pieces" of innovation within a system that itself was unable to respond added further to the growing public and professional disillusionment. Thus, putting more money into the educational system for innovation, and for remediation, has, at best, taught us that we need a new approach to the problems of education in the United States.

Slowly during the 1970s a new public policy began to emerge: *the educational problem is not the fault of the learner, but of the institution.* Consequently, the task is not one of trying to fit the learner to the school, but, rather, the other way around. How can public schools be reformed without dismantling the existing structure or alienating any of those who are part of it? Is there any way that we can deal with the problem constructively while also satisfying the three major criteria: educational soundness, economic feasibility, political viability? It is in this context that educational alternatives and choice begin to enter the picture. The notion that there are a variety of ways in which children learn and can be taught is certainly not new. What is new is the thought that it should be made operational in the schools—not by chance but by choice. If we thought for a moment about the fifteen or so percent of the population that attends private schools, we would see that the idea of options is not far-fetched. If one could afford it, one could purchase educational services in the private sectors. Families, as educational consumers, could select from prep schools, academies, Montessori schools, and the like. Alternatives and choice are available, but not in the *public* sector. For a variety of reasons that will be pointed out in this book, the public schools have evolved as standardized institutions characterized by sameness. As a pluralistic school population began to converge on this public school structure, there were bound to be problems. People are not the same. They are different. They have different styles of learning, and as the need for universal quality education became a necessity, the eighty-five or so percent who depended on public schools began to pose strains on this institutionalized uniformity.

At first, beginning with some pioneer alternative educational experiments outside the system, and slowly inside the public system, options have begun to catch on. We are on the brink of an educational movement that promises to deliver genuine reform by diversifying public education and by providing teachers, parents, and students choices. As someone who has been identified with the so-called "alternative school movement" and written numerous articles and several books on the topic, I have provided in this volume a natural extension of this effort. While my previous works dealt with a general introduction of public school options and choice, this edited work is much more of a technical resource to those who may be either beginning or already into alternative education. As a source book, it is meant to be helpful to parents, students, teachers, administrators, and any other citizen interested in improving education.

The articles have been carefully selected to establish a representative balance in areas that I as the editor view as important in promoting optional learning environments. Obviously, there are countless other articles which are important and could have been utilized. Needless to say, the limits of time and space prohibit additional selections. Those who have contributed to this volume have thought long and hard about educational improvement and the role of alternative education in this process. The reader will be exposed to theoreticians and practitioners alike; they will be exposed to formal and informal prose. Hopefully, the reader will find much in this collection that will be useful. For in the final analysis, this book will have value to the extent that it reaches people of good will who want to do the right thing for learners—regardless of age and background.

Section I

THE ALTERNATIVE MOVEMENT: BACKGROUND, PHILOSOPHY, AND CRITICISM

As the concept of alternative education began to creep into the literature, it was found to trigger serious reaction. There were those who saw it as a new pattern for reform, others who were much more cautious, and those who were downright critical. What is this thing called alternative education? Where did it come from? What's it look like? Where's it going? Why? These are obvious questions that follow any serious attempt at change.

The articles that have been selected in this section are from some of the most astute observers of the educational arena. The different ways in which each author views the same phenomenon should, in itself, solicit some critical thought in the reader. There does not seem to be a right or wrong answer and certainly the writers deal with fundamental questions of value. There are those observers, such as Illich, whose view of alternatives is significantly different from that of Fantini. And then there are others, such as Gene Maeroff, Education Writer for the New York *Times,* who pleads to keep the traditional school among the alternatives. Since the trend toward options is relatively new, it is useful to see how the different authors begin to construct their notions of alternative education and its place in a broader philosophy of education in the United States.

This section will deal with such questions as:

Is there an alternative schools movement or is it just a passing fad?

How did alternative schools start in the first place?

Why are options catching on at this time?

Should we have schools at all? What would replace them?

What is the hidden curriculum of our schools? What effect does it have on students and teachers?

What are schools within schools?

What are the problems surfacing from those who are implementing alternatives?

Are there ground rules for playing the alternatives game?

THE WHAT, WHY, AND WHERE OF THE ALTERNATIVES MOVEMENT*

BY MARIO D. FANTINI

There is an alternative schools movement beginning in this country that could very well become the major thrust of reform in the decades ahead. This trend toward educational diversity has grown out of several decades of frustration: We tried to make a monolithic public school system work for everybody. We were preoccupied with improving a single model of education. We updated courses of study, such as new math and new physics; we introduced new technology and new devices, such as programed learning, team teaching, and nongradedness; and for those who were the most obvious casualties of the schools, we mounted compensatory programs of remediation. In short, we spent our fiscal and human resources attempting to improve a uniform nineteenth century institution. The result is, at best, an improved outdated institution.

Our compensatory, add-on efforts at reform are now slowly being assessed as general failures. President Nixon rendered the verdict on compensatory education in his 1970 Education Message. Disappointment in the results of these innovations is best depicted in the 1972 Ford Foundation Report entitled *A Foundation Goes to School,* which reviewed a decade of investments in school improvement efforts that utilized many of these innovations, with less than satisfactory results.

The problem of providing a pluralistic, technologically advanced society with universal quality education continues to be a problem requiring a basic reform of our educational institutions. Because quality education has an important survival value in today's world, the absence of it becomes increasingly a matter of personal urgency. Quality education has become a value to most American households. However, it is difficult, if not impossible, for a monolithic system of public education to respond to the different conceptions of quality education held by a pluralistic society, and consequently these differences result in increased confrontations.

We can trace the roots of the current alternatives thrust in large measure to the civil rights movement of the 1960's. As the quest for desegregation gained momentum, parent, teacher, and community boycotts of public schools led to the establishment of temporary freedom schools in storefronts and church basements. Teachers, community residents, parents, and college volunteers collaborated to continue the education of black children in the "freedom schools."

An excerpt from a memorandum to Mississippi freedom school teachers participating in a summer project during the mid-1960's illustrates the departure from the standard program of the public schools:

> *"The purpose of the freedom schools is to provide an educational experience for students which will make it possible for them to challenge the myths of our society, to perceive more clearly its realities, and to find alternatives and, ultimately, new directions for action."*

For many blacks and whites alike, the freedom schools provided a glimpse of alternative programs tailored to their perceived needs, which included sympathetic adults working with children, curriculum specifically geared to the self-determination concerns of black people, and involvement in the immediate political life of the community.

To pursue these educational concerns, those involved departed from established procedures by assuming a flexible stance that advocated expanding the boundaries of schooling to include the community and its resources, establishing smaller educational units to humanize the experience for those involved, and relating educational experience to the life of the community. These ingredients remain prevalent in the current alternative schools movement.

Another social trend that continues to contribute to alternative education is the so-called counterculture movement. Viewing public schools as repressive and authoritarian institutions reflecting the deteriorating values of the dominant society, members of the counterculture have attempted to sponsor alternative institutions that are free to develop new learning environments that are personally liberating and geared to individual and group life styles.

Participants in this search were quick to embrace the new educational philosophies of A. S. Neill, Ivan Illich, and a host of the so-called romantic education writers, such as Paul Goodman, John Holt, Herbert Kohl, Everett Reimer, and George Dennison. Underlying this philosophy is the central concern with individual freedom. A. S. Neill states his philosophy clearly: "My view is that a child is innately wise and realistic. If left to himself without adult suggestion of any kind, he will develop as far as he is capable of developing."[1]

To Illich and Reimer, schools, especially public (but also, perhaps, free schools) get in the way of real education. To them, the best idea, one that maximizes both freedom and individual development, is one that gives each person the right and the means for orchestrating his own distinctive plan.

Another movement stimulating alternative education grows in part out of the British experience (including the World War II years) supporting the progressive principles of education articulated by John Dewey. This is the currently popular view of education variously called "British infant," "integrated day," "open," or "informal" education. While not as radical as the alternatives embraced by those in the counterculture category, the open classroom has become increasingly prevalent within the public system of education. Such books as *Crisis in the Classroom,* by Charles E. Silberman, helped popularize this philosophy with the general public. Moreover, teachers, school administrators, and professors have embraced it, rekindling a new interest in John Dewey and the progressive education movement of the earlier part of this century. While the open classroom advocates believe in giving the learner more freedom, they limit this freedom when it comes to determining the common content areas for which the school is responsible, such as the three R's, science, languages, and so forth. Open classrooms have become alternatives in which the learner is free to explore these academic areas in a more natural, personal, and experiential way. Teachers are more likely to be resources to the learner in these settings. In other words, there are still schools and classrooms, only now the structure is more informal.

These major movements helped highlight other alternatives that had either been around for years or were in recent operation due to growing consumer dissatisfaction. For instance, Montessori education became an important alternative. In New York City, Harlem Prep and the Street Academy became prominent specimens of schools that took public school casualties and made them successful college bound students. In Philadelphia, a school without walls triggered a nationwide awareness of the concept of the city as a classroom.

One other project, the voucher plan has significantly influenced alternative education and deserves comment here. Growing out of free market economics, this idea was formulated by Milton Friedman at the University of Chicago and Christopher Jencks at Harvard University. Several Office of Economic Opportunity experiments in voucher education are currently in progress—for example, in Rochester and New Rochelle, New York, and Alum Rock, California.

In brief, the voucher plan calls for recasting education into a free market system in which each family is given a voucher worth a certain sum of money (usually enough to cover basic tuition) for each school-age child. This voucher is redeemable in any private or public school the family may choose after shopping around. Vouchers increase the purchasing power of the consumer and provide him with the right of choice.

Predictably, the voucher plan has elicited stormy, critical resistance from professional educators—especially those within the public schools, including the two major teacher organizations (NEA and AFT), who view the plan as a serious threat to public schools. However, the threat of having a voucher that would stimulate alternative schools *outside* the framework of public education has encouraged a movement for alternatives *within* the public schools themselves. Ironically, as an external threat, vouchers have helped to generate an internal reform effort, thus fulfilling in part their original purpose.

If we put these developments together, the alternative schools movement appears to fall somewhat as follows.

External Free School Alternatives— Toward Radical Reform

Free schools have sprung up from coast to coast in the past five years. Estimates show that over 400 such schools exist. The life span for free schools is about two years, and their average enrollment is estimated at thirty-three students.

The turnover rate of both students and teachers is high. Yet these schools have at times captured a spontaneous quality that any educator would applaud. Allen Graubard, in his book *Free the Children*, provides numerous examples of this quality. To cite one illustration, financial problems prompted a free school to use the public park as its educational setting. The facilities of the park—grassy grounds, trees, picnic tables, fireplaces, electric outlets, sinks, and sports fields—were fully utilized. Graubard quotes one of the leaders in this school as remarking:

> *"The great virtue of the park has turned out to be its openness, which has greatly improved communications among and between the teachers and students. Everyone can see everyone else; we know where the students are and what they are doing and they know where we are and what we are doing. This has eliminated the need we felt last year for schedules. Furthermore, the teachers, instead of being sequestered to [their] rooms, with [their] groups of students, are now all together in the equivalent of one big room with all the students. The result is that we tend to work more closely together, to plan together, and coordinate our efforts much more than we ever did before. We don't, moreover, have to pay the price usually paid by large groups of people together in a big room—noise."*[2]

The free school movement includes two wings. The free schools embracing an A. S. Neill philosophy that "freedom works" are primarily white middle class. The other wing of the free school movement emphasizes the school as a political environment in which to prepare the next generation for the active transformation of society. Obviously, those who consider the present fiber of society oppressive and unjust want to use free schools as the vehicle for societal renewal. In certain quarters, free schools reflect this political orientation. Some nonwhite schools as well as countercultural white schools have developed such formats. Descriptions of these schools can be found in the writings of activists such as Herbert Kohl, Jonathan Kozol, and Larry Cole, who themselves have developed free schools.

Free schools are not free in the financial sense; tuition is charged in most of them. Rather they are free from the ponderous bureaucracy of the massive public schools. They gain their momentum from the dedication of staff and parents.

Teachers, for example, often work round the clock for subsistence wages. The important point is that there is a flexibility about these schools that represents a refreshing departure from the uniformity of public schools. Yet despite their aspirations of love, independence, self-direction, tolerance, and social responsiveness, their real impact, like that of the voucher plan, has not been to achieve radical reform outside the system of public schools, but rather to stimulate a more progressive, albeit moderate, reform effort *within* the public school system.

Alternatives Within Public Schools— Toward Progressive Reform

Eighty-five percent of the nation's children attend public schools, and the bulk of our support for school improvement has been with this public education sector. Yet, while polls reveal that from 60 to 70 percent of those who use public schools express satisfaction with them, a critical mass of over 30 percent do not.

At a time when quality education is critical to the survival needs of the individual, the inability of our public schools to deliver quality education to significant numbers of users has resulted in frustration and retaliation. Many of those who are dissatisfied with the services of public schools and cannot afford private schools are now placing pressure on the public schools to change; those who are satisfied are trying to keep them as they are. This tug-of-war is beginning to affect everybody, sometimes disturbing the climate for those students who are profiting from standard school programs.

Caught in this cross fire are the professional educators, some of whom want to change the system, while others want to keep it the same. The result of these developments is an arena of power politics. Teachers, parents, and students are organizing into groups in order to achieve their own objectives. Desperate attempts to achieve quality are proposed; vouchers, performance contracting, and decentralization are fiercely opposed or supported. But each proposal is embattled by the politics of contemporary public education.

All the while, the costs of education rise as the results decline. A public that needs quality education demands accountability. The professionals—caught in the middle, trying to play

by the norms of a system that was forged in the last century—
resist this public review, become defensive, and look to their
professional organizations for protection.

It is at this point that alternatives enter the picture. Catching on to the possibilities of developing other ways of educating a pluralistic student body, many teachers, parents, and students have begun to plan and implement alternative public
school. Teachers and administrators are swarming to workshops on open education. Hundreds of open classrooms have
sprung up across the nation. (For instance, half the public
schools in the state of North Dakota are considered to have
open education. Dozens of cities have begun their own versions of a school without walls.

These new alternatives differ sharply from the options traditionally available in public schools, such as vocational and
special education, schools for dropouts and unwed mothers—
tracks that carried with them a psychological classification that
was negative when compared to those in the academic track.
Moreover, these options were based more on chance than
choice.

Before the alternatives movement, the child was assigned
to a teacher whose teaching style may or may not have been
congruent with the child's learning style. Some students responded, others did not, but neither teacher nor child had any
choice in the matter.

Alternatives provide new opportunities for a match in
teaching and learning styles. Choice lets students select programs that best fit them. Parents, who have played key roles
as teachers at home, are in a good position to help select
the alternative that best suits their child's distinctive pattern
for learning. Similarly teachers can select the alternative that
best supports their temperament and approach.

On a national basis, public school alternatives fall into several categories:

Classroom alternatives. Some alternatives are found at the
classroom level of neighborhood schools. For instance a first-
grade teacher who favors open education may be the only
one of three or four teachers who does. Hence she offers an
option to any first-grade parents who wish an open classroom.
The same principle applies at any grade level and with any
legitimate educational pattern. A teacher may offer, for ex-

ample, a Montessori, behavior modification, or a multiculture alternative classroom.

Alternative classrooms have certain advantages. They start slowly. Parents and students are introduced to options gradually and within the confines of their own neighborhood school. No one is forced to participate, and even if no overwhelming dissatisfaction with the school exists, alternative classrooms provide a choice to those parents or teachers who are dissatisfied.

Schools within schools. Another manifestation of alternative education is the idea of schools within schools, or minischools within a formerly single school. Any neighborhood elementary, junior or middle, or high school can become two or more smaller schools, each school emphasizing a distinctive pattern of education. Each subschool is made available to students, parents, and teachers by choice. There are many such schools, both urban and suburban, in various stages of development. Examples are:

• Haaren High School in New York City has a mini-school arrangement. This boys school is organized into a complex of fourteen mini-schools within a single building. Each mini-school has its own coordinator (who is responsible to the principal), 5 teachers, 1 street worker, and from 125 to 150 students.

• Walt Whitman High School in Montgomery County, Maryland, a middle class suburb, was one of the first to consider schools within schools similar to that of Haaren.

• After comprehensive planning, the high school in Quincy, Illinois, is now developing subschool alternatives. With extensive faculty, student, and community participation, a range of alternatives were sketched. The Education by Choice planning team proceeded to propose seven options, in terms of learning environments as follows: 1. primarily teacher-directed; 2. direction from both teacher and student, but for the most part, teacher-directed; 3. students and teachers together plan the experiences for the participants; 4. primary focus on considering the various areas of learning in relation to the arts; 5. primary focus on career orientation and preparation; 6. learning environment for special education students; 7. learning environment for dropout prone students.[3]

• Jefferson Elementary, a K-3 school in Berkeley, California, offers three distinct options: traditional, individualized, and multicultural.

Schools within established schools have certain advantages: 1) they are convenient for parents, students, and teachers; 2) they provide opportunities for staff and community to participate in the development of alternatives; and 3) by using the facilities of an established school, they can make fuller use of existing resources such as physical education, music, and art facilities and counselors.

Their disadvantages are the problems that arise when any established social system is disturbed. There may be serious resistance by those who perceive alternatives as a threat to existing arrangements.

Separate alternative schools. A popular mode for alternative education is the development of a new public school in a facility separate from existing schools. The Village School in Great Neck, New York, is housed in a church basement. An abandoned missile base in Long Beach, New York, houses the Nike School. The Brown School in Louisville, Kentucky, uses a downtown office building for its location. Such descriptions are repeated across the country:

• The St. Paul Open School is actually a three-story former factory building now brightly decorated. This alternative school does not mandate attendance. Each student pursues his own tailored plan. The major learning areas—humanities, math, science, and industrial arts—make up the organization. Teachers serve as learning facilitators. The classrooms have an informal, family-type flavor to them (armchairs, sofas, tables, lamps, and so forth).

• The Murray Road Alternative School in Newton, Massachusetts, is located in a former elementary school and has about 115 college bound high school students and 8 teachers who participate in an informal educational community. With only British and American history required, there is great freedom to pursue individual interests and concerns.

Separate alternative schools have advantages. For one thing, they can start from scratch. Away from traditional constraints, they are free to mold new concepts of teaching and learning with sympathetic participants. However, disadvantages may arise if a separate alternative school becomes the only experiment in optional education, thus leaving out other parents, teachers, and students.

Systems of alternative schools. Several school systems have attempted to transform significant portions of their districts into alternative school patterns. For example, the Berkeley Unified School District in California has generated over twenty distinct alternative schools. Such alternatives fall into four broad patterns:

• *Multiculture schools.* These schools include children carefully selected on the basis of diversity of race, socioeconomic status, age, and sex. During part of the school day the students meet and work together. At other times they meet in their own ethnic, social, or educational groups, learning their own culture, language customs, history and heritage, or other special curriculum; later, these aspects are shared with the wider group.

• *Community schools.* The organization, curriculum, and teaching approach of these schools comes from outside the classroom—from the community. There may well be total parent involvement, with both the school day and week being extended into shared family life. There will be use of courts, markets, museums, parks, theaters, and other educational resources in the community.

• *Structured skills training schools.* These schools are graded and emphasize the learning of basic skills—reading, writing, and math. Learning takes place primarily in the classroom and is directed by either one teacher or a team of teachers working together.

• *Schools without walls.* The focus of these schools is the child and his development. The staff deals with the child rather than the subject. The schools are ungraded, and typically their style and arrangements are structured. Their goals are to have the students grow in self-understanding and self-esteem, learn how to cope with social and intellectual frustration, and master the basic and social skills through their own interests.

The School District of Philadelphia has a director of alternative programs who is coordinating the development of more than fifty alternative learning environments. These are modeled after open classrooms, schools without walls, and mini-schools, and include schools for students with special problems (such as gifted learners, academic failures, and disruptive and pregnant students).

The Minneapolis Public Schools have initiated a Southeast Alternatives Program serving all students in that area of the city. Elementary students can attend any of the following four types of schools:

1. A contemporary school, Tuttle, which offers curriculum innovations but maintains a teacher directed, structured curriculum and grade level school organization.

2. A continuous progress school, a part of Pratt and Motley Schools, in which each child advances at his own pace without regard to grade level and in which instruction is by teams and based on a carefully sequenced curriculum in basic skills.

3. An open school, Marcy, which combines flexible curriculum, scheduling and age grouping in the style of the British infant schools. Children take a great deal of initiative for their own education with the emphasis on pursuing their own interests.

4. A free school, the Minneapolis Free School, which extends through the twelfth grade. Students, parents, volunteers, and faculty develop the courses and much off-campus experience is included. The initial enrollment of 70 students will be expanded to 150 during 1972–73, and, according to school officials, a more structured, content oriented program will be developed.[4]

It should be clear by now that, educationally speaking, alternatives run the entire gamut from student directed to teacher directed. On the one end, there are alternatives that accord the learner considerable freedom to determine how he will learn, what he will learn, when, where, and with whom. On the other end, these elements are predetermined by the school itself. In between, there is a vast range of possibilities. With such a perspective, we can see the overall pattern into which are fitted free schools, open classrooms, ungraded schools, schools without walls, prep schools, and so forth.

A few words on the politics of the alternative schools movement are always appropriate. We have learned that any change involves politics. Alternatives as a change effort is significantly different from many other reform plans in that it is based on choice and is, therefore, voluntary. It is chosen by teachers, parents, and students by attraction; it is not superimposed. The "something for everybody" flavor of alternatives reduces the inevitable political conflict that results when people have no choice in the reform proposal being implemented.

No real reform can be achieved without the support of the front line agents—teachers, parents, and students. Alternatives are grassroots oriented and cater to these three basic publics. The role of the school administrator is to provide an enabling structure. This means giving basic information on alternatives to interested parties and arranging and facilitating meetings among teachers, parents, and students.

Alternatives often run into resistance when they make exaggerated claims following a negative diagnosis of the standard process in the public schools. Such behavior by advocates of alternative schools only solicits resistance. First, the "blasting" of what exists makes those associated with standard education feel inferior, a mood hardly conducive to cooperation. Second, projecting high expectations of the proposed alternatives serves both to increase the resentment of those in the standard process and plants the seeds of frustration for those participating in the alternative itself. No one alternative can do it all.

It would be a far better approach for those in the alternatives movement to indicate that the standard process is an alternative that works for many, but not for everyone. There are teachers and students who would profit from an entirely different educational approach. Whatever the proposed alternative, it is, at best, another legitimate way of offering a choice. Since each alternative is aimed at the same common educational objectives, the idea is to develop different means to common ends. Evaluation, of course, should be built into all alternatives, including consumer satisfaction.

In very practical terms, preventing political resistance may mean something as simple as avoiding a particular label for the alternative, such as "humanistic," "open," or "individualized," which implies that other alternatives, including the standard, are "inhuman," "closed," or "unindividualized"—a verdict certain to cause defensiveness.

Most important, a proposed alternative should not carry a price tag that makes it more expensive than what already exists. Strong attempts to keep the per student expenditure the same will enhance its attractiveness. Furthermore, wherever possible, alternatives should help use existing resources differently and more effectively. Some alternatives actually cut certain costs. The School Without Walls in Philadelphia, for example, does not need a school building and can save on construction costs. The St. Paul Open School reports that because it utilizes many volunteers and student self-direction, the per pupil cost is actually less than the average for the city.

By far the greatest danger facing alternatives is that the movement will be viewed as a fad. Education has had its share of them: team teaching, programed instruction, humanizing the schools, and so on. Ironically, these movements were all intended to be services, but unfortunately we have fallen into the box of thinking up a theme for each year, as though by discussing it we had taken care of the matter. It would be tragic for the alternatives movement to fall victim to such faddism. Certainly educators like John Bremer and organizations like the National Consortium on Options in Public Education at Indiana University are emphasizing the virtues of alternatives in educational reform.

Significant numbers of individual teachers, parents, and students could be attracted to alternative education if given the opportunity. But teachers belong to strong professional organizations that must also be supportive if alternatives are to have a chance of working. Thus far, the NEA has generally favored alternatives and has featured the theme in its meetings. The AFT has remained somewhat neutral. However, as alternatives within the public schools grow, and as more teachers become involved actively, the attitude of both major teacher associations is bound to be affected. Their leadership will certainly be welcomed during the year ahead.

On the other hand, if teacher organizations turn against the alternatives movement, then conflicts among teachers, parents, and students are sure to follow. Such collision can hardly serve the best interests of children, the public, or the profession.

During the remainder of this decade we should see more growth in alternative education. What can result is a gradual expansion of the framework of public education to include many former alternative private schools. Over time, we could emerge with a redefined system of public education that is diverse, self-renewing, and responsive to a pluralistic society.

FOOTNOTES

1. Quoted in Graubard, Allen. *Free the Children: Radical Reform and the Free School Movement.* New York: Pantheon Books, 1972. p. 11.

2. Ibid. (See footnote 1), p. 81.

3. "Education By Choice." Application for Operational Grant under Elementary and Secondary Education Act, Public Law 89-10, Title III. Submitted by Quincy Public Schools, Quincy, Illinois. January 1973. pp. 31–32.

4. National School Public Relations Association. *Alternative Schools.* Washington, D.C.: the Association, 1973. p. 23.

THE TRADITIONAL SCHOOL: KEEP IT AMONG THE ALTERNATIVES*

BY GENE I. MAEROFF†

Bayside High School, in New York City's second-largest borough, Queens, contains no minischools. Its academic calendar is based not on modules but on standard semesters. Desks are bolted to the floors and the closest the school comes to having an open classroom is the informality of an art or home economics course. There is a dearth of independent

* Reprinted by permission of the author and Phi Delta Kappa, Inc.

† Gene I. Maeroff, national education correspondent of the New York *Times,* is the co-author of *The New York Times Guide to Suburban Public Schools.*

study and individualization is unusual. Students are more or less outside the decision-making process and they are monitored at assemblies by faculty members who tell them where to sit, when to be quiet, how to salute the flag, and what to do when the assembly ends. All in all, in the opinion of the school's social studies chairman, the 3,800-student school is a place that does not welcome "change for the sake of change."

Bayside also sends some 80% of its graduates to post-high school education and produces championship football teams. It is safe and secure by comparison with most of New York City's 94 high schools and attendance figures rank among the highest. It has one of the city's finest honors programs and its advanced placement program has been one of the most successful. The emphasis in music is on Bach, Beethoven, and Mozart, and study can be pursued in eight foreign languages. There is sufficient ability in the student body to warrant the offering of such courses as nuclear chemistry, calculus, and microbiology.

Not counting such special institutions as the Bronx High School of Science, Bayside is perhaps one of the city's best examples of a traditional high school. Even the appearance of Bayside's sprawling, 3-story brick and stone building with its long, narrow windows invokes the classic image. Inside, the picture is reinforced by clean, quiet corridors in which art can be hung on the walls without being consumed by the graffiti that seem endemic to many New York City high schools. An air of venerability is lent by the fact that the school has had no renovation and little new equipment since its opening almost 40 years ago.

Across the street from a shady park, in a solid middle-class neighborhood, the school is more than 15 miles from trouble-plagued Manhattan. It serves predominantly the children of parents who still think that teachers are right and kids are wrong. Bayside, which once even imposed a ban on *Catcher in the Rye*, fits the no-nonsense concept of what its community thinks a high school is supposed to be. And a succession of nose-to-the-grindstone principals has endeavored to keep it that way.

"I was there for six years and inherited a good traditional school from my predecessor," says Abraham Margolies, who retired as principal last spring. "We kept the skeleton and added new courses without changing the basic structure. In a pure sense, the word 'traditional' is great. We make a great mistake to go in for a completely innovative school without reference to the past. It is gimmickry without substance. My great complaint with all those who have contempt for traditional education is that they think the word 'traditional' is something to be sneered at."

Lester Speiser, a tall, broad-shouldered former English teacher who enjoys writing poetry in his spare time, has taken on Margolies's mantle. "Tradition has become a dirty word in certain circles," says the mustachioed Speiser, himself a product of the New York City public schools. "It's very important not to run a popularity contest in education and pick up the latest fads. You have to examine and use what's good for your particular youngsters. Alternative education means different ways of approaching the understood goals of education. And we have to recognize that youngsters have different needs than they did 20 or 30 years ago. But educational experiments are not something to be accepted naturally, the way you would accept polio vaccine. The greatest creativity is not through mechanical structures and various alternatives but through a creative teacher. And we have many of them at Bayside. I don't believe the teacher should be made into a master of ceremonies. I'm not ashamed to say to kids that I think we know more than they do. I don't want an automaton, but I do want a student who will meet us halfway. I believe the teacher-pupil relationship is a great tradition."

Teachers count at Bayside. The faculty of 175 is an essentially experienced one and good teaching is valued. Excellent younger teachers—dedicated and enthusiastic—such as Alan Brodsky have joined and blended into the faculty, maintaining the accent on quality teaching. In a typical meeting recently of one of Brodsky's beginning chemistry classes, the students eagerly waved their hands, straining for recognition and a chance to join a discussion on the properties of metals. The youthful-looking Brodsky, wearing a white laboratory jacket and standing front and center in a small, tiered lecture hall that could just as easily have been in one of New England's leading prep schools, deftly ran through a series of experiments for the attentive students, questioning them carefully each step of the way, drawing into the conversation those few who were not bursting to participate. There was learning, as well as teaching, taking place that morning in Bayside High School.

Most Bayside teachers can expect to have many bright, responsive, well-prepared, highly motivated students. It is almost as if the majority of the students would succeed regardless of who was standing in front of the classroom and, if necessary, despite the teaching. As indeed they probably would. To its teachers, certainly to the veterans, Bayside is proof that the traditional approach deserves to be represented in the educational spectrum. "When you talk about alternative education," says Mark Yohalem, the school's science chairman, "one of the alternatives should be traditional education." But Bayside is by no means idyllic. It has its disquieting side.

Of the approximately 20% of the school's seniors who do not go beyond high school, woefully few are prepared to enter the job market with salable skills. Moreover, some Bayside graduates who become college dropouts may have belonged in postsecondary technical school, not in college, and they might have known it had they gone to some other kind of high school than Bayside. The school's vocational and technical education offerings are sorely limited. Its cooperative work-study program includes only about 70 youngsters. Some students at Bayside are clearly ill-served.

"There is an element here that we are not equipped to handle and that we don't know how to handle," says Larry Ganeless, Bayside's English chairman. "There is no use sweeping it under the rug. We just don't know how to handle them. Some of us say that maybe they can't be handled."

A substantial portion of "they" are black. More than 700 black youngsters from the impoverished South Jamaica section of Queens attend Bayside under the city's school integration program. The Bayside neighborhood itself has only a handful of blacks. A large number of the South Jamaica students, as well as some white youngsters, bring to the school educational deficiencies that cause them serious problems. "When we get them and they are reading below a fifth-grade level, our type of education doesn't work for them," says Yohalem. A remedial reading teacher claims that when he asked a class of incoming blacks to write the alphabet, one-half were unable to do it.

Pronounced disparities in background often separate the

school's white students from the blacks and, sometimes, those with public school training from those with parochial school training. Also, the school has a sizeable contingent of "hitters" —no one can say where the name comes from—white youngsters who in dress and mannerisms try to emulate the "greasers" of the fifties and display an uncommon fondness for souped-up cars. Such divergencies seem to tear at the very fabric of traditional Bayside, which has been dependent on a degree of homogeneity in its student body.

Illustrative of the differences, an elementary school that feeds some of the white public school youngsters into Bayside, P.S. 184, led the city's 632 elementary schools in reading attainment this year and was second each of the last two years. A staff member at P.S. 184, which is itself operated along traditional lines, describes the pupils as "bright, willing, obedient, and neatly dressed"—attributes that should stand them in good stead at Bayside. By comparison, a test given to Bayside's ninth-graders, almost all of whom are black, showed 24% reading two or more years below grade level. Because of the integration plan and the zoning setup, most blacks enter Bayside as ninth-graders (along with a scattering of white parochial school transfers) and most white public school graduates begin as tenth-graders.

Having an overwhelmingly middle-class student body allows Bayside to benefit from almost none of the programs for the disadvantaged. Only four remedial reading classes at the school are paid for through federal funds. At the expense of the regular program, in a school that is already overcrowded and on double sessions, the faculty has on its own added three other remedial sections of reading and 10 of math.

Bayside's difficulties have not escaped Principal Speiser's attention. "This is part of the problem that a school like Bayside with an academic tradition has," he says. "Our obligation is to try to reach those youngsters who are in various states of miseducation. One of our problems is that we get increasingly more youngsters like this every year and we do not receive the money for the special services that should accompany them. It is like 'Catch-22.' The reasoning is that Bayside is a good school and doesn't need Title I money, so therefore it's all right to have 20% Title I kids without the money." Personnel services of all kinds are limited at Bayside, for neighborhood students as well as those who are bused in, by a budget that permits the hiring of only three guidance counselors for the entire school. "We have to constantly resort to outside agencies for services that should be available within the school," says one teacher. There is a widespread belief among faculty and administrators that "because Bayside is stable and not on the verge of exploding it is ignored by the board of education and inadequately financed in all respects."

If one listens carefully at Bayside he may also detect some discord among the students themselves. There are youngsters such as Ira Peppercorn, an eleventh-grader, who complains: "Things are still going on here the way they were 30 or 40 years ago. It is very, very structured. There is a system and you can't move out of that system."

Or, there are the comments of Debbie Lewis, an eleventh-grader, and other girls in Mrs. Hazel Kidd's sewing class, who wonder why the marvelously open environment they experience in that course cannot be duplicated in the mainline subjects. "There is more freedom and less pressure in here," says Debbie. "It is possible other subjects could be this way. I was in an ecology class in junior high that operated like this. We sat in small groups and talked. People were interested and they got good marks. In here we are free to sit where we want—with our friends—instead of in assigned seats like in other classes. We can talk and there isn't homework unless we want it. Kids would like it more and it would be better if all classes were like this."

Nonetheless, Bayside is not likely to undergo any sort of radical alterations in spirit in response to such observations. Counterbalancing such opinions as Debbie's are those of a student such as Howard Speicher, who thinks that "what a student gets out of Bayside depends on his goals." Howard's are academic, and for him the school has been "successful."

"There is an excellent faculty here," says Howard, who is a twelfth-grader with a 92 average and editorship of the student newspaper. "There is nothing like marks as a stimulus. I find it necessary to have a traditional atmosphere and marks spur me on. I experienced independent study in junior high school and it was nice to goof off and get good marks, but it just didn't work."

While the pace of change at Bayside is not expected to be rapid, there is a feeling shared by the principal and others that carefully chartered steps in new directions would not compromise the commitment to traditional education. "My definition of tradition," says Ganeless, the English chairman, "includes a place for innovation. My experience at Bayside has been that the so-called traditional curriculum in the hands of a good, resourceful teacher has meant exploiting every avenue at hand in terms of content and method."

The school already has a standing committee investigating possible curricular innovations. An expanded effort in vocational and technical education is being planned. A consultative council with the potential of bringing students and the community in on policy making has been formed. If money can be found, there are hopes of strengthening the remediation efforts. If such steps lead to more of the students and faculty sharing Speiser's sense of what education should mean, it could be a good thing. "I'm one of those," says the baldish, graying, 46-year-old principal, "who is lucky enough on Sunday night to look forward to Monday morning." One almost couldn't ask any more of education than that.

SCHOOLS WITHIN SCHOOLS: SOLVING THE PROBLEM OF DIFFERING NEEDS*

BY MARIO D. FANTINI

Neil is a senior at a high school where he spends most of his time pursuing his first love—dramatics—and through acting, script writing and directing is getting knowledge and skills in history, English, science and other academic fields.

Cindy is a senior at a high school where her academic schedule is different each week, depending on her program interest and personal progress. She may take history for one 55-minute period first thing in the morning and spend the rest of the day in the library working on her major project in science.

* © 1975 by The New York Times Company. Reprinted by permission from *The New York Times* (January 15, 1975).

Larry attends a high school that enables him to spend half the day as a student interne working with computers in a local business while the other half of his day is spent in related academic work back on campus.

While attending different schools, these students actually go to the same Quincy II High School in Quincy, Ill. They are part of a growing national trend to establish more personalized educational programs through schools within schools.

Quincy II has gained recognition for its pace-setting format, offering each of its 1,500 students, 80 teachers and parents a choice from among five distinctive subschools. These choices followed a period of cooperative planning and evaluation involving parents, students, teachers and administrators.

Selection of Program

Quincy's plan allows students to select the program that best suits their style and motivation. Choices include a traditional school for those students who need structure, an open model for those who like to design their own programs, a flexible pattern for those who are somewhere between these two, a fine arts option for those who want to pursue in more depth their skills in music, art and theater, and a career alternative for those who want to explore a talent in business, child care, computers, etc.

Schools within schools are not the only way of offering options. Some school systems have established alternatives housed in their own separate buildings. For example, Shanti, situated in an old railroad station in Hartford, Conn., offers an individually tailored program for each of its 95 regional high school students. The Houston school system has a High School for Health Professions, which is situated on the campus of the Baylor Medical College.

From nursery through secondary schools, optional education can be found in some of the most prestigious school systems: such as those in Newton, Mass.; Webster Groves, Mo.; Mamaroneck and Great Neck, N.Y.; Beverly Hills, Calif., as well as in our biggest cities: New York, Los Angeles and Philadelphia.

Reaction to Old System

This trend toward alternative schools is a reaction by parents, students and educators to both the bigness and rigidity of a uniform system of public education. Before this current expression for variety within public schools, the only options were to be found in private schools that were usually limited to those that could afford them.

In addition to the kinds of alternatives pioneered by Quincy, several other types are in practice nationally. These include "schools within walls" where students take classes in museums, hospitals or TV studios, taught by the experts themselves; New York's City as Schools, Chicago's Metro and "multiculture" schools in which the curriculum emphasizes the language and culture of the students, as found in Berkeley's Agora option or the Pilot School in Cambridge, Mass.

There are several reasons why alternative public schools are catching on. For one thing, whether one is an educational conservative or liberal, there is something for each.

Also, little additional costs are involved. After the usual start-up costs for planning, which most school budgets allow for, the actual per-student expenditure is the same. Since schools within schools make use of existing facilities and personnel, there is merely a reutilization of available resources.

Too, graduates of alternative schools are entering colleges with no apparent difficulties. In fact, the personal nature of these programs gives students an advantage in discussing their specific college aspirations with easily available teachers and counselors.

Successful alternatives seem to depend on careful planning involving all concerned parties, an emphasis on quality, clarification of program objectives and methods, maintaining traditional programs among the options, working out common guidelines and continuing evaluation.

This movement toward greater educational variation and choice is not without its problems. Some programs have promised more than they could deliver, disillusioning many supporters.

Other alternative schools have been developed on a loose definition of student freedom. One teacher involved in such a situation summarized her feelings this way: "Of what benefit is a school that says anything is acceptable?"

Perhaps the major weakness so far is that many school districts view alternatives as "dumping grounds" for special cases. When this happens, parents are left with the impression that these programs are not for the average child, but only for those so-called difficult students.

Despite these problems, alternative schools are gaining wider acceptance. A Gallup Poll conducted in 1973 indicated that the majority of parents and professionals support the idea. Moreover, it is difficult to ignore the many testimonials from all those who have been helped by diverse education.

During the first graduation of the Schools Without Walls in Philadelphia, held on the steps of that city's Arch Museum, a parent, with tears in her eyes, expressed to a group of visitors what has now become a familiar refrain in alternative education: "If it were not for this school my daughter would have dropped out. Now she is graduating and going to college."

How to Choose a Program

Which alternative is best suited for your child?

If you have a child who does not have to be told what to do all the time, enjoys going off alone to work, figures things out for himself, can stay with one thing for a long time—then perhaps you would want to consider a school that is flexible or open and provides opportunities for the student to work out his own schedule.

If your son or daughter is the type who seeks the approval of the teacher, enjoys knowing what is expected of him or her at all times, likes things neat, quiet, and orderly, then perhaps the style most compatible is the traditional school with teacher direction.

If your child has not yet cultivated a talent that he or she would enjoy doing as his or her life's work but wants to be sure to satisfy college entrance requirements, then maybe a career-oriented option might be considered.

If the child already has a strong interest in something like science, art, music, photography, etc., and would really like to advance in his or her talents without losing out on the other subjects, then a talent-based alternative may be suitable.

It is important to remember that if one option doesn't work
out, the child has a right to another, and if necessary, still
another. That's what alternatives are all about.

ALTERNATIVE EDUCATIONAL PROGRAMS: PROMISE OR PROBLEMS?*

BY MARIO D. FANTINI

Is there a full-fledged alternative schools movement in this
country that has the promise of achieving genuine educational
reform? Can alternative education accomplish what other reform efforts did not, indeed, could not or is it merely a passing
fad? Will alternatives or options, as they are also called, produce desirable change without surrendering the best of what
we have, or alienating the professionals who are associated
with the existing pattern of public education?

These are some of the questions which alternative schools
have triggered in different quarters of the country. Some
camps view alternatives as the most constructive trend in decades, others are cautious, still others are pessimistic. Where
are we with this recent development? Certainly the theme of
alternatives has become popular in professional and public
circles. The major professional organizations include this subject in their publications and as major topics at annual conferences. A Gallup Poll conducted in 1973 reflected support
for the idea of alternatives by both the lay public and professionals (62 percent of parents, 80 percent of professional educators indicated that it is a good idea).[1]

In order to deal with some of these issues, it may be useful to give a brief overview of alternative education as it has
unfolded over the past decade. First, it should be noted that
there are differing conceptions of "alternatives" among those
who are or have been associated with this activity. One branch
views the concept as alternatives *to* education. In a practical

* Reprinted from *Educational Leadership* 32(2): 83–87; November
1974. Copyright © 1974 by the Association for Supervision and Curriculum Development.

sense, this means alternatives *to* established public and private schooling. The idea was popularized by Ivan Illich, Everett Reimer, John Holt, and others. Among other things, the notion here is to have each person assume the right to orchestrate his or her own education and that schools as such may actually interfere with real education.

Another arm of the alternatives trend bases its concept on the theories of A. S. Neill and his Summerhill experiment. The assumption here is that "freedom works" and a "school" or "educational community" should be an environment in which the learner is free to pursue his or her own learning with minimal adult supervision.

Still another wing led by people such as Jonathan Kozol and Herb Kohl views alternatives as an opportunity to incorporate into the educational process political and cultural orientations that differ from established societal norms. The Civil Rights movement with its history of temporary "freedom schools" and the so-called counter-cultural aspirations of the 70's are connected to this view of alternatives.

Alternatives in the Mainstream

Yet another branch is connected with the modification of the standardization within public schools through plural education. This group, of which I am a member, composed mostly of persons within the established system of public schools, would legitimize a broad range of options—from open to standard to multicultural to Montessori. This latter group has stimulated many of the public school alternatives and has the most to do with whether options become a serious movement or passing fad. This group deals with the mainstream current of public education. The mainstream parents, students, and teachers are the ones we must reach for they are the political gatekeepers of educational reform within our public schools.

Because of the range of participants in alternatives and in the light of their differing philosophical and political orientations, the tendency for mixing all of these into one overall notion of alternatives has led to confusion—especially for those parents, teachers, students, and administrators who are associated with public schools. Because the mainstream is beginning to consider optional learning environments, it has become crucial on educational, economic, and political grounds for this activity to be handled seriously and sensitively.

We now know that for many middle Americans alternatives conjure up a vision of a "free" school with its permissiveness and perceived lack of formal structure. To others, alternatives imply a "hippy type" school with its counterculture flavor. I have been to alternative school conferences in which parents and teachers from the mainstream, seeking more information, were forced to wonder by the climate generated by the most vocal participants at these sessions, whether optional education had anything to do with them—"us straight types."

This perceptual confusion has been fanned also by the widespread use of the term alternative in describing "special" education programs, that is, students who are classified as "atypical" (alternative schools for the emotionally disturbed, retarded, delinquent, dropout, and unwed mother). While this pattern of alternatives is understandable (since there has been a tendency to permit deviations from established practice for those students who do not respond to established practice), it has caused considerable problems with both mainstream parent and professional.

To repeat, it is precisely the mainstream—the middle class parent and professional—who need to be reached if alternatives are to generate into a genuine reform movement. What is being suggested here is crucial. Since our early experience with alternatives is based largely on "fringe" or "atypical" elements of the population, they may have at best few, usually negative, connections with the middle class. If middle class parents, for example, perceive alternative education as something that happens with students who have "special" problems or for students who are "radical" then they as educational consumers, with considerable political clout, are not likely to be attracted to the concept.

Seldom are programs for the "fringe" perceived to be models for the middle class. Moreover, it should be clear to most of us working within established educational institutions, that the *serious* development of alternatives within the public schools will depend a great deal on the acceptability of the idea by mainstream parents, teachers, and administrators.

Problems in the Movement

Consequently, there is at one level a general "image" problem associated with some alternative programs. To counter this, a number of alternative school leaders have emphasized the college-bound nature of many of these programs and the success of the alternative school graduate in entering some of the country's top colleges and universities. Further, there is an attempt to highlight alternatives within so-called "affluent" or "prestigious" school districts such as Newton, Massachusetts; Great Neck, New York; Webster Groves, Missouri; Prince Georges County, Maryland; Beverly Hills, California; and the like. Further, emphasis is given to the reputable aspects of the programs, such as Montessori Schools, Prep Schools and Academies (formerly expensive and exclusive private schools), and British Primary Schools (borrowed from the English experience).

At another level, there are substantive shortcomings associated with certain alternative schools. For example, they promise to do everything, that is, "their" alternative would solve all the problems and be vastly superior to standard education. We have witnessed the rather common occurrence of a small group of dedicated professionals literally working around the clock to keep an alternative program together. This tendency has not only led to a cycle of high expectation, low achievement—resulting in frustration for both the practitioners and the users of alternative schools—but also, in certain cases, has alienated professional and lay colleagues who happen to prefer standard education.

On this latter point, one of the major weaknesses of the public alternative school trend thus far is that many of those leading the way have "written off" the standard pattern of schooling. That is to say, in order to legitimize new alternative approaches, they have made the existing pattern look bad by comparison. However, standard education is a legitimate option. It is also the one most parents, teachers, and students know best and prefer. To engender such internal antagonism among alternative schools within the public school community swims directly against the cooperative spirit which optional education embraces. This matter can be solved in part by maintaining that standard education is a legitimate option—

in fact, it has been the basic pattern of public schooling which has carried the weight of responsibility thus far. With the advent of universal education, this pattern has been overloaded. However, those parents, teachers, and students who prefer this option have the right to it in a system of public schools of choice.[2]

A brief word about something as routine as the labels used in classifying alternatives may be illustrative of the sensitivity which needs to be considered. At times, in an eagerness to communicate the distinctive flavor of the option being proposed, a label is tagged on which alienates those not associated with the program. For example, a proposal for a "humanistic" alternative elicits strong reaction from other sources who maintain that their approach is also humanistic or that by implication ongoing programs are "dehumanistic." Similarly, the word "open" might trigger the reaction that other programs are therefore "closed."

Another major source of difficulty is procedural and deals with the process of legitimizing options. What constitutes a legitimate option within our public schools? What are the criteria which school districts need to employ in considering options?

What Are the Options?

Many anxieties and concerns which are a natural concomitant of innovation, but which if not relieved can serve to thwart change also accompany alternative school proposals. By considering and agreeing on a set of common ground rules many of these fears can be alleviated among laymen and professionals alike. We now have enough experience and have profited from some of the early alternative school efforts so that we may suggest a set of ground rules for engaging in this new system of educational options.

Alternatives within public schools:

1. Are not superimposed, but a matter of choice for all participants—teachers, parents, and students.

2. Are viewed as another way of providing education alongside the existing pattern, which continues to be legitimate. Alternatives are different from special programs for dropouts, unwed mothers, and the like.

3. Do not practice exclusivity.

4. Do not make exaggerated claims of accomplishments that may be deceptive in the long run.

5. Are aimed at a broad, common set of educational objectives, not just limited objectives. Alternative public schools are responsible to the public for comprehensive cognitive and affective goals that cannot be compromised, including basic skills, learning to learn skills, talent development, socialization of basic societal roles (citizen, consumer, worker), and self-concept development.

6. Do not cost more money than existing per student expenditures.

7. Are evaluated.

It is clear also that sufficient time is necessary for the key participants to engage in planning. Too often, alternatives are mounted "on the backs" of those who are also engaged in carrying the "normal" full-time responsibilities. Teachers especially cannot keep an existing program going while, at the same time, being expected to make some kind of quantum leap into an educationally sound alternative environment. They need released time for planning, for involving parents and students in the development.

If school boards or school administrators give priority to alternative education, then they need to provide some "seed" money for planning and development purposes. This may mean rearranging the priorities for existing resources. Certainly this does not preclude initiating enabling state legislation which can provide "conversion capital" to other school systems interested in initiating options within public schools.

Perhaps the biggest problem is to foster professional leadership in advancing options and choice in public education. On balance the public seems willing to consider this plan because it appears both reasonable and constructive to them. Most teachers feel it is a good idea because alternatives hold the promise of providing opportunities for them to choose the type of educational environment that supports their style. In one sense alternatives can be a liberating force for teachers and other professionals who may feel victimized by the constraints of the uniform structure of our public schools.

Professional educators—especially administrators and supervisors—have the responsibility for opening a serious dialogue on alternative education in their communities. Most teachers, parents, and students will turn to them for leadership and validation of this new proposal. Leadership is needed which can keep the lines of communication open among the basic interested parties and can assure their participation in planning and development. Leadership must also reveal clearly just how alternatives relate to what is best for the learner: individualizing and personalizing the learning process, providing teachers, students, and parents with more choice among legitimate optional learning environments, utilizing existing resources differently, perhaps more wisely—in short, establishing the educational, political, and economic rationale for alternative education.

Perhaps we all need to remember the life and death cycle which characterized progressive education earlier in this century. We can "kill" alternatives by having them fall victim to faddism. We can compromise the conception of alternative education to such an extent that implementation will become so watered down as to be a matter of ridicule or a mere relabeling of existing educational practices. Or, we can profit from our past experiences and parlay these lessons into a timely opportunity for genuine school reform, which options in public education have the promise of becoming. Professional educators, after a decade of criticism, need to advance a concept of public education worthy of their noblest values. We need a plan around which people of good will can rally.

While we are calling for professional leadership, it may make good sense also to remind ourselves that while we are trying to come to grips with pluralism in education, another trend is gaining momentum before our very eyes. It is a trend which grows out of public dissatisfaction and a demand for accountability and which stresses a single no-nonsense return to the 3 R's—strict adherence to standardized measures of achievement, ability grouping by IQ, nonpromotion policies, lowering the compulsory school attendance age, placing more police guards in schools. In short, this trend calls for a return to the way schools were earlier in this century.

The ability of the public school to deal effectively with such contemporary ideas as universal equality of opportunity and cultural diversity has led to serious student reaction. This has been interpreted by members of the general public as "permissiveness and lack of discipline" in the schools. Their proposal for school improvement is based on what they know best, what they themselves have experienced as students in such schools. They call for more uniformity supported by a law and order policy within the schools.

In brief, this growing trend, which can swing into a full-fledged movement at any time, would establish more standardization and conformity. It would convey a notion of child growth and development in which there were "winners and losers"—with the latter receiving the verdict that the problem was theirs, not the schools.

It is difficult to see how such a trend will promote the noblest values of human growth. Consequently, there is a sense of urgency in considering alternatives at this time and this is why I have written two books on the subject. This is why the special call is made for professional leadership—including that of our giant teacher organizations. We are close to the proverbial crossroads—one road leading to variety in education and to a concept of growth in which each child is provided an environment that best supports his or her learning style and personal development, in which there are no student failures, only program failures. The other road establishes one right way, with clear norms, with learners competing for the right to be considered "winners," with the losers relegated to an underclass status. Which conception of personal growth and development (the heart and soul of education) will we support?

The former should warrant the full mobilization of our professional energies—as an antidote to the latter.

FOOTNOTES

1. Fifth annual Gallup Poll of public attitude toward education. 55 (1): 43; September 1973.
2. For an expanded discussion of alternatives within public schools see: Mario D. Fantini. *Public Schools of Choice*. New York: Simon and Schuster, Inc., 1974.

THE ALTERNATIVE TO SCHOOLING*

BY IVAN ILLICH†

For generations we have tried to make the world a better place by providing more and more schooling, but so far the endeavor has failed. What we have learned instead is that forcing all children to climb an open-ended education ladder cannot enhance equality but must favor the individual who starts out earlier, healthier, or better prepared; that enforced instruction deadens for most people the will for independent learning; and that knowledge treated as a commodity, delivered in packages, and accepted as private property once it is acquired, must always be scarce.

In response, critics of the educational system are now proposing strong and unorthodox remedies that range from the voucher plan, which would enable each person to buy the education of his choice on an open market, to shifting the responsibility for education from the school to the media and to apprenticeship on the job. Some individuals foresee that the school will have to be disestablished just as the church was disestablished all over the world during the last two centuries. Other reformers propose to replace the universal school with various new systems that would, they claim, better prepare everybody for life in modern society. These proposals for new educational institutions fall into three broad categories: the reformation of the classroom within the school system; the dispersal of free schools throughout society; and the transformation of all society into one huge classroom. But these three approaches—the reformed classroom, the free school, and the worldwide classroom—represent three stages in a proposed escalation of education in which each step threatens more subtle and more pervasive social control than the one it replaces.

* Reprinted by permission of Saturday Review, from the June 1971 issue of *Saturday Review of Education.*

† Ivan Illich is author of *Celebration of Awareness, De-schooling Society,* and *Tools for Conviviality.*

I believe that the disestablishment of the school has become inevitable and that this end of an illusion should fill us with hope. But I also believe that the end of the "age of schooling" could usher in the epoch of the global schoolhouse that would be distinguishable only in name from a global madhouse or global prison in which education, correction, and adjustment become synonymous. I therefore believe that the breakdown of the school forces us to look beyond its imminent demise and to face fundamental alternatives in education. Either we can work for fearsome and potent new educational devices that teach about a world which progressively becomes more opaque and forbidding for man, or we can set the conditions for a new era in which technology would be used to make society more simple and transparent, so that all men can once again know the facts and use the tools that shape their lives. In short, we can disestablish schools or we can deschool culture.

The hidden curriculum of schools

In order to see clearly the alternatives we face, we must first distinguish education from schooling, which means separating the humanistic intent of the teacher from the impact of the invariant structure of the school. This hidden structure constitutes a course of instruction that stays forever beyond the control of the teacher or of his school board. It conveys indelibly the message that only through schooling can an individual prepare himself for adulthood in society, that what is not taught in school is of little value, and that what is learned outside of school is not worth knowing. I call it the hidden curriculum of schooling, because it constitutes the unalterable framework of the system, within which all changes in the curriculum are made.

The hidden curriculum is always the same regardless of school or place. It requires all children of a certain age to assemble in groups of about 30, under the authority of a certified teacher, for some 500 to 1,000 or more hours each year. It doesn't matter whether the curriculum is designed to teach the principles of fascism, liberalism, Catholicism, or socialism; or whether the purpose of the school is to produce Soviet or United States citizens, mechanics, or doctors. It makes no difference whether the teacher is authoritarian or permissive, whether he imposes his own creed or teaches students to think for themselves. What is important is that students learn that education is valuable when it is acquired in the school through a graded process of consumption; that the degree of success the individual will enjoy in society depends on the amount of learning he consumes; and that learning about the world is more valuable than learning from the world.

It must be clearly understood that the hidden curriculum translates learning from an activity into a commodity—for which the school monopolizes the market. In all countries knowledge is regarded as the first necessity for survival, but also as a form of currency more liquid than rubles or dollars. We have become accustomed, through Karl Marx's writings, to speak about the alienation of the worker from his work in a class society. We must now recognize the estrangement of man from his learning when it becomes the product of a service profession and he becomes the consumer.

The more learning an individual consumes, the more "knowledge stock" he acquires. The hidden curriculum therefore defines a new class structure for society within which the large consumers of knowledge—those who have acquired large quantities of knowledge stock—enjoy special privileges, high income, and access to the more powerful tools of production. This kind of knowledge-capitalism has been accepted in all industrialized societies and establishes a rationale for the distribution of jobs and income. (This point is especially important in the light of the lack of correspondence between schooling and occupational competence established in studies such as Ivar Berg's *Education and Jobs: The Great Training Robbery*.)

The endeavor to put all men through successive stages of enlightenment is rooted deeply in alchemy, the Great Art of the waning Middle Ages. John Amos Comenius, a Moravian bishop, self-styled Pansophist, and pedagogue, is rightly considered one of the founders of the modern schools. He was among the first to propose seven or twelve grades of compulsory learning. In his *Magna Didactica,* he described schools as devices to "teach everybody everything" and outlined a blueprint for the assembly-line production of knowledge, which according to his method would make education cheaper and better and make growth into full humanity possible for all. But Comenius was not only an early efficiency expert, he was an alchemist who adopted the technical language of his craft to describe the art of rearing children. The alchemist sought to refine base elements by leading their distilled spirits through twelve stages of successive enlightenment, so that for their own and all the world's benefit they might be transmuted into gold. Of course, alchemists failed no matter how often they tried, but each time their "science" yielded new reasons for their failure, and they tried again.

Pedagogy opened a new chapter in the history of Ars Magna. Education became the search for an alchemic process that would bring forth a new type of man who would fit into an environment created by scientific magic. But, no matter how much each generation spent on its schools, it always turned out that the majority of people were unfit for enlightenment by this process and had to be discarded as unprepared for life in a man-made world.

Educational reformers who accept the idea that schools have failed fall into three groups. The most respectable are certainly the great masters of alchemy who promise better schools. The most seductive are popular magicians, who promise to make every kitchen into an alchemic lab. The most sinister are the new Masons of the Universe, who want to transform the entire world into one huge temple of learning. Notable among today's masters of alchemy are certain research directors employed or sponsored by the large foundations who believe that schools, if they could somehow be improved, could also become economically more feasible than those that are now in trouble, and simultaneously could sell a larger package of services. Those who are concerned primarily with the curriculum claim that it is outdated or irrelevant. So the curriculum is filled with new packaged courses on African culture, North American imperialism, women's lib, pollution, or the consumer society. Passive learning is wrong—it is indeed—so we graciously allow students to decide what and how they want to be taught. Schools are prison houses. Therefore, principals are authorized to approve teach-outs, moving the school desks to a roped-off Harlem street. Sensitivity training becomes fashionable. So, we import group therapy into the classroom. School, which was supposed to teach everybody everything, now becomes all things to all children.

Other critics emphasize that schools make inefficient use of modern science. Some would administer drugs to make it easier for the instructor to change the child's behavior. Others would transform school into a stadium for educational gaming. Still others would electrify the classroom. If they are simplistic disciples of McLuhan, they replace blackboards and textbooks with multimedia happenings; if they follow Skinner, they claim to be able to modify behavior more efficiently than old-fashioned classroom practitioners can.

Most of these changes have, of course, some good effects. The experimental schools have fewer truants. Parents do have a greater feeling of participation in a decentralized district. Pupils, assigned by their teacher to an apprenticeship, do often turn out more competent than those who stay in the classroom. Some children do improve their knowledge of Spanish in the language lab because they prefer playing with the knobs of a tape recorder to conversations with their Puerto Rican peers. Yet all these improvements operate within predictably narrow limits, since they leave the hidden curriculum of school intact.

Some reformers would like to shake loose from the hidden curriculum, but they rarely succeed. Free schools that lead to further free schools produce a mirage of freedom, even though the chain of attendance is frequently interrupted by long stretches of loafing. Attendance through seduction inculcates the need for educational treatment more persuasively than the reluctant attendance enforced by a truant officer. Permissive teachers in a padded classroom can easily render their pupils impotent to survive once they leave.

Learning in these schools often remains nothing more than the acquisition of socially valued skills defined, in this instance, by the consensus of a commune rather than by the decree of a school board. New presbyter is but old priest writ large.

Free schools, to be truly free, must meet two conditions: First, they must be run in a way to prevent the reintroduction of the hidden curriculum of graded attendance and certified students studying at the feet of certified teachers. And, more importantly, they must provide a framework in which all participants—staff and pupils—can free themselves from the hidden foundations of a schooled society. The first condition is frequently incorporated in the stated aims of a free school. The second condition is only rarely recognized, and is difficult to state as the goal of a free school.

The hidden assumptions of education

It is useful to distinguish between the hidden curriculum, which I have described, and the occult foundations of schooling. The hidden curriculum is a ritual that can be considered the official initiation into modern society, institutionally established through the school. It is the purpose of this ritual to hide from its participants the contradictions between the myth of an egalitarian society and the class-conscious reality it certifies. Once they are recognized as such, rituals lose their power, and this is what is now beginning to happen to schooling. But there are certain fundamental assumptions about growing up—the occult foundations—which now find their expression in the ceremonial of schooling, and which could easily be reinforced by what free schools do.

Among these assumptions is what Peter Schrag calls the "immigration syndrome," which impels us to treat all people as if they were newcomers who must go through a naturalization process. Only certified consumers of knowledge are admitted to citizenship. Men are not born equal, but are made equal through gestation by Alma Mater.

The rhetoric of all schools states that they form a man for the future, but they do not release him for his task before he has developed a high level of tolerance to the ways of his elders: education *for* life rather than *in* everyday life. Few free schools can avoid doing precisely this. Nevertheless they are among the most important centers from which a new life-style radiates, not because of the effect their graduates will have but, rather, because elders who choose to bring up their children without the benefit of properly ordained teachers frequently belong to a radical minority and because their preoccupation with the rearing of their children sustains them in their new style.

The hidden hand in an educational market

The most dangerous category of educational reformer is one who argues that knowledge can be produced and sold much more effectively on an open market than on one controlled by the school. These people argue that most skills can be easily acquired from skill-models if the learner is truly interested in their acquisition; that individual entitlements can provide a more equal purchasing power for education. They demand a careful separation of the process by which knowledge is acquired from the process by which it is measured and certified. These seem to me obvious statements. But it would be a fallacy to believe that the establishment of a free market for knowledge would constitute a radical alternative in education.

The establishment of a free market would indeed abolish what I have previously called the hidden curriculum of present schooling—its age-specific attendance at a graded curriculum. Equally, a free market would at first give the appearance of counteracting what I have called the occult foundations of a schooled society: the "immigration syndrome," the institutional monopoly of teaching, and the ritual of linear initiation. But at the same time a free market in education would provide the alchemist with innumerable hidden hands to fit each man into the multiple, tight little niches a more complex technocracy can provide.

Many decades of reliance on schooling have turned knowledge into a commodity, a marketable staple of a special kind. Knowledge is now regarded simultaneously as a first necessity and also as society's most precious currency. (The transformation of knowledge into a commodity is reflected in a corresponding transformation of language. Words that formerly functioned as verbs are becoming nouns that designate possessions. Until recently dwelling and learning and even healing designated activities. They are now usually conceived as commodities or services to be delivered. We talk about the manufacture of housing or the delivery of medical care. Men are no longer regarded fit to house or heal themselves. In such a society people come to believe that professional services are more valuable than personal care. Instead of learning how to nurse grandmother, the teen-ager learns to picket the hospital that does not admit her.) This attitude could easily survive the disestablishment of school, just as affiliation with a church remained a condition for office long after the adoption of the First Amendment. It is even more evident that test batteries measuring complex knowledge-packages could easily survive the disestablishment of school—and with this would go the compulsion to obligate everybody to acquire a minimum package in the knowledge stock. The scientific measurement of each man's worth and the alchemic dream of each man's "educability to his full humanity" would finally coincide. Under the appearance of a "free" market, the global village would turn into an environmental womb where pedagogic therapists control the complex navel by which each man is nourished.

At present schools limit the teacher's competence to the classroom. They prevent him from claiming man's whole life as his domain. The demise of school will remove this restriction and give a semblance of legitimacy to the lifelong pedagogical invasion of everybody's privacy. It will open the way for a scramble for "knowledge" on a free market, which would lead us toward the paradox of a vulgar, albeit seemingly egalitarian, meritocracy. Unless the concept of knowledge is transformed, the disestablishment of school will lead to a wedding between a growing meritocratic system that separates learning from certification and a society committed to provide therapy for each man until he is ripe for the gilded age.

For those who subscribe to the technocratic ethos, whatever is technically possible must be made available at least to a few whether they want it or not. Neither the privation nor the frustration of the majority counts. If cobalt treatment is possible, then the city of Tegucigalpa needs one apparatus in each of its two major hospitals, at a cost that would free an important part of the population of Honduras from parasites. If supersonic speeds are possible, then it must speed the travel of some. If the flight to Mars can be conceived, then a rationale must be found to make it appear a necessity. In the technocratic ethos poverty is modernized: Not only are old alternatives closed off by new monopolies, but the lack of necessities is also compounded by a growing spread between those services that are technologically feasible and those that are in fact available to the majority.

A teacher turns "educator" when he adopts this technocratic ethos. He then acts as if education were a technological enterprise designed to make man fit into whatever environment the "progress" of science creates. He seems blind to the evidence that constant obsolescence of all commodities comes at a high price: the mounting cost of training people to know about them. He seems to forget that the rising cost of tools is purchased at a high price in education: They decrease the labor intensity of the economy, make learning on the job impossible, or, at best, a privilege for a few. All over the world the cost of educating men for society rises faster than the productivity of the entire economy, and fewer people have a sense of intelligent participation in the commonweal.

Recovery of responsibility for teaching and learning

A revolution against those forms of privilege and power, which are based on claims to professional knowledge, must start with a transformation of consciousness about the nature of learning. This means, above all, a shift of responsibility for teaching and learning. Knowledge can be defined as a commodity only as long as it is viewed as the result of institutional enterprise or as the fulfillment of institutional objectives. Only when a man recovers the sense of personal responsibility for what he learns and teaches can this spell be broken and the alienation of learning from living be overcome.

The recovery of the power to learn or to teach means that the teacher who takes the risk of interfering in somebody else's private affairs also assumes responsibility for the results. Similarly, the student who exposes himself to the influence of a teacher must take responsibility for his own education. For such purposes educational institutions—if they are at all needed—ideally take the form of facility centers where one can get a roof of the right size over his head, access to a piano or a kiln, and to records, books, or slides. Schools, television stations, theaters, and the like are designed primarily for use by professionals. Deschooling society means above all the denial of professional status for the second-oldest profession, namely teaching. The certification of teachers now constitutes an undue restriction of the right to free speech: the corporate structure and professional pretensions of journalism an undue restriction on the right to free press. Compulsory attendance rules interfere with free assembly. The deschooling of society is nothing less than a cultural mutation by which a people recovers the effective use of its Constitutional freedoms: learning and teaching by men who know that they are born free rather than treated to freedom. Most people learn most of the time when they do whatever they enjoy; most people are curious and want to give meaning to whatever they come in contact with; and most people are capable of personal intimate intercourse with others unless they are stupefied by inhuman work or turned off by schooling.

The fact that people in rich countries do not learn much on their own constitutes no proof to the contrary. Rather it is a consequence of life in an environment from which, paradoxically, they cannot learn much, precisely because it is so highly programmed. They are constantly frustrated by the structure of contemporary society in which the facts on which decisions can be made have become elusive. They live in an environment in which tools that can be used for creative purposes have become luxuries, an environment in which channels of communication serve a few to talk to many.

A new technology rather than a new education

A modern myth would make us believe that the sense of impotence with which most men live today is a consequence of technology that cannot but create huge systems. But it is not technology that makes systems huge, tools immensely powerful, channels of communication one-directional. Quite the contrary: Properly controlled, technology could provide each man with the ability to understand his environment better, to shape it powerfully with his own hands, and to permit him full intercommunication to a degree never before possible. Such an alternative use of technology constitutes the central alternative in education.

If a person is to grow up he needs, first of all, access to things, to places and to processes, to events and to records. He needs to see, to touch, to tinker with, to grasp whatever there is in a meaningful setting. This access is now largely denied. When knowledge became a commodity, it acquired the protections of private property, and thus a principle designed to guard personal intimacy became a rationale for declaring facts off limits for people without the proper credentials. In schools teachers keep knowledge to themselves unless it fits into the day's program. The media inform, but exclude those things they regard as unfit to print. Information is locked into special languages, and specialized teachers live off its retranslation. Patents are protected by corporations, secrets are guarded by bureaucracies, and the power to keep others out of private preserves—be they cockpits, law offices, junkyards, or clinics—is jealously guarded by professions, institutions, and nations. Neither the political nor the professional structure of our societies, East and West, could withstand the elimination of the power to keep entire classes of people from facts that could serve them. The access to facts that I advocate goes far beyond truth in labeling. Access must be built into reality, while all we ask from advertising is a guarantee that it does not mislead. Access to reality constitutes a fundamental alternative in education to a system that only purports to teach *about* it.

Abolishing the right to corporate secrecy—even when professional opinion holds that this secrecy serves the common good—is, as shall presently appear, a much more radical political goal than the traditional demand for public ownership or control of the tools of production. The socialization of tools without the effective socialization of know-how in their use tends to put the knowledge-capitalist into the position formerly held by the financier. The technocrat's only claim to power is the stock he holds in some class of scarce and secret knowledge, and the best means to protect its value is a large and capital-intensive organization that renders access to know-how formidable and forbidding.

It does not take much time for the interested learner to acquire almost any skill that he wants to use. We tend to forget this in a society where professional teachers monopolize entrance into all fields, and thereby stamp teaching by uncertified individuals as quackery. There are few mechanical skills used in industry or research that are as demanding, complex, and dangerous as driving cars, a skill that most people quickly acquire from a peer. Not all people are suited for advanced logic, yet those who are make rapid progress if they are challenged to play mathematical games at an early age. One out of twenty kids in Cuernavaca can beat me at Wiff 'n' Proof after a couple of weeks' training. In four months all but a small percentage of motivated adults at our CIDOC center learn Spanish well enough to conduct academic business in the new language.

A first step toward opening up access to skills would be to provide various incentives for skilled individuals to share their knowledge. Inevitably, this would run counter to the interest of guilds and professions and unions. Yet, multiple apprenticeship is attractive: It provides everybody with an opportunity to learn something about almost anything. There is no reason why a person should not combine the ability to drive a car, repair telephones and toilets, act as a midwife, and function as an architectural draftsman. Special-interest groups and their disciplined consumers would, of course, claim that the public needs the protection of a professional guarantee. But this argument is now steadily being challenged by consumer protection associations. We have to take much more seriously the objection that economists raise to the radical socialization of skills: that "progress" will be impeded if knowledge—patents, skills, and all the rest—is democratized. Their argument can be faced only if we demonstrate to them the growth rate of futile diseconomics generated by any existing educational system.

Access to people willing to share their skills is no guarantee of learning. Such access is restricted not only by the monopoly of educational programs over learning and of unions over licensing but also by a technology of scarcity. The skills that count today are know-how in the use of highly specialized tools that were designed to be scarce. These tools produce goods or render services that everybody wants but only a few can enjoy, and which only a limited number of people know how to use. Only a few privileged individuals out of the total number of people who have a given disease ever benefit from the results of sophisticated medical technology, and even fewer doctors develop the skill to use it.

The same results of medical research have, however, also been employed to create a basic medical tool kit that permits army and navy medics, with only a few months training, to obtain results, under battlefield conditions, that would have been beyond the expectations of full-fledged doctors during World War II. On an even simpler level any peasant girl could learn how to diagnose and treat most infections if medical scientists prepared dosages and instructions specifically for a given geographic area.

All these examples illustrate the fact that educational considerations alone suffice to demand a radical reduction of the professional structure that now impedes the mutual relationship between the scientist and the majority of people who want access to science. If this demand were heeded, all men could learn to use yesterday's tools, rendered more effective and durable by modern science, to create tomorrow's world.

Unfortunately, precisely the contrary trend prevails at present. I know a coastal area in South America where most people support themselves by fishing from small boats. The outboard motor is certainly the tool that has changed most dramatically the lives of these coastal fishermen. But in the area I have surveyed, half of all outboard motors that were purchased between 1945 and 1950 are still kept running by constant tinkering, while half the motors purchased in 1965 no longer run because they were not built to be repaired. Technological progress provides the majority of people with gadgets they cannot afford and deprives them of the simpler tools they need.

Metals, plastics, and ferro cement used in building have greatly improved since the 1940's and ought to provide more people the opportunity to create their own homes. But while in the United States, in 1948, more than 30 percent of all one-family homes were owner-built, by the end of the 1960's the percentage of those who acted as their own contractors had dropped to less than 20 percent.

The lowering of the skill level through so-called economic development becomes even more visible in Latin America. Here most people still build their own homes from floor to roof. Often they use mud, in the form of adobe, and thatchwork of unsurpassed utility in the moist, hot, and windy climate. In other places they make their dwellings out of cardboard, oildrums, and other industrial refuse. Instead of providing people with simple tools and highly standardized, durable, and easily repaired components, all governments have gone in for the mass production of low-cost buildings. It is clear that not one single country can afford to provide satisfactory modern dwelling units for the majority of its people. Yet, everywhere this policy makes it progressively more difficult for the majority to acquire the knowledge and skills they need to build better houses for themselves.

Self-chosen "poverty"

Educational considerations permit us to formulate a second fundamental characteristic that any postindustrial society must possess: a basic tool kit that by its very nature counteracts technocratic control. For educational reasons we must work toward a society in which scientific knowledge is incorporated in tools and components that can be used meaningfully in units small enough to be within the reach of all. Only such tools can socialize access to skills. Only such tools favor temporary associations among those who want to use them for a specific occasion. Only such tools allow specific goals to emerge in the process of their use, as any tinkerer knows. Only the combination of guaranteed access to facts and of limited power in most tools renders it possible to envisage a subsistence economy capable of incorporating the fruits of modern science.

The development of such a scientific subsistence economy is unquestionably to the advantage of the overwhelming majority of all people in poor countries. It is also the only alternative to progressive pollution, exploitation, and opaqueness in rich countries. But, as we have seen, the dethroning of the GNP cannot be achieved without simultaneously subverting GNE (gross national education—usually conceived as manpower capitalization). An egalitarian economy cannot exist in a society in which the right to produce is conferred by schools.

The feasibility of a modern subsistence economy does not depend on new scientific inventions. It depends primarily on the ability of a society to agree on fundamental, self-chosen antibureaucratic and antitechnocratic restraints.

These restraints can take many forms, but they will not work unless they touch the basic dimensions of life. (The decision of Congress against development of the supersonic transport plane is one of the most encouraging steps in the right direction.) The substance of these voluntary social restraints would be very simple matters that can be fully understood and judged by any prudent man. The issues at stake in the SST controversy provide a good example. All such restraints would be chosen to promote stable and equal enjoyment of scientific know-how. The French say that it takes a thousand years to educate a peasant to deal with a cow. It would not take two generations to help all people in Latin America or Africa to use and repair outboard motors, simple cars, pumps, medicine kits, and ferro cement machines if their design does not change every few years. And since a joyful life is one of constant meaningful intercourse with others in a meaningful environment, equal enjoyment does translate into equal education.

At present a consensus on austerity is difficult to imagine.

The reason usually given for the impotence of the majority is stated in terms of political or economic class. What is not usually understood is that the new class structure of a schooled society is even more powerfully controlled by vested interests. No doubt an imperialist and capitalist organization of society provides the social structure within which a minority can have disproportionate influence over the effective opinion of the majority. But in a technocratic society the power of a minority of knowledge-capitalists can prevent the formation of true public opinion through control of scientific know-how and the media of communication. Constitutional guarantees of free speech, free press, and free assembly were meant to ensure government by the people. Modern electronics, photo-offset presses, time-sharing computers, and telephones have in principle provided the hardware that could give an entirely new meaning to these freedoms. Unfortunately, these things are used in modern media to increase the power of knowledge-bankers to funnel their program-packages through international chains to more people, instead of being used to increase true networks that provide equal opportunity for encounter among the members of the majority.

Deschooling the culture and social structure requires the use of technology to make participatory politics possible. Only on the basis of a majority coalition can limits to secrecy and growing power be determined without dictatorship. We need a new environment in which growing up can be classless, or we will get a brave new world in which Big Brother educates us all.

CBE VIEWS THE ALTERNATIVES*

BY MORTIMER SMITH†

In any discussion of alternative schools we must begin by defining what we mean by schools. Dr. Johnson said that

* © 1973 by Phi Delta Kappa, Inc. Reprinted by permission of the author and Phi Delta Kappa, Inc.

† Mortimer Smith is the author of several books about public educa-

definitions are hazardous, and he might have added, especially those definitions which attempt to state the purposes of social institutions. In a fragmented society such as ours, where to a large degree we have lost a sense of community and shared purpose, we cannot assume that everyone means the same thing when the talk is about the use of any of our institutions. To make my own position clear at once, my view of the purpose of schools is that proclaimed by the Council for Basic Education when it was founded more than 16 years ago: "They exist to provide the essential skills of language, numbers, and orderly thought, and to transmit in a reasoned pattern the intellectual, moral, and aesthetic heritage of civilized man." Although such a definition of purpose is in some circles considered quaint, if not actually antediluvian, perhaps a majority of Americans are still able to accept it, are still willing to say that while schools may have peripheral purposes their chief purpose is to make young people literate in word and number and in historical knowledge.

Now to accept this traditional idea of the function of schools does not mean that one accepts as sacrosanct their present structure and organization. Schools don't have to be run on a 10-month, 9-to-3 schedule. Reading, the social studies, and English don't have to be taught by methods devised by educationists in the 1940s and 1950s. The road to teaching does not have to be only through certification based on a training that is long on education courses and short on academic preparation. More lay participation in the conduct of schools, performance contracting, even voucher plans, should not make educators blanch, nor should programs that combine part-time work and part-time study. The site for learning does not have to be an either-or matter—old-fashioned egg-crate building or the new open type which resembles an air terminal with wall-to-wall carpeting.

In schools particular programs or arrangements or organizational patterns are not important. The important thing is the human element—teachers who combine a sense of humanity and justice in dealing with young people with the requisite knowledge and teaching skills. My point was summed up a few years ago by William H. Cornog of New Trier High School: "We think our school's central task is to train youth

---

tion. Now retired, he was for many years Executive Director of the Council for Basic Education and editor of its monthly *Bulletin*.

in the use of the mind. We assume that this can still be done in box-like classrooms, if the right people are put in the right boxes and get their minds agitated by subjects, or the ideas in them."

The view of the Council for Basic Education is that the more alternatives we have the merrier, as long as they are alternatives to conventional arrangements and not to the historic function of schools. Unfortunately, I see very little in the present leadership of the movement for alternative schools that encourages me to think that the new arrangements will foster rather than discourage the old purposes. Some of these leaders are cultists rather than serious reformers. Read Peter Marin's article in the *Saturday Review* ("Has Imagination Outstripped Reality?" July 22, 1972) about a representative group of radical deschoolers and free-schoolers who gathered at a New Orleans conference and you will see that many of them are prima donnas who can't agree among themselves and show little grasp of the pragmatic reality of schools. Some of them want schools to liberate the blacks or the poor (liberators are apt to have generous traveling grants); some want schools to foster the counterculture; others are social perfectionists who can't bear to face the fact that joy and ecstasy are not constant factors in the lives of teachers and school-children; still others want the schools to help overthrow the present economic order.

Most of the reformers described by Marin are on the far-out fringe of the alternative schools movement, but even among the more reasonable advocates there is a tendency to erect hypotheses and conjectures about learning and the nature of youth into a fairly rigid set of neoprogressive doctrines. The foremost doctrine, especially on the elementary school level, insists on the necessity for "informality." Its lack, according to Charles E. Silberman, has made American classrooms dour places, "killers of the dream," and its presence in some British primary schools has turned them into places of great joy and spontaneity and creative activity. Silberman is unable to point to any data suggesting that informal schools increase achievement, but then he agrees with an English research report which suggests that "the consequences of different modes of schooling should be sought less in academic attainment than in their impact on how children feel about themselves, about school, and about learning."[1]

This last remark suggests another item in the doctrinal litany of many alternative-schoolers: the importance of "feeling." One would suppose that children who achieve well academically would have a good feeling toward themselves, toward schools, and toward learning, but those who are keen on "affective" learning—I use the currently popular jargon—rarely see that it is enhanced by accomplishments in the "cognitive" realm. Some of the alternative school prophets seem to think that there is a fundamental conflict between emotion, or feeling, and intellect, failing to perceive what would seem to be an obvious truth: Feeling and intellect complement each other, the mind providing a guide for the feelings.

After "informality" and "feeling" come a string of doctrines: Children should be allowed to do their thing as the spirit moves them; they are naturally good until corrupted by the outside world; they must never be told things but should discover them on their own; the teacher who asserts authority, either over conduct or in teaching subject matter, is no better than an authoritarian dictator; the right relation between teacher and pupils is that of equality and palship; and—one of the hoariest of the progressive bromides—the school must bring "real life" and "the real world" into the classroom.

With such a set of governing doctrines many alternative schools tend to be anti-book learning and indifferent to the basic skills and to any kind of "structure." Many go in for no grades and no failures, no bells between classes, handlooms and gerbil cages, and guitar playing in the halls. The "educational" program runs heavily to courses in macrame, tie-dying, karate, yoga, urban renewal, and wilderness survival. And over all there waves that banner with the strange device: Relevance!

Not all alternative schools, of course, are such caricatures of real education. Strangely enough, Jonathan Kozol, who considers our school system, to say nothing of our society in general, to be rotten and corrupt, runs his free school in Roxbury, Massachusetts, along rather structured lines, teaching the basic subjects in a purposeful and sequential manner and soft-pedaling the paeans to Joy. He knows that the parents of the poor black children who go to his school want them to learn skills and he is impatient with young affluent white teachers who think such children will be better off making clay vases, weaving Indian headbands, playing with Polaroid cameras, and climbing over geodesic domes.

Several public schools that claim to present alternatives have also managed to be innovative and to meet the interests of students without abandoning the school's fundamental purpose of education. And of course many of the original alternative schools—the private schools—have for a long time been combining learning with practices that would be considered unorthodox in the public school system. With honorable exceptions, however, the alternative school movement seems to have fallen into the hands of either the more *avant garde* of the free-schoolers or the neoprogressives who are busy rediscovering William Heard Kilpatrick.

The alternatives movement in my view falls far short of providing the realistic reforms that many educators and laymen have long been demanding. Consider a little history. In the 1950s it became apparent that American public education was badly in need of change. There was widespread evidence of lowered academic achievement, eroded standards, poor teacher preparation, the proliferation of trivial courses, and the domination of the schools by an unimaginative and standpat establishment consisting of the schools of education, national teacher associations, state departments of education, and the U. S. Office of Education. An amorphous something known as "life adjustment education" was in the air which seemed to be reducible to the notion that the majority of American youth were uneducable and that therefore the schools must provide a substitute for education for this majority. The founding of the Council for Basic Education in 1956 was the first organizational effort on a national scale to call attention to these conditions and to suggest plans for reform. After the alert of the first Sputnik, even before, many academicians who had formerly been aloof from the schools started work on curricular changes, especially in math, in the sciences, and in languages. Some of the reforms of the fifties and early sixties had an impact and some never got off the ground, but there is no doubt that the agitations of the period did much to stem the anti-intellectualism which stressed the social adjustment function of the schools over the primary educative function.

In the middle sixties (roughly) we discovered the "disadvantaged" and the reform clock was turned backwards. For every educator like Kenneth Clark, who considered our first duty was to teach black children to read and write so they might enlarge their horizons, there were a dozen, usually white, who assured us that what we needed to stress in ghetto schools was informality, nongrouping, unstructured programs, the dialect of the streets, and the supposedly superior energy and spontaneity of the culture of poverty. This attitude was infectious and many educators began to apply these criteria for ghetto schools to all schools. In other words, they joined Silberman in suggesting that universally the consequences of schooling should be sought not in academic attainment but in how students feel. This seems to be the attitude of perhaps the majority of the philosophers of the alternative school movement.

The turn that much school reform has taken in the last five years or so cannot but make unhappy those of us who still believe that the schools must fulfill their obligation "to provide the essential skills of language, numbers, and orderly thought." We agree with the alternative schools advocates that many schools (surely not all) are dreary places that fail to reach the students, that many schools are bad schools run by administrators and teachers who are indifferent to, or contemptuous of, the students, and that public education often presents a bureaucratic side that is repellent. We cannot agree that the solution is to insist on a false teacher-student equality or to let the kids run the school or to foster feeling over thought or to value lightly the role in education of books, language, standards, and disciplined knowledge.

Those of us who cling to the historic idea of what schools should be are having a rough time of it these days, battered on the one side by the joy-and-ecstasy boys and on the other by theorists like Christopher Jencks who tell us that what the schools do doesn't make any difference to the future lives of those who attend them. The Council for Basic Education will continue to hold to the faith that true education is essential for all youth and it will continue to point out that if schools are to foster such education they cannot be indifferent to change and innovation but must at the same time operate within some rational organizational framework. I know that such a word as *efficient* will cause some of the advocates of loosely organized schools to bristle, but if we are to have efficient schools—i.e., functional schools—we must find some operating principles on which the majority of reformers can agree.

Sentimental utopians and perfectionists (and they abound in the alternative movement) will be in pained disagreement, but I suspect that pragmatic reformers can agree on certain propositions about schools: 1) While independent schools should be encouraged, a public system of compulsory education is a social necessity and convenience and will continue for a long time to come to be the dominant system. 2) Schooling has to be formalized, with required attendance and sequential courses and schedules, but the formalities should be governed by common sense, flexibility, and sympathetic understanding of the child. 3) Inescapably, the teacher is an authority and not an equal partner of the student. 4) The economics of the situation determine that some large-group instruction is inevitable. 5) Ability grouping in one form or another is fair and beneficial to all students. 6) Examinations and other forms of measurement are essential for judging the effectiveness of instruction. 7) Schools must provide a background of common knowledge if they are to play their proper role in helping to form a community or society of shared interests and ideals.

These are some of the necessities we must face in devising any program of realizable reform for the schools. There is no indication that any considerable number of the advocates of alternate schools would find these propositions congenial. Until they do, and until they are willing to acknowledge that the school's main function is the training of the mind, their movement will remain well-intentioned but essentially quixotic.

It is hard to judge whether or not the movement is a permanent one. Innovations in education have a habit of flourishing for a period and then gradually withering away, and founders of glamorous alternatives to conventional schools tend to weary after a while and move on to new schemes of regeneration. I wish the idealism and energies of the advocates of reform could be enlisted in behalf of changes for which there is an imperative need and for which there can be reasonable expectation of success. We need desperately to improve reading instruction, to devise workable programs based on higher aspirations for children of the ghetto, to establish clearer and better measures of academic achievement, and to give more attention to critical evaluation of current innovations before we move on to new ones. Above all, we need to give serious thought to the greatest of our problems, how to find good natural teachers and then change our present unsatisfactory way of training them.

In education we need always to reexamine our practices and to be willing to change them when necessary. Not to do so would be foolhardy, even suicidal. But change must be based on something more substantial than the slogans, ideological zealotry, and utopian sentimentality that all too often mark the movement for alternative schools. I think it would be unfortunate if this sort of change gained wide favor, for there is a Gresham's law in education, too, where bad reform drives out good.

FOOTNOTE

[1] Charles E. Silberman, *Crisis in the Classroom* (New York: Random House, 1970), pp. 228 and 262.

Section II

FREE AND INDEPENDENT ALTERNATIVE SCHOOLS: OUTSIDE THE SYSTEM

EDITOR'S COMMENTS

An important development in alternative education began as a parallel to the public schools. In other words, these are alternatives *to* the public schools. In some quarters, these alternatives are given the label "free" schools. They seem to borrow heavily from the philosophy of A. S. Neill, who founded Summerhill, a type of therapeutic community in England. Their concern was the lack of freedom in the public schools. For them, freedom works as a natural and basic motivator of learning. That educational setting is best which frees the learner to pursue his own educational diet. There are other "free" schools that have a different connotation: free to them means political freedom, free from the oppression of a public school system that reflects the political interest of those who control society. In one sense, the public schools are viewed as oppressive, and the learner needs to be liberated. Certain carry-overs of the civil rights movement and the freedom of blacks and other minorities would be included in some of these schools. Sensitive writers, such as Jonathan Kozol, seem to reflect this basic notion of free schools. Allen Graubard, considered by many to have done the most definitive work on free schools (*Free the Children*), i.e., alternatives to the public schools, tries to present a picture of what these schools are like.

Other alternative schools do not necessarily carry the caption of "free." Rather, they are considered independent alternative schools, differing also from the so-called "established" private schools. Many of these schools reflect the changing life-styles of the educational consumer, his concern for openness and humanism.

Eventually the free schools have to deal with such mundane

questions as finances and survival. Can they survive? How will they deal with the economic constraints inevitably surrounding them? The Egan proposal for independent public schools is intriguing but fraught with difficulties. As we shall see a little later in Section III, some alternative private schools have found their way into the public school framework.

This section deals with such questions as:

What social factors instigated the movement?

What kinds of alternatives exist outside the system?

Where are they?

How is the philosophy reflected in the curriculum?

What impact have they had on the public school system?

How fast are the schools growing?

Who is involved?

What are some of the problems?

How do these schools combine freedom and instruction?

Why do some students respond?

Can they become part of the public system?

THE FREE SCHOOL MOVEMENT
—A PERSPECTIVE*

BY LAWRENCE A. CREMIN†

About a decade ago, I published a study of the progressive education movement of John Dewey's time. I am often asked, Is there any relation between that movement and the free school movement today? Is there anything to be learned from a comparison? And if so, what? My answer is that we can learn a great deal.

In my study of the progressive education movement, titled *The Transformation of the School,* I put forward a number of arguments:

First, that the movement was not an isolated phenomenon in American life, not the invention of a few crackpots and eccentrics, but rather the educational side of the broader progressive movement in American politics and social thought.

Second, that the movement began in protest against the narrowness, the formalism, and the inequities of the late nineteenth century public school.

Third, that as the movement shifted from protest to reform, it cast the school in a new mold, viewing it as (a) a lever of continuing social improvement, (b) an instrument of individual self-realization, (c) an agency for the popularization of culture, and (d) an institution for facilitating the adjustment of human beings to a society undergoing rapid transformation by the forces of democracy, science, and industrialism.

Fourth, that the movement was exceedingly diverse, enrolling men and women as different as Theodore Roosevelt, Jane Addams, Booker T. Washington, and Samuel Gompers, but that one could discern at least three major thrusts: a child-centered thrust, which peaked in the 1920's; a social-reform

---

* Reprinted with permission of the author. This paper was presented at the Institute of Philosophy and Politics of Education at Teachers College, Columbia University.

† Dr. Cremin is Frederick A. P. Barnard Professor of Education, Teachers College, Columbia University.

thrust, which peaked in the 1930's; and a scientific thrust, which peaked in the 1940's.

Fifth, that John Dewey saw the movement whole and served as the chief articulator of its aspirations—recall his little book, *The School and Society* (1899), in which the first essay reflected the social-reform thrust; the second essay, the child-centered thrust; and the third, the scientific thrust.

Sixth, that the movement enjoyed its heyday during the 1920's and 1930's, began to decline during the 1940's, and collapsed during the 1950's for all the usual reasons—internal factionalism, the erosion of political support, the rise of an articulate opposition associated with post-World War II conservatism, and the sort of ideological inflexibility that made it unable to contend with its own success.

In the original plan of my study, I included a final section addressed to the question, "Where do we go from here?" But when the time came to write it, my thoughts were not clear, so I decided to end on a "phoenix in the ashes" note: if and when liberalism in politics and public affairs had a resurgence, progressive education would rise again.

Now, I did manage to work out that last section in 1965. I had a chance to give it initially as the Horace Mann Lecture at the University of Pittsburgh and then published it in a little book called *The Genius of American Education*. I argued there that the reason progressive education had collapsed was that the progressives had missed the central point of the American educational experience in the twentieth century, namely, that an educational revolution had been going on outside the schools far more fundamental than any changes that had taken place inside—the revolution implicit in the rise of cinema, radio, and television and the simultaneous transformation of the American family under the conditions of industrialism and urbanization. The progressives had bet on the school as the crucial lever of social reform and individual self-realization at precisely the time when the whole configuration of educational power was shifting radically. And what was desperately needed, it seemed to me, was some new formulation that put the humane aspirations and social awareness of the progressive education movement together with a more realistic understanding of the fundamentally different situation in which all education was proceeding.

By the time I wrote *The Genius of American Education,* a new progressive education movement was already in the making. I would date its beginning from precisely the time I was wrestling with that last section of *The Transformation of the School* which I found I could not write. I would date it from the publication of A. S. Neill's *Summerhill* in 1960. (Incidentally, nothing in Neill's book was new; most of what he recommended had been tried in the progressive schools of the 1920's and 1930's.)

The new movement began slowly, with the organization of Summerhill societies and Summerhill schools in different parts of the country. It gathered momentum during the middle 1960's, fueled by the writings of John Holt, Herbert Kohl, George Dennison, James Herndon, and Jonathan Kozol. And it manifested itself in the appearance of scores of new child-centered schools of every conceivable sort and variety.

Simultaneously, growing out of the civil rights movement, there arose the political programs of black and ethnic self-determination and the so-called community free schools associated with them—Harlem Prep in New York, the CAM Academy in Chicago, and the Nairobi Community School in East Palo Alto.

By the summer of 1971, Allen Graubard (whose book, *Free the Children,* is one of the more recent efforts to state the history and theory of the movement) was able to identify some 350 such schools. And these are what Graubard calls "outside-the-system" schools, so that we must add many more schools, schools within schools, and classrooms within schools that are part of the public school system and variously referred to as alternative schools or community schools or open schools.

Also, during the last five or six years, we have seen a fascinating interweaving of the child-centered and political-reform themes in the literature of the movement, so that open education is viewed as a lever of child liberation on the one hand and as a lever of radical social change on the other.

At least two of the three themes of the first movement, then, the child-centered theme and the social-reform theme, have emerged full-blown in the present-day movement. Interestingly enough, however, the scientific theme of the first movement has been noticeably absent from the present version. In fact, there has been an active hostility on the part of many free school advocates toward present-day efforts to apply scientific principles to the techniques of instruction and evaluation. Whereas the progressive education movement reached a kind of culmination in The Eight-Year Study in which Ralph Tyler and his associates tried systematically to assess the outcomes of progressive methods, latter-day advocates of free schools have seemed on the whole uninterested in such assessment.

Interestingly, too, the radical side of the current movement has been much more sweeping in its radicalism than was earlier the case, culminating, I would suppose, in Ivan Illich's proposal that we deschool society completely. There were radicals in the 1890's who were fairly skeptical about educational roads to reform—one of them once told Jane Addams that using education to correct social injustice was about as effective as using rosewater to cure the plague. But I have yet to find a radical at that time who wanted to do away with schools entirely; it was rather the reactionaries of the 1890's who sought that.

What is most striking, perhaps, in any comparison of the two movements is the notoriously atheoretical, ahistorical character of the free school movement in our time. The present movement has been far less profound in the questions it has raised about the nature and character of education and in the debates it has pursued around those questions. The movement has produced no John Dewey, no Boyd Bode, no George Counts, no journal even approaching the quality of the old *Social Frontier*. And it has been far less willing to look to history for ideas. Those who have founded free schools have not read their Francis W. Parker or their Caroline Pratt or their Helen Parkhurst, with the result that boundless energy has been spent in countless classrooms reinventing the pedagogical wheel.

Further, the movement has had immense difficulty going from protest to reform, to the kinds of detailed alternative strategies that will give us better educational programs than we now have. Even Jonathan Kozol's *Free Schools*, which was written explicitly to help people found alternative institutions, is egregiously thin in its programmatic suggestions; while Joseph Turner's *Making New Schools*, which pointedly proffered a rather well-developed reformist curriculum, has not even been noticed by the movement.

Finally, the current movement has remained as school-bound as the progressive education movement of an earlier time. Even Charles Silberman's *Crisis in the Classroom,* surely the most learned and wide-ranging analysis to be associated with the present movement (though it did not emanate from the present movement), begins with a lengthy discussion of how television writers, filmmakers, priests, rabbis, librarians, and museum directors all educate, but it then goes on to propose the open classroom as the keystone in the arch of educational reform.

Ironically, the one book to come out of the movement that appears to have comprehended the educational revolution of our time is Ivan Illich's *Deschooling Society.* But the appearance is deceptive. Illich would like to abandon schooling in favor of what he calls educational networks, but he does not deal with the inevitable impact of the media and the market on those networks.

It is easy enough to criticize, and my remarks should not be taken as a defense of the educational status quo. At the very least, the advocates of free schools have cared enough about human beings to try to make education more humane and that is to be prized. Where they have failed, it seems to me, is at the point of theory; they have not asked the right questions insistently enough, and as a result they have tended to come up with superficial and shopworn answers.

Let me then put my question once again: What would an educational movement look like today that combined the humane aspirations and social awareness of the progressive education movement with a more realistic understanding of the nature of present-day education? What if free schools (and all other schools for that matter) were to take seriously the radically new situation in which all education inescapably proceeds? What would they do differently?

Let me venture three suggestions:

First, classroom teachers have to begin to contend with the fact that youngsters in the schools have been taught and are being taught by many curriculums and that if they want to influence those youngsters they must be aware of those curriculums. The Children's Television Workshop has a curriculum. The *Encyclopaedia Britannica* has a curriculum. The Boy Scouts and the Girl Scouts have curriculums. Our churches and synagogues have curriculums. And each family has a curriculum, though in many instances that curriculum may do little more than leave youngsters to the fortunes of the other educators.

To understand this is to force educators to change fundamentally the way they think about education. It means, as James Coleman and Christopher Jencks—and one should probably add Plato—have pointed out, that the school never has *tabulae rasae* to begin with, that when children come to school they have already been educated and miseducated on the outside, and that the best the school can do in many realms is to complement, extend, accentuate, challenge, neutralize, or counter (though in so doing the school does crucially important work). It means that one of the most significant tasks any school can undertake is to try to develop in youngsters an awareness of these other curriculums and an ability to criticize them. Young people desperately need the intellectual tools to deal critically with the values of a film like *Clockwork Orange* or with the human models in a television serial like *Marcus Welby, M.D.* or with the aesthetic qualities of the music of Lawrence Welk. None of this can substitute for reading, writing, and arithmetic to be sure; but reading, writing, and arithmetic are no longer enough.

Incidentally, if one accepts this line of argument, it is utter nonsense to think that by turning children loose in an unplanned and unstructured environment they can be freed in any significant way. Rather, they are thereby abandoned to the blind forces of the hucksters, whose primary concern is neither the children, nor the truth, nor the decent future of American society.

Second, once educators took seriously the fact that we are all taught by radio and television, peer groups and advertising agencies, libraries and museums, they would necessarily become interested not only in alternative schools but in alternative education of every kind. It may well be, for example, that the most important educational battle now being fought in the United States is over who will control cable television, who will award the franchises, and what will be the public requirements associated with a franchise. Once 40 to 50 channels are readily available to every American home—some of them with the capacity for responsive interchange—then what comes over those channels in the form of education or miseducation will profoundly affect *all* teaching in schools and everywhere else. There is simply no avoiding this and educators had best face it.

Further, if educators were to take seriously what Urie Bronfenbrenner has been saying about the extraordinary power of the adolescent peer group in American society and the need for a greater variety of adult models in the life of every child, they would press for a host of innovations, both inside the school and out. They would be more interested than they seem, for example, in peer-mediated instruction or in summer camps or in arrangements under which children spend time in factories, businesses, offices, or shops, with real adults doing real work, along the lines of the experiment Bronfenbrenner carried out with David Goslin at the *Detroit Free Press.*

Third, once educators took seriously the fact that we are living through a revolution in which opportunities for education and miseducation are burgeoning throughout the society, they would give far more attention to the need to equip each youngster as early as possible to make his way purposefully and intelligently through the various configurations of education, with a view to the kind of person he would like to become and the relation of education to becoming that kind of person. In other words, they would do all they could to nurture an educationally autonomous individual.

In conclusion, I should note that as critical as I have been of the progressive education movement of yesterday and the free school movement of today, I find myself much more in sympathy with the authentic aspirations of both movements —at least as articulated by Dewey—than I am opposed to them. In the last analysis, my critique is simply an effort to call the free school movement to the service of its own best ideals, and it can only learn what those ideals are by studying its own history.

THE FREE SCHOOL MOVEMENT*

BY ALLEN GRAUBARD†

About nine of every ten American school children attend the public schools. The great majority of the remaining ten per cent satisfy the compulsory school attendance laws in parochial schools, although this number has declined sharply over the past few years. A small number of children are educated in private "prep" schools, which are often small, expensive, and elite. The economic troubles of the past few years have been an important factor in the decline in both the number and enrollments of these non-public schools.

Yet, while the customary American private school education has begun to decline, a very special kind of private school has appeared and grown astonishingly in numbers. These schools have received increasing attention from the media and from people interested in educational reform. They are most frequently called "free schools," though they are also known as "new schools" or "alternative schools." In five years the number of these free schools has grown from around 25 to perhaps 600; around 200 have been founded in the past year alone. These schools are usually very small: in absolute numbers of participants—students, parents, and staff—the phenomenon is very limited, but their public impact and symbolic significance are relatively great.

This essay presents some objective data about free schools along with a discussion of the various educational and social change concepts which underlie them. Particular emphasis is given to the extent to which differences of social class, ethnicity, and political perspective contribute to the variation of styles within the broad free school movement. My purpose is to give an overview of the movement, to analyze its sig-

* Allen Graubard, "The Free School Movement," *Harvard Educational Review* 42, August 1972, 351–73. Copyright © 1972 by President and Fellows of Harvard College.

† Allen Graubard is the author of *Free the Children: Radical Reform and the Free School Movement.* He has taught philosophy and social theory at M.I.T. and has been active in educational reform activities.

nificance, and to speculate about its future, especially in relation to reform within the public school system.

The basic theoretical concept is, naturally, freedom. The literature of radical school reform associated with free schools vehemently opposes the compulsory and authoritarian aspects of traditional public and private schools. This literature attacks the emotional and intellectual effects of conventional pedagogy and projects a radical theory in which freedom is the central virtue. The most uncompromising form of both the attack and the theoretical alternative is found in A. S. Neill's *Summerhill*. The small number of free schools which existed in the U.S. before the current wave began are almost all explicitly Summerhillian schools. In recent years, the writings of Paul Goodman, John Holt, Edgar Z. Friedenberg, George Leonard, Neil Postman and Charles Weingartner, George Dennison, Herbert Kohl, Jonathan Kozol, and others have popularized the general notion surrounding free schools: that children are naturally curious and motivated to learn by their own interests and desires. The most important condition for nurturing this natural interest is freedom supported by adults who enrich the environment and offer help. In contrast, coercion and regimentation only inhibit emotional and intellectual development. It follows that almost all of the major characteristics of public school organization and method are opposed—the large classes, the teacher with absolute power to administer a state-directed curriculum to rigidly defined age groups, the emphasis on discipline and obedience, the constant invidious evaluation and the motivation by competition, the ability tracking, and so forth.[1]

We can see in this central concept of freedom two distinct ideological sources for an alternative school movement, one political and one pedagogical (or more broadly, cultural). These sources are in real tension, sometimes even contradiction. By the *political* source, I mean the spirit behind the first "freedom" schools—those in Mississippi, in 1964—when groups of people sought control of the oppressive educational processes to which they and their children were being subjected. This spirit is seen in the movement for community control. It views the public schools and most professional educators with great hostility, and it articulately opposes indoctrination in the content and method of the public schools. This spirit has been most extensively expressed in black communities' struggle for control of public schools. But over the past few years some minority community groups have turned their anger and energy toward starting their own alternative schools, despairing of the possibilities of working inside the system.

These schools emphasize control by the local community, black (or brown or red) consciousness in the curriculum, and the schools' participation in the political and social struggle for equality; the pedagogical idea of allowing each child the freedom to unfold his or her individuality is not given so dominant a position as in most middle-class free schools. So, in many of the black community schools, there is a good deal of structure and organization, including, sometimes, required classes, well-organized compulsory activities run by the teacher, intensive drilling in basic skills—items which contradict in varying degrees the more strictly pedagogical concept of freedom.

If one looks back about six or seven years, one can see the two strands in the earliest days of the free school wave—there were a few Summerhillian schools (e.g., Lewis-Wadhams in New York State, founded in 1963) and a few black community schools starting in the ghettos (e.g., Roxbury Community School, 1966).

Each kind of school is an alternative, articulating a profound opposition to the methods and results of the public schools (this is not true of most private schools); each is a "free" school. But one trend emphasizes the role of the school in the community's struggle for freedom and equality (the freedom of the "Freedom now!" cry of the civil rights movement), while the other represents the strongest possible claim for the individual child's freedom from coercive approaches to learning and social development as expressed by the organization and techniques of most public schools.

The complex differences and possible tensions between these two sources of freedom make it difficult to specify clearly what is a free school and what is not. All of the institutions reasonably included in the class oppose the public schools; but the political and pedagogical sources of this opposition are expressed in varied ways across the range of new schools. (See the typology of free schools below.) Moreover, these tensions exist *within* schools and even within individuals, providing a constant source of serious discussion. (For example,

Jonathan Kozol's recent acerbic criticisms of counter-cultural, apolitical free schools [*Free Schools*, 1972] were the occasion for renewed intense debate among free school people.)

Free Schools: Some Data and a Typology

The complicated problem of definition should be kept in mind in approaching the data that follows. How "free" must a school be for it to count as a "free school" pedagogically? And if a black school is militant and community-controlled, but has rather traditional pedagogy and methods, is it a "free school"? For most of the schools, identification is not a problem. But there are fairly significant grey areas which have occasioned some subjective judgments in gathering the data. Consequently, the data, though it looks precise, being numbers and percentages, should be taken softly, and it is offered in this spirit. It was gathered between March and August, 1971, by the New Schools Directory Project,[2] a group of free school people who wanted to compile an accurate and detailed directory of existing alternative schools, since no real data seemed available and a good deal of dubious information was being widely quoted as fact (e.g., that the average life of the schools is 18 months or that there were 1600–2000 new schools).

The Project proceeded as follows: a small central group went over every existing listing of "free schools" to contact free school people in different areas of the country, including regional free school switchboard people. These contacts gathered some rough "objective" information by checking the local lists and visiting other free schools in their area. All leads were checked in an effort to find previously unlisted schools. Rough as the methods were, I think we missed only a few of the free schools then in existence. (Some 200 schools opened in September 1971, and most of these were not included in the survey.) My own check of the data indicates that the range of accuracy was 80–90%.

The survey limited itself to "outside-the-system" schools. Free school-type programs within the public school system have proliferated rapidly, with important implications for the free school movement. But the concern of the survey was with the grass roots movement that had begun outside of the state-controlled system.

The number of free schools has increased dramatically during the past five years, especially in contrast to the decline of parochial and traditional private school education.

A few very progressive or Summerhillian schools (less than five) were founded every year during the early 1960's. Then, in 1966 and 1967, the real rise of free schools began, simultaneous with the growth of a widespread movement for social change and an increasingly radical critique of American institutions. Around 20 free schools were founded in 1967 and 1968. Over 60 were founded in 1969. By 1970, the number was around 150, and, as mentioned before, the number of new free schools begun during 1971–72 is substantially greater.

A considerable number of free schools close after one or two or three years of existence. Although the existing data does not present an entirely accurate picture, my sense is that the oft-quoted figure of an eighteen month average life-span is very wrong. Since most of the schools are less than two years old, it is difficult to get a meaningful figure, but it seems that at most one out of five new schools closes before the end of its second year, and perhaps not more than one out of ten.

Given the difficulties of starting schools, this dramatic rise in the number of parents, students, and teachers who are willing to make the enormous commitment needed to start their own school is significant far beyond the actual numbers. It is obvious that if there were a free-choice tuition voucher plan or the widespread possibility of alternatives inside the public school system, the number of new free schools and participants would be much greater than at present.

Clearly, the data is heavily dependent on the kind of definitional problem described above. We tended toward a relatively strict conception of "free school"; that is, we wanted the selection to reflect as much as possible the sense of being part of a conscious movement to create schools very different from the normal public and private schools. This selection process was often quite difficult—almost arbitrary at times. For example, we excluded Shady Hill School in Cambridge and Miquon School in Philadelphia, two well-known and established "progressive" schools, but included Miquon Upper School, a free high school started by Miquon last year.

Such decisions are obviously complex; in general, we tried to avoid inflating the figures by including schools which, though progressive, are not really participants in this new wave of radical school reform.

Distribution by State. Thirty-nine states have at least one free school. It should be noted that four states—California, New York, Massachusetts, and Illinois—have fifty-two per cent of the total surveyed. California alone has twenty-seven per cent. There appear to be several particular areas of free school concentration—the San Francisco Bay area, the Chicago area, the Boston area, Madison-Milwaukee, and Minneapolis-St. Paul. There is good reason to think that cosmopolitan urban areas, especially those with high concentrations of university and college-associated people, generate the critical masses of people who share the philosophy of free schools and have the willingness and capability to commit the necessary time, energy, and resources to such efforts.

Staff Characteristics. The data on staff are especially vague. In most free schools there are part-time and volunteer teachers, as well as parents, who participate in teaching and other staff activities. In many schools some of the volunteers and part-time teachers share community governance and policy-making with full-time staff. It is impossible to ascertain precisely either the number of volunteers or the time that part-time and volunteer staff put in. What can be said is that free schools generally emphasize the importance of individual attention and small intimate groups, and the staff-student ratios bear this out. A rough estimate which included all volunteers and part-time staff would be about 1:3, while a figure which involved only full-time staff would be 1:7.

Black teachers are concentrated almost completely in the relatively small number of black community schools and street academies. It is obvious that free school teachers are a considerably younger group than teachers in general. As compared to the national mean age for teachers of thirty-seven years, almost seventy per cent of free school teachers are below thirty, and it is safe to say that at least eighty-five per cent are below the national mean age.

This age distribution suggests some fairly obvious specula-

tions. First, a significant part of the free school movement
is related to the youth and student movement of the 1960's,
both political and cultural. Second, many schools are started
by young parents of very young children, and some of them
become the teachers. Finally, the financial situation of most
free schools makes it difficult for older people with families
to participate, given their need for job security and dependa-
ble income. Young people, mobile and without encumbering
family responsibilities, constitute the most obvious pool for
very low paid and volunteer staff.

School Size and Finances. The data on school size and finances are especially interesting and revealing. A discussion
of these figures will serve as a basis for a detailed typology
of the free schools.

Most urban Americans think of schools as institutions
housed in large expensive buildings, containing anywhere
from a few hundred students (elementary) to two, three, or
four thousand students (high schools). In contrast, the average size for the free schools in this survey is approximately
thirty-three students. Approximately two-thirds of the schools
have an enrollment of less than forty. The fact that two-thirds
have enrollments of under forty can be explained mainly as
a conscious commitment to a special kind of intimate community. Many free school people value the idea that everyone
in the school knows everyone else fairly well; that staff people
can truly relate to each other and to all the children, thus
avoiding the impersonality associated with mass education
institutions. Many free schools refuse to expand beyond thirty
or forty, fearing that some of the essential qualities of the
free school atmosphere would be lost. Some schools have
actually decided to reduce enrollment from around thirty
down to twenty because the people involved felt that even
thirty was too large a group.

All of the schools with enrollments of around 100 and up
deviate from the mean for specific reasons. Some, like Peninsula School in California (230 children) or Shady Lane
School in Pittsburgh (101) are fairly established progressive
schools that have stayed sufficiently experimental and innovative to justify inclusion in the study. Others are predominantly black or integrated community schools, which
emphasize community participation, service in the larger com-

munity, and parent involvement in governance. These schools place a much lower priority on a warm, intimate, personal atmosphere than do the more numerous and smaller white, progressive, middle-class, and often isolated free schools.[3]

The data on school finances needs especially careful interpretation since free schools do not, in general, keep very accurate, detailed, or complete financial records. Since resources come from very diverse sources—tuition paid on a sliding scale (and often irregularly), small contributions, a very few large contributions from individuals and foundations, bake sales, rummage sales, donated equipment, and even, in the case of one school, panhandling—accurate accounting is not often available.

The main source of income, as one would expect for non-public schools, is tuition. Eighty-one per cent of the schools charge tuition, with almost all of them stating that they give scholarships. Since the great majority of these schools use a sliding scale for tuition, the concept of "scholarship" is quite hazy. Most schools ask people to pay what they feel they can afford, hoping there will be enough high tuition payers to balance the people who can afford little. This is important since most free schools do not want to see themselves as "elite" private schools providing a special form of education for those who can afford it. Tuition for most traditional private schools ranges from $1500 to $4000 per year, while a sampling of schools in the survey shows that the normal range for free schools would be $0 to about $1200 per year. It is impossible to determine the average paid tuition, as we were unable to get accurate data concerning how many paid what.

Almost all the schools which do not charge tuition are true community schools and street academies serving poor and minority groups. There is no tuition because the people starting the schools intended to involve groups who can not afford it. The founders wanted to provide true alternatives to the public system rather than private schools that are alternatives only for those who can afford them (and a few scholarship cases). A good example of the tuition-free school is the Children's Community Workshop School in Manhattan. An elementary school with around 125 students, it is completely integrated racially and by class, and is parent controlled, with many poor black and Puerto-Rican parents involved. The school has been supported (with a large, well-paid staff) by contributions from foundations, but financial hardships during the past year have threatened its survival. However, the local school board has voted to grant the Workshop School "public" status, and stability may be achieved with public money.

Other tuition-free community schools include Highland Park Free School, Roxbury Community School and the New School for Children, the three schools forming the Roxbury Federation of Community Free Schools. Over the past couple of years, they have managed to obtain substantial foundation help, including a $500,000 grant from the Ford Foundation, and thus to stay in operation without charging parents. Some dropout-oriented free high schools also do not charge tuition: Genesis II in Springfield, Mass., Independent Learning Center in Milwaukee, Independence High School in Newark, Freedom House in Madison, Wisc., City Hill School and Northside Street Academy in Minneapolis, and Harlem Prep in New York. Funding sources for such schools are diverse: local, state, and federal programs for delinquency prevention, Model Cities and other poverty agencies, church groups, foundations, and corporations. But such funding is difficult to find and very chancy. For example, the Providence Free School began with the hope of being a tuitionless community school supported by individual contributions and foundation help. By the second year they were forced to charge tuition in order to stay in existence.

The data on free school expenditures are very revealing. The mean and median are somewhere in the $500 to $600 range, closer to $600 per year. The curve, however, is far from the normal bell-shaped distribution that would be expected for the public schools in any given state. Instead we find a relatively even distribution all along the spectrum. Rather than a rapid tapering off at the high and low extremes, one finds a distinctive peak in the highest range (over $1000), with nineteen per cent of the schools in this category. At the other extreme, although the curve does taper off slightly, twenty-nine per cent of the schools report per capita expenditures below $300 and twelve per cent report below $100.

It is hard to compare these figures to public school data. For free schools, rent is a major expense, while public school figures, as usually reported, do not contain an equivalent charge. Even so, we do know that the public schools show much greater expenses in general (as do traditional private schools). For example, at the top of the public school scale, localities like Beverly Hills spend $2000 per student per year while urban averages usually fall in the $1000 to $1500 range (if some category equivalent to rent were added in, these figures would be even higher).

Although there are some public school districts in the $500 to $1000 category, there is no parallel in the traditional public and private school experience to the fact that more than a quarter of the free schools work on less than $300 per student and more than one out of ten report less than $100. Moreover, these new schools value individual attention to student needs and desires—i.e., teacher-student ratios on the order of 1:5 to 1:10, versus the 1:25 or so that generally obtains in public schools. This consideration makes the contrast in per capita expenditure figures even more extraordinary.

Of course, many free school teachers work for very little money, often for room and board or less. In addition, many free schools use volunteers from local communities and nearby colleges and universities. Parents often take major roles in the classroom and especially in administration, fund raising, and building maintenance. Students, parents, and staff donate or scrounge up much of the material. Thus, the financial figures as represented on the graph systematically understate the resources used by free schools. If one could assign true value to the work of the teachers, the time of the volunteers and parents, the homes often used for classrooms, the gasoline and cars volunteered, the out-of-pocket unreimbursed expenses of volunteers, and the donated materials, the cash value of resources invested in the schools would be much higher than the actual money figures.

Still, the survival of most free schools depends on the fact that many people, often highly qualified and capable of holding teaching positions in public schools and elsewhere at $9,000–$15,000, are willing to work, for at least one or two years, at salaries in the $2,000–$5,000 range or even lower. Also, of course, there are often more than enough willing and able volunteers.

It should be noted that, with very few exceptions, free school workers are not voluntary ascetics. Their salaries are low because there is no money. The very few schools that have obtained large foundation grants or government help have tried to pay salaries comparable to the public schools, and the poorer schools wish they could. Ideally, free schools would have well-paid teachers and still maintain their low teacher-student ratio without exceeding public school expenditure levels. They would accomplish this by their use of volunteers, community resources, and inexpensive facilities, and by eliminating vandalism by hostile students, massive testing and grading programs and expensive standardized textbooks, and practically the whole full-time public school administrative apparatus.

Types of Free Schools. Within the summary data presented above it is important to distinguish among several different types of free schools: The "classical" free school, the parent-teacher cooperative elementary school, the free high school, and the community elementary school.

The *"classical" free school* is the Summerhillian-influenced community, usually quite small and enrolling students of all ages. Many of these are boarding schools that aim to be truly self-sufficient, intimate, even therapeutic whole communities. As the Summerhill Ranch School in Mendocino, California, wrote in its brochure:

> Educationally, this school can be described as 24-hour life tutorial, where students and staff learn in accordance with their own interests . . . our emotional developments remain primary. Self-awareness, individuality and personal responsibility to oneself and to others here are most important. We have not the rewards and punishments nor the competitiveness of public schools. Many of us regain self-confidence and awareness here, both of which aid us in dealing with the impersonal real world.

These schools are almost exclusively white and middle-class in their constituency, and, when boarding schools, they are naturally quite expensive. They emphasize the emotional and expressive aspects of the personality rather than the formal academic curriculum or job preparation. Development replaces achievement as the primary purpose. Collective decision-making often plays a central role in school activities.

A second type, which overlaps the first, is the *parent-teacher cooperative elementary school*. These schools are formed by parents, especially young, white, liberal, middle-class parents who do not want their children subjected to the regimentation of the normal public schools. They read John Holt's books and Joseph Featherstone's articles on the open classroom as it has developed in the British Infant Schools. Some parents call others; they organize a meeting and decide to start a free elementary school. They find sympathetic teachers who are willing to sacrifice financial reward for the satisfaction of the job. Often one or more of the parents will be full-time teachers in the school. A parent board officially controls the school and participates regularly in school activities, though the staff handles much of the day-to-day operation. Tuition is paid on a sliding scale and usually some minority students are admitted free or almost free; but in general, these schools do not really appeal to poor-minority parents, and in any case, they are not intended to confront the problems of ghetto families and their children.

These parent cooperatives differ from the relatively new, very progressive elementary schools which are on the fringe of the free school development, such as Shady Lane in Pittsburgh and Fayerweather Street School in Cambridge. Like the older progressive schools, these schools, though rather libertarian in pedagogy, are well-organized, well-equipped, fairly expensive, and rather professional about staffing. In contrast, parent cooperatives tend to have looser organization, less equipment, and fewer "professional" teachers.

Another type, the *free high school,* includes several variants, again determined by the social class constituency and the way the political and the pedagogical aspects of the "freedom" idea interact. They are high school counterparts to the Summerhillian schools, oriented toward the white middle class and hip youth counter-culture. In contrast with the types mentioned above, prospective students usually provide the initial impetus, along with some committed adults who are potential staff. Deeply disenchanted with the public schools, these young people want to be involved honestly in the planning and governance of their own school. Several of these middle-class high schools project a politically radical perspective in their rhetoric, curriculum, and other activities. This does not mean that all the young people in such schools are activists, but that some of the originators and staff are, and that activism is in the atmosphere. These schools often participate in anti-war and civil rights activities, and the classes often focus on the Vietnam War, draft resistance, women's liberation, and the legal rights and difficulties of youth.

In the past couple of years, several white working-class high schools have formed, a development with no parallel in the earlier progressive education movement. These schools involve mainly drop-outs and potential drop-outs who feel very hostile to their public high schools. Whereas the middle-class high schools can charge tuition, working-class schools do not have this option, for neither the students nor their parents have the money. Moreover, their parents do not usually find the political and pedagogical style of such schools familiar or appealing. The permissiveness of the free school is often congenial to progressive middle-class parents, but has much less appeal to working-class parents who suspect that such experimental schools will not serve the needs of their children. (Neither do the public schools, of course, but parents persist in the hope that the American dream of working hard, getting skills and credentials, and making it in the world will somehow come true for their children.)

These working-class schools differ from their middle-class counterparts by directing a much greater focus on vocational help and remedial work and by exhibiting a real concern with thinking through what it means to be of the working class. For example, "Self Worth and Competency of Working Class Youth" is the name of a summer course at the Group School in Cambridge. According to the course description, "Self Worth" was

> originally conceived with two express purposes in mind. Because of the obvious lack of information relating to the working class struggle in American history, both in elementary and high school curriculum, it was felt that an objective labor history course was necessary as a foundation for viewing working-class competency and self worth. Once a basic historical foundation was laid, it was hoped that the class could begin to tackle the more personally related questions of 'how does it feel to be a kid without a history?' or 'if I as a working-class youth have never learned about my history, whose culture have I adopted?' (from the Group School summer course brochure).

The working-class schools—with their constituency of public school "drop-outs" and "push-outs"—thus directly confront the tracking function of the public schools which "prepare" these students for the lower rungs of the social and job hierarchy. In contrast, students in middle-class free schools have been slated for college and high career achievement. For them, the free high school is a way to get off, for a while at least, the beaten path to college and beyond.

Another variant of the high schools for drop-outs, more established and larger than the white working class schools, are the street academies for poor minority youth. The most famous of these is Harlem Prep, with over 400 students, but there are such places in most large cities. They are organized by adults, often with the support of community groups (e.g., the local Urban League). They seek to reawaken motivation in young people who have been completely turned off by school. While there is an atmosphere of discipline, the students do not perceive it as the same sort of discipline they experienced in the public schools. Instead, street academy discipline comes from having staff who can relate well with the students, and from the idea of black people "getting it together."

The street academies have a sense of participation, though far from the Summerhillian image of community, participatory democracy, and almost unlimited individual choice. The pedagogy with its emphasis on skills is more conventional, and the strong commitment to getting the young people into colleges differs from the mood of the dominant free high school culture.

The *community elementary schools,* as noted above, tend to be much larger and more highly organized than the average free school. More than the middle-class groups, the people who start community schools see the struggle for community control of the public schools as a vital goal; for them the politics of control are more important than the pedagogical emphasis of middle-class reform groups. These community schools put great stress on skills and on cultural consciousness and pride. Low-income parents, wary of romantic "freedom and spontaneity" rhetoric, often seem to support the more traditional classroom approaches, including strict discipline. Nevertheless, there is still a good deal of pedagogical innovation and libertarian atmosphere in these community schools. The implication here is that when the parents and community people feel they are in control, they are more open to "experimentation" than when it—like all the other school stuff they know—is imposed by the system which has been failing their children for years. For example, most of these schools share an aversion to fostering individual competition by means of grades; instead, they stress giving each child a sense of his or her own worth and capacities. In these schools, as in the public community controlled schools such as CCED School in Boston or Morgan Community School in Washington, D.C., one finds variations of the open classroom.

Free Schools and Social Change

The classification above describes ideal types. Many of the schools, of course, combine aspects of different types. For example, the New Community School, a high school in Oakland, has a large white middle-class group, but provides a strong Black Studies program for its large minority of poor black students. Behind the different schools stand a variety of conceptions, not only of education but also of social change and how educational reform relates to more general political and social issues.

Within the Summerhillian tradition there is a definite "apolitical" quality. The school-community deliberately looks inward, sometimes consciously disengaging itself from the larger community and its affairs; the public schools are simply ignored. This perspective makes a minimal political demand on the larger society: to be left alone by the authorities—for instance, health and fire officials who don't like "hippie schools"—so that those who share the philosophy can "do their own thing."

A more social change-oriented expression of this apolitical perspective conceives of the free schools as exemplars and models of what good schools could be like, moving others, even in the public schools, to change. Another more radical rationale conceives of the growth of these free schools as a kind of strategy to attack and weaken the public school system as more and more people withdraw from it to start their own free schools. Throughout, one underlying view of social change is that the libertarian pedagogy and the schools based upon it will develop children who are joyful, cooperative, and peaceful, neither racist nor sexist nor repressed—and the more people like this, the greater the progress toward solving social ills and building a humane, just society.

This view is more often implicit than explicit. For most middle-class elementary schools, whether staff-run or parent-cooperative, the emphasis is on a small group providing for themselves the kind of education they want for their children. They don't like the kind of education offered in the public schools—at least for their own children—but they don't see that they can or should do much to change the public schools, and they refrain from a political analysis of the role of those schools. The following excerpt from a brochure expresses a fairly common situation:

> My wife and I started the school, with the help-support of a few parents dedicated to the no-pressure idea, in fear and trembling since it was beyond our ability, and is not our responsibility—we pay taxes for suitable schools. Fed up with the degrading and humiliating experience of our children in 'the system' we determined to at least have a 'school' for them—others joined us from a small newspaper ad.

Speaking of tuition, these school organizers write:

> Sometimes we have felt rather crass. We charge at about the 'going rate' for the area. This rules out many who are sold on the principles of free education. Our justification goes like this: this is not our responsibility—if the system listened and acted in accord with the desires of people, there would now be available voluntary participation schools to which we would send our children.

Schools like this can afford only a limited number of scholarship students. Many of the parents—including those just quoted—would be completely satisfied if there were a voucher system or easily available "open classroom-free school" options within the existing public school system.

The more politically oriented middle-class free schools would not be so easily satisfied. There we find strong elements of counter-cultural and counter-institutional feeling, as well as a real and justifiable fear that the system will attempt to coopt educational innovations and water down their efforts. The dream of the counter-institutional "greening of America" perspective is that the dominant institutions will collapse as more and more people go off and build their own good places, self-sufficient and uncompromised by the taint of corruption in the dominant institutions. In a more immediate sense, this vision sees free school education as a way of breaking down the socialization function that most public schools serve. That is, simply being what they are, free schools accomplish a worthwhile moral and political goal by helping some children escape the "brainwashing" of the public school system.

For example, students of the Exploring Family School in San Diego wrote about the role of the public school as they see it:

> . . . after graduation from school the students go out into the world trained to fit into society. Our economic system must create men and women to fit its capitalistic needs. The system has to have men and women who have the same values, who feel free and independent, but who will nevertheless do what is expected of them, people who can easily be controlled.

So stark a political analysis would make many people in free schools rather uncomfortable. They are against indoctrination, and they do not want to think that there is a hint of this in their own schools which are committed to the freedom of the child to learn and think and see in his or her own way, shaped as little as possible by adults. The Exploring Family School is mainly white and middle class, K-12, with as libertarian a pedagogy as any. But many of the people involved share a radical political perspective, and this makes the school somewhat atypical. More than most, the school attempts to relate to sympathetic public school teachers and gets involved in community political activity.

This approach is more typical of the community school, of course. For black community schools, there is little ambivalence in setting forth a strong political analysis and reflecting it in the spirit and curriculum of the school. Whereas most brochures of middle-class schools emphasize the pedagogical flaws of public schools, e.g. unnecessary regimentation, too large classes, and insufficient scope for creative and emotional development, the minority group community schools concentrate on the political inadequacies. The Nairobi Community School in East Palo Alto writes in its brochure:

> The destruction of our minds is planned, programmed. The racist school boards, teachers, administrators conspired to waste our precious youth, who knew they would force the change, plan, learn how to make the radical complete breakaway from systems of white control, manipulation and destruction. We went through the stages of seeking

solutions, such as attempting a futile integration and sneaking into white neighborhoods to attend their schools of white supremacy, only to experience—death at an early age.

The white middle-class schools are clear in theory on what they are *not* going to do (be authoritarian, repressive, etc.) but they often have very serious problems deciding what they *are* going to do. This is less a problem for the black community schools. For example, the curriculum at Nairobi High includes African history, black current events, and Black U. S. history, as well as physics, math, algebra, science, communications, reading, art, music, and French. It is designed to "produce black problem solvers, to produce young black community scholars, who recognize our slave condition and the necessity of breaking these chains on our minds, to heal these scars on our backs and souls." This type of curriculum and this clear sense of purpose typify the new black community schools.

Clearly, minority groups that see themselves struggling to end racial and economic oppression will insist on fighting a school system that they see as part of the process of oppression. They see themselves engaged in political struggle, and they want the community schools they run to prepare their young people for participation in this struggle. From this perspective, the pedagogical free school ideas of not structuring, pressuring, or inculcating social and political beliefs will seem neither relevant nor serious. Whereas A. S. Neill claimed that Summerhill students did not know his own political or religious beliefs, it would be odd for black community school people to avoid projecting their belief in the black revolution or black consciousness. To see this as "laying a trip on the kids" would be to press some of the pedagogical concepts to a dubious extreme.

The political strand in the education reform movement insists on the essentially political nature of the educational system. In particular, it stresses the way the groups in control of the major institutions of society use the school system and other institutions to help maintain the status quo. (This assertion need not evoke a plot; it is true about institutions in any social order.) From this point of view, the very concept of educational reform presents ambiguities. Black and other minority communities either start their own community schools outside the system or try to exert enough political power to get control of the public schools in their communities. They want to make schools major instruments in the struggle for freedom and equality. But many of the problems of the schools are not the product of the schools alone. The value of liberal education, the chance for getting jobs which are intrinsically satisfying and financially rewarding, the sense of growing up in a stable, sustaining social community—these conditions are not readily available to poor and minority youth. Neither community control of schools, nor a really effective alternative school like Harlem Prep, nor the new white working-class high schools can change the basic discouraging social reality that most "lower class" or "disadvantaged" young people encounter. From the political perspective, although these community free schools can often do good things for some young people who were "failed" and unhappy in the public schools, they have only been able to work with a very small number—and they have not been able to "save" all of these.

So, from this perspective, truly liberating educational reform that works for all children can only come with major social, political, economic, and cultural transformations that eliminate not only bad educational conditions but also the roots of those conditions in other institutions.

If these premises are true, then we can expect that serious efforts will be made to coopt the growing discontent with public school education as most clearly and completely expressed by the free schools. Silberman's *Crisis in the Classroom* has been accepted, so to speak, in important areas of the educational establishment, with the result that there is increasing support for public alternative schools and programs. One obvious danger is that, as with many reforms, such reform will blunt and buy off discontent before it can bring about the larger changes which are its goals. Free-type schools supported by the system could be used to siphon off "malcontents," "troublemakers," and activists—among students and parents—and thus ease the spreading troubles in the public schools. Or public alternatives will be closely controlled by the current managers of the school system, so that experiments that are too abrasive and too "radical" can be toned down by threatening to withdraw financial support. (We have already observed this phenomenon in some of the public alternative school projects.)

A similar fear is voiced from the more pedagogical and cultural sectors of the free school movement, but since the demands there are not so extensive, many could be more easily met by a set of open classroom public alternatives or, especially, by a tuition voucher plan.

Looking Ahead. Alternatives inside the public sector supported by local, state, or federal aid, are sure to spread in the very near future. (A recent column by Albert Shanker in the weekly propaganda slot the teachers' union buys in the *New York Sunday Times* confirmed this assertion. Shanker attacks the claims of success for alternative schools—in a misleading and dishonest manner. But his tone is very defensive, as if against a growing trend he opposes.) Many parent groups are organizing to ask the school authorities for alternative public schools committed to libertarian methods. For example, the Cambridge School Committee recently approved such a proposal from the Committee for an Alternative Public School, a group of parents who organized and negotiated for almost two years to get an inside-the-system *free* school. The number of teachers, parents, and students who want such schools is growing, even though most Americans would still say that they basically approve the traditional style of the average public school. As noted, the number of free schools continues to increase rapidly. But contrary to the predictions of some free education activists, this development will not mushroom into thousands of schools and hundreds of thousands of students. As the difficulties of running free schools and scrounging even for meager resources become more widely known, enthusiasm will diminish. And as pressure for reform builds up on the public school system, it will seem more realistic as a strategy to get an alternative public school established, even at the cost of some compromise with the system, than to establish another small and fragile free school that might easily fail after a couple of years. Even now, some schools that started outside the system are trying to figure out ways of being accepted as public schools in some form, without giving up their essential spirit or autonomy. This has happened in the case of the Children's Community Workshop School. For many free school people with a political perspective, the possibility of free schools being alternative public schools will be very attractive, despite the constant danger of being coopted and controlled. As part of public systems, reformers will be able to gain more visibility and influence for their innovations. Also, public financial support will enable schools serving poorer communities to achieve the stability needed to attract parents to what might at first seem a dubious experiment.

Some free schools will prefer to maintain their independence so as to ensure freedom from the pressures and compromises inevitably imposed by involvement in the public system. This stance includes both politically and pedagogically oriented school reformers, since it is obvious that there are free schools expressing both strands that would be too "far out" for any state system to tolerate.

Within a few years the free school movement has emerged as a significant phenomenon, if not for its actual numbers, then for its symbolic significance as representative of the spreading popularity of radical reform ideas. There have been other movements of radical progressive reform; movements that do not seem to have accomplished the serious changes of the sort they initially envisioned. We can hope that the new wave of radical school reform will find ways to avoid repeating this melancholy history.

FOOTNOTES

1. Clearly, these ideas overlap with aspects of the progressive education movement of the early 1900's, which spawned a number of experimental "progressive" schools. But in this current revival of the progressive school reform spirit, we find more emphasis on *participation* in the "freedom" notion—the idea that parents and students should have a much greater part in all aspects of educational institutions. This clearly implies a negative attitude toward professional educators and teachers, whose authority stems from a dubious though certified claim of expertise.

2. Funded by HEW.

3. In this category are Michael Community School in Milwaukee, formerly a Catholic school, now a community school moving rapidly to libertarian methods (290 students), the New School for Children, a black community school in Roxbury, Mass. (140 students), and East Harlem Block Schools, a group of mainly black and Puerto Rican elementary schools in New York (a total of 220 students in four sites). A related category is that of predominantly black street academies for high school people, such as CAM Academy in Chicago (250 students) and Harlem Prep (500 students). A very special category is that of experimental demonstration schools run by colleges which, after some serious hesitation, were included in the study—Margaret Sibley School for Educational Research and Demonstration, Plattsburgh, N.Y. (275 students), run as part of the state university system, and Webster College School, St. Louis (150 students), are examples.

SELECTIONS FROM "I WILL MESS UP ON MY OWN": AN ANALYSIS OF THE FIRST SIX MONTHS OF PENN CIRCLE COMMUNITY HIGH SCHOOL*

BY DAVID ZAREMBKA†

On the typical school day one might be able to count several hundred high school students in the East Liberty shops and streets. Nevertheless more than two thousand more students, i.e., the large majority, might be found inside the school, attending classes, performing their assignments, and working diligently towards their high school diplomas. The problems at the high school are formidable: the school is more than seven hundred students above capacity, has three study halls in the auditorium each period, and yet must try to meet the needs of two thousand seven hundred varied students.

About one out of every four students who starts the high school in the ninth grade drops out before he has completed his requirements for his diploma. Officially about half of these students withdraw because they have "passed the age of compulsory attendance."

The East End Cooperative Ministry (EECM), a social action alliance of twenty-two churches in the East End area of Pittsburgh, runs a free breakfast program every school morning at the Pittsburgh Theological Seminary for local high school students. The staff of the EECM, Burt Campbell and Jud Dolphin, found that each day forty to sixty of the two to three hundred students who came to the breakfast never went across the street to school. For awhile they congregated at

* Reprinted with permission from David Zarembka, Penn Circle Community High School, Pittsburgh, Pennsylvania.

† David Zarembka is Director of the Penn Circle Community High School. He spent five years teaching and administrating in East Africa and has been instrumental in starting a number of alternative institutions.

the lounge reserved for seminary students. When the truant students were forbidden to use the lounge, the EECM staff wondered what could be done for these students.

They began to work closely with about fifteen of the truant students and tried to understand their problems. They found that these students felt they were not able to cope with the situation at the high school. They complained of the bigness of the school, the impersonal relationships with teachers and other students, the confinement brought by numerous rules, and the structure which left them no independence.

As a first step the EECM staff conducted a survey of forty truants who came to free breakfast and with the cooperation of the administration at the high school surveyed the records of fifty comparable truants. They found considerable numbers of failing grades, troubles with the law, and/or family problems at home. Many tended to come from large families and/or tended to be a younger, if not the youngest, member in the family. Their IQ scores, surprisingly enough, reflected the general range of scores in the high school; more than half of the truants had scores above 100, indicating that lack of intelligence had no correlation with truancy.

Armed with these statistics the EECM then approached administrators in the Pittsburgh Board of Public Education to ask them what might be done for these students. While the officials were sympathetic and cognizant of the problem, they felt that the Board of Public Education could do nothing at that time.

The EECM staff were concerned about the truants whom they knew well and who were not receiving any education. So they decided to found an alternative high school, Penn Circle Community High School, for these students. They put together a rather unusual combination of forces in order to launch the school:

1. A grant of $7000 from the East End Cooperative Ministry to run the school for the first six months (January to June, 1973).

2. Five VISTA volunteer certified teachers.

3. School accreditation by becoming an extension to Sacred Heart High School and thereby under the auspices of the Catholic Diocese.

4. Educational expertise by obtaining the assistance of Lester Jipp, a member of an EECM church and assistant professor of secondary education at Chatham College and later Co-chairman of the Penn Circle Community High School Board.

5. Acceptance of the school in EECM's member churches and the surrounding community through the business clubs and other civic organizations.

In October, 1972, the author was hired as Director and on January 2, 1973, Penn Circle Community High School opened with forty students.

Student Self-Direction in Learning

To begin with I always hated high school, even though I was great in grade school. I couldn't hack being forced to do something, like the school making my schedule, the school picking my classes, my teachers, and I had to follow it or else get into trouble. So I started cutting. First I was cutting classes, then days. Well, for two and a half years I've been cutting school, getting suspended, getting detention, fines, and a lot of hassle from my parents.

Now that Penn Circle Community High School has started I have a chance to learn something, to do it without the hassle of my parents, the high school, or the law. I won't have to cut to see my friends. I won't have to cut because I hate the classes they assigned me. I can pick my own schedule, my own classes. And if I mess up I will mess up on my own.

A PENN CIRCLE STUDENT

One of the primary goals of Penn Circle Community High School is to turn students on to education. This is done by developing student interest, by giving the students a lot of choice, and by letting them make their own decisions.

The basic means of implementing this goal of student self-direction is through mini-courses and contracts. All courses last only three weeks, meet four hours per week, and are worth one-tenth of a credit (12 hours out of 120 hours needed for one Carnegie Unit of credit). At the beginning of the year the teachers posted on the wall a description of a number of courses in which they thought the students might be interested. The students then picked their own courses working them into a schedule. Classes like "Rock Poetry" and "Why Psycholog?" were the most popular; others had no student interest and were dropped.

At the beginning of a course an individual contract is signed between the student and teacher. The contract outlines the content of the course, the work required by the student, and the method of evaluation. There are no grades and credit is received by the student if he fulfills the terms of the contract. At the end of the three weeks the teacher and the student fill out evaluations on the work accomplished.

At the completion of the mini-course, three alternatives are open to the teacher and student: (1) the course can be dropped as interest has lagged, (2) the course can be continued with a new contract, or (3) a new course can develop from the interests of the first. For example, one mini-course was "Criminology." From this the students decided to study "Violence," a class which was renewed twice for a total of nine weeks.

As the year progressed two developments indicated the growing ability of students to direct their own course of study. First was the rise of independent studies. More and more students decided to take independent studies in areas that interested them. One student, for example, decided to read *Inside the Third Reich*. Another student studied Renaissance art and for her evaluation drew a picture in the Renaissance style.

The second change came at Easter time when students began to complain that the teachers wrote the contracts and *they* had to sign them. Therefore it was decided that at the first or second class the teacher and students would discuss the terms of the contracts and students who were no longer interested in the course as it developed had the option to drop it.

The last reason the school was able to develop student involvement in learning was the absence of hassling. Students are allowed to smoke, eat, and drink soda whenever they wish. They can sit on a table, chair, or floor. When they are not in class, they are allowed to play ping-pong, pool, or records. Due to this freedom more than one visitor to the school had concluded that Penn Circle was a play school. It is surprising that, when treated as responsible people, privileges are not abused; interest in ping-pong and pool declined as the months progressed. Listening to records is a good relaxation between challenging and intense classes. But most important an informal, tension-free atmosphere, a prerequisite to turning students on to learning, develops.

In order to indicate what happens in a Penn Circle classroom, excerpts are given below from a report on classroom observations made by Alice Troup, a teacher trainer from the University of Pittsburgh.

> The students at Penn Circle are here, I believe, because they have had difficulty in the public school system. Their difficulty has been identified by the symptom of withdrawal —class cutting or truancy. In short, these students have been identified as problem students.
>
> This designation is difficult to reconcile with the cooperation and even enthusiasm demonstrated by the students in their classes. For example,
>
> In a highly teacher-directed, lecture-explanation psychology class, on modes of learning (physical maturity levels, past experiences, etc.) the demeanor of the class was highly positive. When the teacher asked for examples to support or elaborate a point, at least a third of the students responded verbally. During the presentation of the material, the students were very attentive. When the teacher momentarily had a problem with correctly spelling a word on the board (magic marker and taped paper) the students corrected her in a helpful way (no laughing, no ridicule, no "jesse" looks, etc.).
>
> Perhaps it is easier to identify what did not occur in the class. There were no looks of boredom. No heads were down in crooked arms. No horseplay was present nor was there small group whispering. Phrases like "stop it", "may I have your attention", "please be quiet" etc. were not used, nor were they in any way necessary.
>
> The attentive faces, the teacher-student cooperation, the willingness of the students to respond to the direction set by the teacher impressed me—particularly because these students have been characterized, I suspect, in opposite terms . . .

In a class on Classical Egypt, there were two quiet, unsure, young men. Each had identified a research topic, "Who built the pyramids" and "How were they built". A filmstrip on Egypt was shown. Even as a teacher I have rarely seen students discuss a filmstrip in process (especially when the words are at the bottom of the frame)! The young men, however, took notes during the filmstrip, asked questions, made comments, and asked that several frames be shown again.

In a class in Black Studies, on Abolitionists, one student had prepared and presented material on the reason for the abolitionist movement. Another student presented a report on the origins of the Quakers of Germantown, and their creation of the underground railroads.

In another psych class, with four students, a definition of psychology, in conceptual terms, was being established. As part of the process (aside from brainstorming) small excerpts from a college psych book were read aloud by students. The first student was a confident and smooth reader. The second student also volunteered to read. He had much more difficulty. The students on both sides of him came in close, and followed his reading, and helped him with the words he stumbled on. The teacher interrupted frequently to ask the students to translate into regular words, the phrases used in the book ("living organisms" as animals, "extra organic stimuli"—or some such phrase—as environment, etc.). I suspect that this student, if given a reading assignment would not be able to read it, at least not with meaning. If asked to read aloud in a regular classroom, he would, I suspect, have refused. In this case, however, I repeat that the student volunteered—in the context of very strong emotional and tangible support from his peers.

At the beginning of school students had been tested for reading ability. Twelve who read at the eighth grade level or below were placed in a remedial reading class which met twice a week. In retrospect the staff realized that two sessions per week were not enough, since to function adequately at Penn Circle, the student needs to be able to read well. Therefore during the summer the poorer readers will be required to attend a Reading Clinic where they will be saturated with reading and writing remedial development. Students who do not reach adult reading levels by the fall will continue until they do so.

A second group was those students who, as they had been long accustomed, wished to be told what to do and how to do it, who preferred to be passive recipients of teacher guidance. Here all we can hope is, as was told to us at an alternative school in Philadelphia, "It takes a year or two for students to become accustomed to and to take advantage of an alternative learning experience."

THE INDEPENDENT PUBLIC SCHOOLS*

BY SUSAN S. EGAN†

It may seem strange to begin a discussion of independent schools by considering the public schools and the problems they have. The two have always been considered separate school systems with different problems and different interests. In fact, the distinction between them is less and less valid.[1]

Until very recently, there were only two kinds of independent schools: parochial and private. The private schools were, and are today, high tuition institutions which admit students on a selective basis, according to their previous academic success or tests which indicate that students are likely to be successful. For the most part, private schools have white, upper-middle and upper class populations, which are fairly uniform ethnically and religiously. The parochial schools are sectarian institutions, dedicated in one way or another to providing children with a religious education.

About six years ago, groups of parents who felt that the public schools were not effectively educating their children, who were not interested in a sectarian education, and could not afford to send their children to private schools began to start their own schools. Committed as they were to the idea of public education, they made their schools tuition free, sought financial support elsewhere and opened the schools to anyone who wanted to come.

Now there are approximately 120 such schools in New

* Reprinted by permission of Current History, Inc. (August 1972 issue of *Current History*), Wilton, Connecticut 06897.

† Susan S. Egan was the Director of the Committee of Community Schools for two years and then consultant to the Rochester, New York, Board of Education for the preparation of its voucher program proposal to the Federal Office of Economic Opportunity. She is currently associated with a law firm in New York City.

York State alone. Typically, each is run by a board of directors elected by the parents of students in the school. All policy matters are determined by the board, including curriculum, hiring and firing and fiscal procedures. Sometimes teachers sit on the board; sometimes representatives from the community in which the school is located and sometimes professionals, like lawyers or public school administrators, take part.

Because of parental control, educationally, the schools tend to be as different as the parents who run them. They run the gamut from very traditional to way out. Some are college preparatory or vocationally oriented. Others work with drop-outs, or with students with learning problems. Some are Montessori schools: some are Summerhillian; many have open classrooms. Because these schools are tuition-free, nonsectarian and open-to-all, they are called independent public schools. They are also variously known as alternative, community or free schools.

The existence of the independent public schools has precipitated something of a crisis in traditional thinking regarding public and private education. While the existence of a policy-making board of directors would suggest that these schools are private, the policy they are making is public. The reactions to the development of this definitional neverneverland have been widely varied. Private school advocates see independent public schools as a justification for public funding for private schools. Had it not been for private school tradition in this country, they say, independent public schools would never have developed.

The public school advocates, on the other hand, see independent public schools as a demonstration of the breadth and intrinsic flexibility of the concept of public education. The mere fact that independent public schools exist, they say, is the best reason why public funds need not be made available to private schools. In fact, independent public schools are neither public nor private, as those words have typically been defined. Interestingly, the New York State constitution does not define public schools. It provides that:

> The legislature shall provide for the maintenance and support of the system of free common schools, wherein all children of the state may be educated. [Constitution, Article II, Section 1.]

Legal Definitions

New York State case law, however, has defined public schools as schools which are open to all, have no religious affiliation and are intended for the inhabitants of the district where they are located.[2] *In Roman Catholic Orphan Asylum*, schools maintained in sectarian orphan asylums were held not to be "common" schools. The court emphasized the fact that common schools must be open to all children.[3]

Under this definition of a public school, independent public schools would be considered public if they were to receive public funds. Among the obstacles to public support of independent public schools is the intricate scheme of statutory provisions regulating the administration of the public schools which the legislature has established in order to fulfill the constitutional mandate.

The question of how many of these rules and regulations are really necessary in order that the state insure that the public monies made available for public education are properly spent has never been examined. The state education law has developed without real regard for consistency or relevance. As a consequence, the law now runs to five volumes and includes such inconsistencies as making the elementary school physical education requirement 120 minutes per week in one place and 15 minutes twice a day or 25 minutes a day in another place.

Today, tuition-free, non-sectarian community schools are trying to get tax levy monies (i.e., to become part of the public school system) without abandoning their administrative independence to the vagaries of the rules and regulations which would have to apply to independent public schools as a matter of law and those which apply as a matter of administrative regulation or even custom. It is customary, for instance, that students be given grades. All public schools in New York City are required to administer the Metropolitan Achievement Tests. That is a matter of administrative regulation. That the Board of Education is not permitted to delegate its responsibility for the education of the children in the city is a matter of law. The recurring question is: Is it necessary for a school to give Metropolitan Achievement Tests and grades in order to be designated as a public school?

In the public schools, while the schools are required to administer the Metropolitan Achievement Tests, the students are not required to take them. If a parent chooses to keep her child home on the date the test is given, there is little the school can do about it. What is to prevent all the parents in a school from keeping their children home? And if they all do, does that make the school any less a public school?

Increasingly, in New York, the public schools are not giving grades. Nor are they requiring, with their former rigidity, 4 units of English, 3 units of social studies and 1 unit of science in high school. In fact, some experimental public schools have experimental admission procedures, a deviation from the norm which is far more basic to the concept of "public" school than grades or curriculum. The World of Inquiry in Rochester, New York, admits students on the basis of a computer print out which seeks to replicate the demographies of the city as a whole. When there is a vacancy to be filled at the school, it is filled with a child whose profile fits.

Can that school really be called open to all within the meaning of the law? Is that school any more "public" than a school like Harlem Prep which admits drop-outs, or a school like Children's Community Workshop, which admits students on a first-come, first served basis within three ethnic categories: black, white and Puerto Rican? The distinction between "public" and "private," in the conventional sense of the terms, has lost its meaning.

The principle obstacle to public support of independent public schools in New York is the existence of a board of directors. The state is supposed to manage and operate a system of public schools for the benefit of those children who may attend. Under existing education law, the state is not permitted to delegate that responsibility so that, until the law is changed, boards of directors of independent public schools will not legally be able to undertake the task of educating the children who attend their schools.[4]

An effort is now being made to change the state law. Assemblywoman Constance E. Cook and State Senator Thomas Laverne introduced legislation in 1972 which would permit tax levy funds to go to independent public schools, boards of directors and all. The bill faces some very stiff political opposition, but more importantly, it has intellectual opponents, people whose definition of public education differs from the one suggested by the bill. The bill suggests that public education is a very broad concept; that the obligation of the school system is to provide an education for the public. If the "public" is varied, multi-ethnic and economically diverse, the schools should recognize those differences if there is truly to be a "system of common schools wherein all children of the state may be educated." Public education has always been seen as the "great leveller." Equal educational opportunity has been construed to mean the same educational opportunity.

Independent public schools do not challenge the concept of equal education. They question whether or not such education can be achieved through sameness. They do not question the government's responsibility for the education of all the children of the state, only whether that responsibility mandates a system of hierarchical controls. They recognize the fundamental differences between public and private education. They are not so sure that those differences are absolutes.

If the intellectual controversy stirred by the existence of independent public schools has been troublesome, it is equal only to the political confusion they have caused. Until recently, there were only two positions on aid to non-public schools. Proponents believed in pluralism and in the right of Catholic parents to choose what kind of school they wished their children to attend. Opponents believed that the state's first obligation was to the children who attend its schools and that the separation of church and state is a fundamental principle of American government.

The independent public schools, however, do not seek aid in the sense that parochial schools do. They want to be part of the public school system. They believe in the parents' right to choose what kind of education they want for their child, and believe those options can be offered within the public school system.

There is no longer any question that the current method of financing public education is both inadequate and inequitable. The public schools are starving to death, particularly in the cities. Until *Serrano v. Priest*[5] becomes the law of the land and federal assistance is provided, funding independent public schools will unquestionably be an additional burden; however, so will the return of parochial school students to the public schools.

Additionally, it should be remembered that independent

public schools in New York wish to be integrated into the public school system as schools, not as individuals. Along with the 6,000 children come the buildings (everything from re-modelled supermarkets to second floor lofts), the teachers (usually more per classroom than in the public schools) and the administration, thus requiring a higher per capita outlay than the traditional public schools.

In addition to the problems caused by children returning to the public school system are those caused by the shift of children out to the independent public schools. As alternatives develop within the public school system, students will move over from the traditional schools. In any case, the traditional schools who lose a few students here and there are going to want to keep their teachers. More teachers and fewer students means a lower pupil/teacher ratio. In short, it is entirely possible that in addition to the cost of independent public schools, there will be an increase in the cost of education being offered in the traditional public schools.

If one adds up the cost of new students and schools, resulting additional costs for old schools and an allowance for growth, one suspects that the total comes nowhere near the projected cost to the public schools of the drop in parochial school enrollment. No study has even been made of the comparative costs.

But it is worth noting that the funding of independent public schools is not necessarily in addition to the expenditures required to accommodate parochial school children. We can expect parochial schools, particularly those located in city ghettos where the student population is usually not predominately Catholic, to wish to join the public school system as independent public schools. We can expect it because it is already happening, most significantly in Milwaukee and New York, but in other areas of the country as well.

If parochial schools continue to be turned over to parents for the purpose of running tuition-free, non-sectarian, open-to-all schools, they will enter the public school system as independent public schools, not as parochial schools. To this limited extent, the financial problems surrounding the influx of parochial school children and the funding of independent public schools are the same.

In conclusion, we can form the following hypotheses regarding independent public schools:

Unlike other non-public schools, independent public schools are growing both in size and number. Fitting as they do within the legal definition of public school and recognizing that many of the rules and regulations governing public school administration are not inherently part of that definition, they can be expected increasingly to pressure the public school system for admission on some new definitional and administrative basis.

The independent public schools can expect support from the alternative schools within the system which find that the existing administrative structure is not conducive to the development of the kind of options they would like to see their schools offer. Additionally, they can expect support from the Church, which can no longer support its ghetto-based schools without massive federal and state assistance, which it has no reason to suspect the courts will permit.

The operation of independent public schools within the public school system is likely to provoke an academic and administrative reaction within the public schools, a reconsideration of the kind of option the traditional school wants to offer. Any consideration of the cost of independent public school incorporation must therefore include an estimate of the cost of changes in the traditional schools.

Private school children are likely to return to the public school system when the options their parents have been willing to pay for outside the school system or outside the city begin to appear inside the school system. To the extent that such a migration inhibits middle class movement to the suburbs, we can expect independent public schools to have a stabilizing effect not only on the public school population, but on the city population as a whole.

Whether these projections will be borne out depends in large measure on the willingness of the public school system to experiment, the willingness of the legislature to examine its definition of public education and the capacity of the existing independent public schools to survive until the first two things occur.

Whether or not funds can be found for independent public schools is not a question of whether or not we want a larger school system. The question is: do we want to enlarge the concept of public education? Do we quite literally want to encourage people to be part of the public school system? If the answers to those questions are unclear at this point, we can hardly be surprised. So little time and attention has been given to them. This is clearly the time to reconsider. What is public education? What is the purpose of public education? Just what is a public school anyway?

FOOTNOTES

1. In discussing the developments in independent education in the last several years, we will look primarily at New York State.

2. *People Ex. Rel. Roman Catholic Orphan Asylum v. Board of Education*, 13 Barb. 400, 410 (1851); *Gordon v. Cornes*, 47, N.Y. 608, 616 (1872).

3. 13 Barb. 410.

4. On the other hand, the New York City Board of Education has gone to nearly ridiculous lengths to permit some measure of community control. In Park East High School, an experimental, comprehensive high school on Manhattan's upper east side, the board subcontracted with a community group to provide all the supporting services in the school. Supporting services were defined as all necessary support, including planning, consultants and supplementary staff, facilities, supplies and equipment, except for the furnishing of licensed teachers and core instruction.

5. 5 Cal. 3rd 584. For excerpts see *Current History*, July, 1972, pp. 28 ff.

THOREAU SCHOOL WANTS TO JOIN WALLKILL CENTRAL*

BY KARL RODMAN†

A unique experiment in education may halt soon for lack of funds.

The Thoreau school on Tillson Lake road—essentially a one-room private school teaching 22 students from grades one through seven—will have to close at the end of June because of a money shortage, unless the Wallkill central district decides to accept it as part of its system. Although school owner Karl Rodman was turned down in past requests to enter the

* Reprinted with permission from the *Citizen Herald* (Walden, New York), Letter to the Editor, October 23, 1974.

† Karl Rodman is Director of the Thoreau School, Wallkill, New York.

district, he is now renewing his efforts and as a last resort may ask for a public referendum on the matter.

Located on the grounds of the Thoreau summer camp, the school opened in September, 1973, with 19 pupils, all of whom live within a few miles of the facility. Rodman and Joan Hollister, both certified, experienced teachers, comprise the faculty, but the instruction is augmented by a student teacher from New Paltz, and parents who come in to help.

Although the school covers a standard curriculum, and is checked by the Wallkill district to see that it meets minimum state requirements, it also offers a total "open" classroom wherein several activities can proceed at one time. Children are not grouped by grade, but learn at their own pace. Extensive use is made of nature studies, because of the camp setting, which includes a farm. There is a great deal of individualized instruction, as well as freedom of movement.

Unfunded by any governmental agencies or charities, the school is supported by tuitions that are as low as $1 per day for some, to higher fees. Some children do not pay at all. One set of parents were providing the main funding, but have since moved out of the area—hence the current financial squeeze. Rodman said that parents are now holding Tupperware parties and other fund drives to see the school through until June.

Rodman believes the financial problem could be settled, without adverse effect on the Wallkill taxpayers, if the school were accepted into the district. He points out that the district loses $680 in state aid for each of the 22 students enrolled in his private facility. If the school were to join the system, Rodman would ask only that the district pay for one teacher's salary, which would come to an unspecified amount less than the $15,980 the district would receive in state aid. The Thoreau school would continue to pay for all maintenance, upkeep and operating expenses, he said. Nor would the district have to fund extra buses, he added, as all the children either ride their bikes to class or are driven by parents.

While the district's written denial of acceptance, dated May 22, does not contain any reasons, Rodman said one objection has been that the children at the Thoreau school would be getting something—a special school with a special setting—that other children would not. Rodman says the matter could be resolved by determining geographically who could attend his school. "We're not a parochial school," he said. "We're open to anybody."

Most of the present students are from the neighborhood, and the school is supposed to be a community affair anyway, with many parents participating in educational and extracurricular activities. Rodman noted that if the district wanted to increase the pupil load, to bring it closer to Wallkill's class average, he would go along with that.

"Don't deprive the children of a good experience which will cost you nothing," Rodman said in a letter to this paper this week. "If the experiment proves to have value for many children, perhaps then it should have wider application. But let's give it a chance and find out."

So far he has found that his experiment in education is working quite well. Students who had problems learning within the confines of the normal classroom structure are progressing nicely in his open classroom. And most of the students "are expressing themselves better in writing and thinking," partly due to the fact that at the end of each day, every student writes a letter to the teachers explaining what he or she did that day. These essays are corrected and handed back next day.

Also, "they handle more complicated and abstract thoughts," contended Rodman. "And I find more self-confidence in them—that's one of the big plusses."

In its year, the school has had a "beautiful" relationship with district schools. Although he maintains a well-stocked library, his students are also allowed to use Wallkill's. Classes from Wallkill's elementary schools have visited Thoreau several times on field trips, and once went on a joint trip to the New Paltz planetarium with Thoreau students.

However, assistant Wallkill superintendent Dwight Aller believes that accepting the Thoreau school would present too many problems to make it worthwhile. "You would be opening a Pandora's box," he said. "Any group could begin a school and then ask the district to accept it."

"It's a private school with limited selectivity," he continued. "It would establish a two room school within the lines we've drawn . . . We just closed down a two room school because we felt we could give a better education, more economically."

Aller said he believes that the biggest problem is that while Rodman is now asking for only one teacher's salary, eventu-

ally the district would have to take over the maintenance of
the building, and would end up paying for two teachers' salaries, although Rodman had not suggested this.

The pupil teacher ratio would also have to be altered to
conform with the rest of the district, Aller said. "If you added
more pupils, that wipes out everything they're trying to do
there."

As to what effect the acceptance of Thoreau school might
have on the district's relationship with any parochial schools,
Aller had "no comment."

"There are too many questions to be answered," said Aller
on accepting a school with "questionable benefits." Speaking
for himself, he commented "I can't see where there would
be any benefits to doing it this way."

School Proposal

For the past two academic years I have been running a
neighborhood school. We now enroll twenty-two children,
grades one through seven.

We have petitioned the Wallkill Board of Education that
they take us under their wing, giving us limited financial support and recognizing us as an experimental branch of the public school system.

The Board of Education turned down our request last year,
saying that they were not willing to take us over "at the present time."

I am not sure that the board fully realized that their decision is costing the taxpayers money, while a decision to take
us over would provide a service to parents and children at
no additional cost whatsoever to the taxpayers.

As things stand now, the Wallkill taxpayers are losing State
Aid, amounting to approximately $680 per child for each of
the twenty-two children we enroll. If the Board of Education
would agree to accept us as a part of their educational program this $15,960 would come into their treasury. The pro-
posal I made to them is that if they are willing to pay one
teacher's salary, we here at the school would undertake to
carry the full burden of the physical plant and of operating
expenses.

Certain objections have been voiced to our proposal. One
is that our program is a retreat to the days of the one room

schoolhouse. To this I would point out that it can hardly be considered a retreat if the parents of more children than we have room to accommodate have requested this program, even though it is costing them money. More important, the latest educational concepts of individually paced learning in an open environment are being given a thorough testing here in our farm-school-summer-camp environment.

The other major objection has been "How can public education provide a service to the taxpayers in one part of the town, if this service cannot be available to everyone in the town?" I can only answer that this is a "sour grapes" argument. Don't deprive some children of a good experience which will cost you nothing, just because not everyone can have it. If the experiment proves to have value for many children, perhaps then it should have wider application. But let's give it a chance and find out.

If the Board of Education will, at no cost to the taxpayers, give us funding next year, we will be able to continue. (The legal structure under which they would be permitted to do this does already exist.) If the Board again turns us down we will probably have to close our doors, returning twenty-two, or more, children to the Wallkill Schools, and perhaps necessitating the hiring of an additional teacher anyway.

I am writing this letter now, not to state a gripe, but to try and stimulate some discussion of this proposal. I still do think that it can be a valuable program for Wallkill. I do have great respect for the Wallkill School system and I would like to be able to have my school function as a part of that parent system.

Section III

ALTERNATIVES WITHIN THE SYSTEM

EDITOR'S COMMENTS

Alternatives have found their way into the public schools. Since this is where most of the students are, the trend is beginning to reach the mainstream. It is precisely this "mainstream" that needs to be reached if alternatives are to lead to serious educational reform. While public school alternatives deal with the pedagogical problems of the poor, dropouts, disruptive children, the emotionally disturbed, and the like, this is not the main thrust of the movement. Rather, optional learning environments are beginning to surface in middle-class schools and "regular" children. Such places as Newton, Massachusetts, Webster Groves, Missouri, Scarsdale, New York, Bethesda, Maryland—some of the most so-called "prestigious" school systems—are implementing alternatives. These school districts are important because other school districts are likely to take their signals from them. Consequently, if Great Neck, New York, where over ninety percent of the students go to college, embarks on alternatives, it is likely to influence other school districts with similar school populations.

As indicated in some of the articles in our first section, if alternatives are linked only to students who appear to be having problems, then this trend toward diversity will not likely result in major impact on the mainstream of public education. During the 1960s, we assumed that the education being provided to so-called "disadvantaged" students could become the model for the middle class. This has not been the case because (in a socially mobile society) it actually works the other way around. In this context, the Quincy experience is particularly important. Located in the middle of the United States, with its "typical" middle-America flavor, the thrust toward education by choice has had particular impact on the mainstream.

As one might expect, public school alternatives are some-

what different from the alternatives which were created outside the public school. Nonetheless, first-generation alternatives reflected variety. They have gotten people used to other
educational ways. An entire range of options has surfaced,
all the way from the liberation of teacher style to an entire
school system considering alternatives, such as that being con-
templated in the Cincinnati public schools. In between, we
have ideas for mini-schools, schools within schools, schools
without walls, etc. In this section, the reader will be exposed
to this pluralism and the distinctive features of the different
options.

This section will deal with such questions as:

What kinds of separate alternatives exist within the public
school system?

How are they administered?

Why is matching teaching-learning style a growing alternative?

What is a mini-school?

How can space be used constructively?

What is a school without walls?

How are community resources utilized?

What kinds of courses are offered by different alternatives?

Who plans the curriculum in these alternatives?

What happens inside an open school?

Are alternatives operating at all levels within the system?

Can they operate within the confines of a small district?

Must they require increased student expenditures?

MATCHING TEACHING-LEARNING STYLES*

BY MARIO D. FANTINI

As we can sense, alternate forms of education are based on different styles of teaching and learning. These are now largely hidden by the uniform framework of our public schools. They exist on a random basis. Differences among schools are at this moment more a matter of social class than of program. Differences among teachers are minimized.

Once teachers are certified, they are perceived as being "the same." Teachers, all different people with different styles of teaching, find it natural to close the doors of their classrooms and try to deal with twenty-five to thirty-five learners as a block. They try to deal with these learners by imposing one style of teaching on the group. There are many children who respond positively to this style, and just as many who do not. Those who do not are often called "slow," "deprived," even "retarded." By classifying the children, the teacher is also developing an institutionalized way of thinking about them, and constructing a web of self-fulfilling prophecies: what the teacher expects is usually what she gets.

Many teachers have similar teaching styles. These similar styles, if grouped together, generate similar educational environments. Teachers, individually or in groups, produce different kinds of classroom environments, different types of classroom social structure. Some emphasize a certain approach to learning which is markedly different from that of other groups of teachers with other styles of teaching. We have teacher styles generating "informal" classrooms, "schools without walls," "formal" classrooms, etc. Behind each alternative is a teacher or group of teachers with the same basic style. The liberation of the teacher's style through the sanctioning of educational alternatives may make more visible the existence of legitimate differences among teachers, differences which can help individualize learning, increase educational productivity, and enhance professional satisfaction.

* Reprinted from Mario D. Fantini, *Public Schools of Choice* (New York, Simon & Schuster, 1974).

Note the difference between two elementary school teachers in the same school.

> . . . you might examine a classroom and see the teacher in the front of the room talking to the class. The class might be listening and taking notes; if an assignment is being made, the students might ask questions. Soon the class is over and a new class comes in. The teacher again asks for the homework from the previous day, goes on to some new work, dictates some important facts, asks a few questions on the work which should have been prepared for the day, makes an assignment for the following day, and answers some last-minute questions. Then a new group comes in and the pattern is repeated.
>
> You might then examine another room where the teacher is, at first, hard to find. She is in the background, but the students are moving around freely. Various projects are being undertaken by small groups of students, while other students are working alone. There does not seem to be a routine approach.[1]

Certain educators might consider the first classroom described above as being "teacher-directed," and the second classroom as being more "student-directed." Other schoolmen might prefer the term "subject-matter-centered" to describe the first teacher and "learner-centered" to describe the second. These and other phrases are attempts to capture the main thrust of the teacher's approach in the classroom.

One way to get a handle on the matter of individual teaching style—or student learning style—is to consider the method used for teaching and learning. Classically, methods can be viewed as being either more *inductive* or more *deductive*. In the inductive approach, one proceeds from the specific to the abstract, from particular information to some generalization. For instance, a child may have several objects which he throws into the air. Each drops. After several trials, he may conclude that everything that goes up must come down. Once he has formed such a generalization, he can apply it to other situations.

The important point here is that the learner discovered the broad principle for himself.

In a deductive approach, the underlying principle is learned and then applied to different situations.

Both approaches are valid. No teaching is all inductive or

all deductive. In fact, when these approaches are translated into the school and classroom setting, they could have different meanings.

The deductive approach has come to mean a teacher- or school-controlled structure in which known knowledge in various disciplines is systematically covered. This structure has come to mean studying and mastering the known, where knowledge is more prescribed by the teacher.

Inductive teaching has come to mean generating a structure in which problems are solved by doing, by engaging in hands-on activities that lead to solutions—of finding out about the unknown—of having the student attempt to give order to what may appear to be disorder.

Often in my travels through schools, I note the problems arising from a mismatch of teaching-learning styles. For example, in one classroom, the teacher was using a non-directive, inductive approach, trying to elicit a response by asking questions, without himself giving the answers. About half the class participated, i.e., interacted with the teacher. When we stopped the class to analyze the situation with the students, the non-participating students began to voice their discontent with the teacher's approach. "I came here to listen and to learn something from someone who is an expert—instead, I have to sit here listening to a discussion."

When the entire class was asked to show by raising their hands how many preferred the approach in which the teacher was non-directive, about half the students did so; the other half preferred a type of structure in which the teacher presented his or her knowledge directly to the class, through lectures, assignments, and tests.

In some classrooms in which there is a mismatch of teaching and learning styles, the climate for everyone suffers. That is to say, those who are "turned off" by the style become bored and turn their energies to activities which are disruptive. Some of these mismatched students are then labeled "disruptive" or "slow." But the problem may not be so much with lack of ability as a lack of compatibility between the teaching and learning styles. Teaching style does generate a certain type of social system in the classroom. Some classrooms are informal, with students talking to one another and moving about, while other classrooms are quiet and routinized. Again, certain students may be comfortable with each situation.

Personality is also an element of style. Some learners prefer teachers who are strong, dramatic, or extroverted; others
prefer a quiet, more subdued teacher. Some teachers are
friendly; others are more detached. It is possible to have a
quiet, detached, inductively oriented teacher—and a dramatic,
deductively disposed teacher, and vice versa.

All of us could go on mentioning teachers we have had
who impressed us for one reason or another. The point here
is that since both students and teachers are of many sorts,
it improves learning to seek a more harmonious match between them. This is one of the many ways of individualizing
instruction, and that is one of the cardinal principles of education.

Still another way to categorize different teaching styles is
to place the style of each teacher on a scale-continuum ranging from "formal" to "informal." Some of the characteristics
which differentiate the two extremes of the scale are listed
here:

Open	*Traditional*
Informal environment and human interaction	Formal environment and human interaction
Activity duration is child controlled	Activity time-scheduled by teacher
Teacher structures environment and process	Teacher structures curriculum
Teacher provides guidance, facilitates learning	Teacher provides the sources of learning
Furniture type and arrangement are based on the child's workshop pattern	Furniture type and arrangement follow a standard pattern
Individual or small group activity predominates	Whole-class oriented activity predominates
Children and visitors integrated	Children and visitors segregated
Teacher-pupil interaction individualistic	Teacher dominant, child subordinate
Curriculum is planned to meet children's interests	Curriculum is planned to cover teacher's lesson plan
Emphasis on abundance of concrete materials to manipulate	Dominance of textbook

Teacher non-authoritarian; acts as facilitator	Teacher controls, is disciplinarian
No difference between work and play	Dichotomized work and play
Learning by discovery	Learning by being taught
Grouping for several ages	Grouping for single age
Teacher and children determine pattern for the day	Teacher decides who does what and when
Child's education the child's responsibility	Child's education the teacher's responsibility
Emphasis on affective emotional as well as cognitive intellectual skills	Emphasis on intellectual development only
Evaluation as diagnosis	Evaluation as classification

Under our present structure teachers must now almost "sneak" the freer teaching style into the classroom. Many teaching styles are restricted by the uniform ground rules of the public itself. A teacher whose style inclines toward open education finds that, unless his approach to education is recognized as legitimate and considered bona fide by other teachers, administrators, and parents, he has to camouflage his preference in public and try to exercise his individual method only in the privacy of his classroom.

But through Public Schools of Choice we have an opportunity to encourage teachers to free their teaching styles. Most important, such a new structure also supports teachers whose style is standard. While some learners are attracted to open education, others—indeed most—would continue to profit from the standard. Both styles are needed.

FOOTNOTE

[1] Mario D. Fantini, "Open vs. Closed Classrooms," in *Clearing House*, Vol. 37, No. 2, October 1962.

THE MINI-SCHOOL STORY:
A PLAN TO END THE DROP-OUT RATE*

What is a mini-school? Mini-schools are small educational communities usually within and attached administratively to a parent high school. They are staffed with Board of Education teachers, and streetworkers. Mini-schools are a cooperative venture between public and private parties whose purpose is to create change within the structure of the existing school system.

How do mini-schools foster change? Mini-schools stress flexibility and experimentation under existing conditions for those who desire it. They show how schools can redesign space and use it differently; they encourage curricular freedom; and they employ streetworkers to help build trust between the student and the system.

What is a streetworker? A streetworker is a young man or woman a few years older than the students, who shares a similar background and understands their lifestyles. He or she is the agent through which supportive help can be offered the student.

Who are the students? The mini-school student body was originally made up of potential dropouts, kids who were barely making it within the structure of the large urban high school. Among them are truly gifted individuals who did not have a positive relationship within the system. Now, with Haaren going mini, every student will have a chance to function in a mini-school environment.

What is curricular freedom? Curricular freedom in the mini-school is the ability to achieve recognized academic goals

* Reprinted from *Mini School News*, New York Urban Coalition, New York, N.Y.

through innovative ways. One example is the re-apportioning of the school year into shorter cycles rather than traditional 18 week semesters. Another is the introduction of courses in cooperation with the private sector.

Where are the mini-schools? Harambee Prep, part of Hughes High School in Manhattan, has existed since September 1969 and has 110 students, 5 teachers and 3 streetworkers. Wingate Prep, attached to Wingate High School in September, and has 70 students, 4 teachers and 3 streetworkers.

FOURTEEN NEW MINI-SCHOOLS
ALL SET TO GO*

Fourteen mini-schools, tentatively designed and proposed to students last June, opened at Haaren on September 13. They represent a radical change from the ordinary high school schedule. Students chose their mini-school before the summer vacation and wherever possible received their first choice.

With the exception of College Bound, a federally funded program already in existence at Haaren prior to the 1971 school year with an enrollment of 500, the other thirteen mini-schools will contain 125 to 150 students, 1 streetworker and 5 to 6 teachers.

A description and statement of objectives of each mini-school was submitted by the faculty to the Haaren administration and Planning Committee. Fourteen mini-schools were approved and are functioning around curriculum designed by the teachers in each.

College Bound is a federal program for entering students with academic potential. Graduates of the program are guaranteed a seat in one of 117 participating colleges and universities.

* Reprinted from *Mini School News,* New York Urban Coalition, New York, N.Y.

Aerospace is an inter-disciplinary unit for ninth year students. It teaches the history of aviation and navigation within traditional subject areas.

Correlated Curriculum is a four-year course that leads toward careers in business, electronics, transportation and drafting.

Pre-Technical prepares juniors and seniors for a two-year career program at one of the community colleges in construction; chemical, electrical, mechanical or electro-mechanical technology or design and drafting.

Automotive emphasizes traditional subjects by relating them to the automotive field. For example, automotive electricity, mathematics of the service station business, the impact of the automobile on modern society.

Aviation for entering sophomores uses a correlated approach to teach meteorology, rocketry, navigation and the scientific principles of flight.

Electronics is a pre-vocational program in which students learn to repair radio, television and electronic office equipment.

Mobil/Coop is a cooperative work-study program for juniors and seniors. Students study at Haaren and work in a Mobil station alternate weeks.

TUM, Toward Upward Mobility, is a work-study program that emphasizes basic educational skills alongside of saleable skills for potential dropouts.

Swing Back is designed to motivate the truant to return to school. From Swing Back the student can enter another mini-school.

Traditional Program is organized around school-as-we-know-it in a smaller more intimate setting.

Urban Affairs develops skills through the study of ecology, consumer education, housing and mass media in the classroom and out in the community.

Business teaches inter-disciplinary skills needed for the successful operation of a business within a community. As an adjunct to the program, at least one self-contained retail business will be established.

All available Haaren teachers attended a three-week training program that began on August 9. The session was supported by a New York State Urban Education grant. Morning sessions were held in Haaren's large Assembly Hall and were followed by private planning groups of each mini-school unit.

ALTERNATIVES IN THE PUBLIC SCHOOL*

BY MARIO D. FANTINI

Alternative forms of education are springing up in public schools all over the country. I call my plan for alternatives Public Schools of Choice.

This plan calls for cooperation of teachers, parents, and students in the development of a variety of legitimate educational options within our public schools. Choice is a key term in this plan. Each of the participating groups—teachers, parents, and students (the agents closest to the action)—have a choice of the option that best supports their style.

Public Schools of Choice is also based on the assumption that each teacher has a style of teaching and each student, a style of learning. Providing opportunities for a more compatible matching of teaching-learning styles can help promote further the long-held educational ideals of individualization and personalization. Teachers will perform a key role, not only in deciding which of the alternatives best supports their teaching style, but also in designing options. Since parents, students, and teachers are brought together by mutual con-

* Reprinted with permission from *Today's Education,* September-October 1974.

sent and not by chance, the mismatches of the past which led to frustration for both teacher and student can be avoided.

Public Schools of Choice establishes standard education as a legitimate option. We have overloaded the standard pattern of education, expecting this approach to reach all teachers, students, and parents. No one pattern of education can reach everyone, and in a diverse society such as ours, a responsive system of public education provides a range of options and choices, including the standard.

To get any new system to operate, participants must agree on ground rules. To make Public Schools of Choice work, the following ground rules are essential.

• *No alternative within a public system of choice practices exclusivity.* No school or alternative can exclude a child because of race, religion, financial status, or—within reason—the nature of previous educational background. The schools must be truly open, able to survive on the basis of their educational merits and their ability to meet the needs of the students and the parents they serve.

• *Each school works toward a comprehensive set of educational objectives.* These objectives or educational goals must be common to all schools within the system of choice. They should include mastery of the basic skills, nurturing of physical and emotional development, and vocational and avocational preparation. The student must be equipped with a broad range of skills so that he will have as many alternatives and opportunities as possible for social and educational mobility.

Within a system of Public Schools of Choice, the real issue is not what goals to set, but how best to achieve the goals set. The system itself seeks out new means of increasing the chances for the student to mature as a maker of choices rather than to be a mere victim of circumstances.

• *A ground rule intrinsic to the idea of a free and open society and, therefore, to the notion of Public Schools of Choice is that no person or group imposes an educational plan or design.* Within a system of choice, the consumer shops around as in a supermarket or cafeteria, choosing, testing, and finally settling on a school or learning environment that appeals to him.

If 90 percent of the consumers settle on approach A and only 10 percent want approach B, then 90 percent of the system's schools provide approach A and 10 percent, approach B.

Each community has to determine how many consumers are necessary to warrant setting up a new alternative. The point here, however, is that once the minimum percentage is established, the individual consumer can choose his own option, rather than having to accept one program because there are no alternatives.

Similarly, teachers are free to choose the alternatives that best support their styles of teaching. No one alternative is imposed on a teacher.

Obviously, new approaches will necessitate the retraining of teachers, but this can become an integral part of the staff development program of the school district.

• *Each new alternative can eventually operate on a financial level equivalent to the per capita cost of the school district as a whole.* Although each new option may be permitted some additional costs for initial planning and development, it must conform to the standard per student cost of the total system within a reasonable period of time. This ground rule insures that a public school system of choice results in a wiser, more productive use of existing monies.

Some may ask whether a Nazi school or an antiwhite one for Blacks could exist within the framework of a public system of choice. Obviously, it could not. The concept speaks to openness. It values diversity, is democratic, and is unswerving in its recognition of individual worth.

Within these bounds, however, there is a full spectrum of alternative possibilities with new educational and learning forms. Schools could, for example, emphasize science or languages or the arts; they could be graded or ungraded, open or traditional, technical or nontechnical; they could seek a multicultural approach or work to strengthen particular ethnic and group identities. Each, however, must meet the standard principles which are fundamental to a public school system of choice.

Respecting the rights and responsibilities of others, for example, cannot work if the option being promulgated is based on a system which advocates the imposition of one's own values on others.

• *Each alternative provides another approach to education alongside the existing pattern, which continues to be legit-*

imate. Every legitimatized educational option is equally valid. The standard approach to education, therefore, is an important alternative and should not be eliminated or forced to take the brunt of criticism.

• *Each alternative includes a plan for evaluation.* Since each alternative needs to achieve the same ends, assessment is essential for at least two reasons: to gather evaluation information as a basis for continuing to improve the option and to help determine the relative effectiveness of each option.

What constitutes a legitimate educational option under these rules is a critical question.

Public schools have a responsibility to equip each learner with the skills needed for economic, political, and social survival. At the same time, they must provide him with the tools needed for improving, transforming, and reconstructing elements of the environment generally recognized as inimical to the noblest aspirations of the nation or as detrimental to the growth and development of the individual.

Speaking practically, public schools must provide opportunities for each learner to discover his talents. Our public schools are necessarily talent development centers, linking talent to economic careers. As such, public schools encompass economic "livelihood" objectives as an important set of educational ends. If an educational option discounted this set of objectives, it would be suspect as a legitimate alternative within the framework of public education.

Public Schools of Choice can work only when students, parents, teachers, and administrators all have equal access to educational options at both the conceptual and operational levels. But, unless the parent or consumer is aware of the existence of new alternatives, he is left with only the ones with which he is familiar and is forced to play by the ground rules established by the existing system. Then the question which must be posed is: What mechanism must be developed to bring relevant educational information to the public?

The administration of a school system might assume the leadership role by arranging informational meetings with the groups involved. Such meetings could lead parent associations to hold more meetings to explore educational options. Student groups at the elementary, junior high, and high school levels and teacher organizations could do the same thing. After careful planning, the school system could launch trial programs, either in one school or in a cluster of them. Under certain conditions, a whole district could mount a special program.

While Public Schools of Choice works best when an entire school goes into the plan and provides many options for all students and teachers, it may be desirable to start by trying options not too dissimilar to the school's present operational style.

Developing choices at the individual school level can, however, pose a number of problems. For example, as the different segments of the public explore new options, a group might find itself involved in scanning an almost endless list of reading materials. This would not necessarily be bad, but it could leave the participants with a narrow view of the learning process.

If, on the other hand, a community undertook a conceptual examination of educational alternatives, participants might indeed achieve a better background for decision making. It is one thing to become knowledgeable about a concept or idea and quite another to become familiar with the intricate details that go into making the idea work. While it is obvious that some knowledge of detail is necessary, students, parents, and citizens in general need not be as well-informed about the subtleties of pedagogy as are professionals.

Professional educators have the responsibility for the substance and techniques of education, but the consumers must be responsible for determining the kind of education they want. They must, therefore, have the opportunity to perform this crucial policy role. Thus, a new standard of professional and lay participation could lead to more sensible educational conceptions, supported by both groups.

One way to consider alternatives is to place them on a continuum on the basis of how much freedom a student has to choose the elements of learning, i.e., how much freedom he has to choose the teacher, the content, the learning methodology, the time, the place.

At one extreme, the learner selects what he will learn, with whom, when, where, and how. At this end of the continuum, he has the greatest freedom. At the other extreme, he has no choice of teacher, content, methodology, time, and place. Institutional procedures and requirements predetermine the conditions of learning for him.

Between these extremes, there is a range of possibilities. The learner can be free to choose certain content areas, but not others, which are required for everyone (reading, writing, arithmetic, physical education, health). He may have some freedom in how he wishes to approach these content areas (by reading a book, by viewing videotapes, by doing research, by listening to a lecture, by discussing with others). He may have some freedom to choose the time and place to learn. For example, he may enter into a contract with the teacher to accomplish a project by a certain time.

There are obviously different types of free school alternatives—ranging from an Illich/Reimer model, which deemphasizes schooling, to a Summerhill model, which uses the school as a type of self-governing unit. Free school alternatives are the most difficult to legitimize under a public school framework at this time and will probably remain outside as private alternative schools, since they run counter to the emerging ground rules for alternative public schools.

The open phase of the continuum overlaps with the free, but limits the range of choice the learner has. Thus, while a student can choose when and how he will learn science or math, they are, nevertheless, still required subjects, and the teacher helps guide the student in various content areas.

Such an educational continuum can be charted briefly as indicated below.

The British infant school, Montessori, and schools without walls could be examples under the open category. Ungraded continuous progress, modular scheduling, and behavior modification are possible alternatives under the modified. Formally organized, age-graded schools and uniformly regimented academies tend to fall into standard options.

There are various ways of providing educational options based on choice: Options can be based on (1) existing teacher styles; (2) classroom patterns, e.g., standard, Montessori, behavior modification, British infant; (3) teams of teachers forming schools within schools, e.g., Quincy (Illinois) Senior High II has seven subschools—standard, flexible, independent, fine arts, career, special, and vocational; (4) "new" school options which are housed in a setting apart from established schools. For example, in Los Angeles, there are four "off site" alternative schools located in different areas of the school system.

Once optional education and the ground rules of the choice system are understood, an entire district may want to develop a framework of alternatives for its schools. The following is a typical list from which parents, students, teachers, and administrators can choose.

Alternative 1 is a traditional approach. It is graded and emphasizes the learning of basic skills by cognition. The basic learning environment is the classroom, which functions with one or two teachers instructing and directing students at their various learning tasks. Students are encouraged to adjust to the school and its operational style, rather than vice versa. The students with recognized learning problems are referred to a variety of remedial and school-support programs. A central board of education determines the entire educational and fiscal policy for this school.

ALTERNATIVES ON A FREEDOM-TO-PRESCRIPTION CONTINUUM[1]

FREE   Learner-directed and -controlled. Learner has complete freedom to orchestrate his own education. Teacher is one resource.

FREE-OPEN   Opening of school to the community and its resources. Noncompetitive environment. No student failures. Curriculum is viewed as social system rather than as course of studies. Learner-centered.

OPEN   Learner has considerable freedom to choose from a wide range of content areas considered relevant by teacher, parent, and student. Resource centers in major skill areas made available to learner. Teacher is supportive guide.

OPEN-MODIFIED   Teacher-student   planning.   Teacher-centered.

MODIFIED   Prescribed content is made more flexible through individualization of instruction; school is ungraded; students learn same thing but at different rates. Using team teaching, teachers plan a differentiated approach to the same content. Teacher and programmed course of study are the major sources of student learning.

MODIFIED-STANDARD   Competitive environments. School is the major instructional setting. Subject-matter-centered.

STANDARD   Learner adheres to institution requirements uniformly prescribed: what is to be taught—how, when, where, and with whom. Teacher is instructor-evaluator. Student passes or fails according to normative standards.

Alternative 2 is nontraditional and nongraded. In many ways it is like a British primary school with lots of constructional and manipulative materials in each area where students work and learn.

The teacher acts as a facilitator—one who assists and guides, rather than directs or instructs. Most student activity is in the form of specialized learning projects carried on individually and in small groups. Many of the learning experiences and activities take place outside the school.

Alternative 3 emphasizes talent development and focuses on creative experiences, human services, and concentration in a particular field, e.g., art, media, space, science, dramatics, music. The school defines its role as diagnostic and prescriptive: It identifies the learner's talents and orchestrates whatever experiences seem necessary to develop and enhance them. It encourages many styles of learning and teaching. Students may achieve by demonstration and by manipulation of real objects as well as by verbal, written, or abstractive performances.

Alternative 4 is more oriented to techniques than the others in the district. It utilizes computers to help diagnose individual needs and abilities and provides computer-assisted instruction based on the diagnosis for individuals and groups.

The library stocks tape-recording banks and has carrels in which students, on their own, can "talk" to and listen to tapes or work with manipulative objects. In addition, wide use is made of educational media which enable students and teachers to individualize many of the learning tasks. The school also has facilities for closed-circuit T.V.

Alternative 5 is a total community school. Operating on a 12- to 14-hour basis at least six days a week throughout the year, it provides educational and other services for children of varying ages from the neighborhood and evening classes and activities for adults.

Services in such areas as health, legal aid, and employment are available within the school facility. Paraprofessionals or community teachers contribute to every phase of the regular school program. A community board governs the school.

Alternative 6 has a Montessori environment. Students move at their own pace and are largely self-directed. The learning areas are rich in materials and specialized learning instruments from which the students can select as they wish. Although teachers operate within a specific, defined methodology, they remain in the background, guiding students rather than directing them. Special emphasis is placed on the development of the five senses.

Alternative 7, patterned after the Multi-Culture Institute in San Francisco, may have four or five ethnic groups equally represented in the student body. Students spend part of each day in racially heterogeneous learning groups. During another part of the day, students and teachers of the same ethnic background meet together. In these classes, all learn the culture, language, customs, history, and heritage of their ethnic groups.

A policy board made up of equal numbers of parents and teachers runs the school and is only tangentially responsible to a central board of education.

Alternative 8 is subcontracted. For example, a group of teachers, parents, and students could be delegated authority to operate a particular alternative. Or certain private school alternatives can petition to become part of the public schools.

Alternatives help give new direction to pre- and in-service education of teachers. If some options are in greater demand than others, then certain teachers (perhaps those who express the desire) can be helped to staff them. After all, even if there were no options, teachers would still require in-service education.

Public Schools of Choice can encourage closer ties between community and schools, professionals and laymen. Without professional leadership which promotes cooperation of all parties concerned, alternatives can be imposed and often opposed.

The Public Schools of Choice system would be a renewal system, that is, the options under a broad public framework would be judged by results. As the results associated with quality education were realized more in one model than in another, the attractiveness of the successful model would grow. The options that were more successful would most likely be in more demand, thus triggering a self-renewing process.

FOOTNOTE

[1] Mario D. Fantini, "Alternatives Within Public Schools," *Phi Delta Kappan,* Special Issue on Alternative Schools, March 1973, pp. 447–48.

THE PHILOSOPHY, THE ACADEMIC PROGRAM, THE MAIN BUILDING, SELECTION OF STUDENTS AND STAFF*

The Philosophy

With the many and diverse ideas of education which are prevalent today, many schools have been developed throughout the nation which have discarded the use of the traditional school building. Reacting to high building construction costs and to curricular reform movements, these schools have created educational programs which operate in the communities they serve. They are the "schools without walls."

The idea is not new. The incorporation of school and community in educational programs finds a strong heritage in the early American common schools and has roots even in the medieval concept of apprenticeship. In both of these pe-

* Reprinted by permission of Chicago Public High School for Metropolitan Studies. Staff members Don Baker, John S. Everett, Preston Garnett, and Shelby Taylor worked as a committee on developing this statement. A survey form was completed by the total staff of twenty-five teachers and then the committee compiled, edited, and formulated the final document.

riods of educational history, the community was seen as an integral part of a young person's development. In a non-mobile world, the community was part of education because it was that world about which all life centered.

In our highly mobile world, the new "schools without walls" attempt to fulfill the same function, but for different reasons. Whereas in earlier educational systems, the community was an integral part of the school, the urban school of today has become very separated from the world around it. "Schools without walls" attempt to break down the barriers that have been set up architecturally and educationally. Opening up schools by creating curricula in the community and as a part of the community constitutes the essential mode of this new educational concept.

The idea of a "school without walls" originated in Philadelphia in 1968. The school, called the Parkway Program, was planned around the Benjamin Franklin Parkway, a boulevard leading into the central business district along which are found many of that city's cultural institutions.

A year after Parkway opened, the Chicago Board of Education established a school similar to the Philadelphia experiment, with some major innovations. The Chicago Public High School for Metropolitan Studies, Metro High to the students at the school, opened the doors of its central headquarters in February of 1970. Metro began by developing a curriculum utilizing many of the cultural institutions of the city. What was more important were the many other organizations, especially the business concerns and professional associations, which were made an integral part of this public high school program from the earliest days.

The Academic Program

The Metro program is founded on the premise that the urban school must also have the responsibility to help its students become familiar with the city in which they live. The goals of the urban school cannot be limited just to the successful teaching of a working knowledge of the three r's. For the student who will emerge into that urban world after high school, he or she must become acquainted with the immediate environment outside the classroom. Metro began with the belief that the best way to acquaint the student with that real world is to dissolve the walls separating the student from the city by integrating the world into the student's daily curriculum. If a student wants to learn about aquatic life, the school should develop a class taught by a professional marine biologist at the city's aquarium. If another is interested in economics, a class should be created at a bank or a brokerage house. This basic philosophy allows the student to know that there is a wealth of knowledge to be obtained through countless resources in the city which surrounds the school. The student then must be helped to learn how to tap that knowledge and make it work for him. To implement this philosophy Metro has developed a program which offers an extensive variety of academic experiences.

PRINCIPLES OF ECONOMICS SHELBY TAYLOR with MOLLIE D'ESPOSITO of 1st National Bank, HENRY FREEDMAN of A. G. Becker, JOAN CAMPBELL of Carson Pirie Scott and Co., and WALTER E. FAITHORN of Stewart Warner Corporation

A unit designed to examine the basic structure of our economy taught in conjunction with a stock brokerage, a department store, a bank and a manufacturing concern. Students will investigate the nature of supply and demand, scarcity, the consumer relationship of major financial corporations and other economic principles. During the fourth cycle, many of these same firms will teach individual units in the specific nature of their part of the world of Economics.

Classes taught by the Board of Education certified teachers include the majority of the basic academic disciplines, for Metro does not deny the worth of these instructional areas. Many of these classes are taught in spaces outside the main school headquarters in office conference rooms, meeting rooms, cafeterias and even classrooms that Loop businesses make available for use at specified periods during the day.

ADVANCED FUNDAMENTALS OF WRITING VERA WALLACE

This course considers three concerns of writing; isolation and identification of subject; effective use of language; consideration of the particular class of reader for whom the paper is intended.

NAZI GERMANY   PAULA BARON

Does 'Hogan's Heroes' give a true picture of Nazi prison camps? In this class we will try to understand what fascism means by studying the growth of Nazism in Germany. How did it get started? Why did the Germans follow Hitler? Could it happen here? We will read several short pamphlets and some ditto materials. Each student either individually or as a group, will be expected to take responsibility of at least one class session. There will be several short papers also.

ANIMAL AND HUMAN BEHAVIOR   FRED JACKSON

A course dealing with functions of creatures that respond to stimuli (man and lower animals). We will do case studies on individual animals and write a paper. We will read the *Human Zoo* by Desmond Morris.

Where a student exhibits a marked proficiency in a specific area, he or she may offer a short course in tandem with a staff teacher. Several have followed this lead by teaching elective units in Baking, Popular Music and Home Repair.

FIX IT YOURSELF   VINCE WALDRON (MIKE LIBERLES)

At last a class that will help you in life if modern technology leaves you swearing at your broken telephone, radio, television, stereo or if you'd like to better suit your present appliances to your needs, then this is the class for you! You need not be an inventive genius—all it takes is logic and knowledge of a few basic scientific principles.

But the type of class which makes learning at Metro especially unique is, of course, the unit offered by the cooperating teachers. This professional from the business or cultural community may be teaching for the first time. Usually 30% of all Metro class offerings fall into the category of those taught by participating organizations.

T.V. PRODUCTION   DICK BARNETT of W.M.A.Q. T.V.

How does W.M.A.Q. T.V. run an NBC affiliate in Chicago? What goes into the production of a T.V. show? Here is a unit which will begin to get at some of the questions you have when you watch television.

The learning unit is the basic course offering. It differs from the more traditional school course, since it is divided into ten-week sections or "cycles" of intensified learning and evaluation. It is therefore less broad than the regular academic disciplines and offers students an opportunity to discover basic principles in a manageable block of time.

The learning unit also differs from the standard academic disciplines in that it may be taught by a Board of Education staff teacher or it may be offered by a businessman, an art historian, a doctor or one of the many cooperating teachers who participate in the program. In some instances, a staff teacher and a cooperating teacher will team-teach, offering not only educational, but also professional expertise.

MATH LAB   A. SHARON WEITZMAN, B. KEN LE TRAUNIK, and C. PRESTON GARNETT

A. *Equations*—students will learn about algebraic concepts in solving simple equations.
B. *Circles and Shapes*—students will learn about basic geometric concepts, focusing on the circle and polygons.
C. *Fractions and Decimals*—a new look at strengthening skills related to fractions and decimals.

THE HISTORY OF WESTERN ART   NANCY DENIG of the Art Institute

A survey of Western European Art History taught through the collections of the Art Institute. The class will include slide lectures, viewing the collections and the Kenneth Clark film series "Civilization," reading and demonstration of materials and techniques.

STANDARD AND ADVANCED FIRST AID   GERI ZABINSIKI, VIVIAN JACOBSON of the American Red Cross

You'll learn how to recognize and give first aid for almost any type of emergency you might encounter. All areas of first aid for certification (for those fifteen years or older) will be covered. This is the standard course taught by the Red Cross.

ART AND COMMUNITY   DON SEIDEN of the Art Institute

Coordinated art activities involving students from Metro and teacher education students from School of the Art

Institute. Stress is on aesthetic education through group interaction events, art production, multi-media presentation and environmental awareness.

These classes serve a double purpose. First, they allow our students to become accustomed to looking beyond the high school for the answers to their questions, and thus students become used to dealing with the institutions they encounter as tools for learning. The outside world becomes less formidable, more familiar. Second, the business and institutional world gets a close look at a group of people they rarely have contact with. More often than not, the participating organizations who offer classes for Metro are encountering high school students for the first time in their own offices, on their own ground, and they usually receive as much of an education as the students.

HENRY FREEDMAN, A. G. Becker and Company, Partner
"The first time I addressed a class of Metro High School students I told them that I was not a professional educator and had never taught before, and was greeted with smiles. Whether they were smiles of amusement or relief, they helped me over the first difficult hour. From then on my education proceeded at a rapid pace. Teaching for Metro got me away from my desk at regular intervals, it introduced me to such strange and delightful creatures as the students, teachers and staff members of the school and it stimulated me to think seriously, perhaps for the first time as an adult, about a most important subject . . . the process of education."

In addition to these many choices, Metro students can also initiate independent study projects with staff teachers, develop non-paying work placements and lab assistantships with participating organizations and take classes at one of the City Colleges.

The first nine weeks of each academic cycle are devoted to classwork with the final week being the period during which the students' progress in each class is evaluated. Letter grades are not given. Instead, each student meets with the teacher of each of his or her classes and together they evaluate the student's performance during that cycle. If the student has completed the requirements of the course to the teacher's as well as his own satisfaction credit is awarded. If the student has not completed the course satisfactorily, he or she can arrange with the teacher to complete the requirements within an agreed period of time or can repeat the course for credit.

Each student at Metro is part of a counseling group. These non-credit activities, averaging eighteen students in composition, meet once a week for a variety of purposes. Among them, recordkeeping, academic programming and information dispersing remain the most important. The counseling group was thought to be the backbone of the entire Metro program at its inception. This has not always been the case, for many students sought out different channels for the counseling services, both group and individual, the counseling groups were to offer.

Many alternative group and individual counseling plans have been experimented with since the early days of the school. Where some have failed, new ideas were tried. But the purpose of ongoing meaningful counseling remains a vital part of the school's philosophy.

The Main Building

Though the school is spread out over the entire Loop area through its various course offerings, it is necessary to maintain a central headquarters. To this end, the Board of Education rents three floors of an office building at the south end of the Loop on Dearborn Street. It is here that students relax in the lounge between classes, meet individually with their teachers and use the school's equipment. Some classes are held in this central location including the majority of the mathematics classes which meet in the Math Lab. The building is by intent a casual place, where students can talk openly with their teachers. The watchword at Metro is accessibility, and with a student-teacher ratio of roughly eighteen to one, teachers have the opportunity to get to know their students as people rather than merely as names on a class roster.

Selection of Students and Staff

The first Metro students, 150 in number, were selected by lottery from over 1500 applications the school had received.

The process of selection by lot allowed for a diverse student body, closely reflecting the racial, ethnic and sexual composition of the public school system citywide. Expansion came to the Metro program in September 1970 when 200 additional students were chosen, this time from 2000 applicants to the school's lottery selection. Though the school remains with an enrollment of 350 students, the desire to expand within the downtown area is keen with the teaching staff and student body.

Though some 60% of our graduates are either now attending college or will begin in the fall, college is not the only goal for the Metro graduate. Many are employed now, in jobs ranging from shipping clerk to political campaigner. Several graduates have worked at the school helping to develop programs for the coming year. Two of our graduates have spent the year since their graduation abroad; one attending art school in the Netherlands, the other working in an Israeli kibbutz.

How Others Evaluate

Metro, above all, does not conceive of itself as existing in a vacuum. The innovative nature of our program has attracted educators from some twenty states as well as several foreign countries. The general feeling among these educators has been that Metro ranks among the finest high schools in the nation today. Several have gone so far as to say that Metro is the finest example of experimental approaches to education in the United States. There is no doubt that Metro has helped to establish a precedent for innovation in education that is being followed throughout the country.

EDUCATION BY CHOICE: A PROGRAM OF THE QUINCY PUBLIC SCHOOLS*

BY DR. BRANDT G. CROCKER,
RICHARD F. HAUGH, AND
DONALD A. PRICE†

After giving much consideration to the individual differences of students and teachers, Quincy Senior High II (for juniors and seniors) has developed a program designed to maximize the educational opportunities for students. The program, called *Education by Choice,* will offer to students a series of different learning environments called alternative schools.

Each alternative school will be composed of small groups of teachers and students and will be designed to provide different approaches to learning. While all smaller schools will be seeking similar academic and personal goals, the learning activities and methods of instruction will differ, thereby providing several routes for students to attain common educational goals.

This program has been in the planning stage for over a year as a result of a grant from Title III, E.S.E.A., a federally funded project. It has been developed by secondary teachers through many workshops and planning meetings. Finally, it was felt that this program should be implemented for juniors and seniors. Teachers have submitted a further proposal to Title III, E.S.E.A., in hopes of receiving an additional grant to help initiate the new idea.

* Reprinted from Title III, E.S.E.A. with permission of the authors.
† Dr. Brandt G. Crocker is Assistant Superintendent, Quincy, Illinois, Public Schools. He has been involved in almost every facet of education and has directed the development of numerous exemplary programs in the Quincy Public Schools.
Richard F. Haugh is Director, Education by Choice, Quincy, Illinois, Public Schools. He has served as a consultant to many school districts developing alternative schools and optional learning.
Donald A. Price is Director, Special Projects, Quincy, Illinois, Public Schools. He was director of Quincy's Project to Individualize Education and has been involved as a consultant for school districts throughout the country.

The result of all the planning is that seven alternative schools are being presented to students of Senior High II for 1973–74. Students, with assistance from parents, counselors, and teachers, will choose one of the alternative schools. Every effort will be made to match each student's learning style, interest, and self-discipline with a school which offers him the greatest potential for educational and personal growth. Each small school will offer English and social studies and as many other fields as possible with the teachers in that particular school. In some cases, students will take subjects in one of the schools which is outside his choice. For example, there is only one German teacher so students will have to go to the school in which he teaches.

Why have we developed "Education by Choice" in Quincy? The sixties in education will probably be recorded in the history of education as the "innovative years." Many programs to individualize education have made their way on the nation's educational scene. Our P.I.E. program is one of these. The impact has been so great that education may never be the same again, regardless of what finally happens. This individualized instruction generally means the right of every individual to acquire an education within the school system in his own way and at his own rate of learning. Many innovative schools have emerged to implement a program of individualization but, for various reasons, many of these have reached a plateau and leveled off, or have retrenched. We, in Quincy, believe we can profit from the errors which accompanied massive innovations in the sixties and continue individualization in a more reasonable and effective pattern. One of the leading innovators in education, Donald Glines, writing in the February 1973 NASSP Bulletin, says:

> One method of organization, no matter how innovative or conventional, will not meet the needs of most students. Creative leadership sees to it that optional choices of kinds of schools and school programs are available for the district constituents. Schools-within-a-school and one or more different schools within a district prevent this shortcoming; however, few districts have adopted the concept of options.

Quincy Senior High II, then, will be one of the leaders in developing alternative schools. We feel our staff of teachers has shown the commitment, flexibility, and ability to make each smaller school an important choice for students.

The following sections will give the reader more information about each of the alternative schools proposed for 1973–74. They are:

A. Traditional (typifies education in the past)
B. Flexible (utilizes a flexible modular schedule)
C. P.I.E. (individualized approach)
D. Fine Arts (focus on art, music, drama, and humanities)
E. Career (associated with new vocational school)
F. Work-Study (special program now in operation)
G. Special Education (special program now in operation)

The Traditional School

A. Introduction. The stress of the Traditional School will be on continuation of the fine quality and method of education that have transpired during years past and have proved to be successful for many young people. Realizing that not all students accept the responsibility to work up to their ability, without direction, guidance, and supervision, the faculty of the Traditional School will provide an atmosphere where students can realize their maximum potential.

B. Philosophy. In general our teaching is aimed at preparing the student vocationally and professionally. This preparation should be either for a career immediately after high school or for college.

Above and beyond these immediate goals, each student must be prepared for fuller living. The student should be given some introduction to the cultural aspects of life.

It is the firm belief of the faculty of the Traditional School that the traditional teacher-directed education is best suited for personal, human development, as well as for essential vocational and professional needs throughout life.

C. Curriculum. The curriculum of the Traditional School will be made up of basic courses that will be of value to the college-bound and non-college-bound students. The primary purpose of the curriculum is to develop academic knowledge and vocational skills and interests. The curriculum will be developed so that all students will have a chance to satisfy their intellectual curiosity. The curriculum will be subject to evaluation and revision to assure the best education for the students.

D. Method of Instruction. The Traditional School faculty realizes that no one method of instruction is best for all subject areas, therefore, teaching methods can and probably will differ from class to class.

Each teacher will use whatever method he or she feels will be best for the students. Students will be encouraged to help determine the best method, but the primary responsibility for selecting the method of instruction lies with the classroom teacher.

Some methods that can be expected in the Traditional School are teacher lecture, teacher-class discussions, teacher demonstration, class demonstrations, individual and class presentations, and the use of community resource people.

E. Time Schedule. The Traditional School will use the six (6) 55 minute period school day. The 55 minute period will allow each teacher time to present material part of the hour, and also to help individuals or small groups part of the time. Teachers will try to allow a certain portion of each period for a teacher-assisted study period.

F. Non-Class Time. Students will be encouraged to take as many academic classes as possible, thereby reducing non-class time. Any period of the day students do not have gym or a classroom subject, they will be assigned to a supervised study hall. Proper use of the study hall period will help reduce the students' homework responsibilities. Students will definitely have resource center privileges. Students could also be granted lounge privileges from the study hall. Every attempt will be made to schedule students with jobs so their non-class time can be spent on the job.

G. Attendance and Discipline. All classes in the Traditional School will have required daily attendance. Most discipline will be handled by classroom teachers and the school director. Any problems involving the overall Senior High II will be solved in cooperation with the Dean's Office.

H. Student Evaluation. Periodic grade reporting, using the traditional A, B, C, D, and F grades determined by teacher evaluation of student work such as tests, daily work, term papers, oral reports, and class participation. Periodic reports on student progress will be made between grade periods.

I. Other Significant Points. The basic concept of the Traditional School is more structure for the students and more teacher responsibility for learning. While this parallels much of the education in the past, the faculty approaches the future with an openness to improve their teaching methods within the overall concept of the school.

The Flexible School

A. Introduction. The staff of the Flexible School views education as a lifelong process of the growth and development of an individual's potential. We view our role in that development as one of helping the student acquire specific skills which will enable him to function as a contributing member of his community. We further see our responsibility, as humanists, to encourage participation by students in community affairs and out-of-school activities which will directly affect post-high-school life. The important adult responsibilities of making choices, acting on those choices, and experiencing the consequences of one's actions are a pillar of our school's philosophy.

Through a wide range of activities, our faculty will attempt to meet individual needs expressed by our students. Field experiences, community involvement, individual conferences are only a few planned offerings to enhance personal growth.

B. Curriculum. The regular high school curriculum will be available in this school, complemented by many enrichment programs.

C. Method of Instruction. A key word for this school is FLEXIBLE; therefore, the teaching methods will be flexible. Teachers will take into account student interests and needs and integrate these with the instruction techniques best suited to reach the common goal of pupil learning in a particular

subject. Attempts will be made to match the teaching method
of faculty with the learning style of students.

D. Time Schedule
1. Modular Scheduling
   a. Modules or mods are simply fractions of time. The
      main purpose of this type of scheduling is to pro-
      vide greater flexibility in scheduling classes. Classes
      with different needs may require different blocks
      of time.
   b. This school will be in session for the regular school
      day with sixteen twenty-minute mods (time peri-
      ods). A laboratory class might need to meet for
      more than an hour, requiring three or four mods.
      A more traditional lecture class could meet four or
      five times a week and require only two mods per
      meeting. Students will work out their own lunch pe-
      riod using one or two mods during the time 11:20
      A.M. to 1:00 P.M.
2. Wednesdays: "Opportunity Day"
   Several options could be available to the student as follows:
   a. Students *may* follow a modular schedule on
      Wednesdays similar to the other days of the week.
   b. Students *may* schedule themselves to participate in
      activities such as those listed below:
      1) *Needs* — Life and academic considerations.
         (Consumerism, running a home, and the prob-
         lems of coping with life. Schedule planning, col-
         lege preparations, testing, make-up work, indi-
         vidual teacher help, student-teacher interaction,
         projects, independent study, field trips.)
      2) *Involvement* — Community participation and
         civic activities. (Candy stripers, teacher's aides,
         ecology groups, helping share talents with com-
         munity.)
      3) *Enrichment* — Field trips and projects. (Interac-
         tion with other schools, created opportunities,
         self-improvement in interest areas.)
   c. General comments about "Opportunity Day":
      — All field experiences should be of a constructive
         nature.

— If students need any help in their academic work, they should be encouraged to use this day for individual teacher-student conferences.

— Urgent make-up work should take preference to field experiences. (ex: Work that if not completed would result in loss of credit.)

— Field trips and large group activities should be scheduled as early as possible.

— To avoid students missing field experiences because of conflicts, the director will supervise interdepartmental scheduling.

— Wednesday experiences should not be used for holidays. They are important to a student's education.

E. Non-Class Time

1. Amount
   a. We encourage students and parents to think of this school as a school operating during the full school day.
   b. Students will be scheduled (full time) with approximately 60% of their time in classes and 40% of their time in optional activities.
2. Use of non-class time
   a. A maximum of one mod (twenty minutes) per day for "lounge." This is subject to arbitrary reduction by faculty if this use of time conflicts with the best interests of the student or school.
   b. Students should strive for completion of assigned school work during the regular school day through thoughtful scheduling and use of non-class time.
   c. Students may schedule from a number of alternatives to fill non-class mods:
      1) Conferences (teacher-counselor)
      2) Special projects
      3) Resource center
      4) Individual study
      5) Backscheduling (make-up work)
      6) Lunch
      7) "Nothing" is *NOT* an alternative.

F. Attendance and Discipline. Each individual teacher will handle attendance on an individual basis. While the student is assigned to a specific teacher, that teacher and the individual student are co-responsible for directing and implementing meaningful learning activities. The teacher will know the whereabouts of each student at all times. Special direction in learning activities will be given to the student as the need arises.

The "internal" discipline problems will be handled by the classroom teacher to the best of his ability. The director, or head of the school, may be called upon to aid the teacher where more serious internal problems arise.

The "external" discipline problems (hall traffic problems, parking lot, and those affecting other schools) will be handled by the dean.

The director, or head of the school, may be called upon in some cases to serve as a liaison between the dean and teachers in his school.

G. Student Evaluation. Usual quarterly grades will be given. These may be arrived at by teacher-student formula: i.e., interviews, projects, points, contracts, etc.

The P.I.E. School

A. Introduction. The philosophy of the P.I.E. program is concerned with the personal and academic growth of the individual student. Each student is encouraged to make many choices concerning the learning activities in which he becomes involved. Each individual is considered to be a responsible human being, deserving of respect and capable of making decisions and taking the consequences of such decisions. Because of the student's active involvement in the P.I.E. program, he should develop more positive attitudes toward: school in general, learning activities, the community, peers, teachers, and himself.

In addition to learning in the classroom, the P.I.E. student will have the opportunity to learn outside the classroom. A student will be encouraged to use the school and the community as laboratories for growth experiences. This is in keeping with the belief of the P.I.E. teachers that learning should be connected with living and not take place solely in a classroom. It is felt that many people in the community can and will offer invaluable learning experiences for the P.I.E. student.

B. Curriculum. The curriculum of the P.I.E. School will include offerings in the following academic areas: English, social studies, math, physical education, chemistry, accounting, shorthand, typing, and French. However, equal emphasis will be placed on student growth as a human being. This will be encouraged by teachers who are student-centered in philosophy and who have demonstrated their competency for giving support as the student goes about the difficult task of acquiring knowledge about himself and the world in which he lives.

P.I.E. offers a variety of learning methods designed to meet the learning style of the individual student. Learning activities are often developed as the result of student/teacher planning, and the student is encouraged to actively participate.

As an integral part of the educational program, P.I.E. will offer experiences based on student needs and faculty capabilities. Experiences unique to the P.I.E. student may include: 1) field experiences, 2) experiences in forming values, 3) value clarification, 4) communication, 5) career experiences, 6) student/faculty planning sessions.

A P.I.E. student can expect teachers in the program to demonstrate interest in his growth by participating with him in the tailoring of instruction according to need, ability, and interest level.

C. Method of Instruction. Methods of instruction are largely determined through student desire and learning style. Included in the possible learning alternatives for the P.I.E. student are courses of various lengths, mini-lectures, audio-visual presentations, student/teacher-led discussions, work experiences, learning-by-doing activities, independent study, structured study, learning activity packets, and others designed to make learning meaningful for each student. The student should be able to clarify his educational goals as part of the P.I.E. experience and while doing so can expect help from a teacher-advisor of his choice.

D. Time Schedule. A student will be offered a highly flexible weekly schedule. In the past, teachers have arranged schedules according to student desires and have posted them on a weekly basis. The student has found this to be a highly satisfactory scheduling arrangement. An assumption of the program is that a P.I.E. student will exhibit a high degree of responsibility and self-discipline.

E. Non-Class Time

1. Amount: A P.I.E. student's non-class time will vary according to motivation and need.
2. Options available: A P.I.E. student will be encouraged to pursue class projects during non-class time. Each student may pursue his special interest or vocational desires through the responsible use of non-class time.

F. Attendance and Discipline. Since a P.I.E. student schedules himself into class according to his needs and desires, he is expected to follow the schedule he has chosen. Teachers in P.I.E. are available to assist the student and to help the student fulfill his needs and obligations.

G. Student Evaluation. Each student will receive letter grades plus written statements describing the level of competency he has achieved in academic and personal areas. Evaluation may come at different times: at the semester; at the completion of projects or experiences; on demand from the counselor, student, or parent; but not necessarily at ten-week intervals. A student is offered the opportunity to participate in the evaluation procedures. The P.I.E. program has actively sought methods—including home visits, open houses, and phone calls —to inform parents about student progress. These activities will continue as part of the eleventh- and twelfth-grade P.I.E. program.

H. Other Significant Points

1. A student in P.I.E. has the right to be heard, to question, and to examine self, ideas, and philosophies.
2. A student in P.I.E. has the right to be viewed and treated as a human being.
3. A student in P.I.E. has the right to grow academically, socially, and intellectually.
4. A student in P.I.E. has the right to choose from al-

ternatives in areas of curriculum, course content, and
teacher-advisors.

5. A student in P.I.E. has the right to risk and the responsibility to face the consequences of his decisions.
6. A student in P.I.E. has the responsibility to grow and
   produce academically.
7. A student in P.I.E. has the responsibility to develop
   and clarify values.
8. A student in P.I.E. has the responsibility to acquire
   minimum proficiency levels consistent with his ability.
9. A student in P.I.E. has the responsibility to participate
   in pre-testing, interval testing, and post-testing as it
   relates to the program.
10. A student in P.I.E. has the responsibility to develop
    as a contributing member of society.

The Fine Arts School

A. Philosophy. The Fine Arts School is committed to the right
of each of its students to feel, hear, and see that which lends
color and zest to living. For, to live life to its fullest, a person
must be able to sense the often overlooked artistic experiences
available to mankind.

A purpose of this school will be to develop, in the individual, the ability critically to perceive and understand his
surroundings; and to determine, on the basis of understanding
and perception, what kinds of experiences are of potential
value.

Acknowledging the value of the arts in developing a sensitive, humanistic attitude toward life and the world, being a
student in a school with this emphasis will be an important
experience—no matter what his later plans in life.

The Fine Arts School is committed to the belief that a positive self-image will be developed through programs which
place emphasis upon an individual's strengths rather than his
weaknesses and upon his successes rather than his failures.
Feeling good about what one is, does, and feels is essential
to the well-being of each individual.

Through the programs which evolve from the Fine Arts
School's commitment to serving students' needs, the students
will become committed to sharing with others their acquired
skills and abilities. They will be encouraged to involve them-

selves with other human beings by demonstrating learned techniques, by teaching others, and by working on civic and community projects.

The arts add a quality and dimension to life that is essential and unique to mankind. The study of the world's artistic creations (poetry, painting, song, sculpture, symphony, drama, etc.) gives the individual an understanding of where mankind has been, and gives inspiration and hope for the creation of a better world.

> It is the artists of the world, the feelers and the thinkers, who will ultimately save us; who can articulate, educate, defy, insist, sing, and shout the big dreams. Artists can turn the "not yet" into reality.
>
> —LEONARD BERNSTEIN

B. Curriculum. A student who chooses to align himself with the Fine Arts School will be able to earn credit in all courses necessary for graduation from Quincy Senior High School and, if the student so desires, to qualify him for admission to college. Each student will have the opportunity to leave the Fine Arts School for a part of his day to take part in specialized courses which will be offered in other schools. In addition to the traditional fine arts activities such as music, art, drama, and broadcasting, courses in history, English, forensics, physical education, and psychology will be offered in the Fine Arts School. The relationship of the fine arts to these subjects will be emphasized, as well as the relationship of the various arts to each other.

Students will be held accountable for their own individual development. A student will develop and work toward the perfection of at least one artistic skill. He will also be expected to experience significant work in other areas of the arts.

Several new courses, determined by the students' needs, abilities, and interests, will be presented. Examples of the offerings might include:

opera workshop	play writing
experiencing music	dance
history of jazz	history of America as seen
class piano	through the fine arts
guitar	oral interpretation
non-Western music	scenic design and lighting

Physical education may include four courses each one quarter in length:

- Dancing (choreography for fall musical theater production)
- Mime
- Athletics, gymnastics, etc.
- Physical exercises as developed by Jerzy Grotowski at the Polish Laboratory Theatre.

The Fine Arts School will offer a comprehensive program of study which will allow students to graduate with a well-rounded high school background.

C. Method of Instruction. The method of instruction will vary according to the specific needs of the students. Strong emphasis will be placed upon individual and small group instruction.

D. Attendance and Discipline. Students will be trusted and respected as mature and responsible individuals. Those who demonstrate a lack of responsibility will be counseled and directed as necessary. Teachers will discuss and resolve attendance and discipline problems directly with the student and parents.

E. Student Evaluation. Recognizing students' and parents' need for an honest, in-depth report of each student's progress, the faculty will call upon them for help in examining the strengths and weaknesses which now exist in our grading procedure and in the development of an improved means of evaluation.

F. Other Significant Points
1. Teacher-Advisor: A unique and vital part of the Fine Arts School will be the closeness with which students and teachers work. Each student will have a major voice in choosing a teacher-advisor who will listen to his or her problems and give advice on matters of importance. This person will be responsible to the students, in cooperation with their counselors, for the following:

   a. help in working out schedules and planning for completion of academic requirements

   b. help in working out social adjustments and other prob-
      lems in school
   c. demonstrating concern for student's success—both in
      school and out—before and after graduation
   d. developing with the student a strong personal relation-
      ship so he can become an effective link to other stu-
      dents and faculty members, to the school and its ac-
      tivities, and to the community and its resources

2. Time Schedule: The Fine Arts School will officially be
in session for the regular school day. However, many afternoon and evening hours will be devoted to rehearsals and
work on various individual and group activities. The faculty
will be available to students after regular school hours for
consultation, instruction, direction and for supervision of
work areas.

The school day will be divided into twenty-minute periods
called mods. Classes with different time requirements will
meet for different numbers of mods. At least two mods (forty
minutes) will be provided for lunch each day.

Each student, with help from his teacher-advisor, will determine his schedule for one quarter of the school year at a
time. If the needs of the student change during this quarter,
rescheduling will be possible. Rescheduling each quarter provides flexibility to meet the changing needs of students and
provides for frequent progress and credit evaluation by teachers to the teacher-advisors, the students and their parents. Because of the need for social development, the student will also
be given time to use as he chooses. It is expected, however,
that most unassigned time will be used for participation in
some productive activity.

In order to take advantage of the many educational experiences which are not available within the regular schedule, a
special-enrichment day will be provided each week. Possible
enrichment activities will include:

   a. in-depth studies
   b. community involvement projects
   c. field trips
   d. seminars
   e. showcase productions
   f. major school activities
   g. others

3. What a student can expect in the Fine Arts School: Students can expect their time to be filled with activities in which they conceive, design, and produce. They may expect to work creatively on interesting and stimulating individual and group projects, using all media of the arts.

Students will know their teachers well. Teachers will know their students, call them by name, laugh with them, help them, and share their concerns. Students and faculty will be encouraged to care about each other. Each individual in the school (students and faculty alike) will strive toward developing a commitment to one another. When a student or teacher is absent—he will be missed. When a student or faculty member experiences a lack of success—others will be concerned and work toward a solution.

The atmosphere, both physically and psychologically, will be relaxed, stimulating, and productive. Special consideration will be given to creating, using the school's unique talents, a physical environment which will stimulate students and faculty to be energetic and productive. Students and faculty will be mutually supportive. All people in the Fine Arts School will be respected as human beings. No one will be a cog in a wheel. The uniqueness of each individual is recognized. Hopefully, all students will be helped to find what they can do—do uniquely well—and then do it with all the unique powers that they possess for the benefit of themselves and their community—whether that community is a tiny town or six continents.

The Career School

A. Introduction. The Career School is open to any junior or senior girl or boy. Even though the Career School is being housed in the Quincy Area Vocational Technical Center, this does not mean a student has to be in the Career School to take a vocational course at the center. There will be many students taking vocational courses at the Quincy Area Vocational Technical Center who will not be enrolled in the Career School.

A student wishing to enroll in the Career School must take a vocational course and must also enroll in the English and social studies courses required for graduation from Quincy Senior High School. Upon enrolling in the Career School, a student will be educationally diagnosed: that is, when the student enrolls he will bring with him certain educational strengths and weaknesses. If it is apparent that a particular student may need to strengthen an educational weakness, he will be asked to enroll in a course that will help him in the vocational subject he has chosen. Courses offered in the Career School will include business English, technical English, business mathematics, and technical mathematics. These courses will be related to the vocational course a student has enrolled in and will also relate to the career he has selected.

The student's vocational instructor will act as his advisor to assist him with educational concerns, planning for employment, or planning for further schooling after graduation from high school. The Career School counselor will also play a key role in helping a student plan for his future.

The main objective of the Career School is to assist the student to attain economic independence and to appreciate the dignity of work. It is hoped that upon graduation from the Career School, a student will be able to compete for a well-paying job or feel motivated to receive further specialized education beyond high school.

B. Philosophy. The Career School has been designed for the student who has a concern for what awaits him after graduation from high school. The student, for all practical purposes, has three possible choices facing him once graduation takes place—immediate employment, further education, or the armed services. Most high school graduates will probably have to deal with going to work or enrolling in a business school, trade school, junior college, or a college or university.

The Career School has been established to help the student deal with his concerns about employment or further education. The staff of the Career School is committed to be as flexible as possible in providing the student with the occupational skills, general education courses, and attitudes that are necessary in today's world for a person to be competitive in finding and holding a well-paying job. In addition, a student can expect help on how to decide on the type of employment or further schooling he should consider for the future. The Career School staff feels a responsibility to assist the student to find a satisfactory career. However, the staff also feels that the student enrolling in the Career School should realize that all experiences at the school will be directed toward occupational and educational goals and will expect the student to feel also the need for this type of education.

C. Curriculum. The typical Career School student will be enrolled in a two-hour vocational course. The junior student will also be enrolled in United States history and English, both required for graduation. The typical senior student will have to enroll in a two-hour vocational course. Additionally, students will select other courses from among a variety of electives.

The English, social studies, and mathematics courses of the Career School will be taught somewhat differently than in the past. All of these concerns will attempt to cover basic ideas and concepts that the student should know. However, the student will be taught the types of things that he can use to assist him in his vocational subjects and eventually assist him on the job. Course work should be more relevant to the student who is concerned with establishing and entering a career upon graduation from high school. It should be noted that the English, social studies, and mathematics courses can also be used to meet college entrance requirements if the student feels a need for further schooling.

The staff at the Career School recognizes the value of work experience for students who are career-minded. A course being offered at the Career School and that is also part of the course offerings of the Quincy Area Vocational Technical Center is cooperative vocational education. The staff of the school will assist the student to find part-time employment in the community. The student will be required to work a minimum of fifteen hours per week and also take a one-hour class during the day at the school if he wishes to participate in the work experience phase of this school. The student will receive graduation credit for the work experience and also for the class taken at the school.

D. Method of Instruction. The method of instruction will be geared towards the needs of the student. A student who can satisfactorily meet the objectives of the course with limited teacher direction will be allowed to do so. The student who has difficulty in meeting the objectives of the course will receive the needed amount of teacher direction to help him make satisfactory progress. If the student has successfully met the objectives of the course, as defined by the instructor, that student may do additional intensive study in the course or pursue other educational experiences.

E. Time Schedule. The time schedule shall be the same as established for Senior High II. However, the Career School will attempt to be as flexible as possible in dealing with scheduling problems of the student. In some instances a student will be allowed to start his class at a time different than the regular starting time. The student who has a scheduling problem will be asked to present legitimate reasons to the guidance coordinator as to why he wishes to start the vocational course at an irregular time.

F. Non-Class Time. It is anticipated that the typical junior or senior will have at least one hour a day of non-class time. When a student has non-class time, he will be expected to report to the Career School resource center. At the resource center, the student will have some alternatives to consider. He may stay at the center for individual study, he may sign out to the main resource center on the Senior High II campus, to the student lounge, or to one of the shops or labs in the Career School. If the student is experiencing difficulty in one of his subjects, he will be required to remain at the center for help by the resource center director.

G. Attendance and Discipline. A student will be expected to maintain daily attendance. There will be student regulations that will be jointly developed by a Career School Committee. This committee will be made up of staff members and students.

H. Student Evaluation. A student can expect to receive traditional letter grades plus a report on his competencies, attitudes, and other information that help decide his final grade.

Upon graduation and in addition to his regular diploma, a student will receive a certificate from the Career School indicating the occupational skills he has acquired. This certificate can be used to interview for certain types of employment or in some cases can be used to receive advanced standing at some business schools, technical schools, and junior colleges.

The Work-Study School

A. Philosophy. The basic philosophy of the Work-Study School is centered around the belief that within the right structure and with guidance, every student can enjoy a degree of academic achievement. Emphasis is placed on providing the opportunity for and guidance toward adequate personal and emotional development for our students, knowledge of the world of work, what is responsible citizenship, and how to achieve success in family living.

B. Curriculum. The academic subjects offered are centered around the special needs of students and the vocational application to which they can be made. Prevocational work laboratories of various types are provided to evaluate work habits, attitudes, vocational adjustment, and appearance.

C. Method of Instruction. It is the chief duty of each instructor to see each student as a separate person and to individualize the course material to meet the needs of each student. Homework is kept to an absolute minimum. Emphasis is placed on the completion of as much work as possible within the classroom environment where the teacher is available to provide individual help.

D. Time Schedule. The school is organized around a normal four-quarter, two-semester school year, with the daily schedule structured into a six-period day. All students are scheduled for two hour block classes in English and history.

E. Non-Class Time. Students are scheduled into a supervised resource center during their non-class time. If students conduct themselves well, the teacher may allow them the option to use the school-wide student lounge and/or resource center. Work experience is an important part of this school and every effort will be made to provide out-of-school jobs for students. Students may move out to other schools to take courses not offered by our school.

F. Attendance and Discipline. Attendance will be mandatory and promptness to class emphasized. Student discipline problems will be handled within the school. Serious infractions of rules would necessitate the student being referred to the over-all disciplinarian.

G. Student Evaluation. Student evaluations will be made each quarter in the form of letter grades. Students in the work experience program are evaluated on a twelve-point character-adjustment-achievement scale as to their performance on the job.

H. Other Significant Points. The maximum number of students for each grade level is eighty-eight with referrals from counselors used to compensate for those leaving the school. Credit for graduation is given for work experience. A work experience coordinator is an integral part of the school. The school provides sheltered work areas in the form of school stores, which sell school supplies, a service station, and the Vocational Improvement Program, which concentrates on arts and crafts. The service station and V.I.P. offer a summer program where the students can also obtain credit. Each instructor of a block class will be responsible to the parents of each of his students, in a way that will acquaint them with the school and keep them informed as to the student's progress. All students of the school will be assigned the same counselor.

The Special Education School

A. Introduction. The purpose of this school is to meet the needs (academic, vocational, social, emotional, and physical) of students requiring special education services. For all students in secondary special education, emphasis is placed on the following areas:

1. the attainment of social maturity and vocational competencies
2. the attainment of independent living skills
3. the attainment of a realistic self-concept

To meet these goals, the program includes classroom activities or pre-vocational instruction, practical vocational training, and actual on-the-job work experience.

B. Curriculum

GRADE 11
* Vocational English
* Everyday Business
* Work Experience (1 hr.)
* Multi-Experience Unit
   P.E.
   Foods-Clothing
   Electives

GRADE 12
* Occupations
* Vocational Problems
* Work Experience (1–3 hrs.)
   P.E.
   Foods-Clothing
   Electives

Required courses in Special Education

Within the Special Education curriculum, attention is focused on proper work habits and attitudes, and on the work experience program. A student begins his work experience in an on-campus situation and graduates to a job within the community.

The multi-experience approach simply provides many experiences that are necessary to benefit the special education student in his quest for learning. It includes learning skills needed for employment, as well as home living and maintenance, family budgets, purchasing, and leisure time activities.

Students may select and benefit from courses in other alternative schools. These elective courses must have approval of the special education counselor.

C. Method of Instruction. Instruction is in small groups and individualized. Teachers in the program meet certification requirements for teaching exceptional children and, therefore, use various techniques necessary for the different and individual learning processes.

D. Time Schedule. It will follow that established by the school's central administration. Students' schedules will be flexible to meet their work experience program demands.

E. Non-Class Time. Non-class time will be limited. Students may be released in ample time to meet their employment responsibilities which are coordinated with their school curriculum.

F. Attendance and Discipline. Attendance is *mandatory*. Infractions of discipline will be handled by the teachers and/or coordinator in the Special Education School. In very severe cases or in problems confronting other schools, the discipline will then, and only then, be referred to the Dean's Office.

G. Student Evaluation. It is often difficult to measure adequately a student's growth in social maturity and vocational competencies through written tests and/or verbal expression. Evaluation can best be accomplished through the following:

1. subjective teacher evaluation of student's performance
2. subjective and objective measurement of the skills, attitudes, and work habits demonstrated by the student on immediate job placements
3. report card grades will remain in the form of the traditional A, B, C, D, and F rating
4. a parent may receive a progress report at any time through teacher consultation, either personally or by telephone

SPACE FOR LEARNING*

BY AASE ERIKSEN†

While much attention has been centered on the content, methods, and external environment of alternative schools, very little consideration has been given to the importance of the school's interior spaces.

Indeed, the most common school design component for interior space has been movable wall partitions. But movable walls have been found unsatisfactory on several counts, among them are acoustics problems and the staff's failure to use them creatively.

* Reprinted with permission of author and *National Association of Secondary School Principals Bulletin.*

† Aase Eriksen, Ph.D. AAIA, is architect and educator and is director of Educational Futures, Inc. in Philadelphia, Pa.

Another design of the "open school" is the circle, but it, too, has proved unsatisfactory, in that it is one of the most limiting geometric forms in terms of flexible and changing use.

The real problem seems to be that both architects and educators continue to think of school space in terms of specific functions, functions closely related to traditional subject-matter divisions of the curriculum. This division perpetuates the idea that learning is compartmentalized, attempting to force all students to learn at the same rate and in the same way. Since the structure expresses the curriculum, generations of children will move through the same compartments.

What is needed in order to implement the concept of informal learning on the secondary level is to conceptualize not only learning but also space in new ways. We have begun to recognize that the learning process cannot be compartmentalized into rigidly defined disciplines and that children do indeed learn in different ways and at different rates. We have also recognized that *learning* rather than teaching should be the focus of the educational process.

We need to provide the user with a variety of different kinds of spaces that will suggest various activities.[1] We need to provide spaces for students and teachers in which things can happen. It has been duly noted that there is overwhelming evidence that the layout and symbolic content of the man-made environment can encourage or inhibit certain social activities. The reason is simply that structuring the environment in turn structures the communication processes that form the basis of social interaction.[2] Social science and architectural research have documented the fact that all people respond to the spaces in which they find themselves.[3] This has great implication for the learning process when one considers that, in many high schools, the space given to high school students and teachers is, for the most part, ugly, impersonal, and extremely limiting.

Change of Space Must Occur

An important function of the school is to socialize the young and prepare them for adulthood. Along with this aim also goes the responsibility for supporting and widening the natural learning process through the introduction of specific disciplines and training in basic skills. If a more humane and informal environment is seen to be more conducive to the accomplishment of these functions and if learning rather than teaching is to be the focus of the educational process, then the coming years must see drastic changes in the kinds of spaces available in the secondary school.

While there has been some development of different kinds of learning spaces in elementary schools, virtually nothing of this kind has been done for secondary schools. In part, we may draw on open school and open classroom design for innovation at the secondary level; but, more importantly, we need to think in terms of user needs (both student and teacher). These may be conceptualized in terms of three kinds of spaces: *socializing space, natural learning space,* and *private space.*

By *socializing space* is meant the kind of spatial components that would maximize probability of certain kinds of behavioral patterns related to our cultural codes. The school, as the primary locus of extra-familial socialization, is the initial arena of public performance and training in social participation.

Natural learning space is the kind of space which allows students to learn in ways that are natural and easy for them. The natural learning process calls for different environments depending on the learner, the subject matter, and the level of inquiry.

Private learning space can be of two types. The first is space that enables one to be alone but not completely apart from others. The second type allows for total isolation.

Ways of Seeing Spaces

We could envision, for example, small spaces that would invite conversation between only two people, spaces that would accommodate a few more and would suggest a small group discussion, and larger spaces that would allow for activities in which many people participate. These are spaces which would encourage things to happen, irrespective of subject matter divisions.

In this way, we should think of the school as a learning environment made up of any number of different spaces. Some of these kinds of spaces would respond to the more specialized learning needs required by the secondary school curriculum. Such a learning environment would also have spaces that allow interaction among students and teachers—spaces which promote sharing and an awareness of responsibility and concern for others. Large spaces might offer the possibility of smaller spaces to encourage a different activity. For example, bean bags in a corner could encourage students to snuggle down with a book and yet still to be a part of the larger space. Different levels within a room would also suggest different activities and different positions: learning can take place equally well lying down, sitting, or leaning against a step.

Two Examples in Operation

In the Free Gymnasium in Copenhagen, one can observe such different levels and activities in one large room. It is possible there for students to read or talk quietly in corners on the upper levels. At the same time, others may walk through the room or work around a large table on the opposite side at the lowest level. At the time of the all-school meeting, students cover the several levels of the room, many bringing their bean bags with them. The room seems intimate, although it is large enough to accommodate the entire student body of 175.

Another illustration of the differentiation of internal space to meet user needs can be taken from the West Philadelphia Community Free School, a part of a system of scattered schools.[4] The primary and physical educational unit in this system is the "house," renovated residential or commercial building which accommodates approximately 150 students. The students are encouraged to decorate and name their house, to maintain it, and otherwise make it a place which suits their needs and desires.

Each house has four spatial components: learning-teaching spaces (called fixed and flexible spaces), non-teaching spaces, identity space, and service space, each of which plays an important part in creating a learning environment relevant to student and teacher needs. Fixed spaces are those provided for specific activities which require non-portable facilities and include areas for group and individual study. As part of the teaching-learning space, the reading and writing workshop is an example of fixed space. Though an area such as this has an average capacity of 25, it is capable of containing a maximum of 35 people. It is furnished with tables that are easily moved, bookcases for a central library, and a file cabinet with a minimum capacity for 150 folders, one for each student, containing his work as proof of his progress and development. A number of electrical outlets allow for the easy use of audiovisual equipment by individual students or by clusters of students wishing to work cooperatively. This reading-writing workshop is one of the central learning-teaching places in the school. All the students must spend a certain number of hours in this workshop. The art studio is another example of fixed space, since it requires equipment that is difficult to move.

Flexible space is that which does not require fixed facilities or equipment. As many of a school's facilities as possible should be made portable, thus eliminating the need to physically separate learning activities. An example of flexible space is the language laboratory in the form of a cabinet on wheels containing tape recorders, a film projector, or a small TV monitor, phonographs, and ear phones. Any of these may be plugged into conveniently located electrical outlets and thus may be operated in relative freedom.

Planning of non-teaching space is also an important consideration, as much of the socializing purpose of the school takes place in these areas. The entry to each house gives identity to the house unit and distinguishes it from neighborhood buildings. The living room (or lounge) acts as a transition space between the interior and exterior spaces and is located near the entry. It is important to note here that this space is used by teacher and students together.

Identity space is another important aspect of the West Philadelphia Community Free School, here defined as family space. It is differentiated by differently shaped and colored bulletin boards giving information about activities pertinent to the members of particular family groups. The need for private or personal space, another aspect of identity space, must also be taken into account in designing an educational facility. The design of private space is determined by the user needs (student or teacher) and attempts to incorporate these needs into the structure and implementation of space in the school. The bean bag corners on the upper levels in the Free Gymnasium illustrate one kind of private space. Completely private space, however, would be a place where one can be alone to think, contemplate, read, or practice some of the skills to be developed during the secondary school program.

Private identity space is a place where one can safely store his personal possessions. It might take the form of drawers in walls, or one-foot square lockers placed around rooms or in hallways. Cushions could be placed on top of three or more connected lockers to form benches or individual seats.

The differentiation of space along the lines suggested above is particularly feasible in older buildings other than those built expressly as schools, since these are often filled with a great variety of different kinds of space. However, since many existing schools must and should be used, it will now be important to identify the many kinds of spaces that are needed by students and teachers and to devise ways of introducing these into existing school buildings. Such work is in the early stages of development right now. Some work has been done, for example, in developing movable "props" for use in changing existing structures into new learning environments by Curtis-Smith Associates of Boston; Herman Miller Associates in Ann Arbor, Mich.; and by Ronald Beckman of the Research and Design Institute of Providence, R.I. However, we still do not have much research data or evaluation on the use of space in relation to the new informal learning programs.

Developing Teacher Skill in Using Space

Another problem with regard to the newly developed programs based on the concept of informal learning or open learning are new skills demanded of teachers. Teachers must not only be trained to arrange and use the environment in different ways, but they must also be guided toward a new and expanded conception of their role. The physical environment alone cannot shape the new learning process. The architect can design shells that suggest activities and can also design parts of the furnishings, but in the end teachers and students must, to a great extent, determine how to shape space to meet user needs.

It has been our concern to develop a consideration of what we understand are the positive aspects of the last several years of heated debate about the learning process in the United States. It is clear to us that what we know about learning today carries with it the need to reconsider this process as a total humanizing experience. The key issues that have emerged in the last several years of experimentation have been: the concept of open and informal education, the understanding of the school as a socializing agency, and the realization that *natural learning space* and *socializing space* must be viewed together. Our society needs not only citizens who possess certain basic skills but also human beings who have been taught how to relate in public to other human beings. Learning does not occur in a vacuum, and the importance of the surroundings therefore becomes clear.

If we are indeed concerned with used needs, then we cannot simply consider the shell, the square footage, and the modern equipment contained in the "slick new" school designs. The space is what is important. We must ask what kinds of spaces, then, are necessary—necessary, however, in terms of the activities that are important to people and important to the socializing and learning process, not just the activities we assume will take place in a functional and/or efficiently designed room for a specific discipline.

Disobedience and Poor Grades

Junior high school students who rebel against parents and teachers are more likely to use drugs by the time they reach high school than more conventional youngsters. The rebels tend to smoke cigarettes early, to make poor grades, and to score low on such personality traits as: conscientiousness, dependability, planfulness, thoroughness, efficiency, persistency, and ambition. They use alcohol as well as drugs. The heavy marihuana smokers are also heavy drinkers.

Children who are obedient, ambitious and who make good grades are the least likely to turn to drugs and alcohol. They tend to say "I enjoy being good at things I have to do at school" and "When I'm told to do something by a teacher, I do it."

This information was drawn from self reports, reports by classmates, and school records by Gene M. Smith, psychologist, Massachusetts General Hospital. So far, some 2,200 Boston area students have participated in this five-year study.

FOOTNOTES
1. West Philadelphia Community Free School; Parkway Program, Philadelphia; and Metro School, Chicago; are just a few examples.

2. Jon Lang, "Architecture for Human Behavior: The Nature of the Problem," *Architecture of Human Behavior,* Philadelphia: AIA, 1971.

3. Edward T. Hall, *The Hidden Dimension* (New York: Doubleday, 1966).

Robert Somer, *Personal Space: The Behavioral Basis of Design* (Englewood Cliffs, N.J.: Prentice Hall, 1969).

Royston Landau, "Evolutionary Housing," *Architectural Design,* London: September 1971.

John Zeisel, "Symbolic Meaning of Space and the Physical Dimensions of Social Relations," unpublished paper, September 1969.

Robert Propst, *High School: The Process and the Place* (New York: Educational Facilities Laboratories, 1972).

4. Aase Eriksen, *Scattered Schools,* Report to HEW under Special Opportunity Grant #71-7063071 (1971) reprinted by Educational Facilities Laboratories, 1972.

THE ST. PAUL OPEN SCHOOL*

BY WAYNE JENNINGS†

What makes school exciting?

At first, maybe it's fat orange pillars, and purple, yellow, white, blue or green walls and doors stretching down the corridors.

Maybe it's knowing that students and parents and teachers painted most of them, working together—changing an old four-floor building from factory-drab to bright colors in a few weeks' time.

Maybe it's the exciting exploration you witness in the art area, where learners from 4 to 40 are at work on such projects as ceramics, silk screening, painting, carving, jewelry-making, leather-work, photography, and more.

Or maybe it's the quiet, intense comradeship in a 10-year-old helping a 6-year-old learn to read; a tall redhead showing a small blond tyke how to use a camera; a 12-year-old black girl helping a small boy take his first panful of cookies from the oven.

Whatever turns you on—the St. Paul Open School has got it. A research and demonstration unit of the St. Paul public

* Reprinted with permission of the author.
† Wayne Jennings is the principal of the St. Paul Open School.

education system, the school (which opened in September, 1971) has 500 students, age 5 through 18, representative of the city's geographic areas and its citizens' socio-economic and ethnic backgrounds.

It manages to turn the students on, too—so much, that they showed up in droves a week before opening day when the newly rented building was opened for renovation. On opening day they cheered for minutes at a time when the principal spelled out some features of the school: no report cards; no grades; no required classes; no lecture-memorize-test routine from teachers.

How Does It Work

Without those familiar ingredients, what does go on in the school?

Many things are happening simultaneously. Students are working alone, in groups, teaching one another, making discoveries together, discussing, exploring, watching demonstrations, taking short courses, going on field trips.

The school is organized into major learning areas, or "theaters of learning": art; music-drama; humanities; math-science; industrial arts; home economics; and physical education. Each area has a library-resource center and a "smorgasbord" of activities to choose from—some of which are conducted by volunteers or are out in the community. There is also a central library-resource center. Many areas have rooms for quiet study, short courses, and group or individual projects in addition to large open spaces.

When a student is not actively involved in one of the multitude of activities going on at all times, he may be meeting with his advisor. The two of them together are continually charting his goals and means of achieving them, and evaluating progress. When a given project or course of action doesn't work out, there is no stigma of failure. Instead, either the goals are changed or different ways of working toward them are found. The student learns to know his own strengths and weaknesses, what he needs to work on and what comes easily, what areas he avoids, and how he reacts to different people. Eventually, he comes to know himself well. Students determine their schedules, learn to design their own education on the way to becoming self-initiating learners. Such students will be lifelong consumers of learning.

Do They Really Learn?

This approach integrates learning of many kinds. Basic skills like reading and writing are part of many learning situations, and teachers seek ways to weave them in. In the case of a film project, for example, students read manuals, photo magazines, and books on the subject, keep logs or records, write letters, design instructions for others, calculate distances, arrange demonstrations, purchase materials, determine proportions and ratios for enlargements; and thus constantly use and become familiar with reading, writing and math, at whatever level they're operating at. Every plunge is an opportunity for making mistakes, learning from them, and growing in skills and confidence.

Years of research into educational practices suggest that a setting of intrinsically interesting and extensively equipped "theaters of learning" young people are stimulated and learning occurs more easily, more naturally and more thoroughly than in conventional schools. Psychological research indicates that more learning takes place when an individual is predisposed to want to learn—when his emotional state is ready to grasp new knowledge.

Learning, at the Open School, is conceived in terms not only of the 3 R's and other basic "subject matter" of so many curriculum manuals, but also of the other important qualities needed for living in a rapidly changing society: flexibility, openness, initiative, an appetite for lifelong learning, enthusiasm, constructive human relationships, responsibility, continually broadening perspectives and deepening self-discoveries.

Do Teachers Teach?

Teachers—or learning facilitators as they prefer to call themselves—spend their energy and thought on maximizing learning for students.

They are assisted by aides, volunteers, student teachers and various resource people on call. But more than any others, they are assisted by the students themselves—who, by the very nature of the entire enterprise, are in natural roles of teachers-and-learners. The student deeply involved in an interest area attracts others following an old dictum, one doesn't truly understand an area until one teaches it to another.

Older students serve as a model to younger students by providing leadership and teaching. This responsibility role effectively combats the useless feeling of many teenagers and enables them to spend more of their great energy in creative directions and less in resentful, anti-adult, anti-establishment teen sub-culture so common today in a world with little use for teenagers. Younger children benefit by more individual attention and personal help from others not so distant from their problems as are adults. In turn, young children help even younger children.

Teachers were selected for the Open School on the basis of interest, competence and educational philosophy—a distinct advantage over reassigning or retraining a traditional staff. Democratically organized, the teachers themselves make decisions on additional personnel, training, budget—thus increasing their understanding of these decisions and their feeling of responsibility toward making them work. They agreed with gusto to level with one another, to be open and honest, to welcome suggestions from anyone, of whatever age or expertise. Students and parents are welcome and participate in the frequent faculty meetings. Where staff lack the skill to handle a situation or a task, they help each other—through training sessions or more informal means. They work closely with parents and interested citizens, as well as students, on an elected Advisory Council.

Does Education Cost More This Way?

Seldom have so many exciting features and concepts been put together in a single project. In addition, the economic ramifications are exciting to speculate on.

The staff consists of just 17 professional teachers for 500 students. A principal directs the school, assisted by a program coordinator (teacher on special assignment) and two community resource specialists (ordinary citizens) who coordinate volunteers, resources, information dissemination and visitors.

If quality education is the result, as desired, the Open School will demonstrate that the usual attempted solution to individualizing and improving education—the reduction of class size—is not necessarily valid. In the city of St. Paul, with 50,000 public school students, a reduction of just one pupil per classroom for all classrooms in the system would cost over $1-million. A significant reduction of, say, 5 or 10 pupils would cost between $5- and $10-million. It can be seen that, conversely, if class size is increased, then savings of a similar magnitude are realized.

One of the goals of this project is to demonstrate that, with sufficient equipment and materials, as much learning can take place with fewer professional teachers. Initially, the money saved on teaching staff will be put into the "stuff" of learning. Eventually, it is hoped, real financial savings will result. If, in addition, learning is improved, then a real breakthrough in education will have occurred.

At this point in the St. Paul Open School anything seems possible.

OUTWARD BOUND APPROACHES TO ALTERNATIVE SCHOOLING*

BY JOSEPH J. NOLD†

Each of the OUTWARD BOUND[1] schools uses the same basic curriculum design and conducts courses at various times of the year, though the activities vary according to the locale and season: The Hurricane Island School on the sea, using the vehicle of the pulling boat; Minnesota, the canoe; and Colorado, mountain climbing. In the standard courses for young women, young men, and coeducational groups, there are specific program requirements that participants experience at each of the schools.

During the first week of a standard course, everyone takes part in fitness training and conditioning through such daily

---

* Reprinted with permission of the author.

† Joseph J. Nold is Director of Colorado Outward Bound School Project Centre and of the University of Colorado Outward Bound Master of Education Degree Program in Experiential Education.

activities as running, hiking, ropes course work, swimming or other related events.

All participants also undergo extensive instruction in: specialized safety training required to cope with the environment in which the course is taking place; the use of equipment; search, rescue, emergency evacuation and first aid procedures; field food planning and preparation; map, compass and route finding, traveling skills appropriate to the environment; expedition planning and control; care and protection of the environment to be used by the course; and, training in group effectiveness.

These standard courses vary in length from 21 to 28 days and have a 16½ year old minimum age requirement. After successful completion of the initial training phase, participants, in groups of 8 to 12, take part in the following experiences: one or more short expeditions, accompanied by their instructor, appropriate to the environment (sailing, backpacking, canoeing, skiing, etc.); a solo, which is a period of wilderness solitude lasting up to three days and nights with a minimum of equipment necessary for existence; rock climbing and rappelling; a marathon-type event, differing according to locale and taking place when weather and other conditions permit; a one-day service project performed by all students for the benefit of others; periodic time devoted to meaningful readings and/or discussions designed to help students interpret various course experiences; and a final expedition of up to four days' duration, with a minimum of instructor supervision consistent with prevailing conditions and environment.

Founded on the educational concept of Dr. Kurt Hahn, who wrote, "The aim of education is to impel young people into value-forming experience, to inspire the survival of these qualities: an enterprising curiosity; an undefeatable spirit; tenacity in pursuit; readiness for self-denial; and above all, compassion," OUTWARD BOUND schools have assisted in broadening the concepts of formal and innovative education.

The program adaptions of OUTWARD BOUND concepts and methods are many. This paper focuses on five types: (1) motivational programs; (2) the human relations programs within a school; (3) an alternative to traditional physical education; (4) curriculum enrichment; (5) faculty development.

Motivational programs.
There are pitifully few channels in our society through which young men can move with dignity, success, and a

sense of adventure from adolescence into manhood. Opportunities for positive, character-forming experiences are particularly limited for youngsters of low-income families. They often are the ones who don't or can't respond with success to the college preparatory or highly selective vocational education channels of the schools. They often are the ones who turn from the approved institutions of society to seek adventure and prove their manhood on street corners. They are the ones who most often sink finally into aimlessness and apathy, or who take out their frustrations on the institutions that have failed them in acts of violence and hostility. Perhaps more than anyone else in our society these young men need the experiences that will bring to them the sense of their own competence and capacity, that will assure them that the world has a place for them, that what they have to offer is sorely needed. They need experiences that will show them that they are not so limited as they think, experiences that will give them confidence and enthusiasm for the business of facing life, experiences that will assure them they can make it.

So wrote Greg Farrell, then the Director of Community Action in Trenton, New Jersey, in his application to the Ford Foundation and the Office of Economic Opportunity and Title I ESEA in 1965, for funding for a program within Trenton Central High School. The program began by exposing a cross-section of the educational community to OUTWARD BOUND. Teachers, students, mostly from a black neighborhood, student teachers from Trenton State Teachers' College attended OUTWARD BOUND courses and returned to their communities to be the nucleus for planning and launching projects. They were working on a "critical mass theory," the rationale being that a certain number of energetic, trained and experienced leaders could come back from the wilderness, onto the streets and initiate programs. The focus was on the dropout, the pre-dropout, and the delinquent. The program design was built around three components. There were a number of "ignition" activities of an adventurous nature: rock climbing, bicycle expeditions, canoeing on the Delaware River, so-called "high-risk activities," supervised by OUTWARD BOUND trained specialists. These were designed to involve young men in a dramatic and compelling way, to give them experiences of success, kicks that were legitimate, to establish warm relations with their peers, rival gangs, their teachers. The second component of the program focused on the basic skills of reading and mathematics. These were taught on an individual basis by teachers who opted to work in the program, many of whom had gone through OUTWARD BOUND experiences with their students. Gradually an experience-based curriculum was developed around courses in Black History, the Law and Law Enforcement, field trips to New York, Philadelphia, and Washington related to culture and government; and job opportunities were sought. Throughout the program group counseling sessions were held on a regular basis led by a leader trained in the Guided Group Interaction (GGI) process. The program evolved each year. Service training was added; an emergency room team was organized; excursions were planned with black and white students and local policemen to explore each other's stereotypes; a course was organized in urban outdoor education through Trenton State College. The program continued through four years through June, 1970, when federal funding ended, reaching by this time some 250 students per year in some aspect of the program.

Evaluated by Dr. Robert E. Lee, Department of Psychology, Princeton University, a group of forty inner-city, lower-class, non-achieving high school students were studied. As a consequence of their participation in the OUTWARD BOUND activities the group was found to perceive themselves individually as more active, stronger, more positive, and less alienated. With regard to others, the group demonstrated more capacity to see other people as individuals and a greater tendency to view peers and teachers as more positive and helpful. Finally, the group showed a more mature goal orientation and greater flexibility of means for goal achievement.

An Alternative to Traditional Physical Education: How do you reach every student in the school? For OUTWARD BOUND alternatives to be educationally relevant they must reach more students, a wider cross-section than has been possible in most programs. They must reflect the existing structures within public schools, existing time blocks, staffing ratios, physical limitations. "Project Adventure" in Hamilton-Wenham Regional High School, Massachusetts, addressed itself to this problem. A physical education program modeled on OUTWARD BOUND training concepts that met three times a week during a fifty-minute period was designed that operated on the school grounds. An elaborate "ropes course" was constructed on a wooded lot adjacent to the playing field and a part of the campus. It includes obstacles such as an inclined log, ten to twelve inches in diameter inclined at a 25-degree angle rising to twelve feet off the ground. The object is to walk up the log in an erect position. This leads to a postman's walk, two parallel ropes five and a half feet apart connected between supports that one moves across by walking on the lower rope, using the upper one for balance. The tension traverse is a single semi-taut wireline stretched between two trees, the object being to walk along it using a diagonally attached rope for balance. A leopard crawl consists of two parallel ropes four or five feet off the ground along which a student crawls balancing on the top of both ropes. The Bosun's Chair is a series of small swings five feet off the ground that one pendulums on from one to the next. There are climbing ropes, rope ladders, walking a log six feet off the ground, Tarzan swings, a flea leap jumping from the top of one high stump to another, crossing a Burma bridge thirty feet in the air, descending a zip wire from a thirty-foot platform down to the ground. The wall is an obstacle twelve feet high that requires teamwork to get everyone over, as is the beam, a big circular log attached six feet off the ground.

Instruction is sequential beginning with movement exercises, limbering and flexibility movements, learning to fall and learning to spot others in exposed positions. In all situations where students are exposed to height they are "belayed" tied to safety ropes using the techniques developed by rock climbers. Spotting and belaying necessitate attentive teamwork.

A series of field trips was built into the program: a biology expedition to Cape Cod National Seashore and Acadia National Park involving 150 sophomores; a unit on Colonial Life integrating American History with visits to graveyards, old churches, Salem, and the study of Indian remains. An English class visited Gloucester and interviewed old boat builders and deep sea fishermen. The art department planned a "texture walk" where students explored the natural environment and collected, analyzed, interpreted and organized as many different textures as they could discover in a limited time block. The mud walk provided an experiential immersion in the environment as a part of a study of marshland ecology.

Ellsworth Fersch, Ph.D., Boston University, evaluated the program using a battery of six tests and found the following:

The quantitative data indicates overall positive change in self-concept for the sophomore class. Anecdotal and written materials collected from students, faculty, and parents indicate that Project Adventure was substantially responsible for the changes. The students reported more self-confidence at the end of the year. The students had moved to a perception of less external control at the end of the year. The physical education program seemed to raise confidence in the students because it showed them they could do things they didn't think they could.

The girls showed more significant improved changes in self-concept. On the Tennessee scale, for example, they increased significantly in total positivity, positive identity, positive behavior, moral self and family self, and they showed a significant decrease in self-criticism. The boys evidenced less change, but an important result was a significant decrease in total conflict (conflict in self-perception) as measured on the Tennessee Self-Concept Scale. The decrease indicated a lessening in confusion and contradiction in self-perception. The main factor related to this improvement in self-concept was what was variously called by the staff of the project, enthusiasm for life, or zest, or infectious interest.

Curriculum Enrichment: Dissatisfaction with conventional education is not limited to the inner city school. The disenchantment of youth stems deeply into our suburbs and wealthier communities as well.

Lincoln-Sudbury Regional High School serves an upper middle-class commuter community near Boston. Their NIMBUS program reaches 175 students a year through a series of mini courses lasting 14 days, involving weekday afternoon sessions in basic outdoor skills training from 2:45 to 5:15, leading to an expedition which includes an experience of solitude, as well as a long trek unaccompanied by instructors.

They have found this experience to be both relevant to their lives and an exciting part of their education. The program is based upon the concept of wilderness challenge situations which provide heightened sense of individual self-awareness, compassion, group cooperation and responsibility. It is an action-oriented process of involvement and participation. Nobody stands back and watches; everyone experiences and reacts. It is a very personal thing. People get to know each other better and themselves better. Students see teachers in a different light and vice versa. Communication happens naturally. The value of the total experience for the individual lies within the increased awareness of his physical and mental capability—his self-image. The value to the community of having his children excited and involved toward positive, relevant goals within the high school is self-evident.

The Alternate Semester launched in the spring term of 1972 with 35 Lincoln-Sudbury students and five students from the Copley Square High School, an inner-city high school in Boston, integrated an academic syllabus in English, history, mathematics, science and physical education with a schedule of total immersion experiences away from the school. "The students moved from the isolation and biting winds of the Maine winter, to the crowds, steel, cement of Boston, and finally to the quiet calm of spring in rural New England."

It has been demonstrated that such adventure-centered programs can reach a wide cross-section of student populations in a personal way. Programs have been effective with school drop-outs, delinquents, youth from the ghetto, Black and Hispano minority cultures, boys and girls, students from the upper mobility strata of society in the cities as well as the suburbs. Indeed, many of the most effective programs are in the private schools. Recent programs with junior high school children have also been promising. OUTWARD BOUND type experiences provide an opportunity for developing greater confidence, a greater sense of potentiality and self-worth, a greater sense of control over their own lives.

One of the great discoveries of these programs is the degree to which the same values hold true for adults, both faculty and administrators. This had not been predicted and has opened a whole new realm of educational possibilities.

Second, such programs have emerged as a very effective vehicle for the development of better communications and human relations. Whether it is directed toward interracial understanding, police-community relations, the generation gap, improving communications between students and faculty, within the faculty itself, or between the administration and faculty, the process has helped bridge the distance that exists between one person and another. It is a powerful socializing influence. It lends itself to the problems of how organized humanity interacts in a structured setting to the process of institutional change.

Third, OUTWARD BOUND addresses itself to what is drab, oppressive, and alienating in our society and institutions. It can spark enthusiasm, inspire vision, and bring to the level of consciousness the deep and underlying questions of life and meaning and what is truly educational.

FOOTNOTE

1. OUTWARD BOUND is an educational experience of self-discovery that uses challenges found in a natural setting as the teaching medium. Traditionally OUTWARD BOUND presents a course lasting approximately 25 days that presents a series of progressively difficult physical challenges and problems. OUTWARD BOUND asks people to face many seemingly impossible tasks. Confronting these, participants must call upon individual reserves of strength and perseverance they might not think exist. There are times they may find success requires the help of companions and the reliance upon the overall strengths represented within a group.

There are six schools within America ranging from Maine and North Carolina in the East to Minnesota, Colorado, and Texas, and on to Oregon in the West.

WE HOPE YOU LIKE YOUR SCHOOL AS MUCH AS WE LIKE OURS, ALTERNATIVE SCHOOLS 1975*

BY DONALD R. WALDRIP†

IPSIP

Early years greatly influence the intellectual and emotional development of a child. The richer the environment, the greater the learning. IPSIP (pronounced īp-sīp) is a special kind of kindergarten through grade 3 program where children learn by working, playing, and interacting with children of

* This is reprinted from the Superintendent's Annual Report, 1975, Cincinnati Public Schools, Cincinnati, Ohio.

† Donald R. Waldrip is Superintendent of Schools, Cincinnati Public Schools, Cincinnati, Ohio.

different races and cultures. The program capitalizes on children's social, racial, ethnic, and cultural differences. Selected Montessori equipment, formal reading readiness materials, and manipulative learning aids characterize the framework of this alternative. All levels continue the interracial and intercultural experiences started in kindergarten. The teachers in all IPSIP programs are specially trained and qualified to work with young children. IPSIP affords children the experiences necessary to the development of their social awareness; their attitudes toward school, community, and self; and the tools essential to their future learning.

Parent involvement is central to both the kindergarten and primary grade programs. Involvement and support are gained through volunteer participation in classroom activities.

IPSIP (Impact of a Primary School and Interracial Program) began in the Cincinnati Public Schools in 1970. It was an innovative program funded for three years with federal money. At that time, the program included only kindergarten classes. The decision to expand the program to include grades 1 through 3 came about because the project had shown itself to be a successful demonstration of quality integrated education in action.

Eligibility. IPSIP is open to any child in the district who is eligible for kindergarten, first, second, or third grades. The goal of achieving racial balance in the school will be considered in the selection process. Confirmation will be given after parent interview.

Location. BRAMBLE is at 4324 Homer Avenue between Bramble and Roe, about 10 miles northeast of Fountain Square.

LOSANTIVILLE is at 6701 Elbrook Drive between Vera and Section, about 8 miles northeast of Fountain Square.

Montessori

Programs based on the learning principles of Maria Montessori emphasize the development of the whole child. Montessori education provides experiences in all areas of growth and development. These experiences include motor coordination, cognitive learning, perceptual skills, and social interaction. Throughout these learning experiences each child is treated as an individual with differing needs, learning styles, and rates of growth.

Montessori instruction has been offered to young children for more than two decades. Until now, however, this instruction in Cincinnati has been available only in private schools. Parents and educators have found merit in the Montessori approach; for this reason, Cincinnati will offer it as an alternative within public education. The new alternative will provide a full day program for children five to eight years of age in non-graded classes.

Montessori education emphasizes the growth and development of the individual child. Instruction is organized so that children move forward at their own rate under the direction of specially trained Montessori teachers.

Each child is provided learning opportunities in basic skills and in other areas suited to his/her needs and learning styles. Children work in both small and large group activities. The teachers observe and direct each child's work. They screen, test, diagnose skill levels and prescribe appropriate activities.

Eligibility. Any child eligible to attend a school in kindergarten through grade 3 may apply for enrollment in the Montessori program. A limit of 50 will be placed at each age—five, six, seven and eight years. Parent interviews will be arranged when registrations are received.

Location. MT. ADAMS School is at 1125 St. Gregory Street, approximately one mile east of Fountain Square in Mt. Adams.

Fundamental

A fundamental program emphasizes structure, organization, and discipline in teaching and learning, as well as in behavior. This school provides for those who work best where expectations are clearly defined, where curriculum is logically organized and presented, and where teaching is centered around a class group. The fundamental program stresses basic instruction in reading, language, mathematics, and science, through a traditional style of instruction which emphasizes order and discipline.

Fundamental schools also prize traditional American values in education: patriotism, brotherhood, dignity, pride, and respect for self and others. They establish programs and standards to maintain those values and hold their students responsible for living by them in all of their school activities. They also expect parents to cooperate with the work of the school through reinforcement of school requirements, parent conferences, and involvement in a parent-teacher organization.

A fundamental elementary school will be available next year. Specific plans for its operation will be developed by the staff of the school during the next few months. The school will operate along the lines of schools that most adults remember. You will not find team teaching, open classrooms, student-directed learning, or casual dress and language. You will find emphasis on achievement and enforcement of discipline. This will be accomplished through letter grades, homework, detention, repetition of a school year if minimum standards are not met, dress code, courtesy, and respect for adults.

Eligibility. Children with normal ability in grades one through six are eligible. Upon receipt of application, an interview with parents and child will be arranged to assure understanding of the school's guidelines and endorsement of them. The goal of achieving a racial balance in the school will be considered in the selection process.

Location. Not determined at time of printing.

Multi-Age Non-Graded Magnet

The Multi-Age Non-Graded Magnet School groups children of sequential ages within one class. Children will be able to work in settings which more closely resemble real-life situations.

The multi-age non-graded program places students in primary or intermediate units. The primary unit is equivalent to grades 1, 2, and 3, while the intermediate unit will include students who would normally be attending grades 4, 5, and 6. Within these units, each classroom organization will consist of children of multiple ages so that each child may receive instruction appropriate for him, regardless of age or former grade level. A six-year-old could be working with eight-year-olds in math and with seven-year-olds in reading.

The curriculum is flexible and will be made appropriate to each child's learning style. Children will work individually and in both small or large groups. Flexible grouping offers opportunities for students to help other students. Teachers help the students and each other by working in teams.

Each teacher stays with the same group of students for three years. This permits the teacher to follow the progress of a child and become familiar with his strengths and weaknesses. It also provides consistency in the instructional program and the curriculum and it decreases the need for the teacher to orient the entire class each September.

In addition to work in math and reading, the Multi-Age Non-Graded Magnet School stresses the development of leadership, independent work skills, self-discipline, and respect for others.

The general goal of the program is to focus on the individual child. A gain of one year's growth in reading and math is expected. In addition, students will gain positive attitudes toward school and toward themselves.

Eligibility. All children in grade one through grade six are eligible. Upon receipt of an application, parents will be contacted for an interview. The goal of achieving a racial balance in the school will be considered in the selection process.

Location. CLIFTON School is located at 3645 Clifton Avenue between Woolper and Resor approximately 4 miles north of Fountain Square.

Reading Centers

Each year increasing numbers of students leave school unable to read well enough to function in society. This problem has resulted in a nation-wide demand to offer concentrated programs to help pupils with reading disabilities. Cincinnati's Reading Centers are being established to meet this demand. The Reading Centers will provide intensive help for those pupils who have serious difficulty learning to read and have not responded to regular classroom instruction.

Children who are recommended to the Center will be thoroughly diagnosed by trained psychologists and reading specialists. Results from the interviews, interest surveys, and informal reading tests will pinpoint reading problems, possible visual and motor problems, and problems arising from difficulties with perceptual or eye-hand coordination.

After testing, reading specialists will work individually with the child to build vocabulary, phonics skills, comprehension and interpretation. Language arts, social studies, mathematics, and science will be integrated into the child's reading program. All the courses, together with art, physical education, and music, will stress individual and small group activities.

Each center will include 17 pupils and a teacher specially trained to work with learning problems. Continuous evaluation is made of the child's progress and from this evaluation the staff will seek new ways of challenging students to achieve their highest potential.

When tests and observations indicate that the child has gained confidence and mastered the needed reading skills, he/she will leave the Reading Center. Careful attention will be given to insure a successful return to the home school.

Eligibility. Pupils who are at least one year behind in reading and who have an IQ of 85 or higher are eligible. A child must be recommended by two or more teachers and his principal. Parents are interviewed upon receipt of registration. The goal of achieving racial balance in each school will be considered in the selection process.

Location. MILLVALE is at 3277 Beekman Street between Moosewood and Never. It is about 5 miles northwest of Fountain Square.

PARHAM is at 1835 Fairfax Street between Wold and Fairfield. It is about 4 miles northeast of Fountain Square.

IGE Magnet

Students attending an IGE (Individually Guided Education) Magnet School learn in a program designed for their individual differences. Pupils study in non-graded family units taught by teachers and aides. Each student moves at his/her own pace through a set of carefully prescribed activities in each subject. Individually Guided Education is based on the philosophy that children learn best by working at their own pace. The IGE program has been designed to produce higher achievement by providing for differences among pupils' rates of learning, learning styles, and personal characteristics.

Formalized tests and teacher observations provide continuous measurement of each child's progress. With this knowledge, several teachers work with the child to determine specific activities, materials, and personnel necessary to learn what is needed in each subject. IGE students are encouraged to try a variety of learning sources: textbooks, lecture/discussion groups, independent study, audio-visual equipment, and group research. Tests and observations are made regularly to determine if the child is moving forward and if he is accomplishing his goals.

The Wisconsin Research and Development Center for Cognitive Learning developed the IGE program in 1966. There are over 2,000 IGE programs presently operating in the 50 states. North Avondale has been in the IGE league since 1972, and both Eastwood and North Avondale operated as IGE magnet schools during the 1974–75 school year.

Eligibility. Any child eligible to enter kindergarten through grade six is eligible to enroll. The goal of achieving a racial balance in the school will be considered in the selection process.

Location. EASTWOOD is at 5030 Duck Creek Road between Eastwood and Red Bank, approximately 5 miles east of Fountain Square.

KENNEDY is at 6620 Montgomery Road between Kennedy and Hugh, about 9 miles northeast of Fountain Square.

NORTH AVONDALE is at 615 Clinton Springs Avenue between Washington and Leyman, about 5 miles north of Fountain Square.

Bilingual

The world is becoming a smaller place. Daily, our work, business, politics, leisure, and sports activities are influenced by events in foreign lands. Television, radio, movies, magazines, newspapers, and jet travel make it possible for us to see, hear, and meet people with cultures and languages different from our own.

In the years ahead, understanding other ways of thinking and communicating will be an important part of a well-rounded education, and for many, an important career skill as well.

The bilingual alternatives offer first and second graders a chance to include either French, German, or Spanish language and culture in their daily program of instruction.

In bilingual classes, about one hour of each school day is spent with a specially-trained language teacher in activities designed to develop listening, speaking, reading, and writing skills and to foster appreciation of the culture, history, and way of life of the people who speak the language. The rest of the day is dedicated to the standard school curriculum under the leadership of the regular teacher.

The bilingual program begins with first and second graders because it is easier for younger children to master the sounds and patterns of a second language than it is for older children. Current plans call for the addition of one grade each year so that students who desire may continue their bilingual education. In addition, preparation is being made to permit these students to visit and study with native speakers in exchange programs and schools in the United States and in other countries. The ultimate goal of the program is to enable students to think and to communicate easily in a second language.

The first bilingual program in Cincinnati opened in Schiel and Fairview Schools in September, 1974. First and second graders there have made progress in German beyond the expectations of instructors. Their achievement and progress in the regular curriculum have also met or exceeded expectations.

Eligibility. All first and second grade children are eligible; the students and their parents will be interviewed to acquaint them with the program and its standards. Children enrolled should be free of learning disabilities, vision, hearing and speech defects. The goal of achieving racial balance in the school will be considered in the selection process.

Creative & Performing Arts

Young people with talent or interest in the creative and performing arts should be able to develop those abilities as part of their education in the public schools.

This alternative school offers study programs in the following areas: visual arts, dance, drama, instrumental and vocal music, and creative writing. Study in these areas can be used as preparation for a career or as study to broaden cultural appreciation. In addition to the fine arts and basic skill study, courses are offered in the humanities, the sciences, French, Latin and Italian.

The classroom structure emphasizes teaching students—not merely covering course material. Schedules and classes permit some individualization, but major emphasis is placed on creativity through discipline, study, and performance. Quarterly progress reports are sent to the parents. These cover the student's overall performance in three areas: academic, artistic, and social. If a student at any time appears to be having trouble in any of these areas, a special conference is called between parent and teacher.

The alternative school in the Creative and Performing Arts seeks to unify a study of academic subjects with a study of the fine arts. This specialized education for talented and interested students began in July, 1973, at Mt. Adams School. Because of overwhelming public response to Mt. Adams, future plans call for moving the program to a larger facility. The facility had not been chosen at the time of this publication.

Eligibility. Students in grades 4–9 who reside in the Cincinnati school district are eligible to apply. Enrollment is based upon audition and interview to determine present talent, potential talent, and interest. The goal of achieving a racial balance in the school will be considered in the selection process.

Location. Not determined at time of printing.

College Preparatory Alternative

The College Preparatory Alternative is designed to serve students whose intellectual capabilities may not blossom to fullest potentials without special challenge. This alternative program for fourth, fifth, and sixth grade students will provide accelerated and enriched programs that should prove enjoyable as well as challenging.

Students will develop basic skills in reading and mathematics and be provided opportunities to integrate these skills with in-depth learning experiences in the sciences, the humanities, and the arts. The learning experiences in this program, together with work in career education, will prepare students with the content learning, the academic skills, study skills, attitudes, and social sensitivity which will make their progression into the secondary program for college-bound students a challenging, successful experience.

Eligibility. Selection will be based on teacher recommendations, existing standardized information, and an interview with parent and child. The goal of achieving a racial balance in the school will be considered in the selection process.

Alternative Jr. High College Preparatory

The Alternative Junior High College Preparatory Program is designed for students who desire extra encouragement and help so that they may enter a college preparatory program with confidence. Students in the program include those who failed by a narrow margin to pass the Special College Preparatory Program (SCPP) and those who did pass but who do not wish to enter the Special College Preparatory Program in their local junior high school or at Walnut Hills.

Courses offered in the Alternative College Preparatory Program stress, above all, the upgrading of basic skills in mathematics and English. Specific skills and conceptual deficiencies in math are diagnosed by a computerized instructional management system. This system helps both the teacher and the student to determine prescriptive activities. An English program similar to this will be used as it becomes available.

In addition to upgrading basic areas, the program introduces as much of the regular college preparatory program as is possible and also includes career orientation and development. As students become eligible, they will have the opportunity to be phased into the regular college preparatory program if they choose.

Self-contained classrooms and team teaching techniques are incorporated into the program. The instructional format is different from most programs in that math and science are the responsibility of one teacher, while English and social studies are the responsibility of another teacher. This system reduces the number of teachers a student will meet and provides more opportunities for individualized attention.

This program has been at Gamble, Peoples, and Shroder since September, 1974. Students in each of the three schools have registered impressive gains in achievement in basic subjects, improved attitudes toward school, and increased self-confidence.

The Alternative Junior High College Preparatory program demonstrates that, given the proper school environment, students who were not achieving at their highest level can be brought to attain their full potential.

Eligibility. Those students who are not going into the Special College Preparatory Program but who are specially motivated toward an academic program are eligible. Recommendation by teachers, counselor, or administrator is required. The goal of achieving a racial balance in the school will be considered in the selection process.

Academy of Mathematics & Science

In a recent alternative schools survey, Cincinnati parents and secondary students gave mathematics and science the highest rating of all the alternative proposals. The new Academy of Mathematics and Science will provide an opportunity for students to concentrate in these areas in classes and laboratories.

Most of the activities in this alternative program will be self-paced and individualized to support each student's interests and learning styles. Field experiences will be integrated with in-depth laboratory study. The mathematics and science programs will offer the student increased opportunities to observe and to learn from scientists and mathematicians in the community.

In addition to in-depth studies in mathematics and science, the program will deal with the interdependence of all the fields studied in school. For example, mathematics and science courses might present social implications of applied principles, while an English course might cover the nature of the writings in mathematics and science. As the student continues in the program, specific career emphasis will be stressed.

Because the Academy of Mathematics and Science will be rigorous and demanding, students who apply should have an above-average interest in these areas. The program will begin in September, 1975, with seventh and eighth grades and increase each year until grades 7 to 12 are included.

Eligibility. Understanding that this program will be both rigorous and demanding, all students entering grades 7 and 8 in the 1975–76 school year with an above-average interest in science and mathematics will be eligible. The goal of achieving a racial balance in the school will be considered in the selection process.

Special College Preparatory Program

The concept of a Special College Preparatory Program was developed to provide high-achieving Cincinnati students with an education as fine as that offered anywhere.

The SCPP Program is highly selective. Each winter all sixth grade students take the Special College Preparatory Program (SCPP) test. Trained examiners administer the test and students are notified of acceptance by June. Those who are eligible may attend either Walnut Hills High School for grades seven, eight, and nine, or they may attend the closest district junior high school that offers the program.

After ninth grade, students may continue to attend Walnut Hills High School, or they may return to their area high school. All senior high schools offer college preparatory courses. Unlike Walnut Hills, however, the college preparatory courses offered in the area high schools are open to any student who wishes to be involved.

The SCPP program offers a demanding academic curriculum to its students. There is a strong liberal arts emphasis in the areas of science, music, language, drama, math, history, art, and English.

These special college preparatory students at Walnut Hills and the district schools continue to rank among the top students anywhere in the country in achievement test scores, advanced placement test scores, and college admission test scores.

City-Wide Learning Community

The City-Wide Learning Community is an alternative community resource program offered to Cincinnati students in grades 9–12. The City-Wide experience works to combine learning with urban life. With the help of other students and staff, City-Wide students determine their own school program. A student works in a team of 10–15 students and a staff member. Each student, with the assistance of the staff, decides on a specific area of study. Experiences include individual study, Hughes High School classes, seminars, and contact with resource people. Each course has requirements but these requirements can be met in a variety of ways. Teacher and student negotiate what is to be studied and how the work will be evaluated. Every ten weeks students provide "evidence" of what they have learned. The teacher/coordinator, the student, and other students evaluate the progress. The program meets all state and local requirements. Students receive credit for their work in this school and receive high school diplomas when they complete graduation requirements.

City-Wide utilizes the city and its resources. Students learn to study, make decisions, and to govern themselves. The purposes of this program are 1) to help students become responsible, self-directed learners; 2) to teach students to use community resources; 3) to develop group feelings and social responsibility; and 4) to understand and participate in a dynamic city.

City-Wide opened in 1970 as a non-public resource school. In 1973 some of the staff and students from the non-public school joined the public school system. City-Wide has been based at Hughes High School since that time.

Eligibility. An interview process is used to ascertain each student's preparedness to use the unique structures of this program. The goal of achieving racial balance in the school will be considered in the selection process.

Location. HUGHES High School, at 2515 Clifton Avenue between McMillan and Taft, is about 3 miles north of Fountain Square.

Vocational Education

Vocational Education is one of the oldest alternatives. Today it is one of the most timely. As our economy changes, more people are finding rewarding and satisfying careers with training in job skills that do not require a college background.

Next year, Aiken, Hughes, Western Hills, and Withrow High Schools will have multi-million dollar vocational wings open to students. Plans are in the final stages for an addition to Taft. These facilities provide for students who want to learn job skills, for students who desire higher education in that skill, or for those who plan to go on to college.

In most curriculum areas the vocational wings work independently. They offer similar program opportunities in automotive work, food management, construction, and medical and technical training. Each also offers programs not included elsewhere, such as animal husbandry or horticulture. There are over 23 different occupational programs offered in each vocational wing. Any student attending a Cincinnati high school not offering a certain program may apply to attend a vocational wing that does.

Students attend classes from three to five hours a day. Academic classes are integrated into the student's schedule. Teachers for the vocational classes have at least four years work experience in their fields.

Funds for the construction of the vocational wings came from two sources: one-third from the sale of Courter Technical High School and two-thirds from state and federal vocational funds.

Questions & Answers

Choosing a school program for your child is one of the most important decisions you will make. The following questions and answers may assist you in making this decision.

1. *Will my child learn the basics in an alternative school?*
   Whatever the philosophy, methods, or subjects, all Cincinnati Public Schools are committed to excellence in

the teaching of basic skills. Results to date show that children in alternative schools do as well or better than they did in regular schools.

2. *Who can help me decide which option is best for my child?*

Your child's teacher and principal will be able to help. Specific questions and additional information should be directed to the staff of the alternative school. If you do not know how to get in touch with these people, call the Hotline, 369-4037, for help in arranging contacts. Many of these people will be available at the scheduled meetings.

3. *Who can apply?*

Any child may apply for enrollment in any alternative program or magnet school. Each program has its own eligibility requirements. These requirements are described in this report.

4. *How are students selected for an alternative school?*

All applicants must meet the eligibility requirements set for that program or school. These requirements are applied equally to all children. Every attempt is made to ensure that the population in each program is racially balanced.

5. *If my child or I become dissatisfied with an alternative program, can we return to our neighborhood school?*

If you accept enrollment in an alternative program or magnet school, your child will be expected to complete the school year in that program. In exceptional circumstances, the parents of the child and the principals of the alternative and neighborhood school may agree to a transfer during the school year.

6. *Is it more expensive to attend an alternative program?*

There are no tuition charges for any alternative or magnet school for residents of the Cincinnati Public School District. These are public schools.

7. *Can children who do not live in the Cincinnati Public School District apply?*

Yes. If they are accepted, they will pay a tuition fee of approximately $800.00 per year.

8. *How is the staff selected for alternative programs and magnet schools?*

Staff requirements are determined by the area directors and the personnel department. Staff is then selected from both inside and outside the system to provide the best teachers and administrators available.

9. *Can parents become involved in alternative schools the way they do in neighborhood schools?*

Each alternative program and magnet school values parent support. An outstanding feature of all of the new programs is commitment to parent participation.

10. *Will transportation be provided?*

Transportation for alternatives is the same as that for the neighborhood school. Elementary school children are generally provided yellow school bus transportation to the public school nearest their home. Reimbursement may be provided to parents who drive their children. This is in accordance with state and local formulas. Junior and senior high school children use the Queen City Metro routes and are provided reduced fare tokens in accordance with State and local formulas.

11. *How do I apply?*

Application forms are available from any neighborhood school office or by calling the Hotline (369-4037). Application should be returned before May 2, 1975. The earlier the application is received, the better will be your chances of acceptance. Some programs will be filled well before that date. Programs that do not receive adequate applications by that date may be discontinued.

THE ALTERNATE COLLEGE OF STATE UNIVERSITY COLLEGE, BROCKPORT*

BY ARMAND BURKE†

Introduction

After more than a year of planning activities, The Alternate College enrolled its first class of 275 students in Sep-

* Reprinted by permission of the author.

† Dr. Armand Burke is the Provost of the Alternate College of the State University College, Brockport, N.Y. He has taught English for many years and also served as Dean and Vice-President at Brockport.

tember, 1973. Faculty and students looked forward to the first year with high hopes and expectations. We saw ourselves as an academic community part of, but separate from, a much larger college rich in resources and talent. Yet we all wanted more than a larger college community seemed to offer; we hoped for a person-to-person experience in education with the students more heavily involved in the learning process, with a curriculum that attempted to achieve balance among content, skills, and methodology so that the individual student might better become a self-learner.

To prepare themselves for achieving these goals, the faculty read widely in the literature of higher education, conferred with numerous consultants, and visited experimenting colleges which might provide answers. Then, too, we discussed endlessly and challenged one another's notions about the liberal arts experience. At the same time we realized the necessity of functioning within the context of Brockport and State University.

By September, 1973, The Alternate College faculty had put itself together fairly well and morale was high. As self-selected participants in the new venture, faculty saw opportunities to try many ideas about the learning process with highly motivated students in a favorable environment. They hoped that eventually the outcomes of their participation might lead to constructive changes in curriculum and instruction in the larger college.

The Students

Starting in February 1973, The Alternate College began an intensive campaign to recruit students from the entering freshman class. Our aim was to be non-elitist, hoping to recruit a student body similar in characteristics to the entering freshman class in the four-year college. It soon became apparent, however, that our attraction was strongest with a different type of student. As a matter of fact, approximately 60 per cent of our students selected Brockport because of The Alternate College. They tended to be students with slightly stronger academic qualifications than found among students in the four-year college. (See appendix for an academic profile of the entering class.) On the basis of their response to CSQ Form 1, their unique characteristics might be perceived as follows:

(1)   They tend to be more liberal in political attitudes.
(2)   They usually come from urban or suburban homes.
(3)   They tend to come from families with a higher income.
(4)   They are flexible in their attitudes toward family relationships.
(5)   They have given more thought to the choice of a vocation.
(6)   They are interested in academic challenge and are confident of their ability as students.
(7)   They are not strongly interested in extra-curricular affairs.
(8)   They are strongly interested in pursuing graduate study.
(9)   They favor non-traditional approaches to education.
(10) They have a fairly strong interest in cultural pursuits.

How well did these students function academically in their first year? A fairly detailed analysis of academic performance is presented in the Appendix. For the most part, the better-prepared students were most successful academically. Those with marginal academic qualifications often experienced serious problems, and some were counseled out of The Alternate College at the end of the first semester. Students accustomed to a fairly structured learning environment on the high school level also occasionally had difficulty adjusting to the "open education" aspects of The Alternate College's academic program. And the very bright occasionally criticized the absence of self-pacing as a major possibility in the program. On the whole, however, the students were comfortable with The Alternate College; faculty, on the other hand, tended to be enthusiastic about their students.

The Faculty

Starting with a small planning team, a low-keyed effort at recruitment of faculty was conducted during the 1972–73 academic year. An invitation to consider joining The Alternate College teaching staff was addressed to all faculty members at Brockport. The response was positive initially, but when negotiations were undertaken to move faculty to The Alternate College on a shared, rotating basis, obstacles quickly presented themselves. Among these were programmatic needs in the various academic departments or the tenure or contractual status of the candidate. In all fairness, it should be noted that some suspicion of the new experimental degree program existed in the minds of many faculty, partly because of the way in which The Alternate College had been created as a semi-autonomous unit of the larger college.

Those faculty members who eventually joined The Alternate College were firmly committed to attempting new approaches to instruction and content. They were well qualified, capable, energetic, and eager to begin the new venture. This enthusiasm continued throughout the first year and shows little indication of lessening.

Because of the nature of the curriculum, the faculty worked as discipline area teams with at least three disciplines represented on each team. Most faculty members were functioning outside the supporting framework of the academic department for the first time in their teaching careers; most of them found the experience rewarding. Morale continued high throughout the year, partly because of evidence of strong support from the Brockport administration. For example, no faculty member suffered in tenure, increment, or contract renewal decisions. Actually, some probably strengthened their case because of their relationship with The Alternate College.

Nor did the scholarly productivity of the group as a whole seem to be markedly reduced by the heavy commitment to teaching in The Alternate College. A quick review of the faculty progress report files reveals that eighteen faculty members did these things during 1973–74: published or contracted for five books and fifteen articles, presented two public multimedia productions, and had six grant proposals funded. While some of these accomplishments were the result of ongoing projects, commitment to The Alternate College apparently did not discourage or impede scholarship.

Curriculum

The curriculum design for the first year deviated from the conventional in the following ways: courses were organized in time frames of 16, 11, and 5 week modules; a balance was sought to incorporate content, skills, and methodology; the mentor-tutorial seminar served as an important integrating element in the curriculum; opportunity for drop/adding courses was available throughout the first eleven weeks of the semester; and in almost every course a time block was reserved for independent or directed study.

In retrospect the first month was the most critical period for testing the curriculum, since students and faculty were frequently involved in a completely new learning situation. After some minor curricular adjustments or revisions, the academic program in all discipline areas seemed to move along fairly smoothly. By the second semester most of the "bugs" had been worked out. Fortunately, the faculty were free to make changes in curriculum when necessary, although considerable discussion usually preceded such changes. Perhaps the most interesting of these was permitting students who considered themselves "underemployed" to add a module in statistics, computer, or advanced exposition for which they were given two credit hours retroactively. Because of the heavy reading required in the second semester, very few students considered their workload too light.

During the Spring semester, 1974, Levels II and III general education courses were discussed at some length and planning teams organized to establish a rationale for curricular offerings on each level. A major concern of summer planning in 1974 will be development of these courses. Level II courses offered for the Fall semester, 1974, reflect our interdisciplinary bias, but are considered pilot models at this stage of our curriculum development.

Considerable attention also was devoted to revising the Mentor-Tutorial Seminars for the 1974–75 academic year, since it became apparent that we should focus more heavily on the individual strengths and interests of the faculty in developing the seminar format. Prior to registration this summer, each student will select his or her mentor on the basis of the activities and interests to be pursued in the seminar. All seminars, however, will continue to emphasize academic advisement and counseling as an integral part of the seminar experience.

In addition, an Alternate College faculty member will be in residence in a dormitory unit reserved for students who desire a "quiet" living environment. An effort will be made to develop a living-learning environment which encourages a better integration of the academic-social-cultural experiences of our students, with the faculty member serving as a liaison person.

Instruction

From the start, The Alternate College faculty has been committed to exploring different instructional patterns and techniques in order to create an optimum environment for learning, with the student assuming a major role in the learning experience. Early in our planning, we investigated the merits of self-pacing as practiced in California colleges and elsewhere and reached the decision to make self-pacing part of, but not the dominant instructional mode, partly because of our conviction that learning flourishes best in a person-to-person setting. At the same time, we hoped to encourage the students to reach out, to extend themselves, and to assume responsibility for achieving their goals.

Because of our small classes and the Mentor-Tutorial Seminars, the person-to-person relationship was fostered. Within the classroom setting itself, a variety of learning situations developed, according to the background and characteristics of the students and faculty. Some students were not ready to be self-directed learners; some faculty initially were not comfortable with their new role. Much time at staff meetings and student-faculty workshops was devoted to critical discussion of the teacher-student roles in the classroom.

The instructional pattern followed in most courses moved from acquisition of skills and knowledge of methodology, using a specific body of content as subject matter, to independent or directed study culminating in a critique by the instructor or presentation of the project to a student group. A number of devices, ranging from the computer to simulation games, or media technology, were used to support the learning process and to generate greater student involvement. An effort was made in many courses to stress awareness of the relationship between process and the delivery system through identifying the problem, studying or testing alternative solutions, and reaching a decision. Emphasis was on the need to fail occasionally in order to succeed eventually.

Instruction in The Alternate College required considerably

more student-teacher conferences than are normally expected in undergraduate courses. This practice was facilitated by the physical setting in The Alternate College which has instructors' offices and classrooms on one floor. Actually, this space arrangement proved to be a major asset to the entire academic program.

Evaluation

Besides following the guidelines for academic and financial evaluation suggested by the State University-Carnegie Corporation agreement, The Alternate College also used the Student Instructional Report (SIR), its own course and instructor evaluation form, student-faculty workshops, and staff discussion as evaluation devices. Each device contributed valuable insight to the effectiveness of instruction and curriculum, while also encouraging dialogue involving faculty and students.

The results of the initial evaluation of courses and instructors using an instrument modeled on SIR indicated that all three core areas—Science and Mathematics, Fine Arts, Humanities—were judged from better than average to superior. Not a single instructor was judged inadequate, and some rated very high indeed on the five-point scale. Reinforcement of these positive evaluations was found in the forms used for the final student-teacher conferences.

Ironically, the Mentor-Tutorial Seminars, which received almost uniformly high ratings for the first semester, concerned the faculty most during the second semester. How to sustain student interest beyond academic advisement and how to "get close" to students became the topics for one of our most interesting and soul-searching staff meetings. The outcome has been a major shift in our approach to the Mentor-Student-Tutorial Seminar.

On another ironic note, the grading system—non-traditional during the first semester—proved the focal point for furor until a decision was made to return to conventional grades.

On the whole, the results of our evaluation efforts have sustained fairly well the expectations with which we began the academic program of The Alternate College.

Though we have not completed an exhaustive analysis of the financial cost per credit hour generated in The Alternate

College, the cost analysis study prepared by the Office of Institutional Research for the Fall Semester 1973 indicates an instructional cost of $15.11 per credit hour—second lowest in the college at Brockport.

Looking Ahead

As the reader has probably surmised, we are fairly happy with the outcomes of the first year of The Alternate College and believe that many of our expectations have been achieved —if not fully, at least to the extent that we have not become discouraged. There are, however, certain basic concerns which confront us as we look ahead.

1. Student recruitment and retention: Recruiting new students is recognized as one of the truly difficult problems any college must cope with these days. In The Alternate College the student recruitment program is meshed with the overall efforts of the Admissions Office at Brockport. We do not attempt to recruit a specific student unless and until he or she has been admitted to the college, which is usually in February. This is too late in the recruiting season. We need to become involved in recruiting as a year-round program, particularly if we are to enroll an adequate number of students in our Early Admission program.

In these days of uncertainty, retention of students is just as important—or more so—than recruiting them. At the end of the first semester our drop-out rate in The Alternate College was 5+ per cent and the transfer rate to the four-year college another 3 per cent, for a total of approximately 22 students. The most recent figures available reveal the following attrition characteristics for the 1973–74 academic year:

Transferring to other SUNY units	4
Transferring to non-SUNY units (N.Y. State)	4
Transferring to out-of-state colleges	2
Transferring to the four-year college	10
Dropping out permanently	3
Stopping out temporarily	4
	27

Unfortunately, not all students come for an exit interview with the Provost; nor does the data from Student Affairs reach us quickly. On the basis of other available data, we predict that an additional 20–30 students will leave The Alternate College before September, 1974. Hence we project a total attrition rate of 18+ per cent (including transfers to the four-year college) or 10–12 per cent, excluding transfer to the four-year college.

Why do students leave The Alternate College? Those transferring to the four-year college usually desire more time, have changed career plans, or feel too much academic pressure in the TSD program. Those transferring to other colleges often find the Brockport collegial atmosphere distasteful or wish to enroll in an academic program not available at Brockport. Very few leave because they are unhappy in The Alternate College. Quite the reverse—almost every student has indicated satisfaction with most aspects of The Alternate College; some claim the program has helped them find their career interests.

2. Faculty recruitment and retention—All but two faculty members in The Alternate College are associated with it on a shared appointment basis—that is, they spend one semester teaching in The Alternate College and the next in the four-year college. These one-year appointments are made only after careful consultation with the instructor, the chairman of the department, the dean, and the Appointment-Promotion-Tenure Committee of The Alternate College. Although cumbersome and time-consuming, this procedure has worked to the extent that we have been able to staff The Alternate College with highly competent instructors.

A number of factors influenced faculty in their decision to join The Alternate College staff. Most instructors have enthusiasm for what the new venture is attempting and see themselves gaining new expertise and fulfillment as teachers from the experience; some are also influenced by loyalty to an academic department which needs the credit hours generated in The Alternate College in order to strengthen their status as a productive unit. Because of the criteria for professional advancement prevailing in the college at Brockport, all sense a certain risk element in joining The Alternate College staff, a risk which is compounded somewhat by the need to serve two masters, especially when each unit adopts different criteria for rewarding instructors. In actuality, there is strong evidence to allay the fears raised by the apparent conflict in reward criteria, since instructors in The Alternate College have fared well in the reward game. Yet the very existence of dual criteria probably raises doubt in the minds of some potential candidates.

Another concern is the reluctance of academic departments to make a long-range commitment of staff to The Alternate College. Ordinarily, an instructor should remain with The Alternate College for two or three years, but programmatic demands and course staffing requirements in academic disciplines may make such a commitment difficult.

Thus, an adequate staffing policy becomes an unresolved issue, but one that will undoubtedly be resolved in the future.

3. The Alternate College as an agent for change—Originally The Alternate College was viewed by administration as a project encouraging and fostering change in the large college at Brockport. Whether this goal will be gained remains in doubt, although there are signs that progress has been made. On the whole, though, the faculty of the large college apparently has adopted a "wait and see" attitude toward The Alternate College. So many projects are in the planning or developmental stage at Brockport that priority for attention and support becomes a critical issue. Also, the semi-autonomous status of The Alternate College creates an anomalous image in the minds of some people who often tend to equate high visibility with power and subsequent support.

That The Alternate College has served as an agent for faculty renewal cannot be denied. Whether faculty associated with The Alternate College have much impact on their colleagues in the large college is another matter. How effective communication has been with all levels of the large college also could be questioned, but, again, progress has been made in opening better lines of communication. Given the complex organizational structure of Brockport, we realize the task will require patience and sustained effort.

4. Support—Institutional support for The Alternate College has been excellent thus far. Indeed, it is difficult to identify a reasonable request for financial or academic support that has been denied. Occasionally time and argument have been required to make "reason" prevail, but it is difficult to fault the leadership of the college on this point. With the ending of Carnegie financial support in 1975, we shall have to rely heavily on a continuance of this support.

5. New ventures—Part of the reason for our optimism concerning support and The Alternate College as an agent for change is the number of new ventures with which the program has become involved. One of these, Early Admission, has already been mentioned. Another, a pilot program permitting the interfacing of high school and college courses for degree credit, will begin this fall with 150 students in the Greece Public School System. Our joint effort with Student Affairs to create a living-learning environment also has been described briefly. During 1973–74, interesting sharing arrangements were made with Student Affairs to develop new approaches to student counseling. We are also working with new programs for remediation and developmental skills. Our strength is the capability to mount new ventures quickly and to test concepts and practices in a fairly objective fashion. Thus, The Alternate College becomes the laboratory for innovation anticipated in the original proposal.

APPENDIX

PROFILE OF THE ALTERNATE COLLEGE STUDENT
(Class entered September, 1973)

I. *As They Arrived at SUC Brockport*

The first class of Alternate College students arrived in Brockport in September, 1973. They were unique in several ways:

- they were highly motivated
- they were highly vocal
- they came to The Alternate College for two main reasons, namely, interest in the program and interest in saving time.

Their high school records and performance on several standardized tests indicated that they were definitely of a high calibre. The following tables show a comparison with the regular SUCB freshmen.

COMPARISON OF HIGH SCHOOL AVERAGES

Group	Mean	Minimum	Maximum	Sample N
Regular Frosh*	81.92	64.90	96.70	960
Alternate College	83.34	67.70	95.30	188

COMPARISON OF REGENTS SCHOLARSHIP EXAMINATION (RSE)

Group	Mean	Minimum	Maximum	Sample N
Regular Frosh*	153.59	55.00	262.00	1,118
Alternate College	169.30	58.00	261.00	223

COMPARISON OF CEEB-SAT-VERBAL

Group	Mean	Minimum	Maximum	Sample N
Regular Frosh*	454.78	290.00	700.00	326
Alternate College	490.72	340.00	770.00	69

COMPARISON OF CEEB-SAT-MATH

Group	Mean	Minimum	Maximum	Sample N
Regular Frosh*	504.89	100.00	800.00	337
Alternate College	535.00	360.00	760.00	70

COMPARISON OF DECILE RANK IN CLASS

Group	0	1	2	3	4	5	6	7	8	9
Regular Frosh* (1,219)	0.6%	1.3	3.4	5.0	11.2	16.2	20.3	17.4	15.8	8.8
Alt. College (254)	0.0%	0.8	1.2	2.8	7.5	11.0	16.1	23.2	20.5	16.9

* This group included all entering freshmen for which this information was available, but excluded Alternate College and E.O.P. students.

The first day they spent with us was partially used to administer the College Student Questionnaire (CSQ-1). We found that, compared to both national norms and four-year Brockport students in a control group, The Alternate College students generally

- come from urban/suburban settings. They attended a fairly large high school which they feel did a poor job of preparing them for college. A higher percentage did not come to college immediately upon graduation.
- they see their parents as domineering and unapproving of the student's vocational goal, and they feel less compulsion to satisfy their parents' wishes than other students questioned. They come from slightly more affluent families, have more books in their homes, and have a higher percentage of mothers interested in the arts.
- they attach a higher degree of importance to self-discovery, have a greater degree of academic self-confidence, and worry more about finances.
- they are less interested in extra-curricular activities participation.
- they feel that they have greater freedom in making academic choices, and more have a stated goal in law or medicine. They explored more fields than other students before making their choice, and more express a determination to attend graduate school and obtain a doctorate.
- they hold more liberal political views than others, and are less frightened by the idea of a welfare state.
- they oppose objective testing, and favor essays, especially on original research. An opportunity to do independent, individual study especially appealed to them.

II. *As They Completed The Fall Semester*

In November we asked for their impressions of Brockport and found that they were generally satisfied but not ecstatic about their dorm situation, their living conditions, and the food, but they wanted even more cultural and social events.

At the same time we asked their opinion of what they had encountered and assimilated from the mentor/tutorial seminars. The results were overwhelmingly favorable, and over 90% urged its continuance with little or no change.

When their grades for the Fall semester were obtained, the following results were seen:

SUMMARY OF 11-WEEK COURSE GRADES

	# of A Hours	# of B Hours	# of C Hours	# of D Hours	# of E Hours
GSA (2.67) Fine Arts	216	400	356	52	36
GSH (2.87) Humanities	272	432	280	56	4
GSM (2.93) Science/Math	380	280	324	16	32

(Overall cumulative index, both AC and four-year college grades, was 2.87)

THE MOST COMMONLY CHOSEN DISCIPLINES FOR THEIR OPTIONAL
FOUR-YEAR COLLEGE COURSE

Chemistry	99 hours	Mathematics	30 hours
Psychology	51 hours	Sociology	24 hours
Economics	39 hours	Speech	21 hours
Political Science	36 hours	Spanish	21 hours

AREA OF FOUR-YEAR COURSES CHOSEN BY AC STUDENTS FOR THEIR
OPTIONAL FOUR-YEAR COLLEGE COURSE

Sciences and Math	- AC students carried 224 hours in PC courses
Social Sciences	- AC students carried 111 hours in PC courses
Humanities	- AC students carried 66 hours in PC courses
Fine Arts	- AC students carried 38 hours in PC courses
P.E. and Sports	- AC students carried 9 hours in PC courses

III. *As They Completed The Spring Semester*

During the Spring semester the students were asked to declare a major. An interesting fact is that the majors declared fall into exactly the same areas in the same balance as the Fall semester four-year college courses chosen by the AC students (see table immediately above). The distribution of majors is as follows:

Sciences and Math	- 66 majors	
Social Sciences	- 33 majors	
Humanities	- 22 majors	
Fine Arts	- 14 majors	
Human Services	- 9 majors	(this area was only recently opened
P.E.	- 3 majors	to AC students)

There are also nine students who declared an interdisciplinary major, and several who are still undecided or, at least, undeclared.

However, one of the most interesting facts is the choice of a CAM (Contractual Academic Major) by fifty students. These are highly individualized majors, worked out by the students with their mentor and another advisor, to more adequately meet their academic and vocational goals. They range from a fairly intense but relatively traditional Business Administration major, to such diverse areas as:

- Juvenile Deviance
- Music/Psychology/Speech (toward a career in music therapy)
- Language/International Relations (interested in both law school and foreign service)
- Human Services/Ethnic Minority Clientele
- Child Development (wants career in Day Care Center)
- Related Studies in Sociology, Philosophy and Education (wants to work within non-traditional sociological or educational programs)
- Psychology/Art (wants to understand human development)
- Comparative Modernization (covers several Social Sciences areas), and
- Human Services Administration.

The last piece of information we have acquired for our student profile is that gleaned from our administration of the ETS instrument SUR-2, in late April. We had a control group of four-year college sophomores to use for comparison. The results were:

	Social Science	Humanities	Natural Science
Alternate College students	414	431	479
Control group	406	442	468
National norms	389	421	434

Spring semester grades will be available shortly. It will be interesting to see how our students fared in their second semester.

Submitted by: TERESA KNAPP, May 30, 1974

AN ADDITIONAL NOTE: (6/3/74)

After receipt of grades for courses taken during the Spring semester, eight students will be placed on academic probation, and six will be advised of their dismissal and of their right to appeal this decision.

"FIVE O'CLOCK HIGH"*
LETTER FROM DR. GARY CAMERON,
PRINCIPAL†

Sunset High School
401 South 9th Street
Las Vegas, Nevada 89101
Telephone: 702-384-7147

May 21, 1975

Mr. Mario D. Fantini
State University College
New Paltz, New York 12561

Dear Mr. Fantini:

"Five O'Clock High", or as we call it, Sunset High, was organized and began in the Fall of 1970 for the purpose of providing an additional opportunity for kids who, for one reason or another, found it necessary to leave the normal day school operation.

The program was not initially, nor is it now, set up as a haven for discipline oriented students. The program is simply an alternative during the evening hours. We do have a good share of students who have dropped out and have chosen to return to school.

With the exception of no interscholastic activities and athletics, our program is much like any other comprehensive high school in our District. The requirements for graduation from our school are exactly the same as any other high school in our District.

We have made attempts to individualize our subject matter as much as possible, and we have broken our curriculum into four 9-week quarters. This provides our students the opportunity of realizing success and the accumulation of credit to-

* Reprinted by permission of Dr. Gary Cameron.
† Dr. Gary Cameron is Principal of Sunset High, Las Vegas, Nevada.

wards graduation in small increments, rather than the traditional semester or yearly credits. It also provides us flexibility in students meeting graduation requirements, and allows us the opportunity to enroll new students at the beginning of each 9-week period.

Our basic hours of operation for kids are from 4:30 P.M. to 10:00 P.M., Mondays through Thursdays. School is not in session on Fridays. Initially, kids were required to attend the program on Friday nights but the attendance was so low that we finally received permission to stage our program for four nights a week. We do have an extremely high absence rate, with an average daily attendance running from 70% to 80%.

Our Student Body is made up of Grades 10 through 12, with almost half of our students being seniors.

In addition to the normal academic program, Sunset High School coordinates and supervises a District program for pregnant girls. Next Fall, we will institute an Honors String Music Program, where outstanding musicians from throughout the District may come together in an Honors orchestra.

We have eight full-time teachers and thirty-two part-time teachers. Our curriculum offerings include a normal range of high school level courses, with an emphasis on basic diploma requirements. We do offer some courses above the basic level, but very few of our students are college oriented, and thus we have very few upper division offerings. Less than 15% of our students plan to attend college.

The funding for our school is exactly the same as that of any other high school in our District. We merely receive an allotted amount of money for the various categories of instructional supplies, library books, text books, equipment, etc.

Sincerely,

Dr. Gary Cameron, Principal
Sunset High School

GC:gc

Section IV

IMPLEMENTATION OF PUBLIC
SCHOOL ALTERNATIVES

EDITOR'S COMMENTS

As alternative public schools were implemented, we started to get reports from the field concerning their development. It is one thing to talk about an idea for an alternative school, to articulate a philosophy, and to put into writing what you hope the school would look like; it is quite another thing to try to carry it out. How does one go about designing and initiating a new type of educational enterprise? What are the steps that one has to consider? What are the developmental problems that can be anticipated? In this section, the reader will be exposed to procedures for implementing alternative schools. The articles reflect a range of considerations—all the way from guidelines that school boards might want to consider, to the governance structure within an alternative school. Included also are issues of selection of students, how they are grouped; teachers, how they are selected, oriented, and the like. Naturally, the ideas from this section are just that. There are a few "cookbook" approaches to implementation of alternative schools.

At best, the reader will be stimulated to think about the various aspects which impinge on the development of an alternative school. These elements may look different in different locales. Consequently, one is cautioned against trying to follow step-by-step prescriptions. Rather, the hope here is one of developing an awareness to the dimensions of planning and implementation. There are other aspects in the planning and implementation which may not be fully reflected here, such as political considerations, which will be highlighted in Section VIII. The same can be said for the economic considerations, which will be discussed in Section VII.

Here again, this section will deal with such questions as:

What is the first step?

Who must be involved in the planning process?

Why is active community involvement important?

What are some of the major problems?

Why is a strong leader necessary?

How can visiting existing alternatives help?

What steps did some schools take?

How can planners avoid common problems?

What are some requirements to remain within the system?

How can the program receive accreditation?

DESIGNING AND IMPLEMENTING ALTERNATIVE SCHOOLS*

BY BRUCE HOWELL†

Four components that can be identified in the process of designing and implementing an alternative school are need, interest, organization, and accountability. They interface sequentially and in effect point up the basic differences between the comprehensive and the alternative school.

Emerging Needs of Students

The comprehensive school by definition provides something for everyone through a smorgasbord approach under a single administration. Needs, interest, organization, and accountability for this school have evolved through the inconclusive process of "averaging" the requests of the masses. From this list of "average" requests, the term "average" is fundamental to the design of the comprehensive school. Conversely, alternative schools have emerged as the result of unique and contemporary needs of students.

These needs are identified, then clustered within a narrow scope of specific objectives. For example, an alternative school that focuses on high school dropouts will function under different objectives from one designed for black studies or creative arts. As a result of identifying these special needs the great American dream of education for all has simply been modified from molding all students around the mythical national average where all conform to a common standard, to identifying unique student needs and molding the program and schedule accordingly.

In discussing the grouping of students by identified needs, we must clarify that the need must be that of *students,* not of the *organization.* This aspect became quite evident to Tulsa,

* Reprinted by permission of author and *National Association of Secondary School Principals Bulletin.*
† Bruce Howell is Superintendent of Tulsa, Oklahoma, Public Schools.

Ok. educators in their experience of organizing two quite different alternative schools. The first, a Metropolitan Learning Center, was formed to meet a desegregation order at previously all black Washington Senior High School by encouraging white student enrollment. A more flexible schedule and a unique "living cities" curriculum were used as enticements for enrollees.

The program at the "metro" center did not succeed for several reasons, predominant among which was the fact that it did not focus on the needs of a particular group of students. Instead, it was a vehicle for socioeconomic intermix. This rather unique curriculum was implemented for a heterogeneous student ability and interest range, students whose only common characteristic for enrollment was that they must be white. Tulsans learned that color alone was not a good criterion for the identity of an alternative school student body. The brief duration of the "metro school" made it evident that the foundation of the successful alternative school must be based on student needs, not institutional ones. The second example, a dropout high school, will be reviewed in more detail later.

The Importance of Interest

Identifying everyone's interest in developing an alternative school is just as important as determining the need for such a school. Interest must be evidenced by the administrators and potential faculty members, and equally by students who seek that particular alternative as a learning opportunity. The educator can serve as catalyst for interest in options and he can develop the program, but he cannot ensure student attendance. Assessing interest and ensuring commitment is fundamental to the success of the school.

One indicator of interest is the budget. The budget of an institution will usually reveal its priorities. The commitment that boards of education and communities have toward the alternative school concept can be measured in direct proportion to their financial support. Is the project subject to the capricious funding from some temporary federal source or is it a part of the local funds? The hackneyed phrase "put your money where your mouth is" couldn't be more appropriately applied. Another factor concerning interest regards administrative approval. The assignment of staff, allocation of materials, and the facilities that are provided are all indicative of the committed support given to this type of school.

Lip service has been given to worthy efforts in many school districts, but often these efforts still flounder and fail. Do local educators regard the proposed alternative as just another example of contemporary faddism? Are central office personnel committed philosophically to be liaison agents and expeditors for staff members assigned to the program? Who will be held accountable for the success (or failure) of this project? Are teachers selected because of their interest and competence, or are they chosen from the ranks of those glib job seekers with a missionary zeal who are always available? The degree of involvement, commitment, and organization at the administrative level can either ensure or destroy an alternative program.

To this point, the process for initiating an educational option has focused on commitment, attitude, and understanding through identity of needs and interest. The case for these components cannot be overstated, since the initial implementation of any alternative will, at best, be fraught with growing pains. These crises can only be resolved if there is a sincere and continuing commitment of those involved.

Organization as an Ingredient

Assuming the commitment, organization is the next component to be identified and defined. The new educational endeavor should be developed on the basis of these questions:

- What is the purpose of this alternative?
- What is the program of studies?
- How will it be implemented?
- How will it be evaluated?

Those who organize an alternative school should first state its purpose, then design and implement a support system that will meet that purpose, and finally determine how success or failure will be measured.

Project 12, a second alternative Tulsa high school, implies by name its purpose, which is to provide an opportunity for dropouts to complete 12 grades and graduate. The question that resulted in the program was: How can a program be developed to encourage dropouts who have been "turned off" by the system? A local survey indicated that students dropped out because they were either bored with the set-up, were forced to go too slowly because of group pacing, or were pushed beyond their immediate capacities. Students commented also on teacher apathy and lack of opportunities to participate in co-curricular activities because of minimum grade requirements. It was agreed that Project 12 would avoid these pitfalls.

As a result, two teaching strategies were identified for courses, one that utilized continuous progress and a second, experience spiral, that permitted recycling on a level of increased sophistication. All activities were opened to any student who wished to participate. School rules were developed by a joint committee as needed, but held to a minimum.

A director of the Project 12 alternative school was appointed and assigned the responsibility of serving originally as coordinator and catalyst for priorities, course identity and objectives, staff selection, schedule development, and student selection.

Identifying Quantitative Standards

Upon identifying a procedure for curriculum development and selecting staff, the director was able to focus on identifying three quantitative standards for operation and then developing a master schedule. The first standard concerned student admittance criteria. These criteria included:

- students with the least course graduation needs
- age (21 or younger)
- date of drop (at least six months prior to application to "12")
- identified interest and previous achievement
- a graduate of junior high school.

The second standard regarded course offerings in terms of time duration. In some instances, courses are specifically designated by state or regional accrediting agencies in terms of minutes in session per week. This quantitative regulation presented particular problems with respect to the courses developed for a continuous progress strategy. These courses are designed on a sequence of performance-based criteria that encourage students to advance at their own pace, not in terms of minutes in class. The problem was ultimately resolved by allowing two options to students who satisfactorily met the minimum performance criteria for a course: (1) to either develop an indepth independent study contract with the instructor on an area of particular interest or, (2) to combine the completed course time in the same broad area of instruction with one not yet finished.

The third standard can be labeled legitimization. Legitimization is an extremely important aspect in the process of organization. It is imperative that the alternative school meet the standards of acceptance whether state imposed, community assumed, or peer devised.

In order to centralize records, provide a reference for post high school student needs, and ensure students with a source of accepted identity, a "graduation" high school was identified. The selection of an established comprehensive high school as a "record" center is in keeping with the alternative school philosophy. Educational alternatives must emerge as options when needed, but the school officials must be prepared to dissolve the school when they no longer meet student needs. If this occurs, student records providing pertinent data and evidence of graduation will always be available.

Developing a Master Schedule

After assimilating course objectives, an outline of activities, and quantitative standards, the director of Project 12 then developed a master schedule, determined maximum class enrollment, and projected total student body numbers. In order to ensure an appropriate teacher ratio (1/10) and time block, a simple four-by-four schedule was implemented morning and afternoon for two separate 40-member student bodies. The student enrollment was maximized at 80 at any one time to ensure adequate personal attention. Of course, as students complete requirements on continuous progress or the experience cycle and graduate, new enrollees are accepted and a constant turnover of students occurs.

Determination of a source of funds for an alternative school should be an early step in the process of development. Definition of the amount must be reflected by the details of the plan. The curriculum for Project 12, for example, enables dropouts to obtain high school education in social studies, mathematics, and language arts. Thus, costs are limited, since laboratories, special shops, and facilities for extracurricular activities are not provided. This basically academic focus permits considerable latitude in selecting the facility that houses "12," an unused elementary school annex. The *annual appropriation* for personnel, curriculum development time, instructional materials, and facilities maintenance totals $65,000.

Evaluating Effectiveness

The fourth and final component in the process of implementing an optional school involves accountability. Some system must be developed for evaluating the effectiveness of the alternative design that will pass professional and lay community scrutiny. Occasionally, alternative programs develop a reputation for being playpens for uncooperative students. Because of negligence on the part of some innovators to build a plan of assessment into their program, inaccurate statements by critics sometimes cannot be refuted.

The "12" plan includes the staff position of school-community coordinator. The role of this specialist focuses not only on obtaining community resources, but assessment of student progress as well. While the usual information on cost, attendance, courses completed, and standardized test scores is available, more impressive data are also compiled. For example, the fact that 200 students have been graduated from "12" is important. But even more important is the fact that several of these would-be dropouts have entered college and 60 to 70 percent are currently gainfully employed in various productive occupations. The assimilation of these facts would be difficult without constant follow-up of individual graduates by the coordinator. All of this information provides an effective answer to critics' questions. It is clear to the community that the purpose of this school is to provide a high school experience for students so that they can become productive citizens.

Summary

Need, interest, organization, and accountability are components that should be considered prior to the implementation of any educational option. The process for assessment and development must vary according to the objectives, needs, and resources of individual school districts. Of course, administrators who are considering options in education should review what others have done prior to designing their own process and think outside the lines of convention. The excitement of the alternative movement results from the unique but meaningful purpose designed for each different school. A stereotype of the alternative school doesn't currently exist; if we're lucky, it never will.

De-Bureaucratize Education

We have but three rules in our school. They are:

- Be there (at school or work as you have committed yourself).
- Be a reasonable and responsible human being.
- Learn something every day (to survive in a complex world).

Within that broad framework all human interactions must be negotiated, acted out, and interpreted. It allows professionally trained teachers to function as professionals rather than rule-book quoters. Tough—you bet! But it is a tremendous incentive to know that you—operating as a human being first and a teacher when you are "in contact"—may have a really positive effect on a fellow being.

—KEN OSWALD, Director
Career Study Center,
St. Paul (Minn.) Public Schools

DECISION MAKING IN ALTERNATIVE SCHOOLS*

BY ALLAN GLATTHORN†

One reason many students and teachers opt for alternative schools is a determination to find a better way of making decisions for themselves and their schools. And it well may be that the most significant characteristic of alternative schools is not their curriculum or community involvement but their governance.

Decisions and Human Values

It is easy to understand dissatisfaction with the governance of traditional schools. Because they are large systems and are part of bureaucratic organizations, most conventional public schools are operated on principles of benign despotism. A school board of adults makes basic policy; an autocratic superintendent manages by fiat; and an authoritarian principal gives directions. Sporadic attempts are made to operate more democratically within this autocratic context: parents play a game called PTA; teachers serve on powerless advisory councils; and students operate councils to raise money and hold dances. And all of it is more ritual than real.

Now it may well be that such an autocratic process of decision making is essential in a large system, but it violates several things we have learned about how decisions should be made in a school concerned with human values. After decades of research into how people function best in a humanizing climate, we can state the following principles with some degree of assurance:

* Reprinted with permission of the author and the *National Association of Secondary School Principals Bulletin*.

† Allan Glatthorn is Associate Professor of Curriculum and School Administration at the Graduate School of Education, University of Pennsylvania. He was previously Director of the Alternative Schools Project.

- People learn as they live. Those who live in a democracy learn to operate democratically; those who live in an autocracy learn to operate autocratically. Insofar as is possible, schools in a democracy should operate democratically.
- Boundaries are needed. Every community of individuals (including schools) needs limits. In a democratic community, those limits should be set by those who are part of that community.
- Leaders lead. Even in a democratic community, someone is in charge. It's always healthier if people are honest about the authority they possess and don't play games of participation with those who have less authority.
- There is no monopoly on wisdom. Problems are best solved when all competent and informed people pool their insights.
- Students are people. Like the rest of us, they are more likely to support and implement those decisions in which they have had a voice.

Now none of this is brand new. In fact, it all sounds as if it had come out of a primer on the democratic society. But those of us who have worked in alternative schools have found that these principles are more than rhetoric. They are reliable guides to practice, and, given the appropriate organizational structures, they can form the basis for a self-renewing society.

What are those appropriate organizational structures? Every alternative school develops its own decision-making groups and its own nomenclature, but the following structures seem to be most common and most functional.

The Board and How It Functions

Called variously the "community board," "board of trustees," or "board of directors," this group of individuals determines policy for the school. Even when the alternative school operates within a public school system directed by an adult school board, it will often have its own board making policies that apply only to the alternative school. Typically, board members are elected, not appointed; they operate with their own by-laws and meet periodically to conduct official business.

In many alternative schools board members are elected from the community to ensure community control. In others the board will include representatives elected from among students, teachers, parents, and other constituent groups. (In alternative schools affiliated with public school systems, district administrators and/or school board members often have representation on the alternative board.)

Jonathan Kozol in his book, *Free Schools,* wisely points out the dangers of a large, prestigious board, and advocates instead either a small, benevolent dictatorship of the 8 or 10 core people in a school or a revolving board elected by those who are studying and teaching in the school. His point seems well taken. Large political boards composed of conflicting interest groups often become locked in internecine power struggles. But small boards, drawn from the school's constituencies and sharing common goals, seem to be effective stabilizing forces for otherwise unstable schools.

The Director's Role

In almost every successful alternative school there is some designated leader called director or head teacher. Several alternative schools have tried other leadership patterns; some use a two-man team (an "inside man" and "outside man"), some use a small group of "managers," and others seem to thrive for a while on anarchy. But almost all discover somewhat painfully that there has to be one person in charge.

Two other lessons can be learned about leadership from alternative school experience. The first is that the leader must be an integral part of the community, spending full time in that school. Schools that have operated with a part-time director dividing his time between two or three units or with a remote leader trying to administer from the main building have found out that such schemes just don't work. Even in small alternative schools it is better to have a teacher on site devote part of his time to unit leadership than to have a part-time director run in and out one or two days a week or to have someone out of touch with the unit try to govern it.

The other lesson is that the leader will be more effective if he or she has been chosen by the staff and if there is a specific term for his appointment. It often happens that a skillful leader appointed by some outside authority (such as a district superintendent) can successfully enlist staff support from the outset and in effect function as one of the staff. But the chances for harmonious relationships seem greater if the staff has had an active part in the selection of their director. And a limited term of office, perhaps for two or three years, is one way of guaranteeing self-renewal through leadership change. Even a successful leader should surrender his position simply to ensure that a fresh perspective is brought to the school.

The Group, Family, or Tribe

Somewhat analogous to the homeroom in the conventional school, the group (sometimes called the tutorial, the counseling group, the family, or the tribe) is the basic organizational unit for the school. Like the homeroom, the group is the locus for such routine administrative business as checking attendance and disseminating information. But in the alternative setting, it is different from the typical homeroom in quite significant ways.

First, it meets on a regularly scheduled basis for an hour or two each week. Second, it is a structure where much group guidance takes place. Third, it becomes a significant channel for home-school communication. Also, it becomes the primary group where the student makes friends and builds social relationships. And finally it plays a key part, as we shall see, in the decision-making process.

Clearly, such an organizational structure as the group can discharge all these important functions successfully only if optimal conditions prevail. Teachers should get explicit training in group processes to help them weld a collection of individuals into a cohesive group. The groups should probably be as heterogeneous as possible, reflecting the composition of the entire school. Through such heterogeneous core groups, the staff can probably accomplish a great deal in breaking down the stratification that inevitably develops even in small schools. Finally, the groups should meet on a regularly scheduled basis, perhaps for an hour twice a week—enough time to get important tasks done but not so much that boredom ensues.

The Town Meeting

Sometimes called the forum, the community meeting, or the assembly, the town meeting is the gathering of the entire school community. In some alternative schools, the town meeting meets on a regular schedule, such as the first hour every Monday morning; in others it meets only when there is an important reason for it to meet.

Whether scheduled or unscheduled, the town meeting plays an important part in the life of the community. It is an effective means for disseminating information quickly to a large group. It can be a place where students can have useful experience in leading and directing a large group. It can be the structure through which enthusiasm is engendered and school cohesiveness is developed. And it can play a critical role in the decision-making process.

But in many alternative schools students will freely tell inquiring visitors that the town meeting is a waste of time. And even the sympathetic observer, as he sees the mindless wrangling, the angry speech-making, and the adolescent pontificating, is inclined to agree. But these difficulties can be minimized with some simple precautions. Students and staff can develop some basic groundrules for the conduct of the meeting and the handling of business. Strong student leaders can be given special training to enable them to function more effectively with an audience of 100 or more excited peers. And student and staff observers can take a few minutes at the end of each meeting to give the entire group some honest feedback about the processes used and the progress accomplished.

Committees Are Indispensable

No democratic society can exist without committees, and alternative schools are no exception. In fact it seems at times that every student in an alternative school has his name on at least two committees. Some alternative schools operate with a large number of standing committees, usually in such areas as curriculum, building and grounds, community relations, budget, evaluation, sports and activities, transportation, governance and government, and scheduling. Other alternative schools have few or no standing committees but instead convene *ad hoc* task forces to address specific problems as they arise. "Anybody interested in improving the transportation situation come to the lounge at 2:30 today!"

Whether standing committees or *ad hoc* task forces, these committees as they are found in alternative schools are composed of staff and student volunteers, are often chaired by a student, not a teacher, and do much of the real work of school governance. In fact it is often the case that a few active committees in an alternative school are doing most of the dirty work that needs to be done.

The Staff Meets

Much of the important day-to-day decision making takes place in staff meetings. In fact a common complaint of alternative school teachers is that they spend more time in staff meetings than they do in classroom sessions.

Such a condition is easy to understand. In a small staff of strong-minded adults, opinions are likely to be vehemently expressed and feelings openly vented. With a staff that believes in participatory decision making, even trivial issues seem to warrant extended examination and debate. And with a staff that welcomes students at staff meetings as a manifestation of openness, the large size of the group often inhibits the efficient accomplishment of business.

But such problems can at least be ameliorated. The staff itself can decide that they will hold one required meeting each week for purposes of decision making, with time limits clearly set; others who want to gather to examine their psyches can do so as they please. An agenda can be developed cooperatively, with a time limit set for each item. The person who adds an item to the agenda can be given the responsibility of leading discussion on that item. And some simple means of checking attitudes—such as an informal show of hands or a quick polling of all involved—can cut through the red tape of parliamentary procedure.

So the names may vary, and the details of their operation may be dissimilar. But almost every alternative school develops the same basic organizational structures: a policy-making board, a leader, a staff, a meeting of the entire community, a primary group, and special committees.

How can such organizational structures be made to function

effectively in the decision-making process? Although there is no one best pattern applicable to all schools, a distillation of the experience of successful schools suggests that such procedures as the following will probably work with a high degree of effectiveness.

The Boundaries Are Set

All those who are to play a significant part in the school—students, staff, and parents—meet at the opening of the school to set the broad boundaries in which the school will operate. By meeting in small work groups and then by considering together the recommendations of the several groups, the community develops tentative answers to such basic questions as the following:

1. What general processes should be used in making decisions? What authority will the board have? How much power should the director have? What decisions will be made by the staff? How will major decisions be made by the entire community? In what areas and in what ways can parents be involved?

2. What boundaries already exist for us? What federal directives, state laws, and local ordinances most critically affect us? Is there some superordinate group—such as a school board—to which we are responsible?

3. What basic groundrules do we need for people's conduct and behavior? (Most alternative schools develop one set of rules for students and teachers alike.) What stance should we take on such problems as class cutting, drugs, smoking, stealing, fighting, and vandalism?

4. By what processes and under what policies should we deal with those who consistently violate the boundaries? Under what conditions will we ask someone to leave the school? While some schools desire to be inclusive communities that never ask anyone to leave, most find it essential at some point in time to exclude those whose conduct threatens the existence and welfare of the community. And such a contract needs to be spelled out in advance.

5. By what processes and how often should these boundaries be reviewed and revised? Such a review is so essential that it must be planned and legitimized during this critical boundary-setting process.

In this fashion, then, the entire school community develops the basic contract by which it will live.

The Board Organizes

With this basic contract developed, the board organizes itself for its business, developing its bylaws and electing its officers. Many of the early board policies will be developed simply by ratifying and codifying the major parts of the contract previously developed. But the board will also want to focus more specifically on personnel and fiscal matters that require more official action.

Problems Are Solved

With such preliminary groundwork accomplished, the school can now develop its basic problem-solving and decision-making process, which might go something like this:

1. A problem surfaces. In an open environment problems will readily come to the surface. Sometimes they might get first formal notice in a group meeting, sometimes in a committee meeting, a class, or in a town meeting. Some problems are so small that they get solved at this stage by immediate action. Others are so trivial that they fade away without any action.

2. The problem is brought to the attention of the community. The more serious problems are presented in town meeting.

3. Someone in charge decides how the problem should be dealt with. Some problems require direct action by one individual. ("The toilets don't work." "Get a plumber.") Some can be dealt with on the spot by a quick polling of those present. ("We need more time for this town meeting." "How many feel we should extend our meeting time right now?") But major problems should not be acted on without further study. ("Our evaluation system needs improving." "Let's study it first.")

4. A group of interested people study the problem and get the necessary data. The director or the person in charge either refers the matter to a standing committee or creates a task force to study the problem. "All those interested in studying

ways to improve our evaluation system meet with Warren tomorrow at 2:30 in the lounge. We'll expect a report within two weeks."

5. The task force presents its recommendations. For important and complex problems, where the recommendations themselves are likely to be complicated, it seems best to have the task force report presented in writing to the core groups. In the small group settings time can be taken to be sure that everyone understands what is being proposed, and everyone present can have an opportunity to respond and react. With major questions that will have a significant bearing on the life of the school, the task force will probably want to get feedback from these small groups before developing its final set of recommendations.

6. The recommendations are acted upon at town meeting. By this time, we hope, everyone has had a chance to understand, review, and respond to the recommendations, so that the discussion at the town meeting should be focused and constructive. And in order to avoid the divisiveness that often results from a decision by majority vote, most alternative schools will take affirmative action only if two-thirds or three-fourths of those present in town meeting approve the recommendations.

Such a procedure need not be inflexibly followed, in alternative schools or in regular schools. But all effective decision-making procedures will probably involve some processes where the following steps are taken in sequence:

1. Once a problem has been identified, a decision is made about its importance.
2. For all important problems, data are gathered and alternatives are examined.
3. A specific set of proposals is developed to deal with the problem; these proposals are reviewed and discussed in a small group setting where it is possible to ensure rational discussion and reasoned debate.
4. A final decision is made only when an overwhelming majority of the community is willing to support a position.

As perhaps can be seen, such a decision-making process can be time-consuming and complex. It would be more efficient to have all decisions made by the director. It would be more democratic to have all major decisions thrashed out in town meeting. But neither efficiency nor democracy alone is enough. We must instead develop some decision-making process like the one described above that meets the following criteria:

- It is efficient enough to keep the school functioning effectively without consuming too much time.
- It is rational, examining all alternatives, gathering significant data for each option, predicting the consequences of all actions, and choosing logically that option most likely to bring about desired action.
- It is humanistic, involving all those who will be affected by the decision.
- It is unifying, not devisive. All who care about the issue have a chance to be heard, all sides are carefully explored, and no action is taken unless a substantial majority support it.

Any process that meets these criteria, regardless of the structures used, will be a good one for both alternative schools and conventional schools as well.

SELECTIONS FROM "IT WORKS THIS WAY FOR SOME: CASE STUDIES OF FIFTEEN SCHOOLS"*

BY MICHAEL BAKALIS†

Introduction

It works this way for some is a resource for people who are actively engaged in starting new educational programs in their schools, including parents, students, teachers, school of-

* Reprinted with permission of the author and Center for New Schools, Chicago, Illinois.
† Michael Bakalis is a Visiting Professor of Education at Northwestern University. He is also Director of the Eli Lilly, Northwestern University, Project for Alternatives and Options in Public Schools of Education.

ficials, and community leaders. The book focuses on some of the particular problems facing school planning groups in the Illinois Network for School Development (INSD). However, other people concerned with starting new programs within elementary and secondary systems will find much useful information included here.

It works this way for some describes how people have gone about starting new programs and what issues they have encountered in the process. While plans, descriptions, and evaluations of many school programs are currently available, very little of this information analyzes the nuts and bolts of building a new program. It is this development process that is of most concern to planning groups. This book provides ideas about developing new learning programs that are based on the actual day-to-day experience of the fifteen schools.

The information was collected by visiting fifteen new school programs in Illinois and adjacent states, and by talking with the people who had a direct role in devising these programs. In the course of visits and discussions, three overall topics were explored:

1. What did you do to plan and to set up your program?
2. What problems and what successes did you have?
3. What insights and advice do you have that would be useful to groups who are planning new programs?

The initial plan for this book was simply to present fifteen case study descriptions. As work progressed, it became apparent there was a set of key issues that many schools had faced in planning and in implementing their plans. We decided to raise these issues before presenting the case studies to give the reader a framework for studying the school descriptions and to aid the reader's own planning efforts. Thus, Part One presents the issues that appeared most important to school planning groups. For each major issue there is discussion of the common concerns, difficulties, and pieces of advice that were recorded on our visits. Part Two presents the case descriptions of the schools.

Each of the fifteen schools worked in a unique situation. New planners also have their own specific situations they must consider. Thus, prescriptions from the experience of other planning groups about what you should do could be misleading. This book is not a "how to do it" or recipe book for starting new programs. However, despite local differences, new programs face many of the same issues. Information about what people have done, what difficulties they have encountered, and what advice they would give should be of real help to others planning new learning programs.

It works this way for some is designed to be read all the way through. It is organized so that information about a specific issue can be examined when a planning group confronts that issue. The information presented should help you put a given issue in the perspective of other peoples' experience.

In working toward resolution of a given problem, planning groups should consider other resources as well. Complementing *It works this way for some* is the resource catalogue, *Planning for a Change,* which lists and describes some of the publications, films, and other resources that people who planned new programs said were particularly beneficial to them. Of course, there are many other sources of information that may be helpful, including visits to schools, discussions with people who have planned educational programs, and consultants with specialized skills.

It works this way for some is intended as a conduit of past experience to stimulate, question, and support your planning efforts.

Part One presents several key issues that each of the fifteen schools encountered in planning and carrying out a new learning program. In a brief discussion of each issue, we point out typical experiences other planning groups have had and the lessons they have drawn from their experiences. We hope to alert you to some key ideas you may want to consider in more detail in light of your particular situation.

This discussion of issues also serves to introduce Part Two, where isolated issues are put back into the perspective of real schools.

I. Getting Started

Like your own schools, each of the fifteen schools got started within a unique situation. Therefore, none of the fifteen can be presented as a model for others to follow. However, there are certain issues involved in getting a new learning program started which recur in the fifteen schools and which may be useful for you to consider. Brief histories of how each school got started are included in the school descriptions in Part Two.

Issue 1: Leadership. Strong leadership was crucial in the establishment of every school. Initiators of the idea for a new school program included superintendents, principals, teachers, students, community leaders, and parents. Some initiators had run schools for many years, while others had little previous experience in education. Leadership style varied considerably from those who singlehandedly pushed their ideas through to completion to those who created a planning process which divided responsibility and stimulated the active participation of many people. Given this diversity of successful leadership style, it is difficult to generalize accurately about what aspects of leadership you as a planner should consider. We will chance three observations.

1. If the school or program relies on the dynamism of one person, it will be greatly weakened when that person leaves. An essential outcome of the process of establishing a new program is the translation of the idea into an actual human organization which does not rely on one individual. Still, in many instances, a personal dynamic style of leadership has been effective and was perhaps the only style that could have started the school. If your key leader has this style, you and the leader might give special attention to the question of building an ongoing organization that will not depend so much on the leader for continuation.

2. Sometimes the director who implemented the program was selected at the beginning of the planning process and sometimes during the process. Both of these approaches worked better than selecting the director after the planning process was complete. Direct involvement of the director in planning greatly increased the likelihood that the program would be carried out consistent with the planning.

ITEM: A principal was handed a set of plans by a planning group and told that his job was to implement them. His role in the new school was confusing to him and to others because he had not been involved in the planning stage and neither his understanding of the plans nor his authority in relationship to the planning group was clear.

3. Regardless of the characteristics of the school's director, the full support of the district's school officials greatly eased the planning and implementation process. In the eyes of the people directly involved with the programs, the most helpful district leadership allowed the planning group considerable autonomy to develop their own direction, and then helped the school deal with changes in school system procedures necessary to carry out the program. Supportive district school officials attempted to see the school from the perspective of those who worked in it directly.

Issue 2: The Planning Group. Planning groups were established as part of the planning process at almost all of the fifteen schools. The groups varied greatly in how they were started, who the members were, and what role they played in the planning process. Some groups were intended to legitimize plans developed by a few members of the group or even by people outside the group. These groups met infrequently and reviewed and usually approved plans already developed. In other situations leaders attempted, with various degrees of success, to actively involve a wide group of people in making key program decisions. These groups met frequently, and the meetings focused on the active development of various program possibilities.

Most of the schools, in retrospect, feel that wide involvement in planning is a more advantageous approach. The schools that in fact used this approach recognize the frustrations and difficulties involved in carrying it out. Their reasons for favoring this approach are that meaningful involvement develops strong support for the program, and that the resources of diverse experience, ideas, and energy available for the task greatly benefit the planning process. You might consider the following three areas when thinking about the planning group:

—The segments of the community to be represented.
—The amount of power the planning group has to make key decisions.
—Ways to help the planning group work effectively together.

1. Who should be represented? The four groups of people usually included in planning groups are teachers, parents,

administrators, and students. Teachers in the new program were included because most of the schools developed new roles for teachers, which gave them a great deal of responsibility in shaping the curriculum. Teachers were viewed as key to the implementation, and, thus, their understanding of the new program as it was shaped during the planning process was crucial. A negative example follows.

> ITEM: A new team-teaching approach was designed by a planning group with no significant input from the teachers. When the teachers were asked to implement it the next fall, they were less than willing. Their lack of understanding of how the program was to benefit them, and their feeling that they were being treated as subordinates and not as professionals resulted in only minimal cooperation. As a result, any real team work between the teachers was slow in developing.

Parents were included because of the range of perspectives they brought to the planning process and because of the importance of parental and community support for new programs.

> ITEM: A planning group neither included nor informed parents about a new program to be introduced in their school the next September. Parents were shocked when plans were announced and attempted to prevent the opening of the program through legal action. When a substantial effort was then made to involve them, their resistance faded and many eventually became program supporters.

Administrators were included because their day-to-day support of the programs was considered crucial. If administrators were simply informed of the group's work, they had less understanding of the issues the group was struggling with and less stake in seeing the program succeed. When administrators were excluded from the planning group, the group found it had to direct considerable energy to negotiating the establishment of the school with the district's administrators.

Students were included because some groups felt the best way to insure that the planning group consistently focus on the central issue of improving the quality of education for students was to have them present. Students were included more often in the planning of high schools.

2. The planning group's power to make key decisions. In

some schools, the planning group had the power to make decisions about the establishment of the school. These decisions often included selection of the director, of staff, and of the nature of the educational program. In other situations, the planning group prepared recommendations for others, sometimes the district's superintendent, who then made the final decisions.

It appears that the more decision-making authority given the group, the more effective was the planning process. But whatever the scope of the planning group's power, it appears important that the extent of this power be clear to everyone involved as early as possible.

3. Suggestions for helping the planning group work together effectively. People who have participated in planning with a group which includes parents, teachers, administrators and students make the following suggestions:

a. Provide for strong coordination of the group's work, either through one person or a small committee within the group.

b. Develop as much clarity as possible at the outset as to the group's decision-making powers, its relationship to other involved agencies, the purpose of the planning, the role of people within the group, and procedures for reaching decisions. Clarity does not imply rigidity.

c. Seek people for the group who are respected within their constituency and who have a commitment to the group's task of planning the new program, as opposed to being "drafted" for the task of planning.

d. Develop ways that members of the group can keep their constituency informed of developments; and, wherever possible, involve other people in the group's work.

e. Recognize the different perspectives and experiences that individuals have as strengths for the planning process. One way to put this suggestion into action is to have people take leadership in developing the plans which they perceive will have most direct effect on them. All plans, however, should be subject to final refinement by the complete group.

Issue 3: Setting Goals and Objectives. Virtually all of the people who were involved in the planning felt that the process of setting goals and objectives was a crucial step. It gave clarity and direction to the planning and helped establish a conceptual base for explaining the school to others.

People felt that goals should be as free as possible from educational jargon, and should focus on action, rather than philosophy. Goals stated in terms of what people were expected to do were more useful than those which dealt with ideals or motives. Some groups found it useful to distinguish between kinds of goals. One such distinction is between process goals and outcome goals. Process goals deal with the climate of the school, the way people are treated, the way learning experiences are carried out. Outcome goals deal with the capacities persons would be expected to have acquired because they had been in the program.

Two dangers were raised about goal setting. First, a plan for periodic review of goals should be an integral part of program operation. Experience inevitably suggests new goals or revision of goals that should be formally accepted or rejected. Second, goals and objectives always look good on paper; every school has an impressive list. The hard part is putting them into action.

Some groups carried out formal needs assessment procedures with students and with the community prior to setting goals. Those who took this first step felt it was worth the effort not only because of the ideas they received, but also because it increased involvement in the planning process.

Issue 4: Using Resources Outside the Planning Group. All of the planning groups turned to resources outside the group for help in the planning process. Most brought in consultants. Other ways of getting help included locating resources in the local community, obtaining written materials and films related to the planning group's concerns, and visiting other schools.

Based on their experience, planners had some advice about using consultants. "Before asking a consultant to come in and work, think carefully about what you expect the person to do." They thought it frequently useful to spend planning time with the consultant before his work with the group, discussing your needs and how he can and cannot meet those needs. Consultants were found to be most effective when used to help with a specific problem; for example, developing decision-making skills in the planning group, developing patterns of cooperation among a staff, providing expertise on setting up a particular curriculum such as individualized reading, helping draft a proposal, working on a budget, providing advice on management problems, or designing an evaluation plan.

One-shot appearances are usually not as effective as longer term relationships. A consultant coming in for one day will not have much familiarity with your situation, and will have to present ideas from other situations rather than apply past experiences to your particular situation.

Consider asking other people for consulting help besides the usual professional consultant. One excellent source of people is the planners and staff of an already existing program who are carrying out ideas in which you are interested. Consultants who work from a base of real experience are probably more useful than those who work primarily from theory.

Using resources in the local community proved valuable for some planning groups. Local resources are less expensive and involve more people. Planning groups were able, for example, to find a local businessman to work on budget and management problems, an advertiser to work on public information, and a graphic artist to design an effective brochure about the school plan. Some schools were also successful in directly involving local people in the educational program of the school. Mothers with children in school, college students, older people—all have proven successful if their efforts were well coordinated.

Several planning groups found that visits to new school programs in actual operation were a productive means of getting new ideas and learning about the problems facing a new program. The fifteen schools described in Part Two all indicated they are willing to arrange visits from planning groups subject to limits on their time. Information about whom to contact and about each school's visitation policy is presented with the description of each school in Part Two.

Problems encountered by planners making site visits included the usually very busy schedule of people actually running a new program. People in new programs often feel visitors are nice, but that the school doesn't receive back what it gives in terms of staff time and interruptions that visitors cause. Some groups found they could effectively indicate their appreciation for the help given by the visited school by paying them a small honorarium ($25–$75).

1. One planner who had participated in school visits suggested that visitors should be sure to talk with students regardless of age about what they do. (With, of course, the approval of the host school.)

2. Visitors should be sensitive not to interfere with the daily operations of the school.

3. Another problem for the visiting team to consider is how to share their experiences with people who did not go. When a trip was carefully thought about beforehand by the entire group, and then reported on in detail, this problem was diminished.

4. The problem of receiving visitors is one that a planning group should also consider. Most schools found they had to develop clear policies about visitors to maximize the usefulness of the visit and to minimize the interruption in the school's operation.

Further resources available to you as an INSD Affiliate include the INSD staff in OSPI. Through them the whole range of expertise present in the OSPI staff is available to you. The resource catalogue, *Planning for a Change,* presents films and written material that other planners have found particularly useful. Finally, remember the other planning groups in the Network are wrestling with the same problems as you are, and sharing information with them will be of mutual benefit.

Issue 5: Communicating with the Community. Since all the schools found that community participation in and support of the new program was essential, a good deal of thought and effort has been given to the issue of how to communicate with the community. As described, early direct two-way participation in the planning process and then in the operation of the school greatly enhances community support. Most schools found, however, that they also needed a process for regular sharing of information about the school with parents and the community-at-large. The schools that were most effective in informing their community of their work had a person working half to full time on just this task. Often this person's job was combined with the tasks of recruiting and coordinating community resources, and working with visitors to the school. Some of the specific ways planning groups and operational programs communicated with the community included:

1. Visits to each of the families of students in the school.
2. Carefully arranged small group visits of parents to the school. Great effort was made to insure that every family in the school had visited the new program or was visited at home, if a school visit was not possible.
3. Seminars and workshops for parents.
4. Use of the media: newspapers, radio, and television stories on the school.
5. Frequent public meetings to explain the program.
6. Written descriptions of the plans and of the school's program.
7. Slide tapes, video tapes, and movies of the program available for free showing anywhere in the community.
8. A speakers' program available to community groups.

II. Key Decisions About Students

The planning groups in the fifteen schools made several key decisions about students that shaped later events in their programs decisively.

Issue 6: Selecting Students. Selecting students may not be an issue in schools that serve a set geographic area or already have a student body. Six of the fifteen schools had to devise ways to select students. Different schools used two main criteria for selection: (1) students who volunteered and (2) students selected to match characteristics of the school district's total population on such background characteristics as race, sex, ethnic group, family income level, and previous success in school.

Those who accepted volunteers cite some major advantages. Students who choose to attend a program are more likely to work within it. Further, parents' support is generally stronger if students enter a program voluntarily with parental permission.

Those schools that selected representative student bodies did so either because they saw a diverse student body as an important learning resource for their program or because they wanted to test new ideas with a representative cross section of students, not just a special group.

In practice, accepting volunteers and selecting a representative student body were often combined in a lottery selection procedure. In this method the program was explained to all eligible students, and they were given a chance to volunteer. Students were then selected by chance within categories that reflected the school district's population. Schools felt that random selection has several advantages. It frees administrators or planning groups from going through applications and applying admissions criteria. It also does not discourage present and future applicants, since the only reason a student is not admitted is bad luck.

If you use a volunteer approach, an important problem to consider is whether information about the program really reaches all eligible students. In some cases, administrators and guidance counselors only gave the information to some of the eligible students. In other cases, students who distrusted the school system received the information but did not really see the new program as a real possibility for them.

Issue 7: Grouping Students. All of the schools have attempted to move away from the rigid separation of students by age and tested ability. Some combine students from several age levels into a unit taught by a team of teachers and aides. Within this unit, students are constantly regrouped to learn particular skills or pursue particular interests. Others assign a diverse group of students to one teacher who allows children to work in different learning centers based on their individual needs and interests. Others have created tutoring programs in which students teach each other. Still others have brought together diverse groups of students to discuss personal feelings and problems rather than to study traditional school subjects.

1. Dealing with Diversity: Placing students in diverse groups was valued by all of the schools. The experience of the fifteen schools suggests that creating diverse groups that are effective depends upon many other characteristics of the learning program—the nature of learning materials available, the ability of teachers to keep track of student needs and

interests, the ability of a team of teachers to work together, the ability of teachers to oversee a variety of individual and small group projects going on at the same time. Those schools that were struggling with the problems of working with diverse groups felt strongly that their efforts were worthwhile. Part Two describes many of the specific approaches that individual schools have used to realize the potential of diverse student groups while dealing with the new demands they create.

2. New Purposes for Grouping. While most of the schools are working toward a more individualized program, none is attempting to create a program in which students only worked alone on individual tasks and projects. They have rejected the practice of grouping students merely for administrative convenience, but are seeking new ways in which students can learn together in groups. For example, they are attempting to help students learn to work cooperatively together on a task to see how people with perspectives different from their own view a problem, and to learn to make decisions cooperatively. Thus, group projects and student tutoring are common within the learning program. In addition most schools have created a special kind of group in which students discuss personal interests and concerns, participate in group projects and trips intended to build strong group identity, and get advice to help them make decisions about what they should study.

If you are interested in creating this type of counseling or advisory group, the problem of teacher preparation for working with such a group seems crucial. Several schools originally thought that because a person was committed to being open and human with students, he or she could perform well as the leader of a counseling or advisory group. They found people needed training in specific skills of group leadership, time to prepare carefully for group meetings, and continuing support from people skilled in working with groups.

3. Placing Students in a Group. Very few of the fifteen schools used traditional ability or achievement test measures as the basis for grouping students. Some schools constantly give students specific skill tests and regroup them to learn specific skills which they have not yet mastered (for example, adding fractions with unlike denominators in math). Others

rely more on teacher observations, personal counseling, student and parent choices, or random selection as a basis for grouping. Many schools which started out using one primary method for grouping students are now using a variety of methods, based on what seems most appropriate to a given learning activity.

Issue 8: Developing Student Initiative and Responsibility. A common concern of many schools has been to increase student initiative and responsibility by allowing students to make important decisions about the nature of their own learning program and, in the case of high schools, about school policy.

Several schools were overly optimistic in thinking that responsibility would naturally grow when students were allowed more freedom. In some elementary schools, students were turned loose in a classroom with many materials available and allowed to work with whatever interested them with little guidance from the teacher. In some high schools, students were greeted with a statement something like this: "This is your school. You are responsible for your own learning. You tell the teachers what you want to learn, and they will help find out how you can learn it." No school was satisfied with this approach or continues to operate in this way. Instead, each school offers specific suggestions about how a learning program might be organized to help develop students' capacities for initiative and responsibility for their own learning:

1. Define a clear process by which students can assume increasing responsibility for their own learning. The school descriptions in Part Two contain some examples of the approaches that have been developed.

2. This structure should be carefully explained to students at the outset so they fully understand the freedoms, limits, and expectations involved.

3. Any specific plan you develop will have to be modified repeatedly in light of your own experience and situation. When difficulties are encountered, the school staff should not conclude that students are unable to take responsibility, but rather that a new approach should be tried that is built on past experience.

III. Key Decisions About Teachers

All of the fifteen schools agreed that a most important influence in shaping their programs was the beliefs, commitment, and skill of their teachers. Planning groups made or influenced many key decisions on the teaching issues discussed here.

Issue 9: Selection of Teachers. Teachers in the fifteen schools generally were either selected by the program director or screened by a representative committee which conducted interviews and made recommendations to the director. Current staff, parents, and students were included on the committee. In some schools a subcommittee of the planning group selected the teachers for the first year. In a number of situations, such procedures were contrary to school system policy, in which the central administration made most teacher assignments. People in the fifteen schools emphasized the importance of having those directly associated with the program choose the teachers. Whether selections were made by the director or by a committee the following points about teacher selection were emphasized:

1. Clarity of Expectations: Since new learning programs require teachers to assume new roles and take on additional responsibilities applicants should have a clear understanding of the school's goals and what is expected of teachers. The role of teachers in such areas as planning new learning experiences, making decisions, working cooperatively with other teachers, and working with students in new ways should be spelled out carefully during the selection process.

2. Selecting "Innovative" Staff Members: In choosing a staff, many of the schools were looking especially for teachers who were eager to try new approaches, and who were dissatisfied with conventional education. Based on their experience, the fifteen schools give the following advice to new schools trying to assemble a staff.

    a. In looking back, some people felt they had a narrow stereotype of the type of staff members they were looking for. They felt they had been overly impressed by people who were young, had graduated from well-known universities, and had traveled extensively. They found that in actual practice their most effective teachers came from a much wider variety of backgrounds.

b. Dissatisfaction with conventional education is not enough to make a teacher effective in a new learning program. Effective staff members also could describe, at the time they were interviewed, a number of specific alternative ways of teaching that they were eager to try out. Many had already found ways to try out these new approaches even though they had been teaching in conventional schools.

c. Unique talents are important to a program, but equally important are teachers' abilities to work cooperatively with other teachers and to take responsibility for the operation of the school as a whole. The best teachers combined individual talents with these abilities to work cooperatively.

3. Racial and Ethnic Composition of Staff: Most schools had a commitment to identifying a staff whose racial composition reflected the composition of their student body. In addition, several schools serving significant numbers of students from low-income families or strong ethnic neighborhoods felt it was important to select teachers who had come from similar backgrounds.

Schools found that many people from white middle-class backgrounds applied for staff positions but that they had to persistently recruit teachers from other backgrounds until the staff in fact reflected the desired representation.

Issue 10: Orientation of Staff. The first few days and weeks of a new program are often the most hectic and frustrating for both the staff and students. But this period is critical in shaping the direction of the program and establishing the attitudes of both students and staff.

Several of the programs, usually because of late funding, had to open with little or no orientation or teacher planning period before the school started. These schools feel that lack of staff orientation handicapped their program.

The three objectives of one school's orientation program are representative of those schools that carried out staff orientation.

1. To become familiar with the program. School goals, history constraints and possibilities were explained.

2. To become more effective at interpersonal communication and group decision-making skills. Teachers worked with a consultant in developing these skills.

3. To make specific plans for the school's curriculum. Teachers worked in groups and individually to develop the specifics of what they would teach and what the overall curriculum structure would be.

At the close of the orientation sessions, most of the staff felt the third objective had been more adequately achieved than the first two. They concluded that the first two are long-range objectives and that the orientation provided them with a beginning which needed to be built upon during the year. The staff felt that student participation in the workshop was helpful.

Similarly, other schools which held orientations felt somewhat frustrated that they had not achieved all of their objectives for orientation, but felt the orientation was crucial in allowing staff to develop an initial trust level and the beginnings of a common plan for carrying out the school's program.

Issue 11: In-Service Teacher Education

ITEM: Teachers in an elementary program wanted to find specific ways to share decisions in the classroom with students. Their initial attempts resulted in chaos. They identified a psychologist who had extensive practical experience in helping teachers accomplish this goal. On a weekly basis, he observed in the classroom, and met with the teachers to talk about specific problems they faced and to devise plans for further classroom activity. He continued this process for three years.

This example illustrates many of the characteristics that teachers in the fifteen schools regarded as useful. First the in-service program was in response to a problem they had identified as one with which they needed help. Second, the consultant had both a theoretical and practical understanding of the issues involved in the problem. Third, he combined direct work in the classroom with in-service meetings. The in-service meetings focused on a particular issue yet closely related to the day-to-day realities of working in the program. Fourth, his involvement was both regular and on a long-term basis.

The experience of the other schools suggests that in-service experiences which combine as many of these characteristics as possible are an important asset in the development of a new program, and that resources of time and money should be set aside to create an in-service program of this type.

As in the example above, several schools found that the clear distinctions between in-service education and the day-to-day activities of the teacher diminished. In an environment where people were constantly striving to carry out new ideas, committee meetings to plan curriculum, teams meetings to plan the next day's activities or to discuss the progress of a child, governing council meetings to set school policy, and meetings designed to improve teacher skills or to explore a new idea with an outside consultant all become part of "in-service education" program for teachers.

IV. Key Decisions About the Learning Program

Attempts to change schools have often focused primarily on the non-human aspects of education: scheduling, formal curriculum plans, materials, physical plant, etc. But changes in things don't automatically bring about changes in people—attempts to change schools often exist mostly on paper rather than in the day-to-day activities of teaching and learning. One of the primary reasons that many of the fifteen schools are fundamentally different from other attempts at change is that they have altered the human aspects of education: how students and teachers related to each other in the average classroom on the average day, how teachers and students relate outside class, how decisions are made in the school, how teachers cooperate and share ideas, what part students play in shaping their own education. Curriculum, in the sense of what is planned for students to learn, must be considered, but it cannot be considered in isolation from broader issues of "human reorganization" within the school. Below we discuss some important decisions about the learning program that planners must make in light of the need for broad human reorganization of the school.

Issue 12: Who Decides What Students Should Learn? In most American schools, key decisions that shape the learning program are made by people who do not teach day-to-day. Curriculum guides, materials, daily time schedules, and methods of evaluating student progress are passed down from above. Many of the fifteen schools have now placed these decisions in the hands of teachers and sometimes students. They feel that those most directly affected by the learning program are in the best position to decide how it should be carried out and that teachers and students will take the most initiative and responsibility in creating an effective program when they are acting on their own ideas rather than someone else's.

Many of the schools encourage students to take an active role in making decisions about what they are going to learn. Some approaches worked out by schools with this commitment include: the opportunity to choose between a wide range of courses to meet both basic and elective requirements; individual and group learning projects in areas of student interest; contracts with teachers in which students specify their goals for learning and the activities they will complete to meet them; and courses designed and taught by students.

Schools see several important advantages in student involvement. The student's knowledge of self becomes an important ingredient in designing his or her program. Student motivation to work on a learning task is often greater when he has shaped the task himself. Students learn from the process of making decisions and facing their consequences.

The major problem with involving students in decision making has been described earlier: giving students too much responsibility before they had developed the necessary skills to use it effectively.

Issue 13: The Teacher's Role. All of the schools emphasized new responsibilities for teachers in developing a different approach to learning. In various schools teachers were expected to concentrate on the individual development of each student rather than on the progress of the group; to guide students in self-directed learning activities; to help students deal with personal problems; to work cooperatively as a member of a teaching team; to develop long-term plan for the learning program; to make policy decisions about the school's organization; and to identify and monitor learning experiences beyond school walls.

Teachers found that assuming these new roles was an exciting but often exhausting experience. Many spend a good deal more time at school than others in their school district and emphasize that teachers are willing to commit the extra time which is absolutely necessary to make a new program work. In addition, teachers face constant conflicts about the best way to use their time: should they be checking on absent students, meeting with students on their projects, attending meetings on student evaluation, or planning for tomorrow's math program with their team members?

Issue 14: Selecting and Creating Materials. In all fifteen schools teachers have much greater latitude in selecting materials than in a traditional school setting. Some schools provide each teacher or teaching team with a materials budget they can spend in any way they choose. Many deemphasize textbooks and obtain a rich variety of books, filmstrips, skill kits, and manipulative materials chosen by the teachers and sometimes the students. Some schools have a central resource center that makes such materials readily accessible to teachers and students.

In several schools materials are made by teachers and by students. For example, one school's reading and writing program is based largely on having children write stories and booklets that are then used as reading texts by other students. Such homemade material is cheaper and often more relevant to the students who use it. Furthermore, students and teachers often learn a great deal from the process of creating the materials. However, some feel that an exclusive emphasis on homemade materials can be too time-consuming, and that, in some cases, time is better spent searching for appropriate materials that are already available. Whether materials are homemade or purchased commercially, emphasis is on increasing the variety of materials available and actively choosing materials appropriate for a given child or group of children, rather than passively accepting standard materials that are selected by someone else.

Issue 15: Time Scheduling. New educational concepts create difficult problems concerning the length of class periods, the length of the semester, the best times to offer certain learning experiences, the nature of a teacher's daily schedule, and other issues of time scheduling.

Most schools found it necessary to experiment with different time arrangements before finding one that worked well for them. To achieve scheduling flexibility, some adopted a modular schedule in which the day is divided into (for example) twenty-minute time periods that can be arranged in one, two or more units for different types of classes. Several schools create a new modular schedule for a student each week. Others have created a weekly schedule in which class periods of different lengths occur on different days. Still others have done away with schedules altogether, merely specifying that a student had to complete a certain work contract in a given time or that students had to do a certain amount of math, reading and writing at some time during the day. Flexibility is also obtained by shortening semesters. Many effective means for solving technical problems of scheduling have already been developed. Rather than trying to reinvent the wheel, planning groups should consult books on this subject and, better still, schools that have dealt with scheduling problems similar to theirs.

If teachers are expected to assume new responsibilities, the experience of the fifteen schools insists that time be alloted in their formal schedule for carrying out these responsibilities. For example, teachers developing different approaches to learning need more planning time. Some of the mechanisms schools have used to provide this time have included early dismissal one day a week, scheduled use of substitutes, use of volunteers or aides to replace teachers, and independent study periods or large group presentations that require fewer teachers to be working directly with students.

Issue 16: Using Community Resources. Most schools attempt to make some additional use of community resources, either by bringing them into the school building or by creating learning experiences based in the community. Learning experiences in the community were set up with museums, businesses, hospitals, nursing homes, schools for the deaf, zoos, shops, commercial laboratories, city halls, courtrooms, prisons, and community organizations. Adults with special talents and skills, such as chemists, artists, lawyers, draftsmen, community organizers, auto mechanics, and medical students, worked directly with students either in the school or at their place of work.

In addition to taking major responsibility for learning experiences, volunteers from the community have provided many other types of help to the fifteen schools. They have tutored students, helped teachers in the classroom, made curriculum materials, graded papers, helped with or taken responsibility for public relations, raised funds, written proposals, built furniture, made repairs, and designed new plans for using space.

You might consider the following principles about the use of community resources which are suggested by the experiences of the fifteen schools:

1. If you are going to use outside resources, consider their services as contributing to the basic program, not as an added frill.

2. Provide careful coordination of resources. The programs which used outside resources most effectively have assigned a full-time coordinator for outside resources. The many hours of donated time and the high quality of the learning experiences provided justified the expenses for this person.

3. Volunteers' jobs should be taken seriously by both the school and the volunteer. Volunteers should understand their commitment clearly and be expected to follow through on it.

4. Outside people should be kept informed of schoolwide issues, and assisted to understand how their work relates to other aspects of the school program.

5. Periodic feedback from volunteers on their work and on their observations of the school as a whole should be systematically collected.

An additional advantage the schools have found in making extensive use of volunteers is the increased community understanding and support for the school program that results.

V. Governance

Two key governance issues faced the fifteen schools. One was the extent to which a school could make its own decisions about its operation. The second was how to best develop effective internal decision-making procedures.

Issue 17: Relationship with the School District. For public schools, the local school district's policies toward the school determined the boundaries for the new school's decision making. Some of the local districts required the new school program to follow the same policies and procedures as any other school in the district. Other local districts worked with the new programs to develop special guidelines, allowing the school more autonomy in decision making, but still consistent with the legal responsibilities of the district. In both arrangements, several principles emerged which should be considered by new school planning groups:

1. Develop a procedure to explain the program's purposes and activities as clearly as possible to district officials at all levels. Widespread district support and understanding has greatly assisted those schools that have achieved it.
2. Develop as much decision-making responsibility at the school level as possible. This responsibility should include the design of the educational program, the selection of staff, the methods for reporting student progress, discipline procedures, school calendar, and discretion in spending money within the limits of the school's budget. New learning programs require flexibility in these areas to insure that decisions are directly responsive to the needs of an unconventional program.
3. Clarify as much as possible the limits of decision-making authority that do exist. Frequently, an atmosphere of mistrust occurred between school and district when limits were not clear. These issues should be negotiated by the planners and district officials early in the planning process. The agreed-upon conditions should be carefully communicated to district and school personnel at all levels.

Issue 18: Decision Making within the School. The school descriptions in Part Two provide examples of many structures for internal decision making. In some of the schools the principal maintains formal control, but usually involves other students and teachers in an advisory role. In other cases, the schools have developed a system of governance that places decision-making responsibility with a group or series of groups within the school such as a School Council including teachers, students, and parents or teams of teachers. Regardless of which group or individual has formal decision-making authority, most of the fifteen schools have sought to widen the participation of staff and students in shaping decisions about school policy. (Student participation has been emphasized mostly in the high schools.) Many of the schools believe that staff and students should have a right to shape decisions that affect them and that individuals will take more responsibility in following through on decisions when they have a direct role in formulating them. Many of the schools believe that a basic goal of their work with students is to help them become active, independent, and responsible adults. Direct student participation in decision making is viewed as the most effective means for achieving this goal.

All of the schools experienced significant difficulties in increasing cooperative participants in school decision making.

Most schools have tried several approaches and are still modifying their forms and procedures for governance. Many of the difficulties seem to stem from the fact that neither teachers nor students have had previous experience in cooperative decision making. Another key difficulty has been to develop effective procedures for following through on decisions once they are made.

The following points about internal governance are suggested from the experience of the fifteen schools:

1. Several of the schools started with all-school or all-staff meetings as the formal decision-making body for the school. These meetings proved ineffective as an arena for clarifying issues and making decisions. In some of the schools such large meetings are still held but have become a forum for raising problems, airing complaints, and communicating information, with decision making being carried out by a smaller group.

2. Creating a small, but representative decision-making group, appears to resolve many of the shortcomings of the large group meeting. However, such groups have still experienced formidable problems in making clear decisions and carrying them out.

3. A further problem with a smaller group making decisions is that, while it may include representatives of teachers, parents, and students, it can become cut off from the people it supposedly represents. To deal with this problem, schools have sought to involve many additional people on ad hoc and permanent committees, dealing with such subjects as curricu-

lum, teacher selection, planning the school's anniversary celebration, evaluation, use of the student lounge, and student conduct.

4. In one effective process for reaching decisions, the formal governing group for the school defines an issue that has been brought to their attention. Then, an appropriate committee gathers information about that issue, prepares a series of alternatives, and recommends the policy they favor. Based on this report the governing group makes the final decision, often accepting the committee's recommendation.

5. The relationship of the principal and other administrators to the decision-making process should be clear.

6. Once a decision is made, clear responsibility for carrying it out should be fixed, and the responsibilities it entails for all staff and students should be communicated clearly to them. When decisions are made but not carried out, it undercuts the school's entire decision-making process.

VI. Money

The fifteen schools have experienced problems both in obtaining basic or supplementary funding and in obtaining sufficient flexibility in spending funds allocated to them.

Issue 19: Finding Money. There are no magic formulas for getting money that emerge from the experiences of the fifteen schools. Schools experienced most success in obtaining extra resources locally. Some of the schools were able to secure small grants from local foundations and businesses for specific parts of their program (e.g., a summer workshop, coordination of a volunteer program for senior citizens). Large national foundations are not good sources for funding individual school programs.

One obstacle to securing grants from foundations and businesses is legal prohibitions against their giving money to tax-supported institutions. It might be necessary to set up a foundation independent of the school board to receive such funds. This is not a difficult process and need not threaten the fiscal autonomy of the school district. Foundations set up by state universities can serve as good models and sources of advice. In addition to raising money locally, several schools have been successful in obtaining equipment, material, and services from local businesses.

Issue 20: Spending Money. Schools often found that money allocated to them had to be spent in designated ways, so that they could not obtain what they needed most. Also, they discovered they could not make direct purchases but had to wait months for supplies and equipment to be purchased centrally. Schools that were somewhat successful in overcoming these difficulties and in obtaining some discretion in the use of their budgeted funds then had to develop internal procedures for allocating them consistent with their philosophy about governance. One school allocated a given amount per pupil per class to each teacher. Others gave each teaching team such a budget. Another created a staff-student committee to arbitrate requests for resources.

Changes made by school boards or central staff administrations in the budgets of schools have also caused problems:

ITEM: The planning group of a school built its plans on the assumption that money would be available so that the new school would be housed in a building specially designed for their program. After considerable planning was completed, the district decided that money for the new space could not be justified, due to budget constraints. Since an old high school was vacant, the new program was assigned that space. The planning group then faced the difficult task of reorganizing its proposed program to use the old high school's physical plant.

In light of these problems, the fifteen schools offered several suggestions:

1. Obtain specific formal commitments concerning the total amount of your budget and the amounts allocated to each subcategory.

2. Seek the maximum possible flexibility in spending the amount budgeted. No public school among the fifteen has complete control over its funds. State laws, local laws, and union agreements make such autonomy highly unlikely. However, if you study the school district's fiscal procedures carefully, you should be able to propose several specific changes in these procedures that will greatly increase your financial flexibility. For example, one school district agreed that a

school could employ two teacher aides instead of a teacher. Another school got permission to order materials directly if the total bill for a purchase was less than $200. Another school got the number of central office approvals necessary for purchasing equipment reduced from five to two and obtained permission to "walk their requisitions through" the purchasing department when materials were badly needed.

3. Develop methods for deciding how money will be spent within the school that are consistent with the school's philosophy about decision making and its educational priorities.

VII. Evaluation

The fifteen schools were concerned about evaluation in three main areas: overall program evaluation, evaluation of teacher competence and performance, and evaluation of student progress.

Issue 21: Program Evaluation. Many program participants raised serious questions about the usefulness of typical approaches to program evaluation. Despite their misgivings, they expressed a strong need for ways to collect and analyze information that would aid them in improving their programs.

Some critical perceptions of traditional evaluations expressed by school staff members were as follows:

1. Evaluation is often used as a means for controlling or checking up on a program, not helping it.

2. Tests and scales used as conventional evaluations define learning and achievement too narrowly. These scales ignore important areas of student development that are emphasized in the fifteen schools' learning programs.

3. Frequently schools have been used as sites for conducting research which is more in the self-interest of the researchers than the programs themselves.

4. Evaluation seldom provides staff with an understanding of the activities and processes in the school that produce or fail to produce the results which evaluators report. Thus, it does not help the school determine which aspects of their program should be retained, modified, or dropped.

These doubts about evaluation are also shared by many people working in the evaluation field. Thus, planning groups with similar concerns should not passively accept or adopt a traditional evaluation scheme, but should feel confident that their concerns are valid and widely shared. Evaluation programs should be built to address the key issues of the program perceived by program participants and to provide continuous useful information to local school planners and implementers.

Issue 22: Evaluation of Teacher Performance. Most of the schools found that the usual method in which principals evaluate teachers based on a formalized check list was not beneficial to improving the teaching in the program, nor consistent with program philosophy. If you have come to a similar conclusion, you might consider some of the alternatives that schools have used to evaluate teacher performance.

Some of these schools greatly modified the process by which the principal's judgments about the teacher were made. Modifications usually included more discussion between the principal and teacher about his work. Sometimes other teachers and students also helped evaluate a teacher's performance.

Other schools place the responsibility for teacher evaluation with a master teacher or team leader. While it is felt the team leader had greater knowledge of the individual teacher's performance, some schools think the leader's evaluative functions are inconsistent with the supportive and collaborative roles of the team leader. In other schools, teachers are evaluated in a discussion meeting with fellow teachers. This type of session often begins with the teacher himself reporting on a problem he is facing. Other group members then work to help the teacher solve the problem. A final approach has been to establish a teacher review committee. Committee members represent administrators, teachers, students, and sometimes parents. The committee reviews the work of the teacher with the teacher. In one school this process is the basis for renewing teacher appointments.

Issue 23: Evaluation of Student Progress. Most of the schools deliberately modified traditional methods of evaluating and reporting student progress. Many felt report card grades were both inconsistent with the program's ideas about learning, and that they provided little useful information. If you accept the need to modify methods for student evaluation, you might consider some of the ways schools modified the process.

1. Involving students in the evaluation process.

ITEM: At the end of each course in one high school, the student completes a form about his or her progress in that course. The student's teacher completes the same form independently. The teacher and student would then meet in conference to discuss their assessment of the student's work. Following this conference, a third form is made out jointly. The third form is sent to the student's parents and becomes a part of the student's record.

2. Developing a system that allows for continual evaluation of a student's skill mastery, rather than evaluation after set time periods.

ITEM: In an elementary school, teachers developed performance tests, worksheets, and suggested activities for each of the math skills that a student was expected to master before leaving the school. When a student passes a specific test, the teacher punches a math skill card for the student which lists all of the expected math skills. The card is a convenient record of student progress that is continually up to date. A teacher can quickly determine which students have not mastered a certain skill by pulling out the unpunched cards.

3. Developing systems to record additional information about a student's progress, not reflected in skill mastery.

ITEM: Teachers in one school systematically record daily observations of their students. Observations focus on the successes and problems the students met that day. While academic progress was noted, areas of personal development were strongly emphasized. These daily reports are periodically summarized and discussed with parents and students.

In reporting student progress the schools felt several constraints, including district requirements about how to report grades, parents' expectations that they would receive letter grades, and expectations about what other schools, colleges and employers would require. Schools committed to new systems of student evaluation have been quite successful in convincing school boards and parents that the new methods are more useful than traditional ones, and they have been able to get most colleges and employers to accept their evaluations as a substitute for traditional grading.

VIII. Impact

The Planning Councils for Affiliate programs in the Illinois Network for School Development have been requested to develop ways that successful practices in their schools can be adopted by other schools.

Issue 24: What Makes an Impact Program Effective? The Ford Foundation recently commissioned a study of the effect of its investment of 30 million dollars in education over the last ten years. The report concludes that few of the innovative programs they supported had any influence on educational practices in other schools within their districts. Other studies have reached the same conclusion. Traditional methods of disseminating new practices through reports, articles, and site visits have not been effective. For this reason the Affiliates in INSD have been asked to think about new ways to influence the learning programs of other schools. The Affiliate Planning Council is asked to view their program as part of a district's total effort to provide quality education for its students, and not as an isolated experiment. Only one school has carried out a concerted program to influence other schools in its district—The Teacher Demonstration Center of the Welsh School in Rockford. The experience of the Teacher Demonstration Center, which operated from 1967 to 1971, might be of value to Planning Councils considering how to develop an impact program.

As is indicated in the description of the Welsh School Teacher Demonstration Center in Part Two, the Center's main purpose was to create an effective in-service training program for Rockford teachers. TDC was built around the idea that teachers should first work in a school that was successfully implementing new ideas about learning and then work as part of a team to carry out these ideas in a conventional school. Welsh had eight resident teachers who were considered a permanent part of the school staff. In addition, twenty-one intern teachers worked at Welsh each year. The interns then split into teams to go to seven schools, called factor schools. This pattern was repeated for three years, resulting in 21 factor schools. Factor schools were identified a year before they would actually receive teachers so that the principals could participate in a seminar held at TDC to acquaint them with the total program. Principals were expected to support the teachers who came to their schools in implementing some of the practices developed at Welsh and in working with the rest of the teaching staff.

In addition to the factor school program, Welsh encouraged any teacher in the district interested in visiting the Center to do so. A teacher signed up for a series of three, half-day visits indicating what issues he was particularly interested in. A substitute took over the teacher's class on these half-days. A teacher at Welsh who was working in the teacher's indicated area of interest was assigned to work with the visiting teacher. After the first visit, the visiting teacher would be asked to develop a plan for carrying out a new idea in his classroom and on the second and third visits to indicate what progress and problems he experienced in trying out the new ideas in his classroom. Many Rockford teachers took advantage of this plan. Even though TDC is no longer operating, its impact is still strongly felt in new programs in district schools.

Some principles based on the TDC experience which you might want to consider when planning an impact program are:

1. Impact plans should be considered an integral part of the new school's program with special resources allocated to them.

2. An impact program should be built upon sustained and long-term personal contact between the staffs of the impact school and the new program.

3. The support of administrators in the impact school is crucial.

4. Staff members attempting change in the impact school need ongoing support from The Affiliate school.

5. The impact program should concentrate initially on one or two schools, with lessons learned in those schools applied to later plans for impact.

Part Two: School Descriptions

In Part Two, we present descriptions of each of the fifteen schools. The schools were selected by using the following criteria:

1. There had been a planned attempt in the school to improve the educational experience of students by implementing a comprehensive change in the student's educational program.
2. The schools should be in Illinois and adjacent states to facilitate visits and serve as a continuing resource to INSD Affiliates.
3. They should be representative of urban, rural, and suburban schools, and of elementary and secondary schools.
4. They should agree to participate in the study.
5. While most of the schools should be public, private schools should be included if their programs raise important issues for public school planners.

LOS ANGELES SCHOOL SUPERINTENDENT'S MEMO TO BOARD OF EDUCATION PROPOSING GUIDELINES FOR ALTERNATIVE SCHOOLS*

BY WILLIAM J. JOHNSTON†

TO: LOS ANGELES CITY BOARD OF EDUCATION
FROM: SUPERINTENDENT OF SCHOOLS
VIA: EDUCATIONAL DEVELOPMENT COMMITTEE

SUBJECT: GUIDELINES FOR ALTERNATIVE SCHOOLS

A. *Proposal*

It is proposed that the Board of Education approve guidelines to be used in the development and operation of alternative schools.

* Reprinted with permission of William J. Johnston, Board of Education Report, Los Angeles City Schools.
† Dr. William J. Johnston is Superintendent of Schools, Los Angeles-Unified School District.

B. *Background*

At the April 12, 1973 meeting of the Board of Education, a motion supporting the alternative school concept and recommending the development of District guidelines for alternative schools was adopted. Subsequent to that action, members of the staff have been involved in a cooperative effort with individuals and organizational representatives in the development of guidelines for alternative schools.

The aim of these guidelines, which are contained in ALTERNATIVE SCHOOLS . . . . A POINT OF VIEW, is to provide a basis for the effective development and operation of alternative schools.

C. *Recommendation*

IT IS RECOMMENDED THAT the Board of Education authorize the use of ALTERNATIVE SCHOOLS . . . . A POINT OF VIEW as guidelines for the development and operation of alternative schools.

Respectfully submitted,
WILLIAM J. JOHNSTON
Superintendent of Schools

Presented by:
JAMES B. TAYLOR
Deputy Superintendent

LOS ANGELES CITY UNIFIED SCHOOL DISTRICT

ALTERNATIVE SCHOOLS . . . . "A POINT OF VIEW"

The Los Angeles City schools, consistent with the content of the publication POINT OF VIEW, believe that providing options designed to meet individual needs of students is in keeping with district philosophy. Many of the recent requests by students, parents, and staff for program flexibility and increased educational and instructional options can be met within the district's existing programs. However, to provide additional options which more readily meet the needs of some students, the establishment of district supported alternative schools is worthy of exploration.

The concept of an alternative school offers a potential for the district to provide an educational experience different in process from other programs, but consistent with the goal of providing a quality program of education for the learner. Alternative schools' emphasis on volunteer community participation, assumption of responsibility by students and parents for their education, and local school development of the educational program is consistent with district efforts to expand and improve approaches to learning.

To be effective, the planning process for an alternative school will require cooperation between community and staff and adherence to a common set of guidelines which will include the following:

1. The planning group of an alternative school must have a designated leader who can serve as its contact person and spokesman.

2. There should be evidence that the number of parents committed to the establishment of an alternative school is proportionate to the size of the program being proposed.

3. Administrators and teachers in schools most affected by the formation of an alternative school within a community will have the opportunity to participate in the planning process. They will be informed of the progress of the school proc and assist in keeping their school community informed.

4. The pluralistic composition of our society will be reflected in the student body, staff, and educational programs of the alternative school. Providing multi-cultural, multi-ethnic educational programs should be a major function of an alternative school.

5. The decision-making process of an alternative school shall be a shared responsibility among parents, students, school community, and staff. The administrator must assume responsibility for the administration and supervision of the school.

6. Other than the necessary "start up" costs, the district supported budget for an alternative school must not exceed the current per pupil cost of educating students in the regular program.

7. Each alternative school shall have its own administrator. Where a school site is shared, the regular school principal will be responsible for decisions related to shared facilities and services, the alternative school administrator will be responsible for the alternative school program. If a facility is

established on other than a regular school site, an administrator for the facility and overall program will be designated.

(passed 6 ayes)
5-17-73

8. A completed program plan and feasibility study will be required prior to the opening of an alternative school.

*9. The selection of an administrator and staff of an alternative school shall be based upon criteria mutually acceptable to the area superintendent and the planning group of the alternative school.

10. Consistent with the experimental nature of an alternative school, the district will, when appropriate, waive local policy and request waiver of state policy.

THE ASSOCIATION FOR ALTERNATIVE PUBLIC SCHOOLS NETWORK

Abstract

The Association for Alternative Public Schools Network shall provide regular assistance to the cluster of off-site Alternative Schools now operating within the Los Angeles Unified School District.

The Association for Alternative Public Schools Network is designed to provide the necessary support and training to the local school community—students/parents/staff—to ensure a continuous capacity for self-improvement and sustained change at the local school level.

The Association for Alternative Public Schools Network will produce a monthly newsletter; a series of client-identified problem-solving workshops; develop an exchange bank of student projects designed to facilitate an effective, sustained incorporation of the local school community into the student's innovative educational experience; and will collect and

---

* The Association for Alternative Public Schools has submitted the following recommendation for guideline #9:

9. The selection of an administrator and staff of an alternative school shall be based upon criteria mutually acceptable to the area superintendent and the planning group of the alternative school. *The administrator and staff selected by the criteria shall be acceptable to the planning group.*

(failed 4 to 2)
5-17-73

analyze data concerning the development, operation, governance, and continued success of off-site Alternative Schools
within the Los Angeles Unified School District with the aim
of assessing the effectiveness of the above-mentioned processes.

THE ALTERNATIVE HIGH SCHOOL PROGRAM: DRAFT III*

BY THE STEERING COMMITTEE FOR THE
ALTERNATIVE HIGH SCHOOL PROGRAM,
NEEDHAM, MASSACHUSETTS

I. Introduction

The Alternative High School Program will provide up to
one hundred students the opportunity to develop their own
learning experiences in a democratic fashion. With the aid of
three regular teachers as well as interns and community resources, students will chart their own educational course
within the basic framework of requirements established by the
State Department of Education and the Needham School
Committee.

The Alternative Program community will be housed in two
rooms at the High School where required tutorial and general
meetings will be held.

The success of this program will be gauged, and its implications for other programs in the Needham Public Schools
will be considered through a series of evaluative reports.

II. Rationale

A. Why an alternative program?
1. In today's environment, educational systems need
capacity for growth and change. One way to fulfill
this need is to provide experimental programs involving students, teachers, and parents who anticipate

* Reprinted with permission from Needham School Committee, made
up of students, staff, parents, and administrators.

success but understand and accept the possibility of failure.

2. Different students have different needs and learning styles which require alternative educational approaches.

B. Why the alternative program in Needham?

1. The Needham Public School system is committed to constructive, viable change as evidenced by programs in existence and under consideration.

2. This particular program emphasizes the concept of constant student involvement in determining his own learning experiences.

3. Students in this alternative program are given the opportunity for continued personal interaction and the subsequent close sense of community that develops in a small integrated program within the cosmopolitan atmosphere of a large suburban high school.

III. Guidelines

A. Philosophical

1. In keeping with the philosophy of Needham High School, which states, in part, "Needham High School must provide each student with the opportunity to acquire and develop attitudes and abilities which will enable him to participate most productively in his world. The school must offer a comprehensive program having appeal and meaning for all students . . . ," the guiding principles of the Alternative High School Program shall be that:

a. Each student is a unique individual with his own needs, goals, and individual learning style.

b. Learning experiences should be developed democratically by teachers and students.

c. A sense of community is an essential element of a successful educational experience.

d. The educational experience of each individual should be relevant to the time and place in which he finds himself and to his future goals.

2. Within a responsive environment it is expected that the following objectives met:

a. Personal growth as indicated by:

        (1) Awareness of self
        (2) Sense of perspective
        (3) Self-discipline
        (4) Ability to set reasonable goals
        (5) Sense of life and self-esteem

   b. Cognitive growth as indicated by the:
        (1) Ability to question intelligently
        (2) Acquisition of tools to further independently one's own learning
        (3) Ability for divergent thought
        (4) Specific skills needed in the context of one's chosen life style

   c. Social growth as indicated by:
        (1) Successful development of communication skills
        (2) Sensitivity to and respect for the feelings of others
        (3) Development of meaningful skills of social interaction
        (4) Development of a sense of humanity and social values

B. Operational
   1. The alternative program will be under the auspices of the Needham School Committee and will conform to the requirements established for high school education by the Massachusetts Board of Education and the Needham School Committee.
   2. The program will exist as an optional program of Needham High School and therefore responsible to its administration.
   3. The staff and students will be responsible for the coordination of the program.
   4. Alternative program students will be members of the Needham High School student body, entitled to participate in its programs and expected to conform with its requirements.
   5. Selection: The selections of the students will be:
      a. All students entering their junior or senior years of high school are eligible for the program. Special exceptions may be made by the Needham High School principal.

    b. Students will submit an application, including a statement of parental approval, by a date set by the principal.

    c. If more than the hundred students provided for apply, the selection process will be done by random computer sampling weighted to achieve a balance of juniors and seniors, male and female.

6. Students will be expected to maintain accepted academic and behavioral standards as determined by the staff and students of the program. Failure to do so may mean separation from the program.

7. Alternative program requirements will entail:

    a. Students must attend a weekly general meeting of the staff and student body to discuss problems, determine policy, decide on disciplinary matters, attendance, management, and other procedures.

8. In accordance with state and town academic guidelines, students will graduate from Needham High School after acquiring 84 credits including the following requirements:

    a. One credit each year in some form of physical education.

    b. A total of twenty credits in English.

    c. Five credits in U. S. History.

9. Reporting system:

    a. Instead of a traditional report card, copies of the student's learning proposals, his own evaluations, the evaluations of his teachers, and any grades received in other Needham High School classes will be sent to his parents at the end of each term.

    b. Responsibility rests with the student and his adviser to communicate information regarding the student's work to the parent or guardian.

10. Copies of the proposals, written evaluations, and grades will be kept in the student's file as part of his school record and transcript.

11. The responsibility for complying with the school rules of this program shall rest with the staff and students who are a part of this project.

IV. Planning and Implementation

  A. Selection and scheduling of students
      1. Selection:

Any junior or senior is eligible to apply. He must sign a contract-type of application which will be co-signed by the parent. No applications will be accepted after the final date. In order to provide a random selection that will produce a group reasonably equally divided between boys and girls (representing the division in the school) and an even number of juniors and seniors, all applicants will be divided into juniors and seniors and then into boys and girls. A random selection of twenty-five will be made from each group. This group of one hundred will comprise the first student group.

      2. Scheduling:

Each student selected will have a brief planning conference with one of the staff advisers in the final weeks of school. (He must select any regular course(s) that he chooses to take before the end of this academic year. The exact date will be announced.) During the summer vacation, each selected student will have a more extensive interview with one of the teacher-advisers for the project in order to begin development of his program for the year.

  B. Selection and scheduling of faculty
      1. Selection:

Simultaneous with the selection of students, English and social studies teachers interested in the project will be invited to volunteer. From the list of volunteers one English teacher and one social studies teacher will be selected by the principal, assisted by the Advisory Council of the high school. These teachers will be relieved of their originally assigned classes and of all other assignments in the high school for the coming year, and will be assigned full-time to this project. One additional teacher will be hired to work with the above staff as part of the team. Invitations will be sent to nearby university interns who would work with these three teachers and assist the students in their projects. The three teachers would be expected to develop a list of volunteers from the community who might help in various ways. They would also assist students in approaching community volunteers in terms of supporting and participating in individual or small group-study projects.

2. Scheduling:

The three faculty members of this project will be available for a chosen two-period group meeting each week. The students will be divided into eight groups of approximately twelve students each, with each group meeting for one period each week for a group discussion of the groups' projects. The large group meeting will be held to discuss and determine matters of concern to the group as a whole. During other periods of the day the members of the project faculty will visit and supervise, work on independent projects with students, and teach small-group classes in the subject matter areas as determined through group discussion and decision.

C. Faculty involvement in project development

A faculty member will have the responsibility to work with each student in developing his program, assist the student in identifying community resource people or opportunities, and keep in close touch with the work and development of the project. He will consult regularly and frequently with each one of the estimated thirty-three students directly under his supervision, and will play a vital role in working out the evaluation of projects with the student or (where indicated) any other individual concerned in the project. The student will be responsible for keeping a log of his work. The staff will keep a general log of the program, vouch for the ultimate evaluation, and provide a permanent record of the evaluation and the relative worth of each project or course.

D. Facility development

The rooms can be left as they are. The present equipment, with a few additional chairs, should accommodate the group. It might be useful to add a few tables and a portable partition that permits different configurations in the larger room. The Brookline development revealed the need for a telephone in a lockable compartment so that both faculty and students could have direct access to departments within the building and to people in the community in terms of setting up programs.

E. Behavioral conditions and goals in the contract

    1. Conditions:

An important consideration in the contract application to be signed by both student and parent is an agreement to respect the rules of the school in which the project is housed and to respect all majority decisions of the project group. It is assumed that a student who could not live up to his own agreement made in entering the program might be separated from the program after consultation with his adviser and parents. At certain periods during the year, a student would have an option of electing a return to the regular program if he had a compelling reason to do so and if he could be satisfactorily scheduled into ongoing courses.

    2. Goals:

Certain stipulations would be included in the contract concerning the basic meaning of qualifications for a Needham High School diploma. One stipulation for the student electing this program would be to agree to meet the behavioral goals established in consultation with his teacher-adviser and approved by the principal in terms of qualifying for a diploma and what it would mean in relation to his project. Specific evaluation procedures and goals would be set forth in a separate document and referred to in explication of a contract agreement itself.

V. Criteria for Evaluation

A. Objectives

    1. To define outcomes in terms of behavioral objectives.

    2. To account for the transference of learning.

    3. To determine success—or lack of success—of the program on the basis of anticipated outcomes defined

in the philosophical objectives of this program, Section III. A.2.

B. Approaches

1. The students and staff shall determine the general nature of the program so that a viable conclusion can be drawn as to fulfillment of the stated goals.
2. Provision shall be made for modification of expectations as needed and as determined by the students and staff as the program progresses.
3. The behavioral objectives established for the individual shall be within his particular capacity to achieve.
4. For each particular area of study pursued, the objectives will be clearly stated, the content defined, and the media and methods to be used described.

C. Testing and surveys

1. All students in the alternative program will participate in the regular achievement and diagnostic testing program of the Needham Public Schools.
2. An attitudinal survey will be administered in the fall, at mid-term, and at the conclusion of the school year.
3. A student opinionnaire will be developed that addresses itself to personal expectations of the program and shall be administered in the fall. A companion opinionnaire addressed to outcomes actually realized shall be given to students at the end of the school year.
4. A parent opinionnaire will be developed and administered in the same vein as that proposed in C.3. above.
5. Community consultants, resource teachers, and university interns shall, at the conclusion of their particular involvement in the program, discuss and evaluate their respective performances with the teacher in charge.

D. Supervision

1. The staff shall file monthly progress reports with the high school principal.
2. A mid-year (preliminary) report and a final evaluative report (in narrative form) shall be submitted to the principal by each teacher in the program and shall assess effective and cognitive achievements.
3. The principal or his designate shall observe the pro-

gram formally on at least two separate occasions and file his preliminary and final reports to the superintendent of schools.

E. Community liaison

1. A community advisory committee for the alternative program shall be established by the superintendent with the approval of the School Committee.

2. The membership shall be comprised of a minimum of three citizens, two directors, a staff member in the program, two students in the program, and the high school principal or his designate.

3. The basic function of this committee is to act as an advisory board to the school administration and to:

   a. Report on progress

   b. Assess function

   c. Consider problems, alternatives, and propose solutions

   d. Perform an evaluative analysis for consideration by the School Committee

4. The advisory committee shall meet in regular session at least three times during the school year.

F. Reports to the superintendent and School Committee

1. Progress reports from the professional staff and the community advisory committee shall be submitted to the superintendent at appropriate times.

2. A final report and recommendations from both groups shall be submitted to the superintendent and School Committee early in May.

VI. Implications for the Future

A. Assuming the program succeeds as decided by the evaluative process

1. Implications for the student:

   a. A sense of personal pride in being part of a successful, innovative program.

   b. A feeling of need fulfillment—the attainment of at least some of the objectives stated in the guidelines.

   c. An increased ability to achieve (or the achievement of) a large measure of self-direction and motivation.

       d. For seniors—a feeling of adequate preparation for their chosen goals.

       e. For juniors—a chance to continue in the program through graduation.

  2. Implications for the program:

       a. That pre-planning and changes which occurred throughout the year were well-advised.

       b. That the program be continued as is or expanded for a larger number of students (possibly including sophomores) and teachers.

       c. Possibility may exist for allocation of more funds on the basis of success.

       d. Procedural or structural changes will be made in the guidelines based on the year's experiences. The program should not become unresponsive to new ideas just because of one year of success.

       e. Possible state-wide or national recognition may be realized such as the Philadelphia Plan.

  3. Implications for Needham High School:

       a. For the administration: Pride in being able to meet successfully students' needs through one of the Needham High School programs.

       b. Expansion of the successful elements of the Alternative High School Program to the regular high school program where appropriate.

       c. If the Alternative High School Program is expanded in size, the students from the regular high school may be allowed to take part in the activities.

  4. Implications for the town:

       a. An increased sense of community concern and communication between all age groups.

       b. Greater participation and commitment of government, business, industry, and individual citizens in the process of education.

       c. For community resources: The satisfaction that comes in sharing skills, interests, and excitement in being active participants in a pilot program.

B. Assuming the program fails

  1. Provision for evaluation is made:

       a. To study reasons for failure in order to apply

what was learned in the process to future experiences.

    b. So as not to lose sight of successes which can be applicable to Needham High School as a whole.

2. Failure of this program should not jeopardize implementation of other innovations. Experimentation should continue in other areas.

3. Provision for a second attempt should be made after a year of review and the reworking of philosophy and basic plans (i.e., not complete abandonment of idea).

VII. Statistical Analysis

A. Overall budget implications: None beyond that affecting normal staffing, allocations for materials and equipment on a per-pupil basis, and facilities required if the program were to function on an in-house basis.

B. Staff needs

1. Professional—three certified teachers with special training in English (or language arts), social studies, and/or science and mathematics—at school district expense.

2. Paraprofessional—a cadre of volunteer citizens in the community, university interns, and other nonresident resource people—at no cost to the school district.

C. Supplies and equipment

1. Materials and equipment: Provision shall be made for educational material needed to conduct the program in the amount designated as a pro rata share of expenses attributed to all high school students in the regular school budget.

2. Equipment provision will continue on the basis of present allocation and scheduling as provided through the various departments, high school library, and the central media services.

D. Facilities

1. Provision shall be made at the high school for two rooms (equivalent to three) to be reserved exclusively for the alternative school program.

2. Rooms not fully scheduled during the school day will

be made available providing a request is initiated in advance of any other intended or proposed use of the facilities.

E. Transportation

It shall be the responsibility of the student in the program and the parents to fulfill transportation needs beyond that normally provided by the school district. Regular school busing will be made available during the regular times to the Alternative High School student. (The present state minimum distance—two miles or over —shall be in effect for the school year 1971–72.)

HOW TO CHOOSE A MINI-SCHOOL: A GUIDEBOOK FOR FAMILIES*

Program Types to Choose From:

The 50 mini-schools in the Voucher Program offer 10 different types of educational programs for you to choose from. Each mini-school specializes in one of these 10 program types.

Basic Skills	Bilingual/Bicultural
Fine Arts	Creative Arts
Individualized	Kindergarten
Learn by Doing	Multi-Cultural
Open	Careers

To choose a mini-school, decide which of the 10 program types above suits your child best. Then find out as much as you can about the mini-schools that offer the type of program you want.

Steps in Making a Choice:

50 mini-schools and 10 types of programs is a lot to deal with! To simplify things for you, we've set up three steps to

* Reprinted from "A Guidebook for Families on Selecting Alternative Schools at Alum Rock Union Elementary School" with permission of Sequoia Institute in conjunction with the Department of Research and Education Voucher Demonstration Project.

follow. They'll make it much easier for you to figure out the right place for your child to go.

1. Look at your *child's needs—and your own.*

Decide what you really want from a mini-school—for your child and for yourself.

2. Choose the *type of program* which will meet your child's needs.

Read about the 10 types of programs available and decide on one or two that best suit your child.

3. Choose the *specific mini-schools* which offer the type of program you want.

Read about the mini-schools that offer the type of program you want. Talk to a parent counselor. Visit the schools that sound promising. Then choose the three that you like best and write them down on your voucher.

Looking at Your Children's Needs—and Your Own:

What does your son or daughter need from school? Here are a few ideas to get you started thinking. Some of them may be important to you and some may not. Don't be afraid to add some ideas of your own. As you are reading over this section use the "checklist" to jot down your child's *most important needs.*

Reading and Math Skills. Does your child enjoy reading? Is he or she a math whiz? Or does your child need extra help in either of these areas?

Class Structure. Can your child operate well in an open, informal environment? Or does he or she need structure and rules to feel comfortable?

Work Habits. Can your child work well alone? Or does he or she need a lot of encouragement and attention to complete things? Does he or she make friends easily?

Learning Methods. Does your child learn well from reading and discussing? Or does he or she need to do things in order to learn?

Artistic & Creative Interests. Does your child like to draw, paint or play with musical instruments? Does he or she learn things best through some creative activity like cooking, sewing or shop?

Bilingual & Multi-cultural Interests. Does your child need or want to develop skills in another language? Is your child interested in learning about his or her culture—as well as about other cultures?

Career Interests. Is your child interested in finding out about some of the things people do for a living? Are you a parent interested in this approach to learning?

You've thought about your child's needs (and your own) and you've written down the most important ones in Part I of the "checklist." Now you should be ready to choose the type of educational program that will best meet those needs.

You already know that there are 10 different types of programs to choose from. But do you know enough about each one to decide which will be right for your child?

If you don't, there are a couple of things you can do to find out. The first thing to do is read about each of the program types in the Voucher Choices Directory.

Section V

DEVELOPING ALTERNATIVES DISTRICTWIDE: MINNEAPOLIS STORY

EDITOR'S COMMENTS

There are certain districts which have tried to move toward a districtwide policy on alternatives. Such a district is the Minneapolis public schools. Their primary efforts with the Southeast Alternatives are depicted, which ultimately evolved into such a districtwide proposal. This section will provide a glimpse at the Minneapolis setting. The articles are intended to provide the beginnings of a case analysis of the Minneapolis alternative schools approach. The reader will note that Minneapolis was the recipient of a significant grant which enabled much planning and development to take place. In some ways, the Southeast Alternatives, a complex of four schools, each with its own distinctive educational flavor, became a type of sub-system which worked out the initial idea of alternative schools and fed the results to the rest of the Minneapolis Public School System. The results seem to have promoted the idea that alternatives may be a way of organizing the entire big city school systems. Of course, in this case the sizable grant was an important factor. What would happen in a district where this money would not be available is open to serious question.

Again, the reader is cautioned against a "laundry list" approach to implementing systemwide alternatives. It is important for the reader to identify the ingredients that were considered and to see how his or her own situation may differ from that of Minneapolis.

This section will deal with such questions as:

What is the Southeast Alternatives movement?

How did it get started?

Where is support coming from?

What are some of the alternatives in existence?

How are these alternatives unified through a shared support staff?

What are Southeast Alternatives' goals for the future?

Why has the movement been so successful?

How has the University of Minneapolis helped?

What can a teacher center provide?

What's happening inside these alternative schools?

2 BOARD OF EDUCATION DECISIONS AFFECT SEA*

BY SALLY FRENCH

Approval by the Board of Education on May 29 of the new University of Minnesoto contract with the Minneapolis Public Schools has brought the formation of the cooperative K-12 Teacher Center one step closer. When the contract is approved in June by the Board of Regents the contract will go into effect beginning July 1.

Cooperative efforts will provide support for the new Teacher Center amounting to almost $390,000 next year. The University has committed $150,000, the local school district has committed $50,000 and the Federal contract assures $189,000 for next year's activities.

An administrative committee composed of Dr. William Gardner and Dr. Darrell Lewis of the College of Education and Dr. Harry Vakos, Marsh Kaner and Nathaniel Ober of the Superintendent's Cabinet has been appointed to implement the contract.

The newly appointed Teacher Center Board will make recommendations on the Teacher Center staff, screening of proposals and resource allocations and procedures for operating the Centers pre-service, inservice and community education functions.

There are eight members on the Board, four appointed by the Dean of the College of Education, Dr. Jack Merwin, and four appointed by Dr. John B. Davis. The four University representatives from the College of Education are Dr. Jerry Brunnetti, Dr. G. Howard Williams, Dr. Frank Wood and Dr. Ron Lamburt. (Dr. Robert Dykstra will sit in for Dr. Lamburt during his leave of absence.) The four members representing the Minneapolis Public Schools are Jim Seeden, Marshall-University High School; Ken Rustad, SEA; Art Lakoduk, Tuttle Principal; and Jane Starr, Southeast Council and SEA parent.

* Reprinted from the *Southeast Alternatives,* Vol. 2, No. 5, June 1973.

In addition to space in Peik Hall where the Teacher Center will be housed next year, the University is also making available the Peik Hall annex with the Peik Hall gym and the little theatre.

The contract is for a period of three years and will be re-negotiated during the third year.

The Minneapolis school district will be reorganized and decentralized into a pyramid structure. At its May 29 meeting the School Board approved Superintendent John B. Davis Jr.'s proposal which would divide the city into three pyramids and create the new position of deputy superintendent.

Southeast Alternatives will remain a separate district as it now exists through next year and then it may be incorporated into either the North or East Pyramid.

The new pyramids will be autonomous in deciding what their curriculum would be and other matters within the guidelines of the general policy of the school district. Thus if a pyramid wished to try an alternative system of schools it would have the freedom to make that choice.

The chief purposes of the new decentralization would be to aid the implementation of the desegregation/integration plan and allow the students, faculty and community to more closely participate in decisions that most directly affect them.

The Pyramids will report to Superintendent John B. Davis Jr. through the new Deputy Superintendent for Planning and Instruction, Harry Vakos. The North Pyramid will be headed by Melvin Hoagland and the East Pyramid by Vernon Indehar. A superintendent for the West area Pyramid has not yet been chosen.

The first phase of the plan will begin in July and will not affect where students attend school. It is intended:

• that no additional personnel be required to implement it, and that the central office staff would be reduced and re-deployed in a more effective manner

• that a process of long-range planning be instituted which would more effectively utilize the resources of the entire school district

• that to the extent possible, the decentralized areas would be representative of the racial composition of the city.

SEA NEGOTIATES 3 YEAR THREE MILLION DOLLAR CONTRACT WITH NIE*

BY SALLY FRENCH

A phone call from Cynthia Parsons in Washington on May 22 confirmed that the Southeast Alternative's three year contract with the National Institute of Education had cleared the government contracting office.

The informal phone call marked the end of almost nine months of formal planning involving all levels of the Southeast Alternatives community—administrators, teachers, parents, students, staff, advisory groups, councils, task forces—and endless hours of thought and labor.

In addition to the Minneapolis Public Schools funding received by all schools in Minneapolis, the SEA project will receive $3,036,722 in federal money to cover a 33 month period beginning September 1, 1973 and ending June 30, 1976.

A Grant Then a Contract

The initial money given to Southeast Alternatives in May, 1971 for 3.5 million dollars for 27 months was a grant given on the basis of the proposal written in the spring of 1971. The proposal provided general guidelines for the expenditure of program funds.

The 1973–76 contract negotiated May 8–12 on the other hand has far different parameters.

For the three year 1973–76 contract Southeast Alternatives has written a detailed program budget stating what will be done and how much it will cost program by program, school by school.

Thus, people in charge of individual programs such as art instruction at Marcy, reading at Tuttle, social science at Marshall-University High School, student senate and teacher

* Reprinted from the *Southeast Alternatives*, Vol. 2, No. 5, June 1973.

center, for example, know exactly what federal support will be available over the next three years, to accomplish certain specified program objectives.

Basic Direction

The basic thrust of the federal experiment in testing the effect of comprehensive change will be to continue to refine the two major goals of Southeast Alternatives. These are to offer choices in alternative education to parents, students and faculty and to decentralize the decision making processes so that students, faculty, staff, parents and administrators can be more involved in making decisions about their educational programs.

The 1973–76 program budget provides for a continuation of the five alternative schools that we now have. A K-12 theatre program will be offered, the environmental/science studies will offer a living science laboratory. In the Marshall-University High School secondary program the main emphasis will be to create junior high alternatives available to students coming from a variety of educational experiences as well as to develop further senior high electives.

In order to provide information for decision making the level I evaluation activities will provide student data (surveys, interviews, testing programs) so that better educational decisions about program improvement can be made. The teacher center will be expanded to include University and Minneapolis funds and to concentrate on filling the needs of the project's participants.

Phase In

There is a continuing concern by all those involved in the federal project that Southeast Alternatives continue as a viable program after federal funding ceases in 1976. Therefore, the funding levels have been designed so as to provide a phase-in to the Minneapolis Public School funding levels by the end of 1976.

The effects of this phase-in will be felt in the coming year as funds for supplementary personnel and materials decrease.

The discipline of working with a specific budget affords the opportunity for planning and wise use of available monies.

The clear knowledge of what is available gives the opportunity of making the best possible use of the resources at hand.

Top Quality Staff

In a memo from Cynthia Parsons of the Experimental Schools program there is the following comment, "For all of us, it (the project) is a learning experience. What is particularly exciting is that we all have three more years in which to effect the hoped for changes. Not only that, we have the resources to carry out those changes. We have the tremendous advantage of being able to articulate programs through all grade levels, a built-in evaluation program and a training program with the flexibility to meet schooling demands. And most important of all, a staff dedicated to performing a top quality job."

Budget

A complete program budget is available for reading in the SEA office, public library and the school offices.

SELECTIONS FROM SOUTHEAST ALTERNATIVES, 1972–73*

BY SALLY FRENCH

What It's All About . . . .

Individuals Are Unique. Among the many disagreements over what education should be and can do, there is one agreement and that is that LEARNING IS A HIGHLY PER-

* Reprinted from "What It's All About," "Contemporary School," "Continuous Progress School," "Open School," "Free School," "Marshall-University High School," "Jr. High School," "K-12 Support Staff," "Experimental Programs Promising Practices," from *Southeast Alternatives, 1972–73.*

SONAL INDIVIDUAL ACTIVITY. Learning styles differ greatly. The Minneapolis School System is committed to providing for and encouraging the development of the individual differences that are found in any community.

A major goal of the program is to provide children with the basic skills they need to function in society. However, as our society changes so rapidly, many of those skills which we consider basic may become obsolete. In a rapidly changing age, the desire to learn and to continue exploring possibilities is a necessity. Supporting a desire to extend one's skills beyond the classroom then becomes a matter of prime importance.

Choice making in education has become a way of life for members of the Southeast community. Parents and students select the school and the style of learning that appeals to them and that seems to fit their needs.

Five programs are available for families to choose from. They are: the Contemporary School, the Continuous Progress Primary, the Open School, the Free School and Marshall-University High School.

Putting It Together . . . .

The Preparation. During the summer of 1971, parents, faculty, administrators and students worked to make the Southeast Alternatives program operational.

Every parent in the Southeast area was contacted through mailings, meetings and door-to-door visits to make sure that information about the federal program was understood in order that choices could be made.

Summer workshops and refurbishing of already existing buildings established a fresh atmosphere for fall.

Parents and students who chose the Free School selected their own site and staff for the new school. Together they worked on the preparation of the building and program for fall.

The K-12 supportive staff began drawing together the goals and objectives and operational procedures that would provide guidelines for the months ahead.

Those goals which are given on the following page are in

evidence in the endeavors of every program and option in a degree that varies with the uniqueness of each option or program, but which are nonetheless identifiable.

Contemporary School

Philosophy. The Contemporary School provides an alternative for those students and parents and faculty that stresses the acquisition of basic skills in a contemporary setting. Children work in a classroom with a teacher and their peers much as children do in elementary schools around the city. Priority is placed on the mastery of the basic skills, however, many promising practices and new programs are in effect within the school.

Those involved in the Contemporary School are concerned that the image of the school be that of a contemporary rather than a traditional school. Arthur Lakoduk, acting principal of the school, views change as contemporary and Tuttle is a changing school rather than one that is locked into an inflexible pattern. He also sees that as an alternative within a system of alternatives it does not claim to be experimental, but is in the business of providing a sound educational experience for children.

The Reading Program. The reading program is the core of a total language arts program at the Contemporary School. Spelling, imaginative writing, and listening activities are incorporated into reading instruction.

Instruction in reading takes place in each classroom where pupils are grouped according to scores received on diagnostic tests. Decoding skills are emphasized in the primary grades. At the intermediate grade levels, reading instruction takes place in multiple reading textbooks with an emphasis placed on literature.

Supplementary materials in the form of literature books and audio visual aids are also utilized at the intermediate grade levels.

An intervention and detection program for kindergarten pupils has been developed to detect those pupils who may have later difficulties in reading.

A reading resource center is available. Pupils with serious

reading problems may be referred to the resource center for additional testing and instruction. Two reading resource teachers and the SLBP teacher are available to assist teachers and pupils in the classrooms.

The Mathematics Program—A Model for Contemporary Excellence. Mathematics in the primary grades is taught within the self-contained classroom. In the intermediate grades the students are grouped according to their mastery of mathematic skills. A mathematics specialist assists teachers in identifying and using appropriate manipulative aids, materials and instructional procedures. Additional instruction is also provided for students who need remedial, enriched or more advanced mathematics.

Each intermediate grade student's progress in the mathematics curriculum is continuously monitored. This information is used to describe a student's achievement, assess his needs and to prescribe additional instruction.

A teletype terminal with time shared access to a computer, electronic calculator and games provides added incentive for students to learn new techniques in problem solving.

Contemporary Practices. An interdisciplinary approach is used in Art. Evidence of the success of the Arts program was apparent in the spring of 1972 at the Tuttle Art Fair. A fulltime ceramics teacher conducts classes in a five wheel ceramics workshop.

The Contemporary School houses the Science Resource Center. Designed to serve all elementary programs in Southeast, the Center provides rich sources of materials and units from which teachers may draw. Elementary Environmental Studies also uses the Center as a base to serve elementary and secondary programs.

A well equipped Media Center supplies books, pamphlets, tapes, film strips and the newest devices for assisting children in learning. Multi-media approach serves to provide an exciting, multi-sensory way of learning.

Parents Role. Parents are involved in the school through general and grade level meetings, mini meetings and an active PTA group. A Community Liaison keeps in close contact with parent concerns and interests.

Continuous Progress School

Philosophy. Based on the theory that children learn more quickly and have a high degree of success when they work at their own pace, the Continuous Progress elementary program offers an alternative to children along just those lines. The program is ungraded and adheres to a carefully sequenced curriculum in basic skills. Children are allowed to progress through each sequence without regard to artificial or grade level barriers. No child will spend less than five nor more than eight years in the program.

Primary Curriculum—Pratt School. Mornings are spent in basic skills in math, reading and language arts. Placement is done by achievement levels. Social studies, science, art and music activities are planned as afternoon interest activities for the children. Last year one afternoon a week was set aside for special interests. However, during the year, afternoon interest activities were expanded at Pratt. Mini courses are offered at Pratt, with Friday remaining a free choice afternoon for children to select from high interest activities.

Intermediate Curriculum—Motley School. Placement by achievement levels for morning basic skill classes in language arts and math is also found at Motley. Social studies based on reading achievement will be part of basic skill instruction.

Elective Courses. Tally Time at Motley has been a highly successful approach to exploring many areas usually not touched in elementary programs. Children are encouraged to participate in the development of courses and interest centers. Students teach, as do community members, who come in to work their own particular brand of magic. Offerings last year included Patchwork Quilting, Inflatables, Have Kit Will Fly, Autoharp, Populations, Chess, Swahili, Plot the Lot, Soul Dancing, Fraction Action and many more. Every two weeks students could choose a new course and "tally" their new preference. Community support and student interest are determining factors in the offerings.

Teacher's Role. A team of seven teachers operates in each school with a coordinator to help plan a unified curriculum approach.

Staff developed Mini Music units and Afro American studies units that are available for use during the year. Construction of an attractive study area during the summer provides an inviting place for students to do individual work.

In order to bring the members of the school community closer together at Motley, a Code of Responsibility was drawn up by staff and students and presented to the student body and the parents. After review and discussion, the Code was accepted. There has been extensive staff development in Magic Circle, which deals with affective feelings.

Parents Role. Parents assist in the afternoon interest classes and in the advisory capacity. Parents serve on the Pratt-Motley Coordinating Committee and on the Personnel Selection Committee. A community liaison works with the PTA and the various groups in the school to provide meaningful school community relationships.

Changes for 1972–73. This year at Pratt-Motley, the Minneapolis Pyramid Reading program is fully implemented. Summer staff development for teachers in this reading program and the Individual Mathematics system helped ready these approaches to learning for fall. Criterion referenced testing will be used with city-wide standardized testing throughout the year to evaluate students' progress and to design curriculum to better meet their needs.

Open School

Philosophy. When children help plan their own activities within a rich and carefully planned environment, they not only learn basic skills, but they also learn to take initiative for their own education and achieve a sense of joy in learning. Based on the educational theories of John Dewey and the developmental learning concepts of Jean Piaget, the Open School is structured to provide children the freedom and responsibility to determine the direction of their education.

Goals for the Open School. Goals for the Open School emphasize helping children build self confidence, independence, responsibility and a positive self image as well as a respect for individual differences in each other. By eliminating the competitiveness of a traditional grading system and ability grouping, the teachers are given the opportunity to help students learn honest self-assessment and to set realistic individual goals. There need be no sense of failure, as measured against artificial standards, but rather personalized evaluation of each student's own potential and needs. Socialization skills are important and "family" and community projects foster a cohesiveness in the school community as a whole.

Initially the school created resource areas for children to work in. However, this structure did not foster the close relationships between students and teachers that was desired. Therefore, in January of 1972 a reorganization occurred and children were grouped in multi-age "families". Children and their parents may choose a "family" in one of two models.

Model I. Model I consists of one "family" designed to provide children with the benefits of the Open School concept within a single classroom. About 27 children, ages 5–8 years, relate to a single teacher, assisted by aides and volunteers. Children are free to move within the room to various interest centers during the day.

Model II. Model II has four families, each with about 60 students, ages 5–12, with two teachers, two aides and student teachers, parents and other community volunteers. The "family" in Model II functions like an enlarged open-classroom, sharing two classrooms and the hall space connecting them. In addition to the activities in each family, students from Model I and Model II may choose other options during the day in industrial arts (Hammer Hall), pottery, art, gym and music which are located in other centers within the school. The community becomes a resource area as frequent large and small group field trips help to erase school walls.

Role of the Teacher. Working in teams with aides and volunteers, the teacher serves as a guide and organizer, encouraging children to be active agents in their own learning. The teacher provides a variety of choices in response to the di-

verse interests and educational needs of children. The
teacher functions as a facilitator and is sensitive to the needs
of the children in terms of knowing when and how to intervene, when to propose a new task and when to stay away.

Parent Involvement. Believing that when parents participate
in the education of their children everyone benefits, the Open
School actively seeks parent involvement at many levels. A
coordinator of parents and community volunteers helps to
organize parents and community resources in the school.
They assist teachers in working with small groups of children
in interest centers, prepare materials, accompany students on
field trips or offer specific skills as teachers themselves.

Parents help choose their child's teachers by selecting the
family. PARENT CONFERENCES have become parent,
student, teacher conferences.

On an organizational level, parents, staff and students
work together on committees within the school. The Marcy
Advisory Council composed of students, parents, and staff
works closely with the principal and advises him on matters
of operational and educational policy in the school.

Staff Development. An intensive summer staff development
program provided experiences for parents as well as staff.
Parents and staff have designed a human relations program
for staff that began in the summer and will continue throughout the year.

Parents, administrators and staff attended a graduate seminar on the British Infant School in England. In July staff and
parents attended the Bennington, Vermont, Prospect School
workshop. A number of the staff attended the Glaser Reality
Therapy Workshop in Pasadena, California, in August. These
collective and shared experiences provide a rich resource base
for further developments in the Open School.

University of Minnesota Involvement. Each quarter, student
teachers from the University have a unique opportunity to
work with children in a public open school as part of their
regular practice teaching. Several professors in the Elementary Education Division from areas such as reading, math,
social studies and science work with Marcy teachers in developing skills and curriculum especially for an open class-

room situation—much like the integrated-day model provided by many British Infant Schools.

1972–73 Changes. Mathematics and reading programs will draw on many source materials. There are well stocked banks of materials using various approaches to reading. Materials are shared on a systematic basis with the four families and with Model I. Within the families in Model II, there is now a division of responsibilities for planning curriculum with one teacher responsible for ages 5–8 and one teacher for ages 5–11. There is no grouping within the families, however, on that basis. There is some scheduling within families for use of the outside resource areas. As a result of two summer workshops with parents, the resources available for Marcy are even greater than last year. A workshop was held on replicating and designing materials and a workshop was also held to train parents to work in the schools. A new playground project will transform the asphalt area into a fresh air learning area.

Free School

Philosophy. "Freedom is a process, a continuum through which an individual gains the abilities and makes decisions based on his own desires and the realities of the environment he finds himself in. It involves learning how to relate to others (risk taking), finding real work to do (putting up with some drudgery), and understanding the society we live in (hard thinking). It involves developing traditional capacities for delayed gratification, self discipline and nitty gritty." . . .

Based on this statement of freedom by Tom O'Connell, the Head Teacher of Free School last year, the school seeks to provide an atmosphere for students that will attend to their personal needs and growth in such a way that they may BECOME free. Going far beyond the Summerhillian definition once painted in the front hall of the school . . . "Freedom is doing anything you want as long as it doesn't interfere with others", the Free School seeks to build a confidence and awareness within students so that they will want to learn the skills necessary to survive in today's world. "Feeling good" about themselves, they are able to look outward. The school then becomes not an isolated place but an extension of the community, and in turn, extends itself into the community and environment.

Free School—Year I. Provisions for a Free School in the initial proposal represented an attempt to provide an alternative for elementary and secondary students and their parents who had been actively seeking a more humane and creative approach to education.

Parents and students selected a staff of six teachers, one of whom was to be a Head Teacher, during the summer of 1971. They worked together to prepare a program and the site they had selected—the first floor of the United Ministries Building. The relaxed, colorful, informal atmosphere was a reflection of the students and staff creativity. The continuum provided by the K-12 approach and the community feeling made possible by seventy students and the student-staff ratio of 7-1 created a special atmosphere for change.

The group, augmented by six aides and a large number of volunteers, experimented with a non-structured, highly individualized approach during the first year. Developing a basic skills program for elementary students in language and mathematics was a slow process. However, by the end of the year, a viable program was in evidence.

Secondary students gained cohesiveness in the study of social concerns. Individually or in small groups they engaged in language study, Urban Arts, apprenticeships, tutorials in literature and writing, math, cooking, drama, photography, art, gym, woodworking, classes at Marshall-University High School and the University of Minnesota. Travel proved an excellent way to bring students together. An ambitious trip to Mexico in January and an experience at the Pine Ridge Indian Reservation in the fall provided revealing lessons in other cultures. Extensive environmental studies took place in the woods of Wisconsin.

By the middle of the year, student and staff dissatisfaction with "letting things happen" led to weekly and monthly schedules based on mutual interests.

Glendale Street Academy. The original SEA Proposal set the enrollment for the first year at Free School at 70 students. There were many other students, however, on a secondary level who were not able to function in the options open to them. A private school, the Glendale Street Academy, was formed to meet the needs of some of those students. A successful program began in January 1972 in the Glendale community for 25 students. Financial considerations and a desire for a broader based school community led to a decision by SEA, the Free School and the Academy for a merger of the Free School and the Glendale Street Academy for the fall of 1972.

Governance—Parents. Initially school governance was accomplished by the consensus of those staff and students who met at various times to make decisions. In the spring, a Governing Board of parents, students and staff was organized to plan for Year II and to provide an on-going consistent approach to school governance.

Parents are involved in the school through monthly potlucks, general meetings, small group discussions, as volunteers in language study, music, art, literature and field trips. A parent liaison served in the school full time as a general member of the staff during Year I. A parent is now the school secretary and one parent is a secondary teacher in the school.

Year II. Based on honest assessment of where the Free School ought to be going, the members of the community agreed that the school should look to the needs of a more diverse group ethnically and socially. In accordance with this feeling, the enrollment has doubled (150), a more diverse staff has been hired, and efforts have been directed toward recruiting students from the Black and Indian communities.

While holding to the basic tenets of the Free School philosophy, the program for Year II appears to have a much different organization. Primary students have two teachers, aides, and areas of their own. Middle students also have two generalists and aides and a special area. Secondary students have teachers in mathematics, directed studies, humanities and social perspective. K-12 students share resource areas in language (foreign), art, gym, woodworking, music and science. A darkroom for photography is available. An ambitious addition to the program is a Community Theatre. The apprenticeship program and the travel program have been expanded.

Marshall-University High School

History. Marshall-University High School was created in 1968 by the merger of the public school—Marshall High School, and the University of Minnesota laboratory school—University High School. This unique public school is committed to the concept of experimentation, research, evaluation and demonstration. Strong ties with the University of Minnesota and the addition of alternative status further enhance the creative aspects of Marshall-University High School.

A heterogeneous student population draws 2/3 of its students from Southeast and 1/3 from the metropolitan area. The school strives for a climate where many different types of people may come together in an atmosphere of respect and trust.

Philosophy. The school is dedicated to providing a number of alternatives within the school and the community that will enable students to achieve a diverse educational background.

Program: Senior High. A quarter plan allowing students in grades 9–12 to register for the courses and teachers they wish to study with has been implemented, thus giving students a greater range of courses and options during the year.

Four Alternatives. Four modes of study are available to students at Marshall-University High School. They are the Single Discipline courses, the Interdisciplinary courses, Individual Directed Study and Small Group Counseling.

Single Discipline Alternative. Students explore concepts and themes in a single discipline with a faculty member. Classes may be taught at various sites in addition to the traditional classroom, thus adding further dimension to learning. The single discipline class remains the core of the high school program.

Interdisciplinary Alternative. Combined efforts of faculty members, secondary cadre and administration have made possible a number of interdisciplinary courses. The first of these, "Man, His Feelings and the World", attracted 329 students during the 1971–72 school year.

Project AWARE (A Wilderness Aid Research Experience) is a program of wilderness and urban survival training which had its pilot program in the spring of 1972. Thirty students and three staff members worked together on a full time basis to select projects related to the environment, working on them at school and in the field. A total of twenty-three days was spent in the field studying sites from a historical, geological and geographic point of view. Students researched and documented findings on individual projects. Additional skills in backpacking, camping, canoeing were acquired, along with safety, budgeting and cooking.

"Exposure" piloted spring quarter and focuses on art, music and literature. The course is designed to be experiential in nature with exposure to paintings, sculpture, architecture, drama, poetry and music in the Twin Cities.

Individual Direct Study Alternative. Students may, with parent and faculty consent, engage in independent study. A student may plan a course of study, objectives, content and evaluation working closely with a faculty advisor. In the high school this represents a separate option, while in the 7th and 8th grades, it will take place within the regular program. 150–200 senior high students elect this option each quarter.

O.C.L.E. While many independent study projects are carried on in conjunction with single discipline courses, the Off Campus Learning Experience has become an alternative for earning a quarter's credit at a site other than Marshall-University High School. Students write a contract after choosing the site and project. These, together with the objectives, are approved by faculty advisors. Weekly meetings with advisors monitor the progress of the students. Projects selected last spring were varied. While a number of projects in the pilot program involved academic studies, many more were active participants in the community in dance, television, oceanography, police-community relations, work in schools and hospitals.

This alternative is designed both for students who are disenchanted with the traditional school concept as well as for those who seek enrichment.

Guide Groups—An Alternative for All. A guide group program was researched in the spring of 1972 by a group of faculty and students and parents. The plan for small group counseling models calls for students to meet on a regular basis to deal with educational and career planning, to develop interpersonal skills and to assess past learning experiences. Guides are responsible for aiding students with educational programs, keeping them up to date on records, explaining school policies and relating to parents and students in such a way that a better climate is created for helping students with life goals. There will be an ongoing effort to erase the barrier that often exists between home and school. Formative evaluation will help determine the direction of the program in its first year. Guide groups include all students grades 8 through 12. All GUIDES are certificated staff.

Jr High School

Junior high years are traditionally difficult for youngsters. Revisions in the program approach will have an impact on this critical point of transition for students entering the middle years.

A team approach to the total program concentrates on providing a more congenial and human learning environment. Members of each of the four disciplines—English, social studies, mathematics and science—and the counselors meet daily to coordinate planning and to discuss common concerns. The multiple perceptions give a greater insight into students behavior and needs. At the conclusion of mini courses and quarter programs, student and parent evaluations and conferences help team members measure effectiveness of the programs.

A student's day includes a three hour time block for four courses taught by the team, a two hour time block for selected experiences in industrial arts, home economics, art, music and foreign language, and a requirement in physical education. The junior high school program uses the facilities of both Peik Hall on the campus of the University of Minnesota and Marshall building.

Development of interdisciplinary teaching units and mini courses adds to the effectiveness of the program. Flexible scheduling allows for extended field trips and special-learning opportunities. While skill acquisition remains highly important, fostering positive attitudes toward self, school and peers makes possible a more effective total 7th and 8th grade program.

Special Programs

Special Education. Orthopedically handicapped and hard of hearing students come from the metropolitan area to take part in the Marshall-University High School special education program. Special classes are provided for these students; however, great effort is made to incorporate them into the regular curriculum and school activities.

School and Community Sharing. Learning experiences are often most relevant within a community context. The school extends into the community and makes available opportunities for students in many out of school resources. Urban Arts Program offers courses in drama, dance, art design, broadcasting, architecture, photography and poetry at sites such as the Minneapolis Institute of Arts, School of Design, Children's Theatre and Walker Art Center. The University of Minnesota accepts Marshall-University High School students on a tuition basis providing a smoother transition from high school into college. The Work Opportunity Center provides a city-wide alternative program which exposes students to work experiences and lays a foundation for a career after graduation for students who might otherwise not complete their high school career.

K-12 Support Staff

A K-12 staff provides support and guidance for the project. Each member of the staff serves the faculty, administration, students, and community in individual schools as well as providing a unifying element.

Director. Leadership for the Southeast Alternatives program is provided by the Director. He administers the SEA federal program and is the liaison to the Office of Education. In addition to working with the Superintendents' Cabinet and the secondary and elementary staffs, he also consults with the Community Education Council, the K-12 support staff, community agencies, citizens, parents and students to improve the learning climate for students.

Staff Development. A Staff Development Coordinator assists in answering the needs of components as they request programs that will enrich the staff and faculty. During the course of the year, staff development may be in the form of visits to other programs, it may be workshops with guest leaders, inservice training to increase the expertise of teachers in different disciplines. The extensive summer programs are coordinated by the Staff Development Coordinator. Teacher Cadre is also coordinated through the Staff Development office.

Community Liaisons. Five Southeast parents hold staff positions as Community Liaisons in order to facilitate the communication of information from the community to the schools and conversely from the schools to the community.

It is the role of the Community Liaisons to meet with a wide variety of groups, to provide information and opinions to the SEA personnel regarding the operations of the entire program and its options. They assist in developing wider citizen participation in school affairs and provide input to research and evaluation, staff development and the director of SEA.

Community Education. The Community Education coordinator is responsible for supervision of the community educational program in the SEA schools. The aim of the program is to integrate the regular school and evening program into one educational, recreational, social, cultural needs of the community.

An ACTION volunteer assists in mobilizing the community resources to further benefit the program.

Business Advisor. The Business Advisor provides management consultation and staff development in the areas of program planning and budgeting. He is responsible for supervision of financial affairs and for development and monitoring of material procurement procedures. As an additional assignment he coordinates transportation activities associated with regularly scheduled services and field trips.

Public Information. The Public Information coordinator publishes a newspaper every other month, publishes brochures and information about the program, schedules visitors, produces slide tape shows and video tapes dealing with particular aspects of the SEA program. Informational meetings in the community are also a part of the Public Information responsibilities.

Student Support Services. The Student Support Coordinator provides services to the K-12 program which range from testing programs, coordinating pupil record systems to coordinating the services of the counselors, social workers, school nurses and psychologists in the Southeast schools.

Innovative programs generated by Student Support Services are the Guide Group counseling model now in operation at Marshall-University High School, as well as Sprinthal Psychological Education, secondary, and "The Magic Circle" on the elementary level.

Evaluation Team. The Level I Research and Evaluation team of SEA has as its primary mission the task of formative evaluation to provide feedback to project decision-makers. The task of answering the question "Does evaluation make a difference" is an added emphasis of the team planning.

This year twenty-one tasks, some within individual schools, some cross component, have been set. The evaluation team composed of two research associates, five part-time evaluators hired for specialized tasks, and four research assistants are all involved in the gathering of data, report writing, design planning and observation.

Experimental Programs Promising Practices

Explicit in the alternatives program is the mandate to pursue experimental programs and promising practices.

Experimental programs are found in curriculum areas and in broad areas having to do with the total project in governance, community education and evaluation.

In curriculum areas, some of those programs, such as Guide

Groups, AWARE, OCLE, were included in the section on Marshall-University High School. Other programs within elementary and secondary schools are the K-12 Language Arts program, the Environmental Science program, the Industrial Arts program and the TV Media Studio. Planning is now underway to develop a comprehensive K-12 continuum in many discipline areas.

K-12 Language Arts Program. The Moffet Language Arts program in use at the Open School, the Free School and Marshall-University High School includes all of language discourse—speaking, writing, reading—and involves students in actual activity rather than a study of subjects. It is interdisciplinary, project and activity oriented. As a result of activity involved, there is natural peer group discussion which gives immediate feedback on success and needs.

Environmental Studies. The K-12 Environmental Studies program involves students in activities relating all subject areas to the real world (environment). Studies in the urban community and natural areas develop skills in math, social studies, science, language arts, art, music, and physical education.

Eighty units are available for the elementary classes and new activities are being introduced in the junior and senior highs this year.

Most of the units take the students outdoors for camping, crosscountry skiing, snowshoeing, school site development, and canoeing. The program arms the student with an understanding of environmental interrelationships, the inquiry skills needed to answer his questions, and a sensitivity to the environment and other people.

Industrial Arts. A popular addition to the elementary programs is Industrial Arts. School workshops are equipped with work benches, handtools, drill press and scroll saws so children may learn techniques and safe use of tools in woodworking, metal and leather craft.

TV Media Studio. A sophisticated TV Media Studio involving 5 channel, closed-circuit network TV capable of color television transmission to thirty-five locations at Marshall-University High School was approved by USOE this summer.

Video tapes will be available to teachers and students. Elementary and secondary people alike will have access to equipment for learning media techniques as well as sharing in the products.

The Teacher Center. A Teacher Center now serves as the hub for staff development planning and training for teachers. The Center which became operational in the fall of 1972 is both a place and a concept designed to give a unified approach to staff development. It is controlled by those it serves. It stresses a K-12 organization, trains across schools as well as offering individual programs, provides a link with other organizations outside of SEA and provides access for community people including parents and students to training programs in which they may participate as well as initiate.

A thirteen person Board governs the Teacher Center. The Board is responsible to the Southeast Community Education Council and has three members selected by the Council on the Board. Six members are elected by the school faculties and two students and one administrator are selected by their peers.

Proposals for staff development are brought to the Teacher Center Board where they are acted upon. The Staff Development Coordinator serves the Teacher Center Board and is responsible for the submission of proposed activities and their implementation as approved by the Board.

The Teacher Cadre. To enrich the SEA programs, a Teacher Cadre for elementary programs was formed to supplement specific disciplines and provide ideas for teachers. The Cadre members help develop resource centers, provide unique and special class activities in the schools. Specialists in art, mathematics, music science, industrial arts, environmental education and language arts serve all elementary schools. At Marshall-University High School teacher specialists develop new courses and opportunities such as OCLE and AWARE programs, assist in the Junior High program, media, mathematics and English.

BOARD APPROVES ALTERNATIVE SCHOOLS*

BY GREG PINNEY†

The Minneapolis School Board voted unanimously Tuesday to try to offer alternative educational styles to all elementary students in the city by the fall of 1976.

If the citywide alternatives program is set up as expected, it would be a substantial departure from the traditional structure of American schooling in which an elementary student is assigned to a specific building and takes the program that is offered there.

Instead, each student would choose the style of education he or she wants—with styles ranging from structured to open or radical—and then attend at the school building that offers his choice.

Although no details of the arrangement have been worked out yet, the city may be divided into sections and a range of the most popular alternatives offered at the buildings in each section.

It may be the first citywide alternatives program in any major city school district in the nation.

The author of the plan, board member Richard F. Allen, said in an interview after the meeting that the switch to alternatives and all of the other arrangements that will go with it will amount to "a major change in the school system."

Board members qualified yesterday's action by saying that it could be altered if they do not have enough money to carry it out. The motion adopted by the board simply directs Supt. John B. Davis Jr. and his staff to begin feasibility studies and planning necessary to implement citywide alternatives by 1976.

But it clearly established that the board wants to move in that direction, and Allen said, "I'm very optimistic."

Supt. Davis said, "I can't guarantee we'll be able to meet that deadline, but I'm committed . . . . to the creation of choices and options in our school district."

* Reprinted with permission from the *Minneapolis Tribune.*
† Greg Pinney is a staff writer for the *Minneapolis Tribune.*

A new open school might be launched this fall in northeast Minneapolis, and other alternatives would be phased in during the next three years.

Five of the city's 66 elementary schools—all in southeast Minneapolis—now offer alternative styles under the federally funded Southeast Alternatives program that began in 1971. Southeast Alternatives will serve as a model for the citywide plan, but the offerings in other parts of the city may not be precisely the same as in Southeast.

There was no estimate of how much it will cost to convert the entire elementary system to alternatives, but Allen said "to pick a number, we should put at least $50,000" into the 1973–74 budget to start the planning.

The added costs of an alternative system might be confined largely to the transition period for things such as working out mechanical arrangements, for community planning for the schools and for preparation of teachers, said Allen. Once the new types of schools are set up, they probably will not require any more employees than do the current schools, he said, although they might require more transportation of students.

Secondary schools are not included in the current plan because secondary programs in Southeast have not developed as satisfactorily as the elementary arrangement, Allen said. But a secondary plan may be added later.

During yesterday's late-afternoon meeting at the school administration building, the alternatives plan was supported by all board members including the two conservatives, Philip A. Olson and Mrs. Marilyn Borea, both of whom opposed the idea when Allen publicly proposed it more than a year ago.

However, Olson said he still does not favor "wide-open, do-your-own-thing schools."

Yesterday's action was a personal triumph for Allen, a 46-year-old purchasing agent for the Bemis Co., who was elected to the board in 1969 and who served two years as its chairman.

"These are the things I've mulled over in my mind for many years," said Allen, adding that long before he came on the board, he saw that different kinds of students and parents need different kinds of education. "Part of it is recognizing the differences in my own children," he said.

He said his 13-year-old daughter Hilary, an eighth-grader at Jefferson Junior High, might want a continuous-progress or open program, while his 11-year-old son Jeffrey might want a traditional or continuous-progress school. Jeffrey is a sixth-grader at Douglas School.

Allen did not devise the Southeast Alternatives plan. It was proposed by educators and parents in Southeast. But Allen recognized that it fit his previous thinking, and he soon began talking about spreading alternatives to the entire city.

EVALUATING ALTERNATIVES

EDITOR'S COMMENTS

Inevitably the question arises: Are alternative schools working? The answer to such a question involves evaluation, which is a central concern in alternative education. How are new patterns of education assessed? Do they require different forms of evaluation than is normally customary? Is it too early to evaluate? Do we have any alternatives that have evaluated themselves? Are students in alternative schools doing as well academically? Are they getting into colleges?

Evaluating any effort is a complicated endeavor. Trying to evaluate alternative schools is no exception. Yet, whenever any new effort is proposed to teachers, parents, and students, there is a built-in concern for effectiveness and productivity. Consequently, evaluation becomes an integral part of alternative education. However, as different educational forms are proposed, they may not lend themselves to traditional forms of evaluation. In fact, if traditional forms of evaluation are imposed on alternatives, they may not reveal valid results. Furthermore, since the question of results is paramount in the minds of the key participants, if the wrong type of evaluation is applied, then the results may be inadvertently damaging to the alternative itself and to the movement which it represents.

The articles in this section have been selected with an eye toward trying to clarify the complex issues surrounding assessment procedures. Moreover, certain prominent alternative schools have undergone their first cycle of evaluation. For example, Quincy II, Education by Choice, which has received considerable public attention, has completed its first evaluation. In the light of such visibility, the results of the Quincy experiment will be extremely significant. On the other hand, there are certain other kinds of evaluation which are less formal in nature, but equally important, and aimed at an in-house improvement of the alternative. Both the formal and informal approaches to evaluation are crucial and any person interested in alternatives would have to be sensitive to these forms.

One final point deserves mention. Alternative schools need to go through a period of development. Usually this period of development takes a number of years. Thus, it is important to keep in mind that premature attempts at evaluation of alternatives will lead to premature results. Stated somewhat differently, until an alternative has been fully developed, it is difficult to assess the worth of an alternative. For instance, if you are developing a Montessori educational environment from scratch, it would take a number of years to develop all of the ingredients that would go into a legitimate Montessori environment. If evaluation were to take place prior to this full development, then such evaluation would really be misleading. Evaluation of a development of an alternative school is quite different from evaluation of the impact of a fully developed alternative school. This is an especially important point when one considers the fact that most school boards, in particular, are under heavy pressure to report results of any new programs, including alternative schools, that they may be supporting.

This section deals with such questions as:

Why must evaluation be an integral part of the alternatives movement?

How does a lack of structure in alternatives create problems when standard forms of evaluation are applied?

Why should instructional process instead of outcome be given greater consideration in the evaluation of alternatives?

How should alternatives be evaluated?

Who must be involved in the evaluation process?

What kinds of evaluation have been conducted?

How valid are these evaluations?

THE SHANTI EVALUATION: EVEN WILBUR AND ORVILLE COULDN'T MAKE IT FLY*

BY GENE MULCAHY†

Evaluation is a vital element in the care and nurture of alternative schools. Despite the differences among our schools, it can in general be said that the schools differ from the traditional schools in whose shadow they often operate and to whom they will inevitably be compared. When the alternative school folks understand this, then they can take control of the evaluation and comparison and choose an appropriate methodology and time. When alternative school folks do not understand the various roles of evaluation, evaluation occurs anyway, but when unplanned and not designed, others control the choice of methodology and the design of the evaluation. Frequently, the evaluation is non-systemic. What school board members hear constituents say in supermarkets—for example—what parents hear on the bus or in the carpool, etc. This non-systemic evaluation often has little validity, has no controls and can be disastrous.

The alternative school should take the initiative in evaluation and thereby control the process. The process should meet the approval of other concerned parties. Once the initiative is seized, the question must be faced: What are the purposes of our having an evaluation? Three frequent reasons are: 1. To find out if we're doing what we think we're doing or what to be doing. 2. To prove to somebody else that we're doing what they think we're doing or should be doing. 3. To find out what somebody who knows more than we do (we hope) thinks.

These goals for having an evaluation may not be compatible in a given situation. For example, an evaluation which demonstrates in the final analysis that you are messing up royally

* Reprinted from *Changing Schools,* 4:2, 1975, No. 14, School of Education, Indiana University.
† Gene Mulcahy, Ph.D., is Director of the Shanti School and Special Assistant to Superintendent of Hartford Public Schools.

may be a highly successful and useful evaluation, but could be hazardous to your survival. Or you may have an evaluation which makes your benefactors smile and pant warmly but doesn't tell you a bloody thing you need to know.

So, you need to be very clear about why you're seeking an evaluation and be wary of designs which promise to achieve all your goals for having the bloody experience to begin with. . . . There is a great need for a handbook in lay persons' terms outlining the options for alternative school evaluation for the benefit of the schools themselves. With all the dedicated research and evaluation folks scurrying about after doctorates, I plead that one may see fit to develop an up-to-date down-to-earth summary of the options—their strengths, weaknesses, and cost in money and people.

On the other hand, I, as a consumer, am not sympathetic to evaluator breast beating, bitching and moaning about the imperfectibility of their methodologies and instrumentation. Evaluators are too often hypnotized by their own mystical jargon and quixotic vision. School needs are practical needs, needs to know, and evaluation folks have the sublime arrogance to tell me or to facilitate my telling myself. If they are willing to address that formidable task, I commend and thank them. If they spend their energies refining their own sense of perfection, I encourage them not to involve me and my school in that deliberation. I found in the case in point that the two were not compatible. The evaluators' position seems to me analogous to that of the intellectual literary critics of the nineteenth century who labored to discover who other than Shakespeare wrote his plays. Their irrelevant quest for them made knowing, feeling and interpreting the plays impossible.

As a starter for the layperson's guide to alternative school evaluation, let me share my thoughts on the Fortune-Hutchinson Model as experienced at Shanti School. Strengths: careful and articulated goals process, high-level emphasis of control of data by decision maker on data for decision makers, very thorough; those who participate learn a valuable lifelong process of reasoning and evaluating—year-long—evaluation of the evaluation. Weaknesses: long-suffering and time-consuming, long inflexible, requires constant resources of time and effort, too conscious of itself as a methodology at the exclusion of emphasis on the evaluation of a school.

Indeed my judgments are non-systemic themselves, are subjective and subject to the disagreement of those who identify themselves as expert. They are the judgments of an experienced practitioner intended as guidance to other practitioners. This same experience leads me to render another chunk of advice. Behold Gene Mulcahy's checklist on not getting ripped off by evaluators.

1. Be sure you have your own goals for having an evaluation clear. Get out all the hidden goals.

2. Investigate all the possibilities. There is more than one game in town. There are new Rolls-Royce methodologies and off-the-curb fly-by-night used Ford ones. Get all the information you can. Check out the alternative school clearinghouses. The consortium at Indiana University, the National Alternative School Program at the University of Massachusetts and the Center for New Schools in Chicago are all experienced groups.

3. Be sure that the evaluator's primary goal is to evaluate you—not to prove a point, defend a position, or get a degree. These may be secondary concerns—your primary concern is the evaluation. Make sure the other party concurs.

4. Ask to see previous work. Get an idea of what a previous product looked like. What will the differences be?

5. Check out references. Are those previously served by this person or group pleased? Be thorough. If it's a first run, see what's comparable and check that out.

6. Consult as far as possible everyone who has any relationship to your school and program. What do they think about the options? About your learnings? What are they willing to contribute?

7. Make a decision in favor of one method and/or contractor contingent on a favorable contract.

8. Negotiating the contract—
   a. Make clear the goals of the evaluation.
   b. Define as exactly as possible the resources the school is offering; those the contractor is offering. Be very sure you mean it. Think of those outrageous days and weeks of work and ask—Can I give this even then?
   c. Establish time lines. Determine when each part of the evaluation will be completed. When you will get what data.

    d. Establish legal checks and general accountabilities.
    e. Check the contract out with all those who had defined input.
    f. Establish check points to determine if the stated goals are being met.
    g. Design an inflight correction system—to adjust the contract along the way to changing needs.
    h. Provide for an evaluation of the evaluation.

9. Hold clear and high expectations of the evaluation. Don't get talked into or out of things.

10. Don't get overwhelmed—either by the work or the particular jargon evaluators have invented. If you don't understand, ask and ask further. The problem isn't that you're stupid, but that they're not communicating effectively or don't understand their own business very well.

11. Do the above in a spirit of cooperation and good will but don't exclude steps for these reasons.

In the past several years Shanti has been victim to numbers of evaluations—some highly formal and long-range, some much less formal, for specific purposes. I have also performed evaluations. I ardently hope that my efforts as evaluator have been of greater value than my efforts as evaluatee. Little of the effort we have in four years invested in external evaluation has been worth the time and energy invested. Our own non-professional internal systems are highly efficient, speedy and less effort. I am in the process of preparing some written material on these methods as they continue to serve our needs at Shanti School.

STUDENT EVALUATIONS: FREEDOM, RESPONSIBILITY, AND LEARNING*

When students leave the formal structure of conventional schools and enter the more informal learning atmosphere of most alternative public schools, they are faced with increased

* Reprinted from *Changing Schools* No. 5, School of Education, Indiana University.

freedom and responsibility for their own learning. They are also deeply involved in curricular development and policy decision-making. How do students make such a transition? Four students from Pioneer II, an alternative school operated by the Ann Arbor, Michigan, Public Schools, talk about their experiences:

1. *"Participation in decision-making regarding policies which affect the school community has been a very worth-while learning activity for me. The increased opportunity to make personal choices about how to use my time and avail-able resources has caused me to do much thinking about this and has stimulated my personal growth.* The choice, for ex-ample, about whether to attend classes or to do something worthwhile on my own outside the school premises was the kind of issue that I seldom, if ever, considered in school be-fore. For the most part, I just went along with the routine without giving it much thought.

I think that the most important thing that has come from my experience in Pioneer II has been my personal growth and awareness of others. When I attended the regular school, it seemed to me that I was one person at school and a different person at home. I think that this was mainly due to my feel-ings of being stifled at my old school. *Even now when I go back and walk through those huge corridors with hundreds of kids everywhere, I can feel the confusion and tension mounting within myself. I could have survived my last semes-ter at that school and would have been glad to get out. But now after having experienced the Free School, I know that I could never willingly go back to that impersonal system as a full-time student.*

The lack of structure at Pioneer II was something that took a while to get used to. After spending three and one half months at the school, I feel that I have reached the point where I can use my time and available resources more crea-tively than I ever have done before. *I feel a tremendous amount of satisfaction in thinking that I can take the responsi-bility for my own decisions and function effectively on my own initiative. This is quite different from the process of adapting to a plan and structure created by others.* This I count as one of my most valuable learning experiences of this semester. For some students, it apparently didn't take three and one half months for them to function without structure;

for others, it will take longer than that probably. *But, considering that one has so much structure in public schools for so many years, three and one half months seems a very short time in which to learn to function on one's own initiative.* The lack of structure, initially, made it possible for individuals to take part in the decision-making and the direction of the school."

2. "Last summer, when we were planning the school, I had visions of myself as a free school student. I would be studying hard and independently in pursuit of knowledge; and I wanted to know everything. That was what the school meant to me—an opportunity to learn on my own without pressure or busy work. I wasn't at all worried about myself: I was confident that I would live up to my goals. But I wanted to be sure that all the other prospective students shared my attitude. When we spoke to English classes at the old school, I told them repeatedly that they should not apply for free school unless they could motivate themselves. *Yet now, after a semester, I feel slightly foolish in admitting that I have not been able to fit into my own mold. I have done very little real studying. While I've learned a lot this semester, academically I have lacked direction and motivation. I think that one reason why I accomplished so little this semester is that I adopted a common free school attitude. Many people have said that classes are of minor importance compared with the task of getting to know each other and building a community.*

The success of the school has become very important to me. Much of my time has been devoted to activities concerning the school. Among other things, I have written letters to parents, organized committees, written proposals and attended a seemingly endless number of meetings. A lot of this 'politics' is frustrating but I love doing it. I know I will continue with it as long as I am at the school.

It seems that I have completed a full circle this semester. I started with one philosophy, abandoned it, and now I have more or less returned to my original way of thinking. But I have not accepted my old ideal completely. Again I want to study, and I realize my need for organized classes, but want to continue with the activities of the past semester as well. My goals have become much more balanced."

3. "Standing on the threshold of a new semester, it is a time of looking forward and looking back. A time to attempt

new things without repeating the same mistakes. A lot of mistakes were made in the free school, but I believe I learned more last semester than during any previous school year. More about myself and others and how people relate to one another, mostly non-academic subjects and knowledge, more a semester of feelings than intellectual thoughts which I am glad for . . .

I have had the basic problem of many of the people here—lack of self-motivation, and I have discovered that self-motivation is what makes or breaks a person in most cases, at least among those who really do something. I think maybe I was brainwashed for a while by the notion of being free—but *I am finally realizing that it takes more than one hundred 'free' students to make a school.*

When I was asked to write about the school, I could not help but think of the "Tales of Two Cities"—'it was the best of times, it was the worst of times'—the perfect description. We have tried and failed often, and we have tried and succeeded perhaps less often, but we have always tried and we have always learned."

4. *"Has the free school helped me at all? Yes, I feel like I'm doing the work for myself, not for a teacher, or a grade, or even a college. I'm doing all this (or most of it) for my own edification. Wasn't that supposed to have something to do with education? People used to be proud of self-educated men and women.*

The free school has given me the chance to examine my world in a different light, through more time, less pressure and a constantly changing (or disillusioning or electrifying) atmosphere which requires questioning all the time."

SELECTIONS FROM "POLICIES AND STANDARDS FOR THE APPROVAL OF OPTIONAL SCHOOLS AND SPECIAL FUNCTION SCHOOLS"*

Policies are the adopted procedures and guides to be followed by the Commission on Schools in accrediting member schools. The member school has the responsibility of adhering to those policies directly applicable to it.

Policy I. Definition of Schools Qualifying Under These Standards

An optional school is one that offers students an alternative to the standard school program. It may be either a public or a non-public school. A school designed to meet the educational needs of a particular group of students under very special circumstances also falls under these standards as a special function school.

An optional school must offer a complete educational program for the students it serves. However, a special function school offering only a partial program may be accredited under these standards if its particular offerings constitute an integral part of the student's regular elementary or secondary school program, with the remainder of the program being completed elsewhere.

Public schools established to serve all students within defined attendance areas, college preparatory schools, general program non-public schools, and vocational/occupational secondary schools may not qualify under these standards. Alternative educational programs offered within or through a standard school may not be accredited under these standards, since those programs would be covered by the accreditation of the encompassing school.

* Reprinted from the Commission on Schools, North Central Association of Colleges and Schools, revised for 1975–76.

The Commission on Schools shall make the final determination of the eligibility of a school to apply for accreditation under these standards.

Policy II. Accreditation of Special Function Schools

A special function school seeking accreditation under these standards must specify clearly the special function or unusual circumstances that enjoin a special program for the school. Its students must be selected on the basis of the school's expressed special function and the supporting program for the particular needs of those students.

The school must comply with each of the established standards wherever they are applicable to its operation. If the school feels a standard does not apply to its particular situation, it must explain fully its rationale for that exclusion. The rationale will be subject to the review and approval of the Commission on Schools.

Policy III. Non-Discriminatory Selection of Students

A school seeking NCA membership under these standards shall not discriminate in the selection of its students on the basis of race, ethnic origin, or socio-economic level. Nor shall it discriminate on the basis of religion, unless the school is officially church-related and wishes to recruit its students mainly from communicants of that denomination.

Policy IV. Period of Accreditation

A member school accredited under these standards will be accredited for an initial three-year period, including the year the school is admitted into NCA membership. Thereafter, it will be accredited for three-year periods. However, its certificate of membership shall be valid as long as the school continues to satisfy the conditions for accreditation established by the Commission on Schools.

To be eligible for NCA accreditation, the school must be fully approved or accredited by the legally constituted or recognized educational agency in its state, if applicable.

When a school loses its approval or accreditation by the legally constituted or recognized accrediting agency within the state, it becomes subject to the usual Accredited-Warned and Dropped procedures.

A school admitted during the annual meeting will be considered accredited for the entire year.

Policy V. Review of Annual Reports by State Committees and the Commission on Schools

1. A school desiring to continue membership in the Association under these standards shall submit an annual report and such supplementary reports as the Commission on Schools finds necessary in order to accredit schools.

2. Each fall the State Chairman for each state shall distribute the annual report forms with supplementary instructions and suggestions, check the receipt of reports, and make an initial review of the reports in preparation for review by the State Committee. The State Committee shall examine the annual reports from member schools and make recommendations to the Commission for its consideration during the review of the status of all member schools at the annual meeting of the Association in the spring. The accreditation status of the member school covered by these standards shall not be based on the annual report, but on the periodic examination. However, should the annual report or other information indicate such substantive or fundamental changes in the school as to suggest a special examination, the State Committee may so require a re-examination of the school before the next Annual Meeting.

3. It shall be the policy of the Commission not to take an action affecting the accreditation of a member school which is different from that recommended by the State Committee without first consulting with the State Chairman.

4. Each member school in its annual report to the Commission is required to list all violations of standards cited the previous year, and to indicate what action has been taken to correct the deficiencies.

Policy VI. Accreditation and the Composite Effectiveness of the School

1. The member school shall be judged on the basis of its total effectiveness in meeting the educational needs of its students. Although it is a purpose of an accrediting association to develop certain basic standards for the approval of schools, it is recognized by the Commission that desirable variations will occur in the purposes and programs of institutions. Standards and procedures should be sufficiently flexible to provide for these variations within a framework of common preconditions for quality education.

2. The school shall be accredited under these standards on the basis of the recommendations of a board of examiners appointed by the State Chairman. These recommendations shall be reviewed by the State Committee and the Commission on Schools.

3. The board of examiners shall consist of at least three members (one from outside the state) appointed by the State Chairman. The expenses of the examiners shall be paid by the school being examined. The examiners shall remain in the school as long as necessary to assess it thoroughly, but two days shall be considered a minimum period for the examination.

4. In preparation for the examination, the school shall document in writing how it is meeting the intent of each standard.

5. The Commission on Schools, through research and study, shall continue to seek to improve its standards to make them stimulative and conducive to the educational advancement of its member optional schools and special function schools.

Policy VII. School Evaluation

1. In order to stimulate member schools toward continued improvement in the development of quality programs, each member school shall be evaluated at least once each seven-year cycle, using some appropriate evaluation instrument approved by the Commission. These materials shall be used on a self-study basis, to be followed by an NCA evaluation

team of sufficient size which remains an adequate length of time in the school to observe all phases of its program.

2. When the evaluation coincides with a scheduled examination of the school, the two processes may be carried out simultaneously.

Explanatory Note: A typical schedule might be:

1974–75	Year of initial accreditation, examination.
1975–76	Continuing accreditation.
1976–77	Continuing accreditation.
1977–78	Re-examination.
1978–79	Continuing accreditation.
1979–80	Continuing accreditation.
1980–81	Re-examination and full evaluation.
1981–82	Continuing accreditation.
	(. . . and so forth.)

3. A member school shall be evaluated, insofar as is possible, in terms of its stated purposes and objectives, provided these are in harmony with the particular needs of its students and are in accord with the requirements and expectations of the community, the state, and the nation.

4. Following each evaluation, the principal shall file with the State Committee one-year and three-year progress reports concerning the extent to which the school has been using the results of the school evaluation for self-improvement. This is not a requirement to quantify the number of recommendations implemented or rejected but to report on the steps taken to resolve the major limitations disclosed by the evaluation process or to build new strengths deemed desirable by the school.

SELECTIONS FROM "EVALUATION OF HIGH SCHOOL IN THE COMMUNITY," NEW HAVEN, CONNECTICUT*

BY JOHN D. MCCONAHAY, PH.D.,
SHIRLEY FREY-MCCONAHAY,
EDISON J. TRICKETT, PH.D.,
JUDITH E. GRUBER,
WILLIS D. HAWLEY†

I. Introduction

This is the third in the series of evaluation reports on the High School in the Community, New Haven, Connecticut, an educational experiment that is one of the most highly innovative and carefully studied projects in contemporary secondary education. We have discussed the operating assumptions and basic philosophy of the High School in the Community (hereinafter referred to as HSC) in great detail in earlier reports. In this report we shall limit ourselves, for the most part, to discussing several specific objectives that comprise the Evaluation Design for the 1972–73 academic year. Though the HSC community had identified over fifty objectives with multiple sub-objectives which it sought to attain, limitations upon the resources available make it necessary to limit the 1972–73 evaluation to the objectives below. Other important aspects and objectives of HSC, including the Community Orientation Program, were not evaluated this year because they were covered thoroughly in earlier reports and will be covered again in future years.

* Reprinted with permission of the authors.
† John D. McConahay, Ph.D., is an Associate Professor, Institution for Policy Studies, Duke University, Durham, N.C.
Shirley Frey-McConahay is interested in Program Evaluation, the Politics of Educational Reform, and Adolescent Socialization.
Edison J. Trickett, Ph.D., is Associate Professor, Department of Psychology, Institution for Social and Policy Studies, Yale University.
Judith E. Gruber is a graduate student, Department of Political Science, Yale University.
Willis D. Hawley, Ph.D., is Director of Undergraduate Studies, Institution of Policy Sciences and Public Affairs, Durham, N.C.

As indicated in our summary of activities in Chapter Two, the Educational Research Service (hereinafter referred to as ERS) gathered a great deal of data that do not appear in this report. We will be happy to discuss our other findings informally with persons authorized by HSC to receive this information. Finally, we plan to meet informally in August or September 1973 with the entire HSC staff to discuss those findings reported below and any other matters to which our research or study may contribute.

Overview of the Report. This report has five chapters. In this first chapter, we summarize our basic findings in regard to the product objectives for 1972–73 and we make a series of recommendations of a general nature. Specific recommendations are contained in the objective by objective evaluations in Chapter Three. In Chapter Two we give a brief overview of our methodology. This is written in broad strokes and in non-technical language. Appendices A, B, and C provide detailed technical accounts of key methodological strategies written for those interested in the statistical and research methods employed here. As was indicated above, Chapter Three gives the details of our report. Each product, process, and management objective is reviewed, discussed, and evaluated. Those wishing the details of any objective covered in the summary should refer to Chapter Three. Chapter Four includes the three technical appendices alluded to above. In Chapter Five, we list the references to technical and educational books and articles cited within the report.

Readers should note at the outset that we have used the terms "significant" or "statistically significant" very carefully in this report. Whenever either of these terms is used, it means that according to the statistical test used the relationship reported could have occurred by chance less than *five* times in 100. The term "highly significant" means that the relationship could have occurred by chance less than *one* time in 100. The terms "not significant" or "nonsignificant" mean that the relationship or the difference between the schools was so small that it could have occurred by chance *more than five* times in 100. This is the standard terminology in works where statistical tests are applied to data.

Summary of Findings. The picture of HSC which emerges from the data gathered for the 1972–73 evaluation is quite similar to the one found in the 1971–72 report. The school continues to experience many of the growing pains that any organization encounters at this stage of its development. Once again, student performance in the cognitive aspects of education—reading, written expression and mathematics—matched the performance level of a Control Group, comprised of students from Hillhouse and Cross High Schools, the two schools from which most HSC students are drawn (Hillhouse and Cross are referred to here as "feeder schools"). At the same time, HSC students' interest in school, affection for school, and perceptions that they could influence school policy far exceeded the levels of the Control Group students in these important affective areas. The data show that the general atmosphere of HSC, in comparison to the feeder schools, is one that fosters tolerance, cooperation, and a relaxed, relatively tension-free means of learning and interacting among students, faculty, administration, and parents.

Yet, our observations and surveys also revealed that the Policy Council, a promising and innovative approach to involving students and parents in important school decisions, may be dying a slow death from lack of nourishment on basic aspects of school governance and policy making. Further, many of the management tasks appear to be poorly performed or to be performed in a fashion which undercuts the basic philosophy of HSC—openness and shared responsibility for decision making. In future years, HSC will need to devote more attention to shaping, clarifying, and *performing* these managerial functions if the school is to survive this series of growing pains and continue to thrive as an institution in which learning takes place in a satisfying, democratic atmosphere.

In the next few pages, we shall give a brief objective by objective overview of our basic findings. The details of our evaluation of each objective are given in Chapter Three. In reading this summary and the details in Chapter Three, one should keep two points in mind. First, that evaluation has both an absolute and a relative aspect. Hence, while the format imposed upon ERS and HSC by the Office of Education calls for us to evaluate HSC's progress toward a set of absolutes (e.g., a 17 percentage point increase in reading scores), we must bear in mind that these absolutes are usually very high goals and that one cannot really evaluate HSC's progress unless the progress made by students in schools is known. If HSC had reached all of its objectives and the other schools used as a Control Group had also made the same amount of progress, then there would be few grounds for celebration. If, on the other hand, HSC fell short of some of its objectives and still made more progress than the Control schools, then there would be a basis for feeling that something has been accomplished over the past year.

The second point to bear in mind is that, with very few exceptions, the two units of HSC (even with their different personnel and student bodies) differed very little from one another on most product objectives. When one exceeded the Control Group both exceeded it. When one fell short, then the other fell short. As we indicated last year, this is strong evidence that the concepts and philosophies of HSC are more responsible for producing these results than are a few talented or charismatic individuals.

Objective A: Reading and Writing Performance. On the tests of Reading and Written Expression, HSC and the Control Group seniors did not significantly differ from one another nor did HSC seniors improve significantly from 1972 to 1973. Thus, two of the principal reading and writing performance objectives were not achieved. It must be stressed, however, that this does not mean that HSC students did worse than the Control Group from Hillhouse and Cross High Schools on these tests. The three groups (Units I and II at HSC and the students from feeder schools) performed at approximately the same level.

On the other hand, poor readers (as defined in Chapter Three) improved significantly, indicating that HSC's program in this regard was quite successful. Poor writers (as defined in Chapter Three), while successfully identified and given some remedial help, did not improve significantly. Thus, HSC met one of its reading and writing performance goals and did as well as the Control Group on the other three goals.

Objective B: Mathematical Performance. HSC students did not differ significantly from the Control Group students and HSC students did not improve significantly from 1972 to 1973 in mathematical performance. Furthermore, students with poor mathematical skills did not improve significantly (as a group) despite the special instruction they received. Thus, HSC students did no better and no worse than the Control Group students in mathematics.

Objective C: In-service Training—Math and English. While the objective for training 100% of the English, Math, and Language personnel in the Gattegno Method was not achieved, by the end of the school year 75% of the teachers in these three areas had received sufficient training to employ Gattegno methods in their classroom teaching. This is marked progress over the preceding year.

Objective D: Student Attitudes Toward School Governance and Participation in Policy Making. HSC met both of the product objectives in this section. HSC students scored significantly higher (in this case an average of 19 scale points) than the Control Group students on the scale of "Perceived Ability to Influence School Policy." They were, for example, more than 30 percentage points higher than the Control Group in agreeing with the statement: "I feel that I have a real influence on the way my school is run." Hence, as was the case in 1971–72, HSC students clearly feel that they have some influence at HSC and that their views are taken into account whenever policies are made.

Objective E: Teacher Attitudes Toward School Governance. The vast majority of HSC teachers are satisfied with the opportunities which they have to influence school policy and feel that they have a truly significant impact upon the direction of the school. Thus, while the goal of 100% satisfaction was not achieved (one person responded negatively, two people wanted greater input), HSC's attainment of high teacher satisfaction was impressive.

Objective F: Parents' Attitudes Toward HSC and Participation in Policy Making. HSC fell slightly short of its goal of having 90% of its parents feel that they can influence school policy. However, a substantially greater proportion of HSC parents than those from the feeder schools feel that they have enough of a say about school affairs. Furthermore, a majority of the parents of HSC students feel that they have more influence at HSC than at other schools, that they have enough information about the school, and that they have more contact with teachers than they did at other schools.

Objective G: Classroom Atmosphere, Classroom Attendance, and Student Satisfaction with Classes. Data from a sample of classes at both units of HSC, Wilbur Cross, and Hillhouse strongly confirm that students at HSC perceive classes as more involving and more innovative, and teachers as more personally supportive than do students at the other schools. Further, compared with a sample of over three hundred high school classrooms from several states, students at HSC report their classrooms as being above the 80th percentile on these aspects of the classroom environment. HSC classes are reported as less competitive and with less emphasis on "rules and regulations" than classes in the feeder schools. Again, these differences are highly statistically significant. The reported satisfactions of students with their school, their classes, and their teachers again support the contention that HSC students are more satisfied in a number of areas relating to school than are students at the feeder schools. All parts of the attendance objectives were met. Average class attendance at HSC exceeded the stipulated 80%, poor attenders from last year increased their average attendance by well over 10%, and average classroom attendance was over the 80% goal. It should be noted that these attendance figures are not substantially different from those obtained from the feeder schools.

A final aspect of this objective involved managerial issues designed to create innovative teaching and high student satisfaction. Managerial objectives around teacher and student input into hiring practices were, strictly speaking, only partially met, although a great amount of input was reported. Finally, the managerial objectives relating to the role of the Facilitator were partially met, often on a more informal basis than was described in the evaluation design.

Objective H: Revised Job Descriptions. Job descriptions for Facilitator, Unit Head, Outreach Worker, Unit Aide, Guidance Counselor, and teacher were prepared in the fall and revised during June 1973. Since the objective called for approval of the initial descriptions by the Policy Council and this was not done in the fall, this objective was not achieved technically. Nevertheless, the descriptions are now ready to guide HSC in future years.

Objective I: Implementation of Job Descriptions. Our findings revealed that 87% of the HSC staff had job descriptions which were at least 80% congruent with their reported work time. Most of the remaining 13% were overworked in that they were doing much more than was required of them. The second part of this objective requested that every teacher spend at least 10% of his or her time on administrative tasks. Teacher interviews indicated that this objective was met in spirit but not to the point of 100%. Actually, 77% of the teachers were devoting at least 10% of their time to administrative tasks. On the other hand, the remaining 23% did spend a minimum amount of 5% of their time on administration, but they also tended to devote more time to counseling, extra-curricular activities, and additional classes than most other teachers. Some individuals obviously preferred the administrative tasks (35% of the staff spent well over 10% of their time here) while others were much more likely to be counseling students or teaching additional classes. These results seem to demonstrate HSC's ability to adjust realistically to human differences among teachers as well as students on this point.

Objective J: Post High School Educational Plans. HSC seniors planned to go into formal post high school education (college or vocational school) during the next academic year at a rate which exceeded that of the feeder schools by 15 percentage points. This was somewhat less than the projected 20 percentage points, but came very close to achieving the objective.

Objective K: Student Interest in and Affection for School. HSC clearly achieved this objective. Both units of HSC scored significantly higher than the Control Group students from the two feeder high schools on the scale of "Interest in and Affection for School." In addition, students in their first year at HSC (freshmen and transfers from other schools in 1972–73) increased significantly in their interest in and affection for school during the academic year. This is striking evidence

of the superior job that HSC is doing in interesting students
in school and securing their loyalty to it.

**Objective L: Student Acceptance of Persons of Other Races,
Social Classes, and Life Styles.** HSC was generally, but not
entirely, successful in meeting its three product objectives in
this area. The scores of HSC students on the "ERS Ease in
Interracial Contacts" scale showed them significantly more at
ease than the Control Group with persons of other races.
White students at HSC scored lower in anti-black prejudice
than Control Group students on the "ERS Social Distance"
scale, but HSC and Control Group blacks did not differ in
the amount of anti-white prejudice they displayed on a similar
social distance scale. HSC students were more tolerant of
social and political diversity than Control Group students.

Recommendations. Throughout the body of this report there
are a number of specific issues discussed and recommendations made. Here we wish to bring together and focus attention upon several issues which are dispersed throughout the
report but which should be highlighted. Several issues have
to do with the changing organizational context of the school
as it shifts from the phase of creation to the phase of continuation. Particularly appropriate in this context are a number of issues relating to managerial processes and accountability for the carrying out of certain organizational tasks.

(1) While not dealt with in the discussion of issues or the
reaching of decisions, an area of weakness at HSC is the
process by which decisions or ideas are carried out once they
are made. In some cases projects were abandoned consciously
because they were unworkable or non-productive. More often,
however, good projects or ideas simply atrophied or were
tabled and forgotten. Frequently then, at a later time, it would
be clear that work would be lighter or progress swifter if the
original task had been performed effectively. Thus we recommend the following:

(1) A "program development chart" be maintained to
identify non-routine activities and the stage of implementation each is in. Such a chart should be accessible to all
members of the HSC community and could be either a
wall-size display or a workbook format. It should include

the date the program is initiated, the implementation target date, and person(s) responsible. The Facilitator should be responsible for its maintenance.

(2) Priorities must be established for each new program initiative, and old priorities must be reassessed regularly. Priorities must be assigned at the time decisions are made and the persons responsible for programs should be made explicit.

(3) That the Facilitator be responsible for providing each staff member with a semi-annual written comment on the progress that person has made in carrying out the tasks set out in the job descriptions and providing comment on other responsibilities undertaken. The staff member should have an opportunity to comment on these evaluations and they should be submitted, for information and possible response, to the policy council of each unit.

(4) *Concise* job descriptions should be prepared and distributed to all interested staff, students, and parents to provide an opportunity for more cooperation, understanding, and accountability.

(5) When individuals, because of either personality, training, or ideological reasons, are unable to carry out the tasks incumbent with their positions the Facilitator and the Policy Councils must assist them in either changing positions within the HSC community or finding a more suitable position elsewhere.

(2) The Policy Councils are potentially one of the most innovative and exciting components of the HSC design. In order for the Policy Councils to be strong, functioning components of the school governance structure it is important that they have both an advocate for their interests and administrators within the staff. Thus, it is recommended that a staff member (other than the Unit Head) at each unit be assigned responsibility for the Council. This individual would make sure that meetings were called, members were notified, agendas set, relevant issues brought to the Council, pertinent information provided all members, and that the questions raised were pursued until a conclusion was reached. If this individual ensured that problems which are of concern to all groups in the HSC community were meaningfully acted upon by the Policy Council, and not merely legitimating previous

faculty actions, the Council would be a much more vital body than it is today.

Much more attention needs to be given to different ways that parents and students as a whole can be linked with those persons who actually serve on the Councils. There are no magic answers to how this can be done; it is a problem common to all democratically structured organizations. There is, however, considerable reason for optimism about the future of the Councils. Our surveys show that substantial proportions of students, parents, and especially teachers seem to believe that the Councils should be stronger and that it is worth trying to give them a greater vitality.

(3) HSC should expend additional effort to inform and educate the community at large regarding the actual nature and operations of the school. Our parent interviews and our own informal observations suggest that many people in New Haven feel that HSC is a highly disorganized and undisciplined place. Yet, the data running throughout this report tell a different story. HSC is a relaxed, cooperative institution, but students and teachers do not often find discipline problems that interfere with learning. Furthermore, on the basis of our own experiences in other high schools throughout Connecticut, we think that student misbehavior is, if anything, much less of a problem at HSC than elsewhere. In particular the Board of Education needs to be kept better informed about HSC by both the Facilitator and the Superintendent's staff.

(4) Another recommendation is one geared more toward the next general evaluation design than toward the functioning of HSC *per se*. For several of the evaluation objectives, HSC set up a criterion of successful accomplishment which was not stated relative to the feeder schools but to some absolute standard. The teacher selection process described in Objective G provides one example. In terms of the specified procedure for assuring that prospective teaching candidates were interviewed by teachers, students, and parents, HSC only partially fulfilled this objective. However, without question, the amount of input of teachers and students into the hiring process considerably exceeds that in the feeder schools. The way the objective was stated, however, precluded this kind of comparison as a way of judging achievement. It is thus entirely possible that HSC could not be meeting the objective by absolute criteria and still be coming significantly closer than the

comparison schools. On the other hand, the comparison schools might be succeeding better than HSC. The recommendation, then, is to structure goals—whenever possible—in comparative terms with either the feeder schools or with some norms based on more general data serving as the comparison standard.

Conclusion. There is no doubt in our minds that HSC has earned continuation of its program. Both the hard data and informal observations indicate that HSC is doing as good a job as other New Haven Schools in teaching cognitive skills (reading, writing, and mathematics) and doing it in an atmosphere which is more cooperative, less tense, and more satisfying for both teachers and students than is the atmosphere in other schools. HSC may not work well for all students, but it is unlikely that any one school is optimal for all students. The fact that all students have available to them the option of choosing to learn in an environment such as HSC's undoubtedly enriches the possibilities of student success in other schools as well.

As we think back over the three years we have carefully observed HSC, we are impressed that the staff at HSC is, as it has not been before, optimistic that HSC will really work. There appears to be an increased sense of being able to "get it together." Some of the romance is gone and there is a new toughness about the tasks that need to be done and a sense of direction about how these tasks can be accomplished. There is also a recognition that it is not easy to hold a school like HSC together without holding people accountable and submerging the needs of individual staff members to the needs of students and the organization.

In addition, much better use is being made of available resources both educationally and economically; cooperation among individuals, and especially between the two units, has never been greater or more productive.

As we note in the following pages, problems remain. Problems of coordination and accountability are inherent in nonbureaucratic organizations like HSC and they are, to some extent, the costs one trades for the innovation and commitment that HSC fosters. Nevertheless, there is every reason to believe that the performance that HSC has demonstrated in the past will increase in excellence.

II. Methodology

In order to evaluate the High School in the Community and its program, we engaged in a wide variety of methods, approaches, and activities. One of our principal methods was that of careful, detailed observation. ERS observers attended and took notes at the following HSC meetings and activities: faculty meetings at both units, curriculum meetings, all Policy Council meetings for both units, parent meetings at both units, and portions of the post-semester work period in June 1973.

We also used the method of open and in-depth interviewing. During the year, ERS staff personnel interviewed all HSC teachers and staff and a random sample of the parents of students at both units of HSC, Cross and Hillhouse High Schools, and all parents who were delegates to the Policy Councils.

In addition, by means of combined interviewing, controlled observation, and questionnaires, we assessed the classroom environment and student-teacher interactions and satisfactions in a sample of classes at both units of HSC and the two feeder high schools.[1]

The vast majority of our data on student performance and attitudes were gained in three testing sessions: May 1972; September 1972 (for entering freshmen only); and May 1973. From the data gathered in these testing sessions, scales of reading comprehension, written expression, and mathematical performance and various social and personal attitudes were developed.[2]

Finally, many of the official documents and records of HSC and the two feeder schools were examined to gather the data necessary to evaluate attendance objectives and a number of process and management objectives.

Classroom Environment and Student Satisfaction. The assessment of the classroom environments in the three high schools was accomplished through use of the Classroom Environment Scale (CES), a ninety-item pencil and paper questionnaire developed by one of the evaluators (E.J.T.) and reported in the professional literature (Trickett and Moos, 1973).[3] This instrument measures the amount of emphasis placed on nine different dimensions of the classroom environment: Student Involvement, Student-Student Affiliation, Teacher Support, Task Orientation, Competition, Order and Organization, Rule Clarity, Teacher Control, and Innovation. It is standardized on a sample of over three hundred high school classrooms and has highly acceptable test-retest reliability. The student satisfactions were assessed through student response to a number of specific questions which followed the Classroom Environment Scale. These questions included: (1) In general, how satisfied are you with this school?; (2) In general, how satisfied are you with classes in this school?; (3) How satisfied are you with this particular class?; (4) How much actual material do you feel you're learning in this class?; (5) How easy is it to get academic help from teachers if you want it?; (6) How easy is it to talk with teachers at this school about personal matters?

Sampling of Classes. These two questionnaires (the CES and the satisfaction questions) were given to twenty-one classes at HSC, twelve at Wilbur Cross, and nine at Hillhouse. Students were asked *not* to put their names on the individual questionnaires, thus insuring anonymity of response. A total of 157 students from HSC, 156 from Wilbur Cross, and 121 from Hillhouse completed the questionnaire.

Because the actual sampling procedure differed somewhat from that specified in the evaluation design, it will be specified now. The original methodology suggested a sampling of twelve classes from each of the schools, stratifying by grade. This stratification criterion was made implausible by the number of HSC classes containing students from different years (i.e., sampling only from classes with one year of students would not yield a representative sample of classes). Thus, it was decided to select, on a random basis, one class taught by each regular teacher at both units. Teachers at both units thus submitted the times of several classes to ERS; we then selected on a random basis the class for each particular teacher. This yielded six English classes, six social studies, four science, three language, and two business and technical classes. Since the overwhelming majority of HSC classes fell into the four main departments of English, social studies, science, and languages, it was decided that the twelve classes from each of the feeder schools should be divided equally among those four departments. Rather than stratify by grade, it was decided simply to ask for a random sample of three classes from each of the four departments.

At Wilbur Cross, the actual selection was done by the Department Chairman after a meeting with ERS to discuss the procedure, while at Hillhouse the actual selection was carried out by ERS with the consent of relevant Department Chairmen. Scheduling problems precluded gathering data from the science classes at Hillhouse, thus leaving a sample of twelve classes at Wilbur Cross and nine at Hillhouse.

All data collection was carried out in April and May 1973.

Student Performance Testing and Attitude Survey. The reading comprehension, English expression, and mathematical performance and the various social and personal attitudes of students were evaluated by means of tests and questionnaires. The methods for obtaining these data in May 1972 are given in the 1972 Evaluation Report. We shall describe the sampling of data analysis procedures for the September 1972 and May 1973 assessment sessions here.

In order to control for such extraneous factors as history, maturation, and statistical regression, we adopted a modified form of what Campbell and Stanley call the institutional cycle design. All entering freshmen at HSC were tested as part of their orientation program in September 1972. In May 1973, we drew a sample of students from HSC and from Hillhouse and Cross High Schools.[4] Here it is sufficient to note that it was a stratified random sample drawn in such a fashion that *we can safely generalize from the responses of those tested to all students in the group which they represent.* In addition, the sampled students were recruited for the May 1973 session in such a fashion (confirmed by subsequent interviews) that *motivation for taking the test and answering the questions was equal across the various HSC and Control Groups.*

In order to equate the various racial compositions of the schools, all sampling was done within racial groups, i.e., an equal number of black and white seniors, an equal number of black and white freshmen, etc., and the data were analyzed by means of statistical techniques which gave equal weight (across schools) to black and white responses.

Whenever it was possible scales were created to measure

attitudes and performance because these are more reliable and valid than are single item responses.[5]

For the purposes of data analysis, the samples from Hillhouse and Cross were combined to form one Control Group. This is because preliminary analysis revealed little difference between these two schools and because we were interested in evaluating HSC and not the two feeder schools.

Finally, before deciding whether or not a given objective had been met, we subjected the data to a number of analyses in which we compared scores across schools (HSC with the Control) in May 1973, and in most cases, within schools across time (the changes at HSC from 1972 to 1973). In some instances, we also made comparisons within a given class (tenth graders with other tenth graders) and within years at a given school (first-year students, regardless of grade, with other first-year students or scores for first-year students in May or September 1972 with their scores in May 1973). The results of these analyses are not always reported because they were consistent with the more readily reportable and understandable results in the tables. Hence, the data in the tables should be considered as illustrative and not a definitive demonstration.[6]

FOOTNOTES

1. The details of the methods for these classroom observations are given in a special section of Chapter Two and in Appendix C of "Evaluation of High School in the Community, New Haven, Connecticut, 1973."

2. The details of these procedures are given in the last section of Chapter Two and in Appendices A and B of "Evaluation of High School in the Community, New Haven, Connecticut, 1973."

3. A copy of the paper describing the construction of the scale is found in Appendix C of "Evaluation of High School in the Community, New Haven, Connecticut, 1973."

4. The exact procedures for drawing this sample are given in Appendix A of "Evaluation of High School in the Community, New Haven, Connecticut, 1973."

5. The details of the attitude scales are given in Chapter Three and Appendix B and the performance tests for cognitive skills are discussed in Chapter Three of "Evaluation of High School in the Community, New Haven, Connecticut, 1973."

6. Those wishing the details of these and other analyses should read Appendices A, B, and C of "Evaluation of High School in the Community, New Haven, Connecticut, 1973" and consult with Educational Research Service after obtaining authorization to do so from HSC.

"THE ALTERNATIVE SCHOOL TRANSCRIPT" FROM HOME BASE SCHOOL*

Transcripts are translating mechanisms that are crucial to the future of a student and to the success of a school in providing for its students. The main function of the transcript is to offer a portrait of the student; to reflect and interpret the student's education for people outside the school, specifically for college admissions officers and employers.

Transcripts from alternative schools tend to be bulky, awkward and many times they tell very little about the student. Frequently letter grades are not used; consequently alternative schools often rely on some form of written evaluation to make up a major part of the student's transcript. For students who want to go to college, or are applying for a job, the traditional high school will send a sheet full of records . . . the alternative school will send a record full of sheets. The problem is self-explanatory: students who apply to college from an alternative school may be at a disadvantage only because of the TRANSCRIPT . . . not the SCHOOL or the STUDENT.

College Reactions to Alternative School Transcripts

A number of college admissions officers were asked how they handled alternative school applications. They all responded most positively about alternative school students. Their enthusiasm turned into frustration when they spoke of trying to deal with alternative school transcripts. For example:

> I get piles of evaluations impossible to comprehend. . . . I don't know who is making these comments, and all they say is how *great* the kid is. How can one possibly exercise fair judgment without substantial information of a student's performance and skills?

* Reprinted with permission from Home Base School: Students, Staff, and Evaluation Team, Watertown, Massachusetts, John Sakala, Program Chairman; Joseph Boyce, Chairman; and Dr. Daniel O'Connor, Superintendent of Schools.

Alternative school transcripts are all alike.

Alternative school transcripts do not offer enough information to compare these students with those having conventional records.

Again, it should be stressed that despite their frustration, college admissions officers were very positive about alternative school students. As one director of admissions from a highly competitive school noted,

We may be in a damn mess . . . but alternative education is going in the right direction.

Again . . . the TRANSCRIPT, not the SCHOOL or STUDENT.

What follows is a summary of the items that college admissions officers like and dislike in alternative school transcripts. This listing offers clear-cut objectives for developing transcripts.

LIKES
— Profile and description of the school.
— Explanation of the evaluation and credit procedures.
— Explanation of how the transcript is to be read.
— Subject area designations.
— Counselor's recommendation.
— NASSP student transcript and personality rating forms.
— SAT scores.
— Concise and clear statements of the student's progress, accomplishments and interests.
— Examples of the student's work integrated into the format of the transcript.

DISLIKES
— Incomplete transcripts in which only the years in the alternative school are included.
— Different types of transcripts for students from the same alternative school.
— Missing data such as dates and duration of courses and other pertinent information regarding academic performance.
— Unnecessary bulk, pages of unexplained information.

Evaluations: The Key to Transcripts

Since the transcript is based upon all of the course and project evaluations the student has accumulated, it is to the alternative school student's advantage to have an efficient and fair evaluation process.

Evaluations prepared by each teacher are compiled and recorded by the student's advisor at Home Base. This compilation comprises the student's transcript, the outcome of the student's work while at school. In many instances the evaluations are wordy; say the same things about most students; fail to demonstrate specific performance, skills, or growth; omit important information such as duration of the course, hours per week and subject area; and comment on student personality and behavioral traits rather than course work. The transcripts will remain vague, uninformative and bulky as long as the course evaluations remain that way.

The Improved Evaluation and Transcript Procedure

There are three major steps to the improved evaluation and transcript process: a monthly appraisal (called Interpersonal Memo), a formal final evaluation and a transcript statement. These were developed, through a series of weekly school workshops, to meet the need for a clear, efficient and fair evaluation and transcript procedure at Home Base School. The procedure is constantly being monitored and will be changed as the need becomes clear.

Monthly Interpersonal Memo. The memo is a confidential statement written each month by the teacher of the course or project. It is confidential in order to create an atmosphere of honesty and safety that permits an appraisal of the work in a manner that is positive and personal. The memo is monthly in order to allow for a process of regular communication among the student, the teacher and the student's Home Base advisor, which in turn encourages an ongoing collaboration. Additionally, the memo reflects changes in the student throughout the course or project.

Information in the memo includes the requirements and expectations of the student for the month, appraisal of the work, a record of attendance as well as time and duration of the course and a general course description. The memo process encourages students to finish what they start because the ongoing communication allows for supportive and committed relationships among student, teacher and advisor. Students not taking a course or doing a project for credit do not take part in the monthly memo process. It is a barometer for everyone, student and teacher, because it provides an overview of the course and the student's development through the months.

At regular intervals parents are sent notices encouraging them to inquire about the progress of their student. The advisor in synthesizing these memos can keep parents up to date on how their child is doing.

Final Evaluation. The final evaluation, similar to the monthly memo, includes the requirements for the course and an appraisal of the student's accomplishment of the requirements. Additionally it includes a grade of pass or fail and comments prepared in collaboration with the student concerning the student's strengths and weaknesses, progress, participation and attendance, and effort and consistency. The emphasis is on how well the student met the requirements of the course, not on the subjective impressions of the teacher. This emphasis also helps the teacher organize his course into requirements.

Transcript Statement. The transcript is compiled by the student's advisor as course and project evaluations are completed throughout the year. The teacher of each course as part of the final evaluation process briefly summarizes the specific requirements of the course and evaluates the student's work. It includes the duration of the course or project, hours per week, subject area, attendance and a Pass/Fail grade. Because the summary is the result of the whole evaluation process beginning with the monthly memo, it frequently is specific and thorough yet brief enough simply to be transferred to the transcript with little rewriting by the advisor.

It is also the advisor's task to summarize the comments prepared by the teachers concerning the student's development throughout the year. Guidelines for this include progress, responsibility, acquisition of skills and knowledge, effort and consistency, participation in the school community, etc.

Implications

Several purposes are served through the three stages of the evaluation and transcript process.

1. A thorough record is acquired of the specific work that the student has accomplished.
2. Students are aided and encouraged to finish what they start.
3. A regular process of communication among student, teacher and advisor is encouraged.
4. Resource people are aided in developing and organizing their courses.

The monthly memo is the key instrument that encourages communication and helps develop commitment on the part of the student and the teacher to each other. Because it is written at regularly spaced intervals it is also the means by which resource people are aided in developing their courses and through which staff members can keep accurate and up-to-date records. This provides a means for quality control of courses, projects and teachers as well as offering an overview of the student's progress throughout the months.

The final evaluation is the instrument that illustrates specifically what was *expected* of a student in a course or project, what the student *did,* and *how well* it was done.

The monthly memos are the basis for the final evaluation, which in turn is transferred directly onto the transcript.

The transcript is the mechanism that translates the student's accomplishments during high school for college admissions officers and/or employers. It is crucial to the future of the student and it is essential for the alternative school to have efficient and fair evaluation and transcript procedures.

The revised forms for the monthly Interpersonal Memo, the final evaluation and the transcript statement are available upon request. Most important, however, is the idea behind the revision, which this report has tried to convey. Evaluations that encourage continuous collaboration and fairness plus concise and consistent ways of reporting are the key to this process.

"EDUCATION BY CHOICE," 1973–74 EVALUATION SUMMARY OF QUINCY SENIOR HIGH II PROGRAM*

BY DR. BRANDT G. CROCKER,
RICHARD F. HAUGH, AND
DONALD A. PRICE

Introduction

During the 1973–74 school year, the *Education by Choice* program at Quincy Senior High II focused its evaluation on three specific groups: project students, project teachers, and project parents. The objectives relating to project students were concerned with attitudes toward the educational environment, attitudes toward teachers, discipline referrals, dropouts, absences, and academic performance. The objectives relating to project teachers were concerned with attitudes toward their role in the educational program. The objectives relating to project parents were concerned with their attitudes toward their involvement in the educational program and their attitudes toward the alternative school concept. This summary provides an overview of the results of these objectives.

Project Students

Two instruments were used to assess the attitudes of project students. The first instrument was the *Quincy All-Choice Continuum*. This test was developed in 1970 and has recently undergone extensive study by a doctoral student from Southern Illinois University. The results of this study have confirmed that this instrument is a reliable device for measuring attitudes. The second instrument was the *School Sentiment Index*, which was developed as part of the Instructional Objective Exchange in California. Both of these instruments were

* Reprinted from ESEA 1973–74 Summary Title III with permission of the authors.

administered to project students in May of 1973 as a pre-test and again in May of 1974 as a post-test. This design was utilized to determine the amount of change in the attitudes of students after one year of participation in the *Education by Choice* program. This report includes the scores from the *Quincy All-Choice Continuum* and relates the results of the *School Sentiment Index* to those scores. Each item on the *Quincy All-Choice Continuum* has a possible range of 0 to 20 and responses are always scored with the negative side of the continuum as 0 and the positive side as 20.

The first section of the *Quincy All-Choice Continuum* measures the attitudes of students toward *School in General*. The items and results on both the pre and post assessments are:

Item			Pre-test May 1973	Post-test May 1974
My school experiences help me.	_____	My school experiences do not help me.	10th - 14.5 to 11th - 14.3 to	11th - 15.1 12th - 15.4
My school experiences have no meaning for me.	_____	My school experiences have meaning for me.	10th - 14.2 to 11th - 14.4 to	11th - 15.1 12th - 15.2
I am proud of my school.	_____	I am not proud of my school.	10th - 14.2 to 11th - 13.5 to	11th - 15.5 12th - 15.6
School is not important to me.	_____	School is important to me.	10th - 14.5 to 11th - 14.2 to	11th - 15.4 12th - 15.6
I plan to graduate.	_____	I do not plan to graduate.	10th - 18.3 to 11th - 18.7 to	11th - 18.8 12th - 19.0

The results of this section of the *Quincy All-Choice Continuum* quite obviously reflect a more positive attitude in the individuals responding in 1974 than 1973. On all items, there was a positive increase from the previous year in the attitudes of students toward school. It is also interesting to note that those individuals in the eleventh grade in 1974 responded more positively than those who were in the eleventh grade in 1973. Therefore, not only has there been an increase or change with respect to the particular groups, but comparison across groups also indicated a more positive school climate. The results on the *School Social Structure and Climate Scale* of the *School Sentiment Index* totally support this finding in that definite positive growth has taken place in both grade levels.

The second section of the *Quincy All-Choice Continuum* measures the attitude of students toward *School Work and Assignments*. The items and results on both the pre and post assessments are:

Item			Pre-test May 1973	Post-test May 1974
I think all assignments are boring.	_____	I think all assignments are interesting.	10th - 9.8 to 11th - 9.5 to	11th - 10.5 12th - 10.9
I do more schoolwork than assigned.	_____	I do not do any schoolwork.	10th - 10.1 to 11th - 9.8 to	11th - 10.4 12th - 10.4
I never buy books with my extra money.	_____	I always buy books with my extra money.	10th - 7.6 to 11th - 8.1 to	11th - 8.6 12th - 9.0
I like difficult assignments.	_____	I do not like difficult assignments.	10th - 7.5 to 11th - 8.0 to	11th - 8.7 12th - 9.5
I do not like to do homework.	_____	I like to do homework.	10th - 5.8 to 11th - 5.3 to	11th - 7.4 12th - 7.4

Students involved in the *Education by Choice* program show a definite increase in their attitudes toward learning. In addition to exhibiting positive attitudinal growth, students in the eleventh grade in 1974 again have a higher score than those students who were in the eleventh grade in 1973. This seems to indicate that the total environment of 1974 was viewed by students as being more desirable than that of 1973. The subtest of the *School Sentiment Index* entitled *Learning* also shows positive increases in the attitudes of students. Both sets of data indicate that students involved in the *Education by Choice* program have a more positive attitude toward learning than they did prior to the project.

The third section of the *Quincy All-Choice Continuum*

measures the attitude of students toward *Teachers*. The items and results on both the pre and post assessments are:

Item			Pre-test May 1973	Post-test May 1974
My teachers make their subjects interesting to me.	_____	My teachers bore me when they are teaching.	10th - 11.5 to 11th - 11.4 to	11th - 12.4 12th - 12.8
I have a poor relationship with all my teachers.	_____	I have a good relationship with all of my teachers.	10th - 12.9 to 11th - 12.9 to	11th - 14.0 12th - 14.4
I feel that my teachers are human.	_____	I feel that my teachers are not human.	10th - 15.0 to 11th - 15.6 to	11th - 16.4 12th - 16.5
I never trust teachers.	_____	I always trust teachers.	10th - 12.3 to 11th - 11.9 to	11th - 13.5 12th - 13.6
I love teachers.	_____	I hate teachers.	10th - 9.8 to 11th - 10.3 to	11th - 11.1 12th - 11.2

Students in the *Education by Choice* program have shown a notable increase on each item in the *Teacher* section of the *Quincy All-Choice Continuum*. Along with the definite increases after one year of participation in the project, eleventh-graders in 1974 again show a more positive attitude toward teachers than eleventh-graders in 1973. The results on the *School Sentiment Index* subtest entitled *Teachers* also show positive growth in both grade levels. This data seems to indicate that students in the *Education by Choice* program have a more positive attitude toward teachers than they did prior to the implementation of the program.

The fourth section of the *Quincy All-Choice Continuum* measures the attitude of students toward *Peers*. The items and results on both the pre and post assessments are:

Item			Pre-test May 1973	Post-test May 1974
All students dislike me.	_____	All students like me.	10th - 12.4 to 11th - 12.3 to	11th - 12.7 12th - 13.4
I have many friends at school.	_____	I have no friends at school.	10th - 15.8 to 11th - 15.8 to	11th - 15.5 12th - 15.4

Students at this school are not very friendly.	_____	Students at this school are very friendly.	10th - 12.0 to 11th - 12.9 11th - 10.8 to 12th - 12.7
Other students make me feel good about myself.	_____	Other students make me feel bad about myself.	10th - 13.2 to 11th - 12.9 11th - 13.1 to 12th - 13.1
Other students are always mean to me.	_____	Other students are never mean to me.	10th - 12.3 to 11th - 13.5 11th - 12.5 to 12th - 13.8

In general the results indicate a slight positive trend but not nearly as marked as those found in previous sections. This would be expected because a pattern of peer relationships is usually established by the time individuals get to this age level. The results on the *School Sentiment Index* subtest entitled *Peers* would indicate that there has been an increase in attitude toward peers. The results of this subtest are more substantial than those found on the *Quincy All-Choice Continuum* and appear to indicate that the *Education by Choice* program is having a positive effect on peer relationships.

The fifth section of the *Quincy All-Choice Continuum* measures the attitude of students toward *Authority and Administrators*. The items and results on both the pre and post assessments are:

Item			Pre-test May 1973	Post-test May 1974
Administrators are always fair.	_____	Administrators are never fair.	10th - 10.8 to 11th - 10.3 to	11th - 10.9 12th - 11.0
Administrators are rigid.	_____	Administrators are flexible.	10th - 10.0 to 11th - 9.9 to	11th - 10.8 12th - 11.3
School administrators at *this* school are fair to students.	_____	School administrators at *this* school are unfair to students.	10th - 11.7 to 11th - 11.2 to	11th - 12.4 12th - 12.2
Administrators are not friendly people.	_____	Administrators are friendly people.	10th - 11.3 to 11th - 11.8 to	11th - 12.8 12th - 12.8

Item			Pre-test May 1973		Post-test May 1974
I feel that administrators are willing to try students' ideas.	_____	I feel that administrators are never willing to try students' ideas.	10th - 11.7 11th - 11.4	to to	11th - 12.4 12th - 12.2

The results of this subtest are most impressive since in all instances there has been an increase. A comparison of the scores of eleventh-graders in 1974 with those of eleventh-graders in 1973 tends also to substantiate that the *Education by Choice* program is having a positive effect on student attitudes toward their administrators. Further, through talking with students, it appears that they are very positive concerning the interaction that occurs between them and their administrators. It would seem highly desirable for the project administrators to continue this effort.

The sixth section of the *Quincy All-Choice Continuum* measures the attitude of students toward *School*. The items and results on both the pre and post assessments are:

Item			Pre-test May 1973		Post-test May 1974
I feel I am not important in this school.	_____	I feel I am important in this school.	10th - 9.9 11th - 9.0	to to	11th - 10.7 12th - 10.9
School people see me as a good person.	_____	School people see me as a bad person.	10th - 13.5 11th - 13.5	to to	11th - 13.4 12th - 14.1
I attend all school events.	_____	I attend no school events.	10th - 10.0 11th - 9.8	to to	11th - 10.0 12th - 10.2
At school everyone cares about me.	_____	At school no one cares about me.	10th - 11.4 11th - 11.1	to to	11th - 11.5 12th - 11.5
My school is not a friendly place.	_____	My school is a friendly place.	10th - 12.1 11th - 11.3	to to	11th - 13.4 12th - 13.0

The results on this section of the *Quincy All-Choice Continuum* are generally similar to the results on the other sections. While the positive growth is not as pronounced as in other sections, it does appear that students in the *Education by Choice* program do have a more positive attitude toward their school environment. In addition, the *School in General* subtest of the *School Sentiment Index* supports the results of the *Quincy All-Choice Continuum* by showing positive growth in both grade levels.

The final section of the *Quincy All-Choice Continuum* measures the attitudes of students toward Quincy. The items and results on both the pre and post assessments are:

Item			Pre-test May 1973	Post-test May 1974
Quincy is a good place to live.	_____	Quincy is a bad place to live.	10th - 12.8 to 11th - 12.3 to	11th - 12.1 12th - 12.1
I am not happy in Quincy.	_____	I am happy in Quincy.	10th - 12.8 to 11th - 12.3 to	11th - 12.0 12th - 12.0
There is a lot to do in Quincy.	_____	There is not a lot to do in Quincy.	10th - 8.1 to 11th - 6.3 to	11th - 7.0 12th - 6.5
Quincy has nothing to offer to teenagers.	_____	Quincy has a lot to offer teenagers.	10th - 7.8 to 11th - 7.0 to	11th - 7.8 12th - 7.3
I am proud to live in Quincy.	_____	I am not proud to live in Quincy.	10th - 12.7 to 11th - 12.5 to	11th - 12.2 12th - 12.4

The results of this section show a definite deviation from the trends established by the first six sections of the *Quincy All-Choice Continuum*. While the items on this section do not directly relate to the educational environment, it would appear quite appropriate for the project staff to review these results and consider possible ways to reverse this trend.

Overall, the data provided demonstrate that the attitudes of students in the *Education by Choice* program toward school and school-related activities have definitely improved. The findings of the *Quincy All-Choice Continuum* and *School Sentiment Index* indicate that students have a more positive attitude toward their educational environment than they did prior to the implementation of the program.

A second area of the *Education by Choice* project which related to students was concerned with dropouts. During the

1972–73 school year, 184 students left the eleventh and twelfth grades prior to graduation and without transferring to another school. Of these, 148 were considered to be dropouts. Based on the eleventh- and twelfth-grade enrollments during the 1972–73 school year, the dropout rate for the school year prior to the implementation of the project was 10.67%. During the 1973–74 school year, 186 students left the eleventh and twelfth grades prior to graduation and without transferring to another school. Of these, 110 were considered to be dropouts. Based on the eleventh- and twelfth-grade enrollments during the 1973–74 school year, the dropout rate during the first year of the project was 7.09%.

The results are very encouraging since there was a decline of 3.58% in the dropout rate. This is an outstanding reduction for one year. The project personnel should be encouraged to monitor carefully the dropout rate for the 1974–75 year to see if the reduction is maintained. These results would tend to support other data indicating that students are positively inclined toward the environment available at Quincy Senior High II through the *Education by Choice* program.

A third area of the *Education by Choice* project relating to students was concerned with absences. The 1972–73 data is based on grades ten, eleven, and twelve, and the recordkeeping system utilized at that time prevents the separation of absenteeism for grades eleven and twelve only. During the 1972–73 school year, there were 30,268 student absences in grades ten, eleven, and twelve. The 1973 data is based on grades eleven and twelve, and provides the absences incurred by project students. During the 1973–74 school year there were 23,140 student absences in grades eleven and twelve. From a comparison of the data available during the 1972–73 school year and that of the 1973–74 school year, the results seem to indicate the pattern of absence has not changed as a result of the *Education by Choice* program.

A fourth area of the *Education by Choice* project which related to students was concerned with discipline referrals. The 1972–73 data are based on grades ten, eleven, and twelve, and the recordkeeping system utilized at that time prevents the separation of discipline referrals for grades eleven and twelve only. During the 1972–73 school year, there were 6,002 discipline referrals in grades ten, eleven, and twelve. The 1973–74 data is based on grades eleven and twelve, and provides the number of discipline referrals incurred by project students. During the 1973–74 school year, there were 517 discipline referrals in grades eleven and twelve. While a direct comparison cannot be made, the data would seem to indicate that a definite reduction did occur and that students in the *Education by Choice* program incurred noticeably less discipline referrals than the pattern present in the year prior to the project.

The final area related to students was concerned with academic performance. To assess the academic growth of project students, the Iowa Test of Educational Development, available through Science Research Associates, was used. This instrument was administered to project students in May of 1973 as a pre-test and again in May of 1974 as a post-test.

The results indicate that in each of the seven areas, project students in both grades showed positive growth. Additionally, the results show that students in the project are extremely close to the national mean in every instance. It should be noted that one intent of the project is to provide an ideal learning climate for every student. By providing such a program, those students who are remaining in school and are not necessarily academically inclined will cause the mean scores to be lower than if these students were to leave the educational setting. The results of this study indicate that students in the *Education by Choice* program have shown positive academic growth and maintained their cognitive level as compared to national norms.

Project Teachers

The commitment of teachers in the *Education by Choice* project to involving parents in the educational program was measured in two ways. The first method was to assess teachers in September of 1973 with a series of continuums to determine their feelings toward the involvement of parents in the educational program. The continuums were again administered to teachers in the *Education by Choice* program in May of 1974 to determine if their feelings had changed after participating in the project for a year. As with the continuums administered to students, each item had a possible range of 0 to 20 with 0 always representing the negative side and 20 always representing the positive side. The individual items on this test and the results of both assessments are:

Item		September 1973	May 1974
This past year I contacted all of the parents of my students.	This past year I contacted none of the parents of my students.	7.0	11.8
This past year I made no effort to involve parents in the educational program.	This past year I made every effort to involve parents in the educational program.	8.5	11.4
This past year I was not interested in the opinions of parents.	This past year I was very interested in the opinions of parents.	13.1	14.3
This past year I made parents feel free to contact me.	This past year I did not make parents feel free to contact me.	13.1	15.7
This past year I was not interested in involving parents in the educational program.	This past year I was interested in involving parents in the educational program.	12.3	14.4

Another method to determine the commitment of teachers in the *Education by Choice* project to involving parents in the educational program was to record the number of parental contacts that were made. During the 1973–74 school year, teachers made over four thousand contacts with parents through home visits, phone contact, personal letter, or other methods of contact on a personal basis.

The two sets of data are quite complimentary in that they both indicate that there has been a great deal of contact with parents by the teachers during the year. It is most impressive that there were a large number of different parents contacted throughout the various months of the year. This is most encouraging because in many traditional settings parent contacts occur most often when discipline problems occur within the school.

The responses to the five items dealing with this objective show marked increases. In addition to the increase, special note should be taken that the teachers felt that in the past they had not contacted the parents of their students. This is especially evident in the first item. There have been marked increases in those items where the teachers, in general, were rating themselves low at the beginning of the year. The data available for this objective strongly indicate that the intent of this objective has been met and that teachers are highly interested in involving parents in the educational program offered at Quincy Senior High School II.

The other area concerning teachers that was part of the *Education by Choice* evaluation was their attitude toward their role in the educational process.

In September of 1973, teachers were administered ten continuums to determine their attitude about their role in the educational process. The continuums were again administered to teachers in May of 1974 to determine if their attitudes had changed after a year of participation in the *Education by Choice* program. The individual items on this test and the results of both assessments are:

Item		September 1973	May 1974
This past year I felt involved in the decision-making process of the school.	This past year I did not feel involved in the decision-making process of the school.	10.2	10.7
This past year I felt bad about my role in the educational process.	This past year I felt good about my role in the educational process.	12.7	14.9
This past year I spent no time thinking about education.	This past year I spent all my time thinking about education.	13.5	14.3
This past year I worked hard at my job.	This past year I did not work hard at my job.	17.2	17.5
This past year I spent all my time discussing education with my colleagues.	This past year I spent no time discussing education with my colleagues.	11.7	12.5

Item		September 1973	May 1974
This past year I felt bad about my fellow teachers.	This past year I felt good about my fellow teachers.	13.1	15.1
This past year I felt good about my administrators.	This past year I felt bad about my administrators.	11.3	12.6
This past year I felt as though I didn't know what was going on in the school.	This past year I felt as though I did know what was going on in the school.	11.3	11.6
This past year I felt good about the way the school was run.	This past year I felt bad about the way the school was run.	9.7	12.1
This past year I felt bad about my school.	This past year I felt good about my school.	12.2	14.6

On all ten items there was a positive increase in the teacher responses. The items showing the greatest increase concerned the teachers feeling better about their role in the educational process, feeling more positive toward their fellow teachers, feeling good about the way the school is run, and finally, in general, feeling good about the school. In looking at the response pattern of the items, it is obvious that there was a general shift toward the positive end of the scale from the pre to the post assessment. It appears, therefore, that teachers in the *Education by Choice* project are more positive concerning their role in the educational process than they were prior to the program.

Project Parents

The attitude of project parents concerning their involvement in the educational program was also measured through the use of a series of continuums. In June of 1973, the instrument was mailed to a random sample of parents to determine how they felt about their involvement in the educational program. In June of 1974, another random sample of parents was administered the series of continuums to determine the amount of change that had occurred in parental attitudes after one year of the project. The individual items on this instrument and the results of both assessments are:

Item		June 1973	June 1974
I am never contacted about my son or daughter's progress in Senior High School II.	I am always contacted about my son or daughter's progress in Senior High School II.	10.5	12.3
I feel highly involved in the educational programs offered by Senior High School II.	I feel uninvolved in the educational programs offered by Senior High School II.	9.3	9.2
I feel my son or daughter's teachers are very interested in my opinions.	I feel my son or daughter's teachers are not interested in my opinions.	11.0	11.9
I feel teachers make a serious effort to involve me in the educational program.	I feel teachers make no effort to involve me in the educational program.	10.5	11.1
I do not feel free to contact my son or daughter's teachers.	I feel free to contact my son or daughter's teachers.	15.7	15.7

The item showing the greatest increase substantiates the findings of the teacher data and indicates that the school is making more contact with the home than previously. Additionally, this item indicates that the effort of the school to contact the home is being perceived in a more positive manner by parents. The two continuums concerned with teacher involvement with parents also substantiate previous findings that parents feel teachers in the program are making a greater effort to contact and involve them. On the other two items, it appears that the parents' perception of their involvement in the educational program and their feelings about being free to contact teachers remained unchanged. It should be noted, however, that the pre-assessment regarding freedom to contact teachers was quite high and it is probably unrealistic to expect a sizable increase on that particular item.

The attitude of project parents regarding the alternative school concept was measured in the same way as their attitude toward their involvement in the educational program. The individual items and the results of both assessments are:

Item		June 1973	June 1974
I am well informed about *Education by Choice*.	_____ I am uninformed about *Education by Choice*.	12.7	14.4
I like the idea of *Education by Choice*.	_____ I do not like the idea of *Education by Choice*.	15.0	14.5
I do not feel my son or daughter will receive a better education because of *Education by Choice*.	_____ I feel my son or daughter will receive a better education because of *Education by Choice*.	11.9	12.6
My son or daughter's alternative school is the best one for him.	_____ My son or daughter's alternative school is the worst one for him.	14.1	14.0
I feel my son or daughter's alternative school will help him.	_____ I do not feel my son or daughter's alternative school will help him.	14.1	14.3

In analyzing the data, the first and third items seem to indicate that parents are better informed about the program and generally feel their child will receive a better education because of *Education by Choice*. The last two items show very little change between the pre and post assessments. Since both assessments are quite favorable, it would seem that the perception of project parents regarding the program have continued to be positive throughout the year. The second item showed the greatest decrease and, although it was not extreme, it would be well for the project staff to be aware of this information. It should be noted that even though a decrease has occurred, this item has the highest value of any of the five.

General Summary

There are three significant groups that are part of the evaluation of the *Education by Choice* project. One group is the students who are involved in the program. The results of this study indicate that the students have grown academically and maintained their cognitive level as compared to national norms. There also have been positive increases in measures reflecting their attitude toward the school and school-related activities. All indications are that *Education by Choice* has been beneficial to the students who have participated in it.

A second group that is affected by the project is the teachers. The results of the evaluation indicate teachers have felt that they have been very much involved in the project and the measure of their attitude indicates they are positively inclined toward the Quincy School System. In addition, the results indicate that the teachers feel they are working more with parents than they have in the past. Therefore, a general summary as it relates to the teachers is that *Education by Choice* has been helpful in improving their attitude toward parental involvement in the school and the project.

A third group affected by the *Education by Choice* project is the parents. The results indicate that parents are more aware of what is going on in the schools and feel that the teachers have made a strong effort to keep them involved. The project has also helped to maintain the rather high rating that the parents gave school at the beginning of the year.

Overall, the results of this evaluation are quite positive and indicate that the effort being expended on *Education by Choice* to date be continued.

Section VII

FINANCING ALTERNATIVE SCHOOLS

EDITOR'S COMMENTS

The question of finances escapes very few contemporary programs. The days of "free money" are over. We are in a tight fiscal period which will be with us for the foreseeable future. The educational enterprise, one of the largest in the country, is particularly vulnerable to public scrutiny as far as expenditures are concerned. As mentioned in the introduction, the 1960s were characterized by federal and philanthropic support of innovations, many of which posed additional fiscal funding on the school districts, i.e., when the federal or foundation monies were consumed, the school districts were left holding the tab. What will be different about alternative schools? Will they cost more money? Where is the money to come from?

The crucial questions surrounding the funding of alternative education are of paramount concern. This section begins to deal with some of these issues. In the earlier days, many of the pioneer alternative schools received outside support. However, both the federal government and foundations are not likely to continue to promote experiments which have already been funded. Is it possible that the schools can assume fiscal responsibility on their own, especially during this period of economic restraint? The theme advanced by some of these articles is that alternatives need not cost more money, that they can be mounted with existing resources—if they are utilized differently. If making "wiser" use of existing resources seems to be one basis for support, then the other has to be the notion of vouchers, i.e., providing families with the equivalent of the per pupil cost of educating a child in a form that they can cash in, depending on their choice of education. The other funding possibility has to do with enabling legislation promoting alternatives. All of these possibilities are presented here, with some others. The reader is urged to read and reread this section, since it offers more information on this important area.

This section deals with such questions as:

How can alternative schools cut costs in the long run?

Why invest in alternative schools?

What should be considered in planning finances for alternative schools?

What community and school board questions should you be prepared to answer?

How can schools write proposals which will bring money?

How can schools apply for a planning grant?

What did Berkeley's proposal have that made it take?

What is an educational voucher?

Why has the Alum Rock voucher succeeded?

Why did the Rochester voucher proposal fail?

FISCAL ASPECTS OF ALTERNATIVE SCHOOLS*

BY WILLIAM WHITE †

Proponents of alternative education make a strong point of the fact that options can operate on the same per pupil expenditure as other schools in the district. Whether this is true depends on many factors. This article reports the mixed outcome in the area of budgetary commitment of Jefferson County, Colo.

The elements of a school district budget affected most by the concept of alternative education fall under the categories of staffing, transportation, and administration. Generally costs for such items as curriculum development and textbooks are very small or nonexistent. Conventional curriculum designs are usually abandoned in favor of more unstructured approaches. Since they tend to make extensive use of community resources and employ unstructured learning situations, textbooks have little relevance to the instruction.

In Jefferson County the support services for alternatives are not very elaborate, since the student population is small. Very little investment in pupil personnel, cafeteria services, or maintenance has been required. These are areas where smallness has led to economy. When you take a look at staffing and transportation, however, this has not always been the case. Consider first some situations involving staffing.

Staffing Cost Situations

The district's first alternative school site was the Metropolitan Youth Center, established in 1964 jointly by the Denver Public Schools and Jefferson County Public Schools for the

* Reprinted with permission of the author and the *National Association of Secondary School Principals Bulletin*.

† Dr. William White is Director of Instructional Planning and Development, Jefferson County Public Schools, Lakewood, Colorado. He is responsible for developing the policy on Alternative Education for Jefferson County, where eight separate alternative school sites are presently operating.

purpose of reaching the dropout population of young people between the ages of 15 and 26. The school opened with 32 students and now has more than 1,500 per year.

A classroom rarely has more than eight students at a time and teachers are specially trained to use a completely individualized approach with students working at their own speed. Attendance is voluntary. Although two sponsoring districts share in the costs jointly and some Title I funds are used, the operation requires considerably more dollars to staff than a conventional high school.

On the other hand, it costs no more money per pupil to staff Jefferson County's Open Living School than any other elementary school in the district. This alternative houses 300 pupils, ranging from pre-school to grade 8, on two sites. Guidelines for the school are planned through parent and staff participation. The high degree of parent involvement results in an additional staff gain as parents volunteer to serve as aids, clerks, and even assistant teachers.

When it comes to developing in-school alternatives, however, advantages in staffing ratio do not fare too well. Each of the three projects operating within various high schools in the district at the present time require additional staff in order for the goals of the project to be attained. Arvada's school-within-a-school project, in its second year of operation, has five teachers and 125 students working in a separate wing of the senior high school. Although the 25 to 1 ratio of pupils and teacher meets the district standard, an additional full-time counselor/coordinator was assigned to direct the program, screen applicants, and coordinate the many off-campus activities.

Another school-within-a-school project located at Alameda High School uses a 19 to 1 pupil/teacher ratio for 180 students. A full-time counselor is required to help coordinate the program and work with pupils. The program was designed to help students who had dropped out or were near dropping out of the regular school. Students attend school half day and work on the job the other half. As in many such programs, teachers are inspired to work many more hours than normally expected, making home visits, conducting small group trips, seeing employers, and generally acting as part-time social workers. Teachers in the regular school program have seen the positive results of these efforts and are willing to assume a larger student load in order to free the school-within-a-school teachers.

Per Pupil Cost Considerations

Per pupil costs are difficult to compute in most alternative school projects. This is a result of a constantly changing pupil population in an operation that does not follow the typical school day or calendar year. The Metropolitan Youth Center serves its students year-round and has them in class situations anywhere from one to five days a week for an indefinite period of time each day depending on the individual student's study plan. For planning purposes the school administration reports a cost figure of $2.35 per student per class hour. If this were projected to a normal 180 day school year, the cost would come out about triple the amount of $728.02 per Average Daily Attendance allowed for high school students in the Jefferson County system.

But it must also be taken into account that Metropolitan Youth Center students tend to complete course requirements in one-third less time than the typical high school student and teachers spend more than one-fourth of their teacher/pupil contact time outside the classroom setting. Add to this the fact that Title I funds help to offset one-third of the school's costs and state vocational education monies pay for equipment and teacher time spent in vocationally certified programs. When all factors are considered, the school comes out considerably closer to the going rate for high school education in the Denver Metropolitan area.

Housing and Transportation Costs

Provision for plant facilities has proven to be the one area of alternative school operation where cost savings have been achieved consistently. This is true because most of the projects have used facilities, such as unoccupied portable classrooms, empty elementary cottage school buildings, a church basement, abandoned former high school buildings, and a separate classroom wing in a junior high school. None of these resulted in any extra cost to the district other than maintenance.

Transportation has been one of the more difficult areas for

alternative schools in Jefferson County to deal with. It has been policy to require the student to provide his own transportation when the individual does not attend the school which serves his neighborhood attendance area. Most people have worked out arrangements for transportation to and from the school, and high school students prefer it this way, but the many trips and excursions during the day require a fee that amounts to a considerable sum over a year's time. Fund raising to pay field trip costs has become a regular activity in most of the alternative programs. Arvada's school-within-a-school students raised $3,000 to cover expenses for one trip of a week's duration.

Grants and fund raising have not been too important to the operation of the in-school alternatives, but the separate school operations have for the most part relied upon outside resources. These monies have come from both Title III and Title I grants, from state vocational and special education funds, and from write-offs through local school operations.

No Opposition on Basis of Cost

It appears that options to the standard program of education are here to stay in Jefferson County. The particular form they have at the present time may change but the concept will remain to provide for a diversity of student population too great for any one school. In those areas where costs are high, the returns are also high. There has been no opposition to any of the existing programs based upon their operating costs. As long as they continue to be staffed by dedicated faculty and parent volunteers, as long as parents and students feel that they have a real voice in the type of education which the school provides, and as long as the district is attempting to satisfy their needs, then budgetary problems are likely to be no greater for the alternative school than for any other school.

HUSTLING: HOW TO WRITE A PROPOSAL*

The Grantsmanship Center in Los Angeles has published a short guide for *Program Planning and Proposal Writing* in its newsletter, January 1974, Number 3. Below are the major points made in the guide, with liberal quotes from the article as it appeared.

The Center suggests the following format for proposals:
PROPOSAL SUMMARY
I. INTRODUCTION
II. PROBLEM STATEMENT OR ASSESSMENT OF NEED
III. PROGRAM OBJECTIVES
IV. METHODS
V. EVALUATION
VI. BUDGET
VII. FUTURE FUNDING

Proposal Summary:

The summary is a very important part of a proposal—not just something you jot down as an afterthought. On a federal grant application, there is usually a box provided for the summary. In other cases, a cover letter or a lead paragraph will suffice. The summary should be about a page long.

I. Introduction:

This is a section of the proposal in which you tell who you are. This is the section in which you build your *credibility*. The way a funding source views credibility varies from type to type. A somewhat conservative organization will look for prominent members of your Board of Directors, how long you've been in existence, who else is supporting you with funds. More "avant garde" sources will look for the involve-

* Reprinted with permission from the National Alternative Schools Program, School of Education, University of Massachusetts, Amherst, Massachusetts, from the January 1975 issue of *Applesauce*.

ment of community people in your governing board, and will react more favorably toward new and innovative organizations. Potential funding sources should be selected because of their stated interest in your type of organization. You can use the introduction section of your proposal to develop the connection between the funding source and your own group. Some things to include in your introduction are:

How you got started

How long you've been around

Unique features; things that distinguish you from others

Some of your most significant accomplishments. If you are a new organization, stress the significant accomplishments of your Board members or staff.

Your organizational goals; how you were started.

Indications of support from established organizations; included here might be letters of endorsement from prominent individuals.

You should start a *credibility file* in which you keep copies of newspaper articles about your organization, letters of support, statements of commendation. You can then use this file for the writing of the introduction of your proposal.

II. Problem Statement or Assessment of Need:

This is the section of the proposal in which you clearly define the problem you are going to tackle. Here you build a strong argument for your funding. Narrow down the definition of the problem so that you define something that can be changed in a reasonable amount of time and with reasonable resources. Be specific; don't "overkill".

It is important to carefully *document the problem* so as to convince the funding source that the problem does exist. Use hard data such as statistics, charts, and graphs that are easy to read and are not so voluminous as to turn off your audience. Use discretion; choose only the most important, the most convincing information.

To summarize, you want to:

Make a logical connection between your organization's background and the problem it hopes to tackle.

Support the existence by use of convincing evidence.

Clearly and precisely define the problem with which you intend to work. Make sure that what you want to do is *workable*.

III. Program Objectives:

An objective is a specific, measurable outcome of the program. Look to your problem statement; your objectives should offer some relief to the problem as you've defined it.

Be careful to distinguish between methods and objectives.

One common problem in many proposals is a failure to distinguish between means and ends—a failure to distinguish between methods and objectives.

For example, many proposals read like this:

"The purpose of this proposal is to establish a peer-group tutoring program for potential drop-outs in the _____ area of Los Angeles," or

"The objective of this program is to provide counseling and guidance services for delinquent youth in _____."

These objectives do not speak about outcomes. The fact that a service has been established or an activity conducted doesn't tell that the problem has been solved.

Knowing that something is being planned is not enough. Be sure to state just what will be the results of the planned activities.

The statement of objectives is particularly important because it is usually against these objectives that the program is evaluated.

Therefore, the careful setting forth of objectives serves another purpose as well—one that might lead to continued or additional funding.

IV. Methods:

This section tells *how* the objectives will be accomplished. You should describe the methods you will use in detail. This might take some *research* because funding sources will want to be sure that you have chosen appropriate methodologies from a variety of options. The consideration of alternatives is an important aspect of describing your methodology. Showing that you are familiar enough about your field to be aware of different models for solving the problems, and showing your reasons for selecting the model that you have, gives a funding source a feeling of security that you know what you are doing, and adds greatly to your credibility.

V. Evaluation:

Evaluation of your program can serve two purposes for your organization. Your program can be evaluated in order to determine how effective it is in reaching the objectives you have established—in solving the problems you are dealing with. This concept of evaluation is geared towards the results of your program.

This is called *summative* evaluation.

Evaluation can also be used as a tool to provide information necessary to make appropriate changes and adjustments in your program as it proceeds.

This is called *formative* evaluation. Many alternative schools have opted for this type of evaluation, since it helps the organization as it grows and changes.

Be sure to state which kind of evaluation you intend to use in your proposal so that you will not find yourself in trouble with evaluating agencies of the school system at a later date. Again, the measurable objectives you stated provide the basis for evaluation. Be careful to formulate objectives that say what you mean.

One way to insure that your program receives a fair and objective evaluation and one along the lines that you define is to look to an outside organization to conduct an evaluation for you. You might go to other non-profit agencies, colleges and universities in your community which will work with you in developing an evaluation for your program. Sometimes it is possible to get an outside organization to develop an evaluation design and proposal for evaluation that can be submitted to a funding source, complete with its own budget, along with your proposal. This not only can guarantee a more objective evaluation, but can also add to the credibility of your total application, since you have borrowed the credibility of the evaluating institution.

Some of the organizations listed in this and the past will provide this type of assistance.

VI. Budget

As with proposals themselves, funding sources requirements for budgets differ; foundations require less extensive budgets than federal agencies. The following budget design will satisfy most funding sources. The first section of the budget is *personnel;* the second section is *non-personnel.* Most social service and education programs use 80% of their budgets for personnel.

Personnel:

A. Wages and Salary: Here you should list the title of the position, the per-monthly rate of pay, and the time commitment of the position (full-time, ½ time). To justify the salaries you build into your budget you must obtain information from other local agencies regarding the salaries of person with job descriptions, qualifications and responsibilities similar to those of the jobs in your agency. You might go to the local city and/or county government, the school district, the United Way or United Fund, etc. By comparing the jobs in your agency with the jobs at other local agencies, you plan a salary for each position, and you keep the "comparability data" on hand, should you be asked by the funding source to justify your staff salaries.

B. Fringe Benefits: In this section you list all the fringe benefits your employees will be receiving, and the dollar cost of these benefits. Some fringe benefits are mandatory—but these vary from state to state, so you will have to determine what they are for your agency in your state. Mandatory fringe benefits may include State Disability Insurance, Unemployment Compensation, Retirement contributions, etc. Most nonprofit agencies participate in the Social Security Program (FICA) although non-profit agencies may vote, when they are started, not to participate in Social Security. These fringe benefits are all based on a percentage of salaries. For example, FICA, which is going up, has been based on 5.85% of the first $10,800 of each person's salary.

C. Consultant and Contract Services: This is the third and final part of the Personnel section of your budget. In this section you include paid and unpaid consultants, volunteers, and services for which you contract. It is important to develop as much donated services and equipment as possible. No funding source likes to think that it is carrying the major and complete burden for financing your group.

Non-Personnel:

A. Space Costs: In this section you list all of the facilities you will be using, both those on which you pay rent and those which are being donated for your use. Rent you pay, or the valuation of donated facilities, must be comparable to prevailing rents in the geographic area in which you are located. In addition to the actual rent, you should also include the cost of utilities, maintenance services and renovations, if they are absolutely essential to your program.

B. Rental, Lease or Purchase of Equipment: Here you list all of the equipment, donated or to be purchased. This includes office equipment, typewriters, Xerox costs, etc.

C. Consummable Supplies: This includes all supplies such as paper clips, pens, pencils, etc. A reasonable figure is $75.00 per staff per year.

D. Travel: Divide the section up into local and out-of-town travel. Don't put in any big lump sums which will require interpretation or raise a question at the funding source. Remember, on local mileage all of your staff won't be driving on the job, and not all who do will drive the same amount.

E. Telephones: Remember installation costs. Justify any out-of-state calls.

F. Other Costs: This catch-all category should include the following:

1. Postage
2. Fire, theft and liability insurance
3. Dues in professional associations paid by the agency
4. Subscriptions
5. Publications, the cost of which may be broken up into:
   a. printing
   b. typesetting
   c. addressing, if done by a service
   d. mailing (separate and distinct from office postage above)
6. Any other items that don't logically fit elsewhere

VII. Future Funding

This is the last section of your proposal but by no means the least important. Increasingly, funding sources want to know how you will continue your program when their grant runs out. This is irrelevant for one-time only grant applications, such as requests for vehicles, equipment, etc. But if you are requesting program money, if you are adding to your projects through this proposal, then how will you keep it going next year?

A promise to continue looking for alternate sources of support is not sufficient. You must present a plan that will assure the funding source, to the greatest extent possible, that you will be able to maintain this new program after their grant has been completed. They don't want to adopt you—they don't want you continually on their back for additional funds. Moreover, if you are having problems keeping your current operations supported, you will probably have much more difficulty in maintaining a level of operation which includes additional programs. The funding source may be doing you no favor by supporting a new project, and putting you in the position of having to raise even more money next year than you do now.

What is a good method to guarantee continued support for a project? One good way is to get a local institution of governmental agency to agree to continue to support your program, should it demonstrate the desired results. But get such a commitment in writing. A plan to generate funds through the project itself—such as fees for services that will build up over a year or two, subscriptions to publications, etc., is an excellent plan. The best plan for future funding is the plan that does not require outside grant support.

Federal Information

Factsheet

The Department of Health, Education, and Welfare (HEW) has put together a *Fact Sheet in Sources of Federal Funding,* which generally outlines procedures for awarding funds and cites sources of information which may prove of some use to schools looking for funds in the fiscal year 1975. Below is a summary of the *Factsheet*.

The two major instruments used to award funds are *contracts* and *grants*. A *contract* is used when a "specific product is needed. Through a contract, the Federal government maintains direction and control over the development and timing of the work." A *grant* is used when "HEW wants to provide support for researchers to explore issues of mutual interest with a minimum of supervision and control." Grants are usually awarded to non-profit institutions (like schools).

There are three major ways of applying for HEW funds: (1) *grant competitions*, (2) proposals solicited through *Request for Proposals* (RFP) and (3) *unsolicited proposals*. *Grant competitions* are announced in the *Federal Register* when the office wishes to encourage specific proposals from people in the field. The Register is available for $45.00 through the Superintendent of Documents, Government Printing Office, Washington, D.C. and can also be found in most university libraries. *RFPs* are announced in the *Commerce Business Daily* (CBD) which sells for $63.50 and is also available at university libraries. An *RFP* asks for proposals to do a specifically defined task. A contract is awarded to the bidder who submits the best technical proposal, as judged by HEW. *Unsolicited proposals* are the least likely means to being funded. These proposals are reviewed by HEW and monies are sometimes given. The idea must be "unique and beneficial, and the submitter must be uniquely well qualified."

To obtain the most comprehensive information available on funding through federal sources, consult the *HEW Catalogue of Assistance*, which may be obtained by sending $2.00 to the Government Printing Office.

Acts

The Safe Streets Act of 1968 created the Law Enforcement Assistance Administration within the Department of Justice. The Act adopted the stance that crime is a local problem, and mandated the creation of the State Planning Agencies (SPA). Designated by each governor, SPA's are required to have supervisory boards to review, approve, and provide oversight functions, including grants making and the creation of the comprehensive state plans. When a state has its plan approved, LEAA formula block grants, allocated by population, go the SPA's. Alternative Schools interested in applying for LEAA money would do well to network together on regional basis and approach LEAA for 5–10,000 grants based on the service they provide pertinent to the act.

Some information courtesy of the Alternative School Network in Chicago: watch out for "the new bills signed by Ford ($5.5 billion) creating at least 100,000 public service jobs. You should call your local government to find out how to get a person into your school, if possible. This may come under the Comprehensive Employment Training Act (CETA)—the updated manpower act."

Also, look out for "the Community Development Act—an $11 billion package that may, when the money filters down to the local level, fund some people to do various kinds of services in your communities."

Finally, "your students may qualify for services paid for by the federal government under the Title I for the Elementary and Secondary school Act. A whole list of services are available if the children read or compute below their grade level and they live in a very poor section of town."

St. Louis:
The Danforth Foundation
222 South Central Avenue
St. Louis, Missouri   63105

Pittsburgh:
Richard King Mellon Foundation
525 William Penn Place
Pittsburgh, Pa.   15219

San Francisco:
The San Francisco Foundation
425 California Street
San Francisco, California   94104

New York State:
Rockefeller Brothers Fund
30 Rockefeller Plaza
New York, New York   10020

Indiana:
Lilly Endowment, Inc.
2801 North Meridian Street
Indianapolis, Ind.   46208

Milwaukee:
Faye Mcbeath Foundation
110 East Wisconsin Ave.
Milwaukee, Wisc. 53202

The Milwaukee Foundation
110 East Wisconsin Ave.
Milwaukee, Wisc. 53202

The Walter and Olive Stiemke Foundation
110 East Wisconsin Ave.
Milwaukee, Wisc. 53202

Hawaii:
Mcinerny Foundation
P.O. Box 2390
Honolulu, Hawaii 96804

New Haven:
The New Haven Foundation
1 State Street
New Haven, Conn. 06511

BERKELEY: EXPERIMENTAL SCHOOLS
PROPOSAL ABSTRACT*

BY RICHARD L. FOSTER†

The Berkeley Unified School District proposes to design and establish a comprehensive educational program of alternative schools for 5,318 students which will provide a significant departure from present-day school programs, structures, practices and performance. The district will test the program over five years of development and operation.

The Berkeley Alternate Schools Proposal will adopt as its central theme the issue of institutional racism—one of Amer-

---

* Reprinted with permission from the Office of Project Planning and Development, Berkeley Unified School District.

† Richard L. Foster is Superintendent of Berkeley Unified School District.

ica's most urgent educational problems. The assumption is that racism is inextricably woven into the institutions of this country in their organizational structures, practices and traditions, consistently resulting in an inequitable distribution of "pay-offs" for non-whites. The delivery of basic skills to all children will be a main thrust of the Alternate Schools.

The Alternate Schools will constitute a system of educational options giving parents, students, teachers and administrators a direct voice in educational decision-making and, in addition, propose a new educational structure that will be a radical departure from local school systems as they are currently operated throughout the country.

The Berkeley program is not a piecemeal or individual change component but is, rather, a consistent, comprehensive program that will provide for options throughout the entire school life of a pupil. About 5,318 children, one third of the Berkeley School population, will be involved in the proposed schools.

The project components in which changes are planned will modify activity along the following dimensions:

. . . . organization and administration
. . . . curriculum and instructional patterns
. . . . coping in a pluralistic society

The options represent as many as twenty separate experimental schools. They have been listed under four categories or as variants of four categories even though the divisions are not discrete. The four categories are:

1. *Multi-culture Schools*—These schools will have children carefully selected on the basis of diversity—racial, socioeconomic, age and sex. During part of the school day the students will meet and work together. At other times they will meet in their own ethnic, social or educational groups learning their own culture, language, customs, history and heritage or other special curriculum; later these aspects will be shared with the wider group. Pupils will learn from the strengths and weaknesses of each group. In a deliberate and planned way they would learn to appreciate differences but at the same time to break down polarization. They may well form a model of what all Berkeley may be like in the future. Two schools are proposed; both will be operational in the fall term and will affect 993 students at the K–6 level.

2. *Community Schools*—The organization, curriculum and the teaching approach of these schools come from outside of the classroom—from the community. There may well be total parent involvement with both the school day and week being extended into shared family life. There will be use of courts, markets, museums, parks, theaters and other educational resources in the community. The schools will be multi-aged and ungraded with an emphasis on real-life problem-solving. Emphasis will be on learning together rather than solitary competition, on developing a multi-cultural community of participating families that learn from each other, and for the older children, of working directly in the community in agencies, businesses or projects. Four schools are proposed; three will be operating in the fall affecting 400 children at K–12 levels; one K–3 school for 150 children will open in the following year.

3. *Structured Skills-Training Schools*—These schools would be graded and would emphasize the learning of basic skills—reading, writing and math. Learning would take place primarily in the classroom and would be directed by either one teacher or a team of teachers. Usually the schools will be smaller units with the regular program affording both teachers and students the opportunity of having close personal relationships. Eight schools are proposed; five will be open in the fall with 900 students involved at K–12 levels. Three more will open the following year with 780 students in grades 7–12.

4. *Schools-without-walls*—The focus of these schools is the child and his development. The staff deals with the child rather than the subject. The schools will be ungraded and typically their style and arrangements will be unstructured. Their goals will be to have the students grow in self-understanding and self-esteem, learn how to cope with social and intellectual frustration and master the basic and social skills through their own interests.

The children will be encouraged to assume responsibility for their learning and growth. The teacher's role will be one of facilitating the child's learning and supporting his growth. Six schools are planned for the fall with 1,515 children involved in grades K–12. One is planned for next semester for 150, K–3 children, and one is planned for the following semester for 850, K–12 pupils.

EXTERNAL AND INTERNAL EDUCATION VOUCHERS*

BY MARIO D. FANTINI

Recently the education crisis has been linked to the citizens' pocketbook and, in the face of a tightening economy, the educational consumers have begun to raise questions. Are the federally supported programs in education working? Was there really payoff for the financial investments of the 1960's?

Reports from the field on programs such as Title I of the Elementary and Secondary Education Act of 1965 are far from promising. In fact, President Richard Nixon, in his 1970 Message to Congress,[1] pointed to the failure of compensatory education:

> The best evidence available indicates that most of the compensatory education programs have not measurably helped poor children catch up. Recent findings on the two largest such programs are particularly disturbing. We now spend more than $1 billion a year for educational programs run under Title I of the Elementary and Secondary Education Act. Most of these have stressed the teaching of reading, but before-and-after tests suggest that only 19% of the children in such programs improve their reading significantly; 13% appear to fall behind more than expected; and more than two-thirds of the children remain unaffected—that is, they continue to fall behind. In our Headstart program, where so much hope is invested, we find that youngsters enrolled for the summer achieve almost no gains, and the gains of those in the program for a full year are soon matched by their non-Headstart classmates from similarly poor backgrounds.

Added to this mood of questioning was the growing awareness that add-on, compensatory-type approaches to school improvement really resulted in more money being spent in the same old ways—the very ways which were being subjected to increased criticism by growing numbers of students and par-

* Reprinted by permission of Current History, Inc. (August 1972 issue of *Current History*), Wilton, Connecticut 06897.

ents, i.e., the educational consumers themselves. Any serious reform effort must deal with three fundamental problems: (1) equalizing educational expenditures among public school users; (2) making the most effective use of existing resources in our schools; and (3) delivering quality education to a diverse society.

As Americans recognized the importance of quality education to their own survival needs—at times in desperation—education vouchers entered the picture. One of today's most controversial reform proposals, vouchers are an attempt to generate needed change by altering existing misallocations of resources between rich and poor children. The voucher increases the purchasing power of the educational consumer, usually the poor, for different forms of education in a type of free-market enterprise. However, some families which would likely utilize such vouchers are dissatisfied with public schools. The plan would favor private schools. This is why some use *external* voucher in referring to such a proposal. The Office of Economic Opportunity, which has been testing the feasibility of vouchers, reports:

> It is readily apparent that the education system is failing the poor—both by failing to provide adequate skills and by failing to retain children in school.

> One reason for this disparity could well be that poor parents have little opportunity to affect the type or quality of education received by their children. The poor have no means by which to make the education system more responsive to their needs and desires. More affluent parents usually can obtain a good education for their children because they can choose schools for their children to attend—either by deciding where to live or by sending the children to private schools. . . .

> The Office of Economic Opportunity therefore has begun to seek a means to introduce greater accountability and parental control into schools in such a way that the poor would have a wider range of choices, that the schools would remain attractive to the more affluent. This has led to consideration of an experiment in which public education money would be given directly to parents in the form of vouchers, or certificates, which the parents could then take to the school of their choice, public or nonpublic, as payment for their children's education.[2]

The voucher proposals suggest that monies devoted to the financing of public schools be transferred to the parents in the form of redeemable coupons. These coupons, worth the cost of a year's schooling per child, are to be used to support the schools of the parent's choice—public or private, parochial, profit-making, and so on. Schools would cash in the vouchers at proposed Education Voucher Authorities, which would supervise the institutions participating in the plan.

The voucher idea sounds simple, but presently there is no voucher proposal—and there are several—being offered that is acceptable to all. The problem lies with both the economics and politics of each.

Various Voucher Plans

Milton Friedman, original contemporary proponent of the voucher idea, nine years ago introduced a model in which all parents receive a basic voucher that might be supplemented at will from personal income. Better known as the unregulated voucher model, this plan has come under increased criticism, for wealthy parents could easily match the value of the voucher and thus send their children to better, or at least more expensive, schools. If this occurred, Friedman's model would probably broaden the gap between rich and poor. The plan might operate as a "partial" scholarship for a few of the most talented poor to attend expensive schools, but this does not seem a sufficient incentive to recommend this proposal over the present system.

A second voucher plan developed by former Harvard Dean Theodore Sizer and Phillip Whitten proposes that the value of a voucher be invertibly related to family income. That is, families with incomes below $2,000 would receive vouchers worth a set amount. The value of the voucher would decline to zero as the family's income approached the national average. This sliding scale voucher would help poor families compete with the wealthier families in purchasing private education. It would be a coarse equalizer, however, for it would not consider how much personal income a family is willing to spend on education . . .

. . . such discrimination in favor of the poor not only raises possible equal protection problems, but may also discriminate against the "near poor" or students of more affluent families who fail to supplement their vouchers as much as was "predicted" for their income level.

Furthermore, experience in other subsidized areas, such as food stamps and housing, provides little hope for legislative adoption of a system that effectively enables poor families to compete in purchasing services. Because the Sizer-Whitten model is not proposed as a substitute for the present system of state administered education, but rather is designed as a supplement in which poor families are subsidized in choosing private schools, the proposal does not discuss state involvement in any nonfinancial areas. Educational standards and equality of educational opportunity, for example, are not considered.[3]

John Coons has proposed a voucher model under which parents would choose schools of various expenditure levels to send their children, the lowest level being roughly that of present public school expenditures. The parent would receive a voucher about equal to the per pupil cost at this lowest level, and would have the option of supplementing that voucher. (As in the Friedman plan, the wealthy would be able to choose a more expensive school for their children as they could more easily supplement the voucher.) This system would be combined with a compensatory scheme so that a parent's economic effort in educating his child was measured relative to his income, the result being a wider separation between the "best" and the "worst" schools. Critics of Coons' plan conclude that this model would accelerate the inequalities in outcome of schooling and would penalize children whose parents have little interest in education.

A fourth plan is the achievement model. Under this plan, the value of a student's voucher would be determined by the "success" in educating him, rather than by the student's economic qualifications.

. . . A school's income would be determined by how much progress its students need. That progress would be measured by standardized tests. The difficulty of separating aptitude from achievement in such tests, the questionable relationship between high test scores and later success, and the importance of socio-economic status and race as determinants of test results, are all reasons why this model is found unacceptable. . . .[4]

The voucher proposals that are mentioned here, as well as others, cannot deal in any significant way with the disparity of revenue between school districts either in a state or between states, as long as property taxes are the main sources of school revenue.

Presently, the financing of public schools is derived from three principal funding sources: at the local level, mainly through property and sales taxes; and at the state and federal levels, from individual and corporate income taxes. To all intent and purposes, the property tax is the most basic for American education, especially for local school districts. In 1970–1971, in the nation as a whole, 52 per cent of school revenue was provided by local sources and over 98 per cent of the public school revenues of local tax sources are property tax revenues.[5]

One of the key problems associated with the property tax is that the ratio of assessed values to full legitimate values has declined, thereby reducing significantly the capacity of school districts to tap local funds on a continuous basis. This problem has become more acute with rising school costs.

We have reached a stage in which even the most staunch supporters of public education have been affected by this over-dependence on the local property tax. Citizens cannot continue to have their taxes raised indefinitely on the grounds that without these additional revenues the quality of education for their children will suffer. Obviously, there is a limit to what the taxpayer can afford.

While there is a general mood of discontent toward this over-reliance on the property tax for financing public schools, there is another dimension which may really become the legal basis for reform. This dimension concerns the fact that the way the property tax works within most states results in unequal allocations of educational resources. This unequal allocation arbitrarily discriminates against the poor. That is to say, since property taxes are assessed according to wealth, the "richer" communities receive more revenues; those "privileged" public school districts can actually afford a better delivery of educational services than the poor school districts. This unequal allocation of educational resources is considered by some citizens to be *unconstitutional* on the grounds that the property tax system for financing public schools actually denies children equal protection which is guaranteed under the Fourteenth Amendment.

The problem of differential spending apparently will be resolved by the courts rather than by the use of vouchers. For instance, in a historic decision, the Supreme Court of California, on August 30, 1971, tentatively concluded:

> We have determined that this funding scheme invidiously discriminates against the poor because it makes the quality of a child's education a function of the wealth of his parents and neighbors. Recognizing as we must that the right to an education in our public schools is a fundamental interest which cannot be conditioned on wealth, we can discern no compelling state purpose necessitating the present method of financing. We have concluded, therefore, that such a system cannot withstand constitutional challenge and must fall before the equal protection clause.

This case, *Serrano v. Priest,* has launched a national dialogue on the inequities of the local property tax.[6] New York State and New Jersey have proposed similar plans for full state funding to reduce inequities.

The voucher plan is an attempt at equalization, but it faces many hard problems unless a more equitable school finance framework is developed. Further:

> Carried to its logical conclusion. . . . the parallel-school approach would reduce the scope of public education, if not dispense with it altogether. The establishment of private schools sufficient to handle significant numbers of poor children would require public support and, in effect, establish a private system of publicly-supported schools. Middle-income parents would demand similar privileges. For financial reasons alone, the parallel-school approach is hardly likely to become widespread in the foreseeable future; moreover, the scheme would founder on political, if not constitutional grounds. . . .[7]

At present, it could widen the gap, because the voucher plan can be used to continue economic segregation within the schools. If this segregation occurs, the vouchers would effectively become a subsidy for the rich and middle class.

Also, vouchers could lead to further racial segregation within external schools. Presently, there is no framework outside of the public school system that protects against this happening. This system could also lead to public support of religious instruction which might violate the prohibitions of the Constitution. For example:

> Several cases now in the judicial works will have a bearing on the legal status of vouchers. One of these is *Flask v. Gardner,* which challenges the use of federal funds to pay for educational services conducted in religious-sponsored schools under Title I of ESEA. If the courts should decide that the use of funds in this way is unconstitutional, the legality of the voucher concepts so far as the religious-related schools are concerned would be dubious indeed.[8]

Others question whether parents, particularly low-income parents, are capable or have the desire to choose sources of education for their children. In addition, many wonder whether a voucher system would jeopardize the public schools which might be forced to become schools of the last resort.

The true merit of the current interest in educational vouchers is that it has provided a new way of looking at the problem of delivering quality education to dissatisfied consumers. This new viewpoint has stimulated public schools to develop educational alternatives themselves. In so doing, the external voucher has prompted the development of the internal voucher plan—a plan which does not demand the creation of still another bureaucratic regulatory agency to facilitate its implementation. The public schools have the capacity and the resources to operate such a system internally. The creation of a voucher system of education which operates outside (external) the public school system is less necessary and/or desirable than the creation of options within (internal) a public system of education. The voucher emphasis on alternatives has given the public school mechanism a new mission to use existing resources.

As we have suggested, the voucher concept, therefore, can be viewed as external or internal. The externally oriented voucher system emphasizes access to alternative schools outside the public school system. The internally oriented voucher plan views access to alternatives within the framework of the public school system. Both plans rely on increased consumer interest in alternative forms of education, and acknowledge the intrinsic value of individual choice.

Many teachers, supervisors and administrators feel constrained by the system of public schooling and are eager to join with parents and students in a search for reform. These professional educators have been waiting for a new framework for action. In fact, many have attempted successfully to bring about changes, at times, against major obstacles.

Enough members of the public school establishment have embraced the philosophy of institutional deficiency to sustain an internal effort to create new ground rules for professional action. Considerable inside professional energy could be channeled from trying to improve a single educational process to working out alternative forms of education within the basic framework of public schools.

Public schools have gone through a number of important stages to insure that they would be non-sectarian and non-exclusive, and that they would reflect the basic values of an open, free society. Public schools are mature enough, strong enough to withstand any pressures that might attempt to compromise these values. These professional pressures are critical to the control of schools that might be bent on undermining the basic values of a free society. The point here is that public schools—subject to public scrutiny as they are—are more capable of representing our noblest values than many of our more exclusive private schools. Thus, a quick rise in private sector education without adequate supervision and monitoring might, in the name of responsiveness, create educational structures which would not serve the basic societal values that support a free society.

Furthermore, alternative forms of education, to be legitimized under a framework of public schools, must satisfy other important standards. One criterion in particular deserves mention here. Any alternative mode of education must be capable of addressing a comprehensive set of educational objectives, not merely particular sets. For example, some may advance a "free school," based on the theory that it is complete freedom of the learner that is important—and that happiness, joy and ecstasy are the major objectives of education. This alternative may not be legitimized by public schools because of the emphasis on particular objectives at the expense of others. Public schools have a responsibility—the wide-range objectives of:

1. Basic learning to acquire skills—reading, writing, communications, inquiring, analyzing.

2. Talent development, developing individual creative potentialities.

3. Preparation for basic success in assuming major societal careers: parent, consumer, citizen, self-developing individual.

These can be categorized as "cognitive" (intellectual) and "affective" (emotional) terms if necessary, but they are broad at their base. Public schools are instrumentally related to the fabric of society—economically, as well as politically and culturally. It is difficult, if not impossible, for public schools to ignore or dismiss these ties. Consequently, public schools must also be manpower institutions. Unless a person is independently wealthy, he hopes school will open options for him in the career market; unless a learner expects to secede from participation in society he expects schooling to help him acquire the skills to participate effectively as a citizen with rights.

Therefore, it is possible for certain alternative forms of education to cultivate people who are happy, joyous, ecstatic—but who cannot read, write, or qualify for any realistic economic career. Perhaps, in the name of humanistic education, certain educational options may emphasize primarily affective objectives. The learner who has selected these options may realize too late there are other requirements for full involvement in the multi-environments (economic, political, cultural, social) of modern society. Ironically, in these cases, the very humanization the option sought to realize may, in the end, have produced exactly the opposite effect, i.e., denying the learner options in the real world. Public schools and their traditions of experience are more likely to protect the next generation from these possibilities than their less accountable private counterparts.

If our assumption is valid—namely that the present public school educational process constitutes only one alternative to a common set of objectives, and that a diverse consumer-society is rightfully demanding alternatives to the one—then the basic problem is really in the delivery of an expanded supply of legitimate educational alternatives. In supply and demand terms, we now have a high demand market, but limited supply. The external voucher is a proposal of demand which is expected to affect the supply side.

Under the external voucher plan for education, it would seem that existing private schools would benefit to be sure. New private schools would also spring up, but how could any educational consumer be sure of quality? What would prevent a "fly-by-night" slew of institutions from emerging during high demand-low supply periods? These problems relate to the process of legitimization of educational alternatives. The public schools already have the manpower, the mechanisms, and the knowledge to deliver such a new supply system of safeguarded options at no extra cost to the taxpayers.

For any voucher plan (internal or external) to succeed, enormous attention must be given to parent and citizen education. Unless parents and their children receive basic educational information and understanding, their ability to make wise choices will be seriously curtailed. The heart of any voucher approach is individual choice from among educational alternatives. This means that parents and students, in particular, need to know the theory and practice surrounding each educational alternative. This type of consumer education cannot be left to chance. Consequently, a process must be developed to reach parents and students. Again, it appears that the public schools would be better able to deal with such a massive task at no added cost, for public schools can reach almost all learners and their parents in a matter of minutes, e.g., student assemblies, parent meetings, and so on; they have a built-in mechanism. They also have the manpower, the hardware and the software to educate the consumer.

Furthermore, the majority of Americans still attend and support a system of public schools. They may perceive the introduction of external vouchers as an attempt to weaken the public schools and strengthen private schools—including the highly controversial parochial schools.

The establishment of enough private schools to handle significant numbers of children would require increased public revenue and, in effect, would establish a private system of publicly financed schools. Middle-income parents would demand similar privileges. For financial reasons alone, the external voucher is hardly likely to become widespread in the foreseeable future.

Finally, internal vouchers need not cost more money. For example, it is estimated that "The School Without Walls"— the Parkway Program in Philadelphia, by using the city as the school, actually saved the city 15 million dollars in construction costs.

Internal vouchers are already beginning to emerge. The most advanced illustration is found in the Berkeley Unified School District in California, which now offers over 20 educational alternatives.

FOOTNOTES

1. Richard M. Nixon, *Message from the President of the United States to the 91st Congress,* 2d Session, Document No. 91-267, March 3, 1970.

2. Office of Economic Opportunity, Washington, D.C., January, 1971.

3. Judith Areen, "Education Vouchers," Hearings before the Select Committee on Equal Opportunity of the U.S. Senate, 92d Congress, Part 22, p. 11133. Washington, D.C., December 1, 2, 3, 1971.

4. Irene Solet, "Education Vouchers: An Evaluation," Washington Research Project, Hearings Before the Select Committee on Equal Opportunity of the U.S. Senate, 92d Congress, Part 22, p. 11131. Washington, D.C., December 1, 2, 3, 1971.

5. *Future Directions for School Financing* (Gainesville, Florida: National Educational Finance Project, 1971).

6. 5 Cal. 3rd 581. See *Current History,* July, 1972, pp. 28ff for excerpts.

7. Mario D. Fantini, *Alternatives for Urban School Reform* (New York: Ford Foundation, Office of Reports), pp. 9–10.

8. David Selden, "Vouchers—Solution or Sop?" Hearings before the Select Committee, *op. cit.,* Part 16 D-1, p. 7741.

A SCHOOL VOUCHER EXPERIMENT RATES AN 'A' IN COAST DISTRICT*

BY EVAN JENKINS†

On the east side of this city of half a million an hour's drive south of San Francisco, six schools are finishing the first year of a project that has made them the focus of national attention and controversy.

The project is described as the first experiment anywhere with educational vouchers, the explosive concept that would let parents use public funds to send children to schools of

---

* © 1973 by The New York Times Company. Reprinted by permission from *The New York Times,* May 29, 1973.

† Evan Jenkins is an educational staff writer for the New York *Times.*

their choice, and make the schools compete for pupils and money or fall by the wayside.

If the voucher system became widespread, its friends and enemies agree, it could revolutionize American education.

At the end of the first hectic year of the experiment here, those involved in it see a revolution of sorts in their schools —less absenteeism and vandalism, more variety in educational offerings, more enthusiasm for school on all sides. Their version of the voucher system has widespread local support, partly because it is carefully limited.

In its purest form, known as the Friedman model after the conservative economist Milton Friedman, the voucher concept has aroused fierce opposition from educational groups, civil rights organizations and citizens.

Some Fear Ill Effects

The chief arguments are that unrestricted vouchers would promote racial and economic segregation, provide unconstitutional backdoor aid to sectarian schools and cripple or even destroy public education.

The experiment here is a far cry from the Friedman model —so much so that both supporters and critics of the voucher principle contend that it is not a true test of voucher education. They say it may be seriously misleading as an example of the concept in practice at a time when districts around the country are considering voucher experiments.

Voucher purists think private and parochial schools should be part of the competition they would like to see in education. Here, only public schools are involved. Affluent parents may not supplement the basic sum—the voucher—allocated to each child, as they could under a pure voucher system. Nor may schools choose among applicants.

Moreover, safeguards have been built into this city's program to keep teachers and administrators on the payroll even if their programs are uncompetitive and to give parents the right to keep their children in neighborhood schools.

Abuses Were Feared

Some of the restrictions were placed on the concept by the Federal Office of Economic Opportunity after a study headed by Christopher Jencks of Harvard concluded in 1970 that an unregulated voucher system could lead to abuses and probably would be thrown out by the courts. Other modifications were made at the insistence of local officials for this experiment.

Finally, the unusual nature of the school district and its leadership raise the question of whether anything that happens here can be a lesson for anyplace else.

The six schools in the experiment are among 24 in the ethnically mixed, economically strapped Alum Rock Union School District, where the project and the Federal funds that go with it landed after other places turned the idea down.

With a two-year grant of $2-million from the Office of Economic Opportunity, the six schools have developed a total of 22 elementary education programs, called "minischools." Parents have been given the right to enroll their children in any program they like.

Every child carries with him a voucher, worth $680 a year for children in kindergarten through sixth grade and $970 for seventh and eighth graders.

The amounts represent the average per-pupil expenditure in Alum Rock, one of the poorest districts in California, and the money comes from the regular district budget.

Extra Funds For Food

For children poor enough to qualify for the Federal school lunch program—more than half the Alum Rock children qualify—O.E.O. provides compensatory vouchers worth about a third more. The goal is to encourage school staffs to develop programs that would help and be attractive to the poor.

The range of educational choices starts with the traditional —straight rows of desks, teacher-imposed regimen, structured group learning. With some wrinkles added here and there, each of the six schools in the voucher project offers a traditional program.

At the other end of a spectrum that stops short of radical pedagogy is School 2000 at the Donald J. Meyer Elementary School. Standard subjects are taught in the context of such modern and future concerns as space exploration and ecology, and pupils in a single classroom may range in age from 5 to 10.

Between the two extremes are such offerings as the fine arts minischool, also at Meyer, where Mrs. Bonnie Jacobsen says she finds her pupils more responsive this year because art is an integral part of school and not just a reward for getting through the dull stuff; and the multicultural program at Grandin H. Miller Elementary School, where Ruth Domingo, 11 years old, and Rosalind Wyman, 12, say they enjoy "the cultures"—the supplement to standard elementary fare that involves learning how Chicanos, blacks, Japanese and Hawaiians live.

Parents Were Careful

Faced with such a variety of choices for their children, Alum Rock's parents have reacted conservatively in the first year of the voucher project.

Only about 5 per cent have chosen programs that take their children away from their neighborhood schools, and for them the Federal grant provides transportation money.

Traditional education is the single most popular offering, enrolling almost 1,400 of the 3,800 pupils in the six voucher schools.

The voucher project is to be expanded next year to seven more schools under a new two-year grant, approved in Washington, that will bring the total Federal investment in the program to just under $7-million. And there are signs that the parental caution that marked the first year may be easing.

Paul Hutchinson, spokesman for the nonprofit Sequoia Institute, which administers the project under contract with the school district, said the selection process now under way among parents for next year showed a developing pattern of willingness to leave the neighborhood school—"going with the program instead of the building," as he put it.

Mrs. Thelma Atterbury, who works part time in the voucher project's parent information program, backs the district's experiment on the ground that "there was something wrong in the past, why not try something new." But she chose traditional education programs for her two children this year.

"I felt it would take a year for this thing to get off the ground," she said, "and I was afraid the kids might lose something if they went into a new kind of program. But I plan to change now."

Evaluations Next Year

Are children learning more under the voucher program than they did before?

Detailed evaluations are to be done by the Sequoia Institute and the Rand Corporation, but results will not be known before the end of the project's second year.

No one in more than a score of interviews suggested that the children were learning less, and many thought that there was marked improvement.

Is the Alum Rock experience applicable elsewhere?

Daniel F. Joy 3d, a former official of Young Americans for Freedom and one of the political conservatives now running O.E.O., said he believed that the voucher concept was hardly being tested at all. He was much more enthusiastic about a proposed experiment in New Hampshire that would include nonpublic schools and in general come as close to "pure" voucherism as possible.

Joel M. Levin, president of the Sequoia Institute and director of the Alum Rock project, said he thought that with proper preparation and civil rights safeguards, at least part of the program here could be duplicated anywhere. But he conceded that Alum Rock was in an extraordinary school district.

Harmony Among Leaders

It would be hard to imagine any abuse of parental choice that could lead to segregation here, for example. The district's enrollment is 50 per cent Chicano, 35 per cent white, 10 per cent black and 5 per cent Oriental and other minorities. The ethnic ratios in the voucher schools have reflected those proportions.

Alum Rock also presents a picture of exceptional harmony in its leadership.

B. Luke Levers, head of the local affiliate of the California Teachers Association, shares with the state group and its parent body, the National Education Association, a distrust of the voucher concept. But he feels that the local program is working well, for purely local reasons.

"We're probably unique in our school board," he said. "It's the best I've ever been around. But the key to the whole thing is the superintendent, Bill Jefferds. When he tells you something is going to be a certain way, that's the way it is."

Most observers credit Mr. Jefferds with the success of the exhausting local consultations and negotiations with Federal officials that brought the experiment to Alum Rock.

Augmented Resources

Even before the Federal project came along, though, Mr. Jefferds had proved himself adept at augmenting Alum Rock's meager resources through conventional and unconventional channels. One program, involving use of school buildings for community activities, has financial help from a pair of improbable sources—the Junior League and a Federal crime-control act.

"The justification was that we were helping to prevent juvenile delinquency," Mr. Jefferds said.

Ed Gehrhardt, president of the East San Jose local of the American Federation of Teachers, echoed the praise of Mr. Jefferds. But he said he thought most of the schools opted for the voucher program to get O.E.O. money, and added:

"As a local we're particularly concerned because the experience in Alum Rock might be used to form a conclusion that a less regulated voucher model is workable."

Mr. Jefferds became superintendent three years ago after a career in Alum Rock that included teaching and various administrative jobs. He immediately started a process of decentralization in the district, once so rigidly structured that it was possible to tell at any hour of the day almost exactly what a pupil in any classroom was doing.

Fears Elitism

Mr. Jefferds said he thought two aspects of the voucher experiment—parental choice and educational alternatives—could be introduced in many school districts.

"I'm against the Friedman model because it could produce a separate, élite school system," the superintendent said. "But I'd like to see private and parochial schools involved in vouchers if they had the same ground rules we have—the same resources, the same admissions procedures. I think the public schools could compete very effectively."

"MATTERS OF CHOICE"—A FORD FOUNDATION REPORT ON ALTERNATIVE SCHOOLS*

The long-term solution to the question of survival for most alternative schools is public funding. For all practical purposes that means becoming part of a local public school system. Most viable alternative schools today are incorporated into their local public schools.

In most states, all public schools must abide by regulations about curricula, attendance, budgets, and teacher hiring practices. Both teachers' organizations and local and state regulations impose additional requirements on the operation of schools. Yet alternative public school systems are generally recognized as "experimental" schools which are exempted from many state and local regulations, at least temporarily.

Whether the restrictions placed on public alternatives hinder the operation of the schools depends on the flexibility of teachers' organizations and of local and state educational authorities. For example, community schools which involve a high degree of parent involvement in teacher selection almost invariably find it difficult to function within the public system. Also, parents who teach in community schools are rarely state-certified teachers, which places such schools in direct conflict with teachers' organizations.

Other kinds of public alternatives find it easier to adjust to the restrictions. They may use state-certified teachers but retain some control over which teachers they hire. Or they may use a mix of state-certified teachers, paraprofessionals, university interns, and street workers. Most alternative schools have pupil-teacher ratios below those found in traditional schools. To keep costs comparable, they must either find a way to pay some teachers less than negotiated salary scales

* Reprinted from the Ford Foundation, 1974.

or to trade off facilities and materials to pay prevailing salaries. In their curricula, alternatives generally find a way to meet state requirements without excessively altering their programs.

While some educators feel that only public alternatives can have an impact on the public system, others contend that public alternatives cannot provide genuine options because of the restrictions imposed on public schools. For some private alternative schools such questions are truly academic. The alternatives to public funding are foundation and federal grants, which expire, and local fund-raising efforts such as bake sales and private donations, which rarely yield enough.

Some alternative schools have initiated experiments in public-private cooperation which would entitle them to public funds without requiring that they become part of the public school system. Thus, the East Harlem Block Schools plan to provide training for public school teachers. Yet even these arrangements provide only stop-gap funding until the political climate is such that the schools can be incorporated into the public system without losing their uniqueness.

Going Public

"Here she is! Miss Boston University!" a group of students shout as their friend walks into the headmaster's office at Harlem Preparatory School. Miss B.U., a former New York City high school dropout, twirls around to show off her new self. Another young former student brought her baby girl with her to school because she could not afford a babysitter. Until a year ago, she was working at the telephone company—bored, scared, with no real future for either her or her child. Now she is attending college.

Harlem Prep is a school for dropouts: for the American Indian girl who was told she didn't have enough credits to graduate from public school. ("I got tired of taking courses I didn't like, like home economics, instead of courses I needed to graduate. So I hit the streets. Then somebody told me about Harlem Prep.") Or the aspiring journalist who couldn't convince her former school that she didn't want to become a nurse. Or Ron, a dropout from three New York City public high schools. ("I needed help and guidance from the teachers, but they didn't have time for that. They were the educators and we were just the students. Here, we all teach and we all learn. There's a reason for everything you have to do.") Ron graduated from Cornell in May 1972 and entered graduate school.

In central Harlem alone, some 1,000 teenagers drop out of school every month. "I figured there must be some out of that number who could enter and complete college," says the headmaster of Harlem Prep, Ed Carpenter, a former counselor in a New York City public high school. Harlem Prep opened in October 1967 with forty-nine students and nine faculty members. In 1968, the school moved into its permanent site in an abandoned supermarket. The atmosphere is open and informal. Students and teachers stay after school and have a voice in picking courses and in running the school. But when it comes to learning, Harlem Prep is structured and strict. Teachers take attendance, give homework, and grade students in a traditional way.

To be admitted to Harlem Prep, a student must be at least sixteen years old and able to read at the seventh grade level. Thus, only highly capable students are admitted to Harlem Prep in the first place, even though they are all public school dropouts. Students can be of any race, nationality, or religion. The maximum period of enrollment is two years. To graduate from Harlem Prep, a student must be admitted to a college or university—and 99 per cent do go on to college. For most students, this means getting a full scholarship as well as being accepted. Since its inception in 1967, Harlem Prep has sent 731 former dropouts to college.

Harlem Prep's students are morally obligated to "enter and complete college and return to serve the Harlems throughout the nation." The goals of maximizing service and minimizing materialism are built into the curriculum. "Our students are the have-nots who are going to become the haves—with compassion," Carpenter says. Of Harlem Prep's twenty-five college graduates, several are attending graduate, medical, and law schools, several are teachers, two are writers, two work in government agencies, and four are back at Harlem Prep as teachers.

"This is a school that produces—that sends kids to college, that reduces welfare rolls, that cuts down on narcotics problems, that generates taxes," says Carpenter. "It's profitable for everyone." But Harlem Prep has not been profitable for itself.

Since the school opened, it has been funded by the Ford and Exxon Foundations, Carnegie Corporation, hundreds of corporate grants, and literally thousands of individual contributors. But private funds finally were not enough.

In August 1973 Harlem Prep's board of directors decided to close the school down. But the teachers and administrators voted to stay on with no pay. Some collected unemployment compensation instead. A massive campaign was mounted by the board of directors and by various contributors and politicians who had supported Harlem Prep over the years to persuade the New York City Board of Education to fund the school. The effort was ultimately successful. As of May 1974, Harlem Prep was still negotiating with the Board of Education over such technical matters as teacher certification requirements, but public funding has begun for the entire program.

What public funding will mean to Harlem Prep in the future is uncertain. The board is trying to certify most of the school's present staff, but two teachers without college degrees will not be eligible. However, the agreement with the board will allow Harlem Prep to solicit outside funds, which could pay for uncertified personnel, and since Harlem Prep went public the Exxon Education Foundation has granted $25,000.

Ed Carpenter isn't too worried about losing teachers under the new arrangement. He is worried about constraints on curricula, the number of hours teachers will be allowed to work, and the scheduling of meetings according to union contract. But, noting that public school alternatives have been allowed to retain their individuality, Ed Carpenter says, "I can't really say what will happen, but I'm encouraged."

Quid Pro Quo

One possible long-range solution to the problem of funding private alternatives may lie in cooperative programs with a public school system. In September 1972, the Hawthorne School in Washington, D.C., a private high school with a reputation for innovation, enrolled forty-one public school students. The students were chosen by lottery—three from each high school and one from each vocational school in the city. In return, Hawthorne, then on the verge of closing for lack of funds, was granted the use of an old public school building. Annual tuition for regular Hawthorne students is $1,950, and many have scholarships. Since the public school system couldn't pay the cost of educating the forty-one students, it agreed to let Hawthorne use public school resources such as athletic facilities, counselling services, vocational equipment, and field trips. "But since we wouldn't normally pay for field trips and athletics anyway," said headmaster Alexander Orr, "the arrangement really isn't of any financial use to us." The Ford Foundation granted $31,000 to make up the deficit and to fund a documentation of the three-year project.

"We decided that the best way to help big city education was to make ourselves directly available to the public system," said Eleanor Orr, headmistress of Hawthorne. "We can respond to the need for change faster. We can constantly revise our curriculum. Public school systems have a certain regimented character and there will always be some kids who don't fit there."

At first Hawthorne experienced serious attendance problems with the public school transfers. "The public school kids never saw the connection between being in class and passing," said Mrs. Orr. "In public school, their teachers ignored them. Here, the teachers follow them around. It was hard to get used to." Fourteen transfers returned to public school because Hawthorne was too difficult.

Last year Hawthorne enrolled a total of 120 students. Twenty-four of its forty-one public school students were black. It was the first year that the school enrolled more black students than white students. Hawthorne now faces a serious public relations problem to persuade white tuition-paying parents that Hawthorne still has high academic standards. While as many white families applied to Hawthorne as ever this year, a far smaller percentage decided to enroll their children after they had visited the school. "The parents are frightened," said Eleanor Orr. "They think, 'How can you bring in all those public school kids and still offer quality education?'"

Still, many private alternative schools are in financial trouble. They will have to seek some kind of help to face up to their role vis-à-vis public schools, especially with the proliferation of public alternatives. Eleanor Orr would like to see a system of tuition grants to public school students who need help so that they could take advantage of private alternative school programs: "The best thing would be if the whole city were a set of alternative schools."

Prospects

If the kids have to go back to public school, it will bring about the same situation that spawned the Federation in the first place. But I don't think it could have the same result. These people are tired. They've struggled for seven years to make some kind of change, and the conditions in the Boston public schools haven't changed at all. They're still terrible. Perhaps even more important, while the schools stayed the same, the situation in this community got worse. Federal cutbacks for Model Cities and other programs have turned a poor community into a destitute one. The parents are less and less interested in the schools and more concerned with day-to-day problems of survival. At this point, education becomes an abstraction.

—PHILIP HART
Federation of Boston Community Schools

Conditions at many levels of education discourage the growth of alternative school programs. In many school districts lay boards as well as professional administrators maintain rigidities in curriculum, organization of the school day, the rules governing student behavior. Regulations at the state level often impose another ring of restraints—on what is taught, who may teach, and how teaching may be done, and some union contract provisions hamper the flexibility that is central to the spirit of alternatives. Yet as several projects discussed in this report indicate, there are important exceptions; in various parts of the country the initiative for alternative schools has been taken by professional educators, state education officials, and teacher union leaders as well as by parents and community leaders.

There is much less public support now for reforming inner-city schools than during the "urban crisis" a few years ago. Alternative education, both public and private, is in danger of becoming regarded as a fad—a simplified panacea one day, an expendable experiment the next. If this happens, the Boston Federation will become one of the first victims. The hope that public school systems or federal or state agencies would assume the costs of private alternative programs is no longer as bright as it was several years ago.

CALIFORNIA ALTERNATIVE SCHOOL
ASSEMBLY BILL NO. 1052*

An act to add and repeal Article 2.3 (commencing with Section 5811) to Chapter 6 of Division 6 of the Education Code, relating to alternative schools.

LEGISLATIVE COUNSEL'S DIGEST

AB 1052, as amended, Dunlap (Ed.). Alternative schools.

Defines alternative schools, declares purposes thereof, and authorizes governing board of any school district to establish and maintain such schools.

Specifies maximum average daily attendance of each school district which may be enrolled in alternative schools. Requires any alternative school to be maintained and funded by the school district at the same level of support as other educational programs for children of the same age level operated by the district.

Requires specified notice re alternative schools to be given to parents, pupils, and teachers.

Requires that teachers and pupils be selected from volunteers.

Prohibits racial or ethnic discrimination in operation of alternative schools.

Permits Superintendent of Public Instruction to waive Provisions of Education Code, other than those relating to earthquake safety, in operation of alternative schools. Requires superintendent to make specified reports to Legislature re alternative schools.

Requires Department of Education to institute program to evaluate alternative schools.

Authorizes school districts to provide transportation of pupils to alternative schools or to reimburse parents or guardians for the actual costs of transportation provided for or paid by them.

* Reprinted from the California Legislature 1973–74, Assembly Bill No. 1052. Introduced by Assemblymen Dunlap, Dixon and Vasconellos, April 3, 1973.

Operative July 1, *1975*. Ceases to be operative *July 1, 1979*.

Provides that neither appropriation is made nor obligation created for the reimbursement of any local agency for any debts incurred by it pursuant to this act.

VOTE: majority. Appropriation: no. Fiscal committee: yes. State-mandated local program: no state funding.

The people of the State of California do enact as follows:

SECTION 1.   Article 2.3 (commencing with Section 5811) is added to Chapter 6 of Division 6 of the Education Code, to read:

Article 2.3.   Alternative Schools

5811.   The governing board of any school district may establish and maintain one or more alternative schools within the district.

For the purposes of this article, an alternative school is defined as a school or separate class group within a school which is operated in a manner designed to:

(a) Maximize the opportunity for students to develop the positive values of self-reliance, initiative, kindness, spontaneity, resourcefulness, courage, creativity, responsibility, and joy.

(b) Recognize that the best learning takes place when the student learns solely because of his desire to learn.

(c) Maintain a learning situation maximizing student self-motivation and encouraging the student in his own time to follow his own interests. These interests may be conceived by him totally and independently or may result in whole or in part from a continuous presentation by his teacher of choices of learning projects.

(d) Maximize the opportunity for teachers, parents and students to cooperatively develop the learning process and its subject matter. This opportunity shall exist not only before the commencement of the alternative school but also shall be a continuous, permanent process.

(e) Maximize the opportunity for the students, teachers, and parents to continuously react to the changing world, including but not limited to the community in which the school is located.

5811.5.   The following notice shall be sent home with

each pupil's report card at the end of the third and the fourth quarterly period or once during the month of February and once during the month of June:

"Notice to Interested Parents, Pupils, and Teachers

California state law authorizes all school districts to provide for alternative schools. These schools are defined and procedures described in Sections 5811 to 5819 of the Education Code. Section 5811.5 of the Education Code requires that notice of this alternative educational program be given.

In the event any parent, pupil, or teacher is interested in further information concerning alternative schools, the county superintendent of schools, the administrative office of this district, and the principal's office in each attendance unit have copies of the law available for your information. This law particularly authorizes interested persons to request the governing board of the district to establish alternative school programs in each district."

Further, a copy of the notice shall be distributed to each teacher of the district before March 1 of each year and copies shall be posted in at least two places normally visible to pupils, teachers, and visiting parents in each attendance unit for the entire month of March in each year.

5811.6.   The parent or guardian of any pupil may request the governing board of a school district to establish an alternative school program or programs in the district pursuant to this article.

5812.   Teachers employed and students enrolled in the alternative school shall be selected entirely from volunteers.

5812.5.   Previous classroom performance shall not be a criterion limiting any student from the opportunity of attending an alternative school.

5813.   Each school district may enroll not more than 10 percent of its total average daily attendance during the preceding fiscal year in alternative schools. A district may establish alternative schools in each attendance area or on a districtwide basis, with enrollment open to all students districtwide, or any combination thereof.

5813.5.   The maximum percentage prescribed by Section 5813 may be waived by the Superintendent of Public Instruction on a showing by the district that it has been or is in a position to continue to operate its program in an alternative school manner without the loss of its experimental value.

5814. Alternative schools shall be operated in a manner to maximize the opportunity for improvement of the general school curriculum by innovative methods and ideas developed within the alternative school operation and to improve the general level of education in the State of California as provided in Section 5816.5.

Any alternative school shall be maintained and funded by the school district at the same level of support as other educational programs for children of the same age level operated by the district.

5815. There shall be no racial or ethnic discrimination in any aspect of the operation of alternative schools.

5816. For the operation of alternative schools as herein defined, the Superintendent of Public Instruction may, upon application of a school district, waive any provisions of this code other than those relating to earthquake safety and the provisions of this article.

5816.5. The Department of Education shall institute a program for evaluating the effectiveness of alternative schools. The processes of evaluation shall include but not be limited to teacher, parent, and student input from the alternative school itself. To facilitate the improvement of the curriculum of all school districts, the Department of Education shall disseminate to all school districts information concerning the operation of alternative schools.

5817. The Superintendent of Public Instruction shall establish minimum standards to further implement the definition of alternative schools as used in Section 5811 and may also establish such further guidelines as may be deemed by him necessary to the proper administration of this article.

5817.5. The Superintendent of Public Instruction may authorize any participating school district to contract with other agencies of government, universities, foundations, or nonprofit institutions for assistance in planning the proposed educational reform.

5818. The governing board of a school district maintaining an alternative school may provide in whole or in part for the transportation of a pupil attending the alternative school. In lieu of providing such transportation, the governing board may pay to the parents or guardian of the pupil a sum not to exceed the cost of actual and necessary travel incurred in transporting such pupils in cases where transportation is provided by or paid for by the parents or guardian.

5819. The Superintendent of Public Instruction shall annually evaluate the operation of alternative schools and report thereon to the Legislature on or before January 6th of each year. He shall also provide a final report to the Legislature on *July 1, 1979.*

5819.5. The article shall become operative on July 1, *1975, shall cease to be operative on July 1, 1979, and, as of July 1, 1979, is repealed.*

SEC. 2. No appropriation is made by this act, nor is any obligation created thereby under Section 2164.3 of the Revenue and Taxation Code, for the reimbursement of any local agency because the Legislature hereby determines and finds that in this act there are no duties, obligations, or responsibilities imposed on local governmental entities or school districts.

Section VIII
POLITICS

No educational proposal to reform escapes politics. The politics surrounding the educational alternatives movement is as crucial as any other aspect described so far. Unfortunately, the educational establishment has not revealed fully the unique type of politics played within the educational arena. Questions of power, decision-making, and influence have only recently been considered "fair game" in education. Certainly anyone who has followed other reforms, such as desegregation and decentralization, will have been struck by the politics converging on these issues. As we shall see here, the idea of alternatives has also been linked to education vouchers. The educational establishment has responded negatively to the proposal for education vouchers which would have provided additional purchasing power for the educational consumer—especially the discontented consumer. For many in the public schools, education vouchers signal the beginning of the end for public education, since in their view, dissatisfied consumers would opt for private alternative schools. As we shall see with the review of the Rochester experiment on vouchers, politics can "make or break" a proposed change.

It is also clear that educational alternatives cannot compromise one group in favor of another. This is one of the reasons that public alternative schools have more political support. Teachers and their professional organizations, parents, and students share equally in the right to choose. In brief, it is not at *their* expense. At any rate, the intricate political themes are explored here and, hopefully, will reveal to the reader important insights concerning this unexplored domain. Anyone who is seriously considering alternative education will have to become as knowledgeable as possible concerning the dynamics of political reality.

This section will deal with such questions as:

How has politics been both a stimulus and a drawback to changing schools?

By whom and how are political faction groups formed?

How does the established structure of the system complicate matters?

What are some problems confronting alternatives in meeting state education laws?

What are some common political problems?

What groundwork could be laid down in the beginning to avoid them?

How can students and other support groups help resolve them?

POLITICS, RAGE AND MOTIVATION IN THE FREE SCHOOLS*

BY JONATHAN KOZOL†

Education is always political in one fashion or another. It is political by provoking painful choices. It is political by urging ethical decisions. It is also political, though in a different sense, if it creates a mood or atmosphere in which there are no serious provocations and no ethical decisions to be made. I do not mean that education needs to be political in the sense of New Left, Old Left or Old Right—although this often is the case—but rather, that all of the school-discussion has at its foundation the question of what young people will believe, or not believe, about the way they live, about the way their nation lives, and about the way in which it serves or does not serve the cause of justice.

Most Free Schools begun in ghetto neighborhoods have had, from the first, a strong ingredient of direct, unfalsified political consciousness; this, in most cases, in coordination with a hard-boiled and pragmatic emphasis on skills, effectiveness and realistic willingness for certain kinds of active competition with acknowledged enemies. By and large, Free Schools begun for the children of upper class white people have been not merely non-political, but conspicuously and intentionally anti-political. In many respects, the two movements not only separate but, unfortunately, segregated; yet the fashions from one school drift easily into the other. Therefore, it is essential for the survival of the serious Free Schools of this nation to raise the issue of political participation, or, conversely, of political abdication and surrender.

The issue of "free choice" is of particular importance when we speak of schools that serve primarily children of rich peo-

* This article is adapted from the second edition of *Free Schools* by Jonathan Kozol (Mass., Houghton Mifflin, 1972). Copyright © 1972 by Jonathan Kozol. This article is reprinted from *Harvard Educational Review*, Vol. 42, No. 3, Aug. 1972.

† Jonathan Kozol received the National Book Award in 1968. His newest books are *The Night Is Dark* and *I Am Far from Home*.

ple. It is simply dishonest to lead children to "experience" freedom if, in fact, they *are not free*. In an unjust nation, the children of the rich and powerful are not free in any way that genuinely matters if they are not free to know the price in pain and exploitation that their lives are built upon. To surround these children with the bright and whimsical gadgets sold by groups like Westinghouse and I.B.M. and E.D.C. while innocently pretending to ignore the fact that everybody in this high-tuition Free School is white-skinned, well-fed and middle-class, to offer anesthesia but to call it "freedom," to speak of "options" but to fail to tell the children of the unearned wealth that makes these kinds of options possible for them, and them alone, this does not seem to me to be an honest or a conscientious process.

The heart of the deception is the pretense of free choice within a carefully constructed framework of contrived and managed possibilities. The children can "choose" for Hermann Hesse, for Richard Brautigan or Tolkien, for Mexican sandals, Polaroid cameras or brown rice with mushrooms; but they cannot "choose" for starving and malnourished kids in Harlem, for dying men in Venezuela, or for slaughtered babies in Vietnam, Laos or Cambodia if everything in the air and on the walls and in the meadow and over the river and, above all, in their parents' and teachers' eyes, conveys to them the secret message that such things *do not have credible existence* or, if they do, then only in a way that cannot touch them, or make claims upon them, or intrude upon their dreams, or intervene upon their slumber. To encourage these children to "experience" freedom because they are allowed to choose the water-play unit from Westinghouse above the gerbil-cages or the packaged science-game from E.D.C., if they have *no freedom* to choose to side in spirit and in fact with those who are the victims of the unjust allocation of resources which affords them privileges and pleasures such as these, to offer this "beautiful freedom" in all things pertaining to an immediate kingdom of delight but *no freedom* in terms of access to data and openness to experience which, together, may be able to destroy or undermine the walls of anesthetic self-protection that surround the unreal world in which they live, to offer this kind of falsified freedom, in my judgment, is to purvey a very deep and desperate kind of servitude. A child in a rigorous, old-fashioned public high school would be far more fortunate in several respects. At least he would not be deceived into believing that his choices were his own and consequently would be able to react with secret rage and silent skepticism to the undisguised mendacity around him.

In visiting many of the rural Free Schools in the course of these two years, my wife and I repeatedly ask ourselves this question: Why is it, in so many of these self-conscious, open and ecstatic Free Schools for rich children, everyone boasts that he is doing "his own thing" but everyone in each of these schools, from coast to coast, is doing the same KIND of thing? Why is it, we ask, that "free choice" so often proves to mean the weaver's loom, tie-dye and macrame, that "organic growth" turns out in every case to mean the potter's kiln? How come it doesn't ever mean a passionate and searching look into the origins of unearned wealth that makes this segregated Free School possible? How is it that it never pertains to danger, choice, or confrontation?

It is, of course, because *all* teachers and *all* adults in these kinds of situations do in fact dictate the options and preferences of the children in a number of important and inexorable ways: by the very familiar and predictable clothes they wear and life-styles they foster, by the very familiar and predictable tools, gadgets, gimmicks, and ornamentations they provide, by the physical location they have chosen, by the pupil-tuition they establish, by the race and social class of children they enroll. I do not propose that teachers and parents in these schools ought to exercise *less* power. What I do suggest is that they ought to exercise their power with more conscious recognition of the bias they now serve and that they ought to give more honest and straightforward expression to those deep and oftentimes insuperable barriers of privilege and class which shade their preferences and tarnish and restrict their sense of love, their will to justice or their capability for passion.

Those who adhere with the highest degree of noncritical perception to the notion of impartial, nonpolitical and non-directive education attempt very often to portray themselves as those who are involved exclusively with the child "him-self" and who do not desire, therefore, to bring political or social bias into pedagogic areas. In truth, however, there is immense and serious bias in their prior choice to keep things low-key, whimsical, untouched by anger. The methods with

which they decorate their pedagogic vision and demonstrat
their upper-class sophistication may, from a certain poir
of view, appear to express a nonpolitical preference and
nonideological choice of learning-atmosphere. In fact it i
by no means nonideological or nonpolitical. It is a clea
and obvious choice AGAINST the voice of anger. It is a clea
and obvious choice AGAINST the need for ethical behavio:
It is a clear and obvious choice AGAINST the need for strug
gle, confrontation, intervention.

"Spontaneity" is the magic word among the liberal an
genteel men and women I now have in mind, but the ideolog
cal antisepsis of the kind of Free School they inevitably creat
guarantees well in advance that no child here will ever choos
spontaneously to learn of things which lie outside the provinc
of privilege, the kingdom of trivia, or the boundaries of sel:
gratification.

In certain of the more sophisticated classrooms in some c
the innovative and experimental public schools, children ar
now provided with an opportunity to research and to explor:
without apparent supervision, into a seemingly diverse arra
of books and films, of tapes and magazines and other type
of resource-data. If we look, however, what we find in almo:
every case is that the seemingly diverse resources that th
school purveys are not very different from the unimporta:
options of mass magazines, of TV networks or, at the ve:
most, of the commercialized rebellion of the counter cultur:
These schools do not suppress the revolutionary instincts c
our children; instead, they buy them out.

The Free School that is born of a high consciousness c
struggle is in a unique position to puncture this pretense c
apparent freedom and to expand and deepen the falsified mi
and insubstantial options that now are purveyed as seriou
choices in the public schools. In one Free School that I kne
first hand, teachers bring in materials from the public schoo
in order to give the children concrete data on the ways i
which the public system of indoctrination functions and pr:
ceeds: HOW PUBLIC EDUCATION SERVES THE FLA:
IT FLIES. In the same school—one which is operated in th
Boston ghetto—there is also a semester of math-exercises bui
upon the exploration and examination of the drug-trade i
the neighborhood in which the Free School stands. In anoth:
Free School there is a team of parents, teachers, and chi

dren who look into serious problems such as lead-paint poison in their neighborhood, research the causes, consequences, possibilities of action, call in the press, call out the neighborhood, and launch a city-wide campaign against lead-poison for *all* children.

There must be at least a hundred other ways in which some of the Free Schools I have seen endeavor to expand the sense of option and the possibilities for direct provocation in the course of academic labor. Several, for example, go to great pains to be certain that the casual materials—books, magazines and pamphlets—which are present in the school, in classroom-shelves, on hallway-tables or in whatever passes for a quiet reading place, include such strong, diverse but often unfamiliar items as *Monthly Review,* the English language version of the Marxist daily paper (*Granma*) from Havana; the brilliant, angry and exciting research-bulletins that are prepared and issued by the North American Congress on Latin America ("Tupamaros," "The Rockefeller Empire," "The Great South Asian War"): the documents and data of the African Research Group in Cambridge, Massachusetts, or of the Medical Committee for Human Rights in San Francisco. I go into some detail here in regard to names and titles in order to make sure that I will not be misunderstood, and so that the point at stake here will be absolutely clear: children can only "choose" for what they see *as* choices. Children will never spontaneously ask to learn of things which they have never heard of. We do not awaken one morning, without prior provocation, to a spontaneous and organic sense of curiosity concerning the function of the C.I.A. in Guatemala or the progress of the sugar-crop in Cuba. Nobody walks into an airport and requests two tickets to fly to Rio de Janeiro if he does not first know it is there.

This is, for me, the crucial question in regard to choice and freedom in the Free School: ferment, provocation, liberation or the sense of option does not "happen" by spontaneous combustion. It happens only if the teachers, parents, organizers, leaders, partisans, coworkers, are willing to stand up and defend a point of view, to introduce unusual kinds of catalytic possibilities, to risk the likelihood of error, sadness, anger or upheaval by bringing into the context of the child's education visible and unexpected forms of provocation which he cannot independently discover. Children who read and who have access to a newsstand in the year of 1972 or 1973, might well be prompted on their own to pose a certain *type* of question in regard to Mao Tse-tung or Chou En-lai, or possibly just to ordinary life in Shanghai or Peking. It is obvious, however, that they are going to ask a totally different kind of question and, as I believe, to ask that question from an infinitely less passive and less neutral point of view, if they have also had an opportunity to see a copy of *Peking Review*. It is obvious, again, that children might, by natural processes, be prompted or provoked to ask a certain sort of question in regard to Mexico, Bolivia or Brazil, merely in reaction to the latest issue of *LIFE Magazine* or *Newsweek*. They will, however, ask a far more serious and more searching kind of question if they have also had a chance to read some of the penetrating bulletins from NACLA: still more if they have been provoked to place the versions of the truth as it is documented or narrated or reported by both publications side by side, therein to find that genuine tension and that deepdown sense of intellectual provocation, choice, decision, which never is possible within a classroom that must serve the interests of a single nation or of a single social class.

I do, of course, agree with the point made several times in recent months by certain of my colleagues, that many of these problems are less blatant and less obvious in a Free School which is situated in a neighborhood of Black or Puerto Rican people in the first place: i.e., a Free School that can locate or can ascertain the counterfoil to *TIME* or NBC or CBS merely by pulling up the blinds and looking out the window. Yet even within the most intense and conscientious Free School there are whole areas of intellectual provocation and of political consideration to which no child ever will gain access if his curiosity and his initiative are not challenged by the active and non-neutral intervention of adults.

It is one thing for an alert and serious young woman or man to recognize, on his own and without added information, the grim, archaic, racist and, at times, dysfunctional character of the public high school on the opposite corner; it is another thing to have available *the records of closed sessions of the Boston School Committee,* and to discover in this fashion the deep, deep, cynical, corrupt and conscious processes by which dishonest men defraud the poor and the least powerful of the young while serving their own allies, cronies and ward-organizers. It is one thing to recognize, from repetitive exposure, that medical services in ghetto hospitals like Boston City Hospital tend to be slow, inadequate, chaotic, and disheartening; it is another thing to understand that this is not an accidental, isolated situation, but that every major city in this nation has at least one hospital to give this kind of care to those who have no economic options: that is, that every city offers ghetto medicine to ghetto citizens and makes available its least effective, least reliable and least consistent services to those whom it has come to view as its least valuable children. It is, once again, one thing to live with a low-key, lifelong, unstated recognition that police-collusion or police-collaboration is affiliated in some stupid, gross, informal or disorganized way with the sale of drugs, the sale of sex, and the total climate of corruption, drug-addiction, and violence that now obtains on something close to plague dimensions in black communities of cities such as Boston and New York. It is another thing, however—indeed it is something of a *totally different order*—to begin to understand that wholesale drug-addiction, prostitution, violence on these dimensions COULD NOT CONCEIVABLY EXIST if it were not for the consistent, organized and even disciplined liaison between pushers, prostitutes and cops.

The difference here is something more important, I believe, than a matter of the volume of information or of the level of detective-work at stake, it is the difference, rather, between two levels of incipient perception. The first is discontent, uneasiness and involuted desperation; the second is leverage, potency, a point from which to look down and consider the full view. The first is the sense of inarticulate and as-yet-disorganized rebellion; the second is something more like "functional anger," "passion that can force its path through realistic channels." In my belief, very little of the second kind of insight, leverage or perspective ever takes place in the lives of children within a nation of manipulated will and of stage-managed choice, without the direct risk-taking intervention which is constituted by the actions and examples of adults in a state of ethical rebellion. Inevitably the areas of challenge and of catalytic action that come to my mind are those which voice a New Left bias and a Third World orientation. These are, for certain, the kinds of challenges that I would look for, advertise and foster. The point, however, is less the left-wing bias or the Third World point of view than it is the simple fact of an authentic confrontation among genuine and exciting possibilities.

I have tried to emphasize, at various points within my work, that I do not like the notion of political indoctrination; I think it is an incorrect response to the indoctrination of the state, inasmuch as it confirms the basic character and notion of the process of indoctrination, even if it transforms the subject-matter. I like even less, on the other hand, what I believe to be the ethical abdication or the disguised collaboration of the Free School which denies the struggle for justice and evades or neutralizes the experience of anger. If indoctrination is an incorrect response to pain and mandate, abdication or collaboration is an obviation of the claims of mandate altogether. The perception of pain is not the end of spontaneity; it is the starting-point of motivation. This point, so far as I can understand, must lie someplace close to the heart of any Free School that intends to take its stand in the face of history. This is the case, at least, so long as history remains, as it has been within our lives and in our generation, the chronicle of men who live upon the misery and exploitation of their brothers, yet do not know and oftentimes can never even dream the price that must be paid in hunger, pain and desperation in order to make their sense of private satisfaction possible. There is simply no way in which to disaffiliate entirely from the blood and stench of the times in which we live.

POSTSCRIPT

This is intended as a brief, pragmatic footnote to the larger discussion of political consciousness and provocation in the Free Schools.

The urban Free School has been described by Ivan Illich as a pedagogic Free Zone in a land of intellectual stagnation.[1] The first responsibility of a revolutionary cadre—in the mountains of Bolivia or in the canyons of New York—is to solidify and to secure its borders. It is essential, therefore, both for the symbolic possibilities and for the tactical objectives of the Free School struggle in this nation that we be prepared to offer, both to those within our ranks and to those on the outside, the vision of men and women who can do things right; can start, continue, follow up and follow through; can instigate, promote, excite, inspire, and then can stick with that which we have helped inspire, promulgate, promote, long enough to bring it to at least a tentative level of completion.

The issue is posed for us, in these terms and at this time, because of the very familiar problem of low levels of *consistent* loyalty in many of the Free Schools. The deepest danger to survival, in large numbers of these schools, is by no means —as many of us like to say—the speed with which some of our allies get co-opted. It is the willingness with which we self-destruct. Hundreds of times, by now, we see and recognize the sudden and unnecessary abdication of real power and of real threshold-status in regard to the consummation and completion of a looked-for goal. Right at the edge of action, on the threshold of real generative force, there is a familiar instant of reiterated failure, fractional passage of imaginative loss and of emotional collapse which sometimes seems, remarkably, to yearn to forfeit everything. Time and again we encounter people who get high on abstract possibilities, wax rhetorical on the birth of new conceptions, become exhilarated during the opening hours of a new experience, but lose their steam the moment it appears that something they helped inspire may in fact persist and prosper and survive.

I wonder, though, what kinds of loyalties can be constructed on a groundwork of desertion. There is a black child that I know in Boston who has now gone through four generations of white teachers, organizers, drifters, VISTAS, O.E.O.-supported revolutionaries and what he calls "The Hippie People," all in the course of six years. Peter can list the names of all the young white men and young white women he has known. They give him supper and they buy him shoes and take him out on hikes and sit down on the floor to play with the cuisenaire rods for one summer and one winter, and sometimes for one spring and for one summer once again. Then they switch gears, and they are into a New Thing. They cancel him out, or rather they do not "cancel" him— they cannot quite do that—but situate him in a slot of history or a place of pain known as "the race and conscience bag." They make new friends and read new books, and find a whole new set of slogans and bywords, and they are off to a new dedication.

Peter, however, does not live within the "race and conscience bag." He lives on Columbus Avenue in the South End of Boston. He is a real person and, after they are gone, he is still there.

There is, for each of us, the need to learn and grow—and grow, of course, in terms of our own consciousness of what "school" is about. There is the need, therefore, to open ourselves at all times to new, vigorous and conflicting notions which will challenge those things which we presently believe or which we *think* we understand. There is, however, an even deeper need to find one solid core of concrete action and specific dedication in one neighborhood, or in one city, with just one group of children, and with one group of allies, and with one set of loyalties, and with one deep, deep dream of love and transformation. This is the struggle which large numbers of us in the Free Schools now must face during the years ahead. It is the struggle also of the whole youth movement in this nation. It is the struggle of those of us who have been taught for twenty years how to be non-stop consumers, and now must pause to teach ourselves how to be loyal to one thing that we believe in.

FOOTNOTE

1. In a letter to the author.

ALTERNATIVES: 90% POLITICAL, 10% EDUCATIONAL
THE POLITICAL DEMISE OF MARKLES FLATS*

BY JONATHAN DAITCH, PRINCIPAL†

It seems to me that Markles Flats is a classic case of the politics of alternative education. The school is a parent-student-staff run alternative junior high school within the Ithaca City School District Public School System. It was started a year after East Hill, an elementary public alternative was begun.

* Reprinted with permission of the author. This report is based on a telephone conversation between Jonathan Daitch and Mario D. Fantini.
† Jonathan Daitch is Assistant Professor of Education at Ithaca College and former principal of Markles Flats.

There was, initially a lot of support, the idea for the school came from a bunch of students and faculty in Cornell's Human Affairs Program—a radical, fieldwork oriented interdisciplinary program which got students out into the community. When they, a member of the Education faculty of Cornell, and several public school teachers approached the then Superintendent, Roger Bardwell, they were given a good deal of encouragement, but told they must have parent support. Bardwell really believed in this sort of thing—parents and kids involved. Eventually, with a great deal of parent and student support, the then liberal Board O.K.'ed the school in May of 1970.

The first year was, as is usual in alternative and free schools, pretty hectic. And, in addition to the usual problems of developing a new school, there were staff conflicts stemming from the mix of professional staff and HAP students. The three paid staff were trying to run the school as a group and couldn't get it together. They came into conflict with the HAP students who were bound and determined to make up for all the evils of the public school system. When one teacher emerged as leader he was not able to overcome the split in part because the HAP students were responsible to a Cornell supervisor and not the principal.

Well, the upshot was that support for the school started eroding, and members of the community began pressuring some board members who were never strong supporters to begin with. The school became a big item in the press, and after much vascillation the Superintendent and Board O.K.'ed another year with several stipulations—at least 75 kids, another location, and a new principal—HAP supervisor to whom everyone in the school was responsible. That's when I was hired.

That next year was a good one. With ups and downs the school began to define itself, and we found ourselves involved in a lot of interesting projects and field trips. We were struck a blow though when the Superintendent resigned and was temporarily replaced by a man not supportive of the school. Fortunately, he was not strong enough to act on his feelings. Unfortunately, his administrative weakness allowed an increasingly conservative and aggressive Board to encroach on the administrative process. By summer they were running the District. Support for the school had not yet completely waned, and with considerable parent pressure, and in the light of a very favorable evaluation of the school, the Board was forced to give us another year.

Now the important thing to remember here is that up to this point, with the exception of the initial decision to start the school, all decisions and judgements were political and not educational—pressure, not evaluation determined the outcome. Even the decision to go a third year was not based on the favorable evaluation—it's just that in the light of that evaluation the Board couldn't say no without blowing its cover of educational responsibility and being blatantly political.

That June (1972) a citizen (not in any way connected with the school) brought a suit against the school. The suit was legally not valid: she had no grounds either in process or substance. But what she did accomplish was to alert the State Education Department, and to arouse anti-Markles sentiment in the community. The new Superintendent of schools had previous difficulties with the SED, and was not the kind of guy to make stands. He thought that through his personality, he could satisfy everybody.

O.K., at this time the SED is running scared because alternative schools are bursting out all over the place and there's a problem of how to handle things—how to define, regulate, and control these people who are making some fundamental challenges to traditional school organization, and the SED's cumbersome and inconsistent regulatory process. So when the Superintendent (who is caught between pro- and anti-Markles and won't make a stand) calls the SED and says we have an illegal school here (we did not meet all SED rules and regulations) can we keep it going? Of course the SED is not about to set a precedent and open the flood gates for a bunch of crazy radicals, and says NO! Now the Superintendent can go back to the community and lay it on the SED.

So the evening before opening (September 6) it is announced at a board meeting that until we meet all rules and regulations or get official waivers, the school is closed and will try to reopen on October 2. Markles school people went to the SED with documents, etc. After 4–5 weeks they received a letter from the SED stating that under NO circumstances will they support Markles until the Board of Education backs it. The SED couldn't challenge the substantive material of Markles, so they worked this political move. There was a lot of parent pressure to open the school though, and so there was much back and forth rhetoric, while the Board became increasingly irritated and the Superintendent refused to move one way or the other. Finally, in December the issue was resolved as follows: Markles would reopen in January for only six months, and a committee would be set up to study the needs of alternative education in Ithaca. *The reason given for closing Markles permanently was that its name was too controversial.* Educationally we had met the needs of 100 students, met all local and state requirements, and were a proven education success. Politically, we were too much. Further evidence of this is that only one Markles staff and two parents are on the study committee of about 12 and it is apparent that the new school will not open in September and no current staff will be kept on.

Our educational success is irrelevant in the political arena. We were not doing a proper job of socializing. In Markles, education is not the issue. Style and goals—schooling are. And goal setting is a political process.

THE POLITICS OF IMPLEMENTATION AT "ANY" ALTERNATIVE SCHOOL*

BY ALAN SUGARMAN†

The politics involved in trying to implement an alternative school program are complex and, often, as discouraging as "trying to pilot a plastic raft through a storm around the Cape of Good Hope." This political case study of an alternative program presents real points of view, although locale and names have been deliberately omitted. It is important for you to have a sense of the group dynamics involved when such a program is proposed. This account is written from the point of view of a participating observer.

The idea of alternative education presented an interesting and legitimate possibility of dealing with the overcrowding

* Reprinted with permission of the author.
† Dr. Sugarman is Superintendent of Schools, Connetquot Central School District of Islip, Bohemia, New York.

expected in our senior high school. Here was an opportunity, through voluntary participation, to provide an educational renewal by programming a curriculum having export possibilities.

We spoke with experts, hoping to find practical solutions without raising too many anxieties. There seemed to be some worthwhile spinoff possibilities. The administrative team, comprised of the high school principal, the Director of Secondary Education, the Assistant Superintendent for Instruction, and an administrative assistant, pursued the matter in this way for a three-month period. The concept of several approaches emerged. Originally, we conceived of this plan as a program for the gifted. Ultimately, we decided on a heterogeneous grouping for about 150–200 students. The plan would stress conservative models: interdisciplinary education, personal inquiry, independent study, etc.

We saw the need for participation of parents and students in the committee and were planning to solicit this interest, when a group calling itself PAPER came on the scene. This group sought an alternative plan for the elementary schools: they wanted an open education format to be incorporated into the school district curriculum, and they wanted it soon.

We had not considered possibilities of an alternative program in the elementary schools, since it was overcrowding in the senior high school that triggered our investigation of alternatives originally. However, now we saw the possibility of responsive involvement. The PAPER group provided the needed parent input, and so we decided that the alternative education thrust would include the elementary school component. We enlarged the committee to twenty-three members. To eliminate any charge that we operated covertly, we advertised in the school district bulletin, inviting teachers and principals to join our investigation into alternative education.

We now confronted a major issue: the Curriculum Planning Board. In our district, curriculum is negotiated. The Curriculum Planning Board is a contractual agency to which curriculum innovations and recommendations are usually presented, and is composed of six members of the Teachers Association, six principals, and six Central Office designees. We had decided to avoid involvement with this group, in line with our approach to the whole idea of alternatives: that this involved administrative reorganization rather than being a program change. We thought, as well, that we could avoid Teachers Association politics when we asked for teacher input rather than Association input.

Our situation was further complicated by the resignation of both Directors of Education. Neither of the new people on the scene wanted to pursue alternative education, for a variety of reasons: they had come to the situation "in the middle" and there were other pressing problems to consider. These men had to be convinced.

The parent group was upset at the negative arguments the directors presented. The administration had to explain to vociferous committee members that it was essential for the two directors to present this to the Board with their endorsement as a priority in secondary and elementary education.

Group dynamics and politicking were intricate parts of the picture. Internal problems arose in the upper administrative echelon. The PAPER group was suspicious of the administrator. They felt that he was more committed to secondary education than he was to elementary education. Finally, they realized his honesty and the important position the two directors held, and held down their exacerbation.

At last, the proposal was ready, and we were faced with unanticipated problems: We were planning to house three hundred students in an off-site building that had recently been vacated, but we had not anticipated the financial end. The new alternative program would cost us $400,000 as we had set it up. The administrative cabinet was negative on the presentation of finances, so we decided to go to the Board with the program but not with the finances. Were we to present the finances to the Board, we felt that the proposal would be killed.

As for housing three hundred students in an off-site vacated junior high school building, we faced opposition from a large committee who interpreted the original close of the building as an end to all educational processes that could take place there. Actually, the building had been inadequate to house a sufficient number of junior high school students, and the new building was considered better suited to our program of traditional education. The committee claimed that this constituted an illegal use of the building.

We already had a school-within-a-school (SWAS) operating that was raising more criticism than praise on the grounds that it was too open an operation and too controversial a program. Several Board members used the SWAS controversy as a weapon to neutralize our interest in alternative education in terms of this other model. The Board of Education was split with a conservative minority charging that the entire alternative education effort was illegal: that we had no right to appoint a committee of lay people without Board of Education action. This matter is being pursued by a Board member in the Legal Division of the State Ed. Department. Each review of the Educational Standards Committee was marked by venomous debates. I often wonder, "Was it worth it?"

We were planning a cultural island type operation—a mini system through which we could look at the process of educational renewal and at approaches which could be put into use in the main institution. We hoped for a redesign idea in a voluntary setting, away from the mainstream. We had the format for the possibility of change.

Now, we've had to give up off-site possibilities. We are ready to propose an on-site senior high school program to replace or to be injected into the SWAS. We have a few on-site centers on the elementary school level. We're planning a summer training program for volunteers—a summer school that will generate most of the ideas developed by the Alternative School Committee for Elementary Education. It's not easy to come in with this program when the interest is running conservative. I am not optimistic.

But there are a number of possibilities in the alternative education package which have good exportability for conservative education. At least the hierarchy is getting tuned in to some sound educational approaches. This can lead to some worthwhile curriculum renovation.

We have faced opposition from a number of groups. The Teachers Association was opposed to alternative education on the grounds that we circumvented the Curriculum Planning Board and that we went directly to the teachers instead of working through the Teachers Association. We were condemned for the finances, the educational program, and the process we had adopted for its development. The conservatives on the Board criticized us for catering to a minority. The minority Board members felt that their interests had been shunted aside. We were involved in have and have not politics. These conservatives felt that a program with merit is a program for everyone, not a select few. They insisted that if a choice can't be offered to everyone, then offer it to no one. They resisted the voluntary lottery selection of students. They didn't understand the spinoff implications. They objected to the fact that the Alternative School Committee was not appointed in a legal fashion. We felt we had a right to involve the Committee. The question became "Does the Board have to approve?" Some claimed that the Committee was made up of a select few who were predisposed to alternative education. There were some valid criticisms raised.

Maybe it would have been better to go through the classic route. At the time the idea was initiated, we had no time. We were faced with overcrowding. Now time is not a factor, since the overcrowding is not a reality. We didn't want to get bogged down in contract commitments and organizational restraints—a procedure that might have tied the whole thing up for two to three years. There's a real need to be daring sometimes. Population pressure is a valid need.

Many important questions were raised. What is the prerogative of the administration in setting up an advisory committee with lay people? It's a power question. What is the place of Boards of Education in relation to administration? Who makes the policy and who executes it?

Finance became a real problem—and our main source of concern. Is this the route to austerity? We had three hundred kids and planned for eight to ten teachers, at a salary of $18,000 each. Housing and transportation were problems too. The Business Department refused to endorse any program not meeting its scrutiny. It claimed that none could represent finances without their approval. Perhaps further consultation was necessary. Maybe this alternative program was too conventional and would function simply as another school.

While we recognize that educational innovation is a "must," we must face two problems and deal with them. There is a need for credibility. We must apply a "systems" approach to change through programmed budgeting and performance orientation. We must set up an organization through which, step by step, systematically introduced, we provide assessment in layman's terms.

IS A COLLISION BETWEEN PARENTS AND TEACHERS INEVITABLE?*

BY MARIO D. FANTINI

Powerful, perhaps irresistible, currents are converging on our public school system—some economic, some political, some racial. They seem to herald a storm that will engulf embattled teachers and indignant parents, to say nothing of the children. The threatening storm may be difficult to see in some regions where tranquillity still reigns. But it is only a matter of time before the clouds gather there too. Teachers have found potent weapons in group cohesion and political action. We need only be mindful that an entire educational system can be brought to a halt through strikes.

Sensing the implications of the new forces surrounding them, teachers are becoming aware that they must continue to build political leverage. This means moving from local and state affiliations, and from national organizations such as the National Education Association and the American Federation of Teachers, to what might possibly become the American Teachers Association.

Parents and students do not have the same organizational capabilities as teachers, but they do have access to elected officials and can put tremendous pressure on them. The public is beginning to raise serious questions about what the school is or *is not* doing. There are no villains in this scenario—only people with justifiable concern about what direction education in America should take, who should decide that direction, what the costs it involves will be.

For some of us, the roots of this battle can be found in the nature of the public school itself. An institution formed in the nineteenth century, it still retains much of the structure and objectives of that era. Yet it is now expected to respond to the needs and values of twentieth-century America, with all its cultural diversity and its goal of quality education for all.

* Reprinted with permission of the *PTA* magazine published by American Congress of Parents & Teachers.

The public is expressing its discontent in a manner that is shaking the foundations of public education, even though most school users may still be favorably disposed to the school. To compound the problem, Americans are responding negatively to the spiraling educational costs, especially since the financing of public education is so widely dependent on local property taxes. Even though many citizens value quality education for their children, they feel forced to defeat local bond issues. Tight economics makes parents raise questions about teachers' salaries and tenure. They pay attention to public school failure rates, to student discontent, or to the need for humanizing the educational process.

In the urban centers, parents and students alike are protesting the inequities of education. Because of historical patterns, black Americans have been sentenced to depressed areas and to institutional racism. They are caught in a cycle of despair: poor education leading to poor jobs, leading to poor housing, leading to psychological and social discontent. For many of these Americans, education remains the one hope of renewing their status, cultivating their own culture, satisfying their own aspirations.

The Biter Bit

Where the casualties are greatest, so is the retaliation. Parent and community boycotts and calls for community control of schools have now followed a decade of neglect, of unfulfilled promises, of futile dependence on the people—usually white—who are in a position to improve the lot of minorities. Time has run out.

Soon the professional educator will be fighting for his very life. If the public really comes to support educational vouchers, for instance, the organized professionals cannot sit by and watch their own welfare being compromised. They see such techniques as a ploy to bring about the demise of the public educational system and the people in it. Moreover, they find much that is substantively wrong with these "desperation" efforts at reform.

The ultimate weapon, school stoppage, may have to be used in order to confront the rising storm of public discontent. It is clear that the public cannot do without education, whether it is entirely satisfactory or just so-so. Denial of formal education through the closing of schools—not only state-wide, but conceivably nationwide—can make this point.

Teacher organizations assert that if they had the power, they would use it to reform our entire educational system. It is difficult to see how parents will be convinced by this argument. The teacher shortage of the past decades has ended, and we now have a teacher surplus. Today many people may not be so concerned with professional organizations as they are with being employed. The professional ranks are not easy to keep closed when people are hungry and "hustling" for jobs.

Government policymakers have already begun to set in motion a "get-tough-on-education" policy. In fact, the President of the United States clearly enunciated the new policy in his March 1970 Education Message to Congress: "American education is in urgent need of reform." As a result, the new terms now being employed in the U.S. Office of Education are "reform," "renewal," "redesign."

New policies are bound to affect public school procedures. Professional educators will turn abruptly from the add-on, compensatory approaches of the past. Heretofore they responded to problems of educating the poor by mounting programs of compensation. When the crisis in urban education was spotlighted in the 1960's, they produced remedial programs, mostly for minority groups. Earlier, they responded to society's demands with such reforms as vocational education, adult education, early childhood education, special education.

This add-on strategy will no longer work. Not only are the costs high, but the results are questionable. As President Nixon stated in his message to Congress, "The best available evidence indicates that most of the compensatory education programs have not measurably helped poor children catch up."

Many minority parents, dissatisfied with their schools, want to rely more heavily on black and/or other minority professionals to bring about educational programs that are more responsive to their needs. In so doing, they directly threaten many white principals and supervisors. Given such tensions, educators turn ever more frequently to their professional organizations.

The Difference to Them

For teachers who have attempted to play by the ground rules set by an institution, it is difficult to contend with the demands associated with the new wave of public accountability, demands which appear to them to be unreasonable. A teacher may feel that trying to be a "good citizen" inside the educational institution means closing the door to outsiders and trying to do his best with a group of twenty-five to thirty-five different children. Not having been trained to deal with the problems of cultural diversity, teachers have tried to "make it" on their own. They have had to learn on the job. They think it is the increased number of students who are the problem, who do not adjust, who have "changed," who are not willing to work as other students once did.

In earlier times, the student who did not adjust, who did not keep up with the "standards" of the school, had the "option" of dropping out and going to work. During the first industrial revolution our labor needs made this possible. But now the labor situation has changed. Today, more people have to stay in school a longer time to meet the demands of our advanced technology. Further, to flood the labor market with millions of young people would be disastrous to the economy.

At one time, if a child did not respond to the standard public school program, he was placed in a classroom for slow children, regardless of the stigma attached. Labor needs triggered the development of vocational education, which, to many, was a place for "those who could work with their hands and not with their heads." It was natural to assume that since certain children were making it and others were not, those who were not were "deviant," they were "failures." We began to classify human beings as "slow," "underachievers," "disruptive," or "disadvantaged." A way of classifying human beings is a way of thinking about them. Such classifications spawned a whole psychology of self-fulfilling prophecies.

These ground rules have now become unworkable to all parties: to students, because such rules forced them to adjust to uniformity; to parents, because their aspirations were thwarted by seeing their children "turned off" or tagged as "failures"; to teachers, because they became the victims of consumer discontent and of institutional outmodedness. For teachers, the blow was ironic: Trying to live by the rules of the institution had led to their being used as scapegoats for the system itself.

The teacher does his best to deal with diversity by trying to "individualize instruction." A basic hindrance to doing so, teachers feel, is large classes. Teacher organizations have negotiated districtwide for reductions in class size—from thirty-five to thirty-two, thirty-two to thirty, and the like. To a public already overtaxed, this approach is expensive and is abrasive.

In the standard public school view, some children are disruptive, a term which, in most cities, refers to minority students. This designation foments further bitterness in the minds and hearts of minority communities. And so the battle grows. Moreover, traditional "improvements" are now being challenged not only by the consumer but by the professional himself.

Failure in beginning reading is common in inner-city schools, but in a few cases reading has been taught there with notable success, as shown in a study conducted by the Council on Basic Education. In these cases there was no attempt at a crash program: From three to nine years was devoted to the project. In each case there were strong leadership, high expectations, good atmosphere, additional reading personnel, and indivualization. Surprisingly, certain factors often considered important were absent: small size, achievement grouping, school personnel of the same ethnic background as the pupils, and outstanding physical plant.

The stakes are getting higher because certain communities have a stronger voice in local public school control. Decentralization and community control raise the voice of consumers through their election to local neighborhood boards. This represents a "get tough" attitude toward professional dominance and toward "more of the same." In some urban areas, community participation has led to new forms of accountability. Local neighborhood boards begin to develop policies about hiring, transfer, and dismissal of teachers who are "not productive with children." These new pressures are viewed as unreasonable by professionals inside the educational system trying to make it work.

It seems inevitable that parents and the public will eventually win this "war." The delivery of educational services must go on, preferably within the structure of public education. The stakes are indeed high. They affect not only the future of public education itself, but the whole fabric of American society.

In traditional schools all efforts are aimed at trying to improve the one uniform system and make it better. And we do make it better by lowering class size, team teaching, television, the New Math, program materials, or in-service training. But all of this fails to come to grips with the fundamental problems that schools now face: (1) making the school responsive to diversity and (2) using available resources more effectively rather than always calling for more money to do more of the same.

When Optional is Optimal

Obviously, we need to open up educational options within the framework of public education, *not by chance, but by choice.* Teachers ought to be encouraged to develop alternative forms that fit their own styles of teaching and enlarge the chances for educational productivity—especially if these options are made available to the student. Student-made decisions not only increase consumer satisfaction but offer new learning opportunities to those who have not responded to the standard options, such as open classrooms or multicultural units. Further, these alternatives need not cost more money, since the same teachers are paid in the same way as before.

For instance, the Parkway program in Philadelphia, a School Without Walls, viewed the city as a classroom with a range of learning environments: the art museum, the Franklin Institute, IBM, hospitals. Staff members of the involved institutions became teachers. The students roamed the city, which became a viable alternative *within* the framework of public education. And there were no extra costs.

Other educational alternatives could be developed. Again the costs would not be greater—not if college students are used as teacher assistants and tutors and independent study is encouraged with students assuming responsibility for their own learning. Certain public schools have begun to move in this direction. The Berkeley Unified Public Schools now offer more than twenty educational alternatives grouped in four categories:

1. *Multiculture Schools*—These schools will have children carefully selected on the basis of diversity—racial, socio-economic, age, and sex. During part of the school day, the students will meet and work together. At other times, they will meet in their own ethnic, social, or educational groups, learning their own culture, language, customs, history, and heritage. Later, these aspects will be shared with the wider group. These schools may well form a model of what all Berkeley may be like in the future.

2. *Community Schools*—The organization, curriculum, and teaching approach of these schools come from the community. There may well be total parent involvement, with both the school day and week being extended into shared family life. There will be use of courts, markets, museums, parks, theaters, and other educational resources in the community. The schools will be multiaged and ungraded, with an emphasis on developing a multicultural community of participating families that learn from each other, and, for the older children, on working directly in the community in agencies, businesses, or projects.

3. *Structured Skills-Training Schools*—These schools will be graded and will emphasize the learning of basic skills—reading, writing, and math. Learning will take place primarily in the classroom and will be directed by either one teacher or a team of teachers. Usually the schools will be smaller units, with the regular personal relationships.

4. *Schools Without Walls*—The focus of these schools is the child rather than the subject. They will be ungraded; their goals, to have the students grow in self-understanding and self-esteem, learn how to cope with social and intellectual frustration, and master basic skills through their own interests.

The development of such an alternative public schools plan would not only "save" the public schools through feasible reform, but elicit the support of both parents and teachers. Teacher organizations can use their "power" for statesman-like leadership, which means rising above the environment that now shapes us inside the institution in which we find ourselves; leadership that spearheads the opening of options within a framework of public education.

Money is available, through Titles I and III of the Elementary and Secondary Education Act, that could serve as "conversion capital," transitional money that would allow people to come together, plan new alternative structures, and provide basic information to citizens.

Unless constructive proposals are considered soon, a collision between teachers and parents seems almost unavoidable. Yet there is still time to deal with the common enemy—the restrictive structure of our public schools. After all, teachers and parents want the same thing—responsive education. Professional teacher organizations can lead this reform; parents can help give it shape and stability. To do so, we must resist the temptation of protecting the existing institution and its conventional wisdom.

STUDENTS AT METRO PLAY THE POLITICAL GAME*

BY STUDENTS OF THE CHICAGO PUBLIC HIGH SCHOOL FOR METROPOLITAN STUDIES

The Chicago Public High School for Metropolitan Studies (Metro), Chicago's only experimental public high school, is protesting the unsatisfactory rating given to its principal, Mr. Nathaniel Blackman, Jr., by his District Superintendent, Dr. Bessie F. Lawrence. This rating could result in his dismissal within eight weeks. Students, teachers, and parents feel that this is a direct attack on the school, which throughout its two-and-a-half-year history has been harassed by the Board of Education and particularly by the Superintendent of District 7, Dr. Bessie Lawrence.

Teachers have been trying to engage the General Superintendent of Schools, Dr. James F. Redmond, in some kind of meeting, but so far he has refused to respond. Teachers are demanding the removal of the unsatisfactory rating and

* Reprinted from a report released by Students of the Chicago Public High School for Metropolitan Studies. Nov. 16, 1972.

direct communication between the Board and Metro to help with other difficulties without going through the Board bureaucracy.

Parents have requested meetings with Dr. Lawrence and her superiors, but they have refused to meet. Three hundred of the 350 student enrollment have picketed the Board's headquarters, 228 North LaSalle Street, on Monday, November 13, and another picket is scheduled for Thursday, November 16.

The Chicago Public High School for Metropolitan Studies is one of only two schools of its kind in the country, a "school without walls" with classes meeting at various businesses, museums, and cultural institutions, as well as the main headquarters at 537 S. Dearborn Street. It has been highly praised by educators all over the country.

The continual harassment and negative attitude displayed toward Metro by the Board of Education and Dr. Lawrence is displayed by the differences in the Metro educational program as it now exists and the original goals as set up in September 1969, in the Board of Education Rationale and Program for the Chicago Public High School for Metropolitan Studies.

The document stated that:

a) The school would admit a freshman class of 500 students each September, and by 1973, the school would have an enrollment of between 1500 and 2000. In reality, the present enrollment of 350 falls far short of this estimate, and the school's main headquarters and facilities as they now exist could not possibly handle even half the projected enrollment.

b) The school would provide the Board of Education with a laboratory situation suitable for the field testing of teacher training procedures and "varied curricular approaches." Yet, some staff members have been told by Dr. Lawrence to conform to the rules and regulations of the Board in relation to attendance lists, class curriculum, and other items. The rules and regulations of other Chicago public high schools are not applicable to the Chicago Public High School for Metropolitan Studies, however, for it is attempting to use "varied curricular approaches," the idea expressed in the aforementioned document. The paper also stated "The school will illustrate the school system's potential for innovation given sufficient resources." But it is difficult to achieve this goal when our principal is being threatened with unsatisfactory reports and the staff being expected to conform to the guidelines established for other contemporary high schools.

All this despite the fact that Metro has the highest reading scores of all general high schools in District 7 according to reports issued October 1972. Of the 1973 senior class 7% received Illinois State Scholarships; 7% received National Merit commendations; 1% were semi-finalists for the National Achievement Scholarships. Of our two graduating classes, 68% have gone on to higher education, proving the worth of this program and its effectiveness.

SEATTLE PUBLIC SCHOOLS PLANNING PROCESS FOR ALTERNATIVE PROGRAMS*

General Proposal Format

I. *ABSTRACT*
   Brief summary of all aspects of the program.

II. *NEEDS*

A.   General Needs
   1. Initial statement of the problem.
   2. Brief description of the setting (social, economic, organizational) in which the problem occurs, including constraints.
   3. Description of the previous history of this program (for continuation proposals) or discussion of similar previous programs (for new proposals).
   4. State who was involved in the needs assessment.

B.   Specific Needs
   This should include a statement and documentation of the specific needs of the population which this

* Reprinted with permission of the Seattle School Board.

program is designed to serve. These will be particular needs which will be demonstrably lessened by the successful implementation of your program.

III. *GOALS AND OBJECTIVES*

A.   General Goals

This section of the plan should define and justify (as necessary) the general goals toward which the program is aimed. This section is not intended to define the explicit, measurable objectives of the program, but instead should define a general condition that the program should be facilitating.

B.   Specific Objectives

This section of the proposal should provide a list of those specific outcomes or levels of performance that can reasonably be expected to result from the program. Objectives that cannot reasonably be measured in specific terms should not be included in this section. Objectives should be concise, explicit, assessable, and clearly directed at alleviating the stated needs.

IV. *PLAN**

This section should contain a detailed explanation of the proposed program. This explanation should include the following factors:

A.   Experimental variables, or conditions which will be altered to bring about the changes listed in the OBJECTIVES section. Where appropriate, describe why and how these conditions will be changed.

B.   Staffing and facilities necessary to conduct the program should be described. Provide proposed staff-to-student ratios and indicate roles for paraprofessionals, parents, etc. Include job descriptions and staff selection procedures.

C.   Describe scheduling and procedures for selecting students to participate in the program.

D.   Major anticipated problems and proposed coping tactics.

* See Special Requirements for Alternative School Proposals (attached)

E.   Outline proposed curriculum, proposed activities, special texts or materials to be used in the program.

F.   Explain the proposed strategies for involvement of parents and community in the program.

G.   Timeline for implementation of proposed activities of the program, including evaluation.

H.   Alternative school proposal criteria.

V. *EVALUATION*

This section should describe in detail the proposed evaluation process. It should contain answers to the following questions:

A.   How will on-going evaluative feedback be incorporated into program improvement and modification?

B.   How will the information be collected? What form will the information be in? Who will provide the information? (Where available, attach copies of proposed forms and questionnaires.)

C.   Who will conduct the evaluation, and who will process the information?

D.   How will baseline or comparison data (where appropriate) be collected?

E.   To whom, and in what form, will the evaluative information be reported?

F.   Have all objectives been accounted for?

VI. *BUDGET*

This should include a detailed breakdown of how the requested funds are to be spent. Indicate where applicable the amount and source of other funds which will be used to support this component.

Alternative School Proposal Criteria

The following considerations must be addressed in the *Plan* section of Alternative School Proposals.

1. STAFFING:
   a. State the necessary staff roles in your program.
   b. Develop tentative job descriptions for these roles. Job

descriptions should include statements of the qualifications, duties, and responsibilities of each position.

2. STAFF SELECTION:
   a. The selection of the program manager and/or head teacher is the primary responsibility of the Department of Special Programs. It is suggested that your proposal describe a method by which students, parents, and community persons can develop and submit recommendations for filling the position to the Department of Special Programs.
   b. The selection of all other program staff is the primary responsibility of the program manager and/or head teacher. It is strongly recommended that, where possible, decisions about staff should include students, parents, community, and other staff.

3. STAFF TRAINING:
   Make provision for continuing staff development.

4. STUDENT SELECTION:
   Provide the criteria for selection of students. Describe the student needs that your program can and cannot serve.

5. STUDENT PARTICIPATION:
   a. Specify criteria for continuing participation in the program.
   b. Describe procedures for dealing with non-participating students, including follow-up counseling mechanisms and dismissal procedures.

6. ACADEMIC CREDIT:
   State criteria and methods for earning credit, e.g. contracts, classwork, independent study, etc. Refer to "Conditions for Granting Academic Credit" and "Graduation Requirements for Alternative Schools."

7. FACILITIES:
   Specify minimum facility requirements for your program, including:
   a. amount of space
   b. location
   c. rent
   d. other requirements

Proposal Review Checklist

A. *NEEDS ASSESSMENT*
1. Is needs assessment *process* indicated?
2. Does proposal demonstrate complete and accurate assessment of local and *specific* needs of target population? Specific needs of target population are most important.
3. Community involvement in needs assessment demonstrated?
4. Is target population defined?
5. Is priority given to assessment of *student* needs?
6. Have students, teachers, parents and community contributed input to needs assessment?
7. Does proposal contribute to long-range goals of the district?
   a. Show documentation showing district commitment.
   b. Consistent with institutional needs or goals?
8. Does proposal give evidence of being supplementary, not supplanting?
9. Is evidence provided showing relationship/adaptations to other related programs nationwide? (review of literature)
10. Is focus of project clearly indicated?

B. *OBJECTIVES*
1. Are objectives functionally related to stated needs?
2. Are objectives assessable at relatively frequent intervals?
3. Do objectives include description of:
   a. Performance being observed?
   b. Conditions under which behavior is to occur?
   c. Criteria of acceptable performance?
4. Do objectives indicate changes in student performance?
5. Are staff objectives specified?

C. *PROCEDURES*
1. Is logical progression of events evident?
2. Is the responsibility for procedural steps evident?
3. Are procedures clearly enough described so that an

outside reader could be expected to implement those procedures in very similar form?

4. Are there specific procedures for each objective?
5. Are procedures described to monitor staff activities and responsibilities?
6. Are procedures cost efficient; i.e., would less costly procedures meet minimum requirements of meeting objectives?
7. Is budget consistent with established needs and objectives?
8. Do procedures indicate how evaluation is to be incorporated in on-going program operation?
9. Are procedures capable of being transported?
10. Do procedures lend themselves to continuous evaluation?
11. Is the sequence of events delineated?—timeline?
12. Is evidence given of suitability of necessary resources? (facilities, personnel, staff utilization, materials, etc.)

D. *EVALUATION*

1. Does it contribute to continuous project management decisions?
2. Does evaluation incorporate measurement of each specified objective?
3. Does it measure *progress toward* objectives, not just whether objective was or was *not* achieved?
4. Are provisions made for modification of procedures based on feedback from on-going evaluation?
5. Will evaluation product be understandable to appropriate audiences?

CONCLUSIONS, FEASIBILITY STUDY FOR THE DESIGN AND IMPLEMENTATION OF AN EDUCATION VOUCHER SYSTEM IN ROCHESTER, NEW YORK*

BY PHALE HALE, LARRY O. MAYNARD, AND ELEANOR PECK†

As the Study progressed, the Staff found that most of the individuals and organizations they contacted were generally open minded and honest when voicing either support or opposition to the program. The major exception was the leadership of the Rochester Teachers Association (RTA), which persistently refused to consider the possibility that the program could have any merit.

While the majority of teachers in the Rochester City School District held firmly to the RTA line in their opposition toward any form of voucher demonstration, a significant number of those opposed to the plan said consistently that given more time to study and offer input on successive drafts of the proposed model and considerably more time to plan for implementation, they might become supportive.

Although many community organizations voiced concerns, several publicly stated their support. Notable among these are the Northeast Area Development Association, the 19th Ward Community Association, the Community Schools Council, and the Brookings Urban Policy Conference.

Our Study further indicates that a significant number of

* Reprinted from the Feasibility Study for the Design and Implementation of an Education Voucher System in Rochester, N.Y., Vol. I–III, February 1973.

† Phale D. Hale is Supervising Director, Compensatory Education, coordinating efforts to improve reading and math performance and provide services for non-English-speaking students in the Rochester School District.

Larry O. Maynard is Consultant for Elementary Education.

Eleanor Peck is Communications Assistant for Grants Center.

parents have become aware of the voucher concept, and most have agreed that:

1. Alternative educational programs present a viable educational innovation.
2. The City School District is desperately in need of financial support to continue and expand innovative programs of all types.
3. City School District educators are doing a "fair-to-good" job of educating children.
4. Parents are generally satisfied with the existing alternative schools operating within the City School District.
5. Parents should have the opportunity to choose the educational program and school which they feel best meets the educational needs of their children.
6. The voucher system would not be a threat to teacher performance.
7. The voucher system would not provide a mechanism which would bring about increased school segregation.
8. The voucher system would not be a great threat to the public school system.
9. Technical problems created by the implementation of the voucher system would not be insurmountable.

Our Study shows, however, that many city residents of schoolage children know very little about the proposed voucher model. Because of strong opposition from the Rochester Teachers Association and subsequent newspaper coverage resulting from the controversy generated by that organization, these residents have either voiced modest opposition to the plan or have not taken a stand at all. The RTA had immediate access to ready-made arguments against the general concept of vouchers through its state and national affiliates. Since the voucher Study Staff was attempting to develop a very specific voucher model quite different from other models which have been heretofore proposed, the RTA, in many instances, presented arguments against concepts which, in fact, were never inherent in the proposed Rochester model.

The misinformation generated by other organizations and individuals also created problems. For example, various spokesmen suggested that the Rochester model would "open the door to participation by private and parochial schools," and that "parents would acquire the right to hire and fire teachers." At no time during the Feasibility Study was consideration given to these provisions. In fact, the Board of Education entered the contract to do the Feasibility Study contingent upon OEO acceptance of the concept of an *all public demonstration*. A careful examination of the "Teachers' Rights" and "Parents' Rights" sections of the proposed model (Volume II) should make it clear that in the voucher system, parents *would not* acquire the right to hire and fire teachers.

Opponents of the system raised many other objections which must also be given consideration. The most wide-spread objection was shared by people who otherwise supported the program: the general feeling of fatigue felt by almost every Rochester parent, teacher, and student. The community in general appeared weary from too many educational changes brought about too quickly with too little evaluation before the change occurred. Most people expressed the wish to rest a bit, to catch their breath, before another change was put into effect. Other major objections were voiced as follows:

1. Doubts regarding the stability and longevity of the Federal Office of Economic Opportunity
2. Teacher fears about increased accountability, community control, *etc.*
3. Parent fears that the voucher system would not result in increased parent involvement
4. Teacher concern that parents would not be able to make choices wisely
5. Mistrust of the school district's desire to offer parents real educational alternatives
6. The additional administrative costs that would be required to implement the program
7. The continued necessity to use some local funds to support the already-existing alternative schools

Some of these objections were addressed in successive revisions of the original draft proposal. For example, the "Teachers' Rights" section of the proposal was strengthened in accord with teachers' suggestions. A parent information and training component was added to assist parents in learning how to make informed choices. A "Parents' Rights" section was added to the proposal which guaranteed parents certain rights—most significantly, the right to be involved in program development in their individual schools. In addition, the Staff attempted to minimize administrative costs and to channel the largest possible share of the OEO funds into the participating schools.

ROCHESTER TA DIGS IN FOR VOUCHER BATTLE*

The Rochester Teachers Association is moving to implement the action of its Delegate Assembly, which voted on November 21 to "oppose the Education Voucher as proposed by OEO" for the city of Rochester.

RTA's Executive Council met on Tuesday, November 28, 1972, to formulate plans for a massive campaign in opposition to the OEO plan.

Dave Glossner, president of the RTA, calls the proposed voucher plan, in which parents would be given vouchers to carry to schools of their own choice and design "a grave threat to public education in this city."

Glossner charged that the voucher plan would provide a "million-dollar windfall" for private schools.

"What would prevent wealthy parents who now send their children to private schools from converting those schools into quasi-public schools for the purpose of obtaining voucher money?" Glossner said. "If that occurs—and it probably will —we are talking about a million-dollar windfall for private schools at the cost of the taxpayer and the public schools."

In a late-breaking development, the Brookings Urban Policy Conference in Rochester was reported by the Rochester *Democrat-Chronicle* to have announced a position in favor of "full implementation of the voucher system," one that would include public and parochial schools.

Democrat-Chronicle reporter Kathy O'Toole wrote: "The inclusion of private and parochial schools in the Task Force (Brookings Conference) recommendations gives weight to the RTA argument against the city voucher proposals. The union claims the system would eventually lead to the funneling of public monies into parochial school systems."

* Reprinted from the New York *Teacher,* December 3, 1972.

Glossner also charged that the voucher plan "panders to the separatist mood of Rochester at this time."

"People here are already talking about how they can create their own all-black schools and all-white schools and all-middle class schools under the voucher plan," Glossner said.

NYSUT and NEA staff flew to Rochester on the day of the RTA Delegate Assembly meeting. NYSUT Vice Presidents Dan Sanders and Toni Cortese, and NEA East Coast Regional Coordinator Rudy Lawton, conferred with Glossner and other RTA leaders and staff, and then appeared as a resource panel at the Delegate Assembly meeting.

The NYSUT and NEA leaders urged strong opposition to the plan and promised assistance to the RTA in its campaign against the voucher system.

NYSUT Co-President Thomas Hobart, in his "Where We Stand" column in last week's NEW YORK TEACHER, wrote that Rochester's "current program is designed to bring children *together;* the voucher plan would drive them *apart* . . ."

Hobart added: "We stand solidly behind our Rochester teachers in their fight, which is a fight for all of us."

On Tuesday, November 28, NYSUT Vice President Dan Sanders, returned to Rochester for consultations with Rochester Teachers Association leaders. David Ford, NYSUT public relations man also was in Rochester last week to assist the RTA in developing a comprehensive public relations campaign concerning the voucher proposals.

ROCHESTER VOUCHER PROPOSAL ANALYZED BY NYSUT LEADER*

BY DAN SANDERS†

Overview

The *Draft Proposal* for a voucher system in the City of Rochester calls for a demonstration of a voucher system for

* Reprinted from the New York *Teacher,* Dec. 3, 1972.
† Dan Sanders is Vice-President of N.Y.S. United Teachers.

a period of five to seven years. The recommendation of the committee in the *Overview* states that "if the Board of Education decides to proceed, it would request funding for five to seven years in order to insure the District against any possible disruptions resulting from policy decisions at the federal level." Such a statement is misleading for no federal funding is ever granted for such a long period of time. The reality is that federal funding is normally given for a one or two year period—appropriations of this type are rarely if ever made beyond a Congressional term (two years).

In the *Overview,* eight items are mentioned which "require further study" and do not appear in the draft proposal. All of these items carry tremendous implications and would require detailed analyses and scrutiny if a voucher plan were to be undertaken. The unanswered questions include: which students would be affected by the program and which would not, whether Title I services would be granted in addition to the OEO funds, guidelines for new independent schools, and whether or not such a plan would involve suburban districts along with Rochester.

General Objectives

Goals of the voucher system are listed in the proposal as:

"1. To increase parental satisfaction with the public school system by allowing parents to choose the type of school they feel will best meet their children's needs.

"2. To improve the quality of education by giving teachers additional flexibility and resources to develop educational programs around their particular skills and the needs of their pupils."

It is interesting to note, however, that both of these goals could be met without a voucher system. Open enrollment programs would and do allow parents to choose which school their child should attend. The quality of education could very well be improved by the Board of Education, in cooperation with the professional staff, developing new and innovative types of school programs or "alternative schools" within the basic school system, and without the strictures of federal control. It is an incontrovertible fact that the voucher plan is completely and totally irrelevant to the goals which are listed in the Draft Proposal.

Main Features of the Model

The section of the proposal entitled, *Main Features of the Model,* makes no provision for the special needs of children such as those with specific learning handicaps, physically handicapped children, brain-injured children, children with mentally retarded development, etc. No cost factor is assigned to help these children with special aid. There might be a dozen brain-injured children in a school, but no provision has been made for supplemental funds for them, nor is any provision made to provide decent facilities for children needing special education in regular school settings.

The report states that "Students currently enrolled and their incoming brothers and sisters would be guaranteed the right to remain in the public school they now attend." This statement, designed to allay parental fears, is virtually impossible to implement, for how could 200 or 300 students and their incoming families continue in a public school if a large number of students from their school chose different schools. Would the school system pay the heating bill and expenses of operating a huge three-story building if only the first floor were occupied once the federal government ends the experiment and stops footing the bill?

Item 6 talks about the OEO providing "reasonable funding for each school to develop its program." But development money is one thing, and money to run a program is another! If a participating public school develops a program which would be slightly more expensive but much more beneficial for children there is absolutely no provision in the budget beyond the voucher, so that all the innovation that takes place in any school is based upon keeping costs down, enrichment down, individual instruction down—innovation, giving the *appearance* of progress rather than the *reality*.

Item 7 states that new schools might be set up by individuals, groups of parents, etc. (for a start up in September 1973). Can the author(s) of this proposal be serious in stating that within one-half school year a meaningful school program can be developed and can attract large numbers of children to it?

Item 9 creates a new bureaucracy of paid employees called "community counsellors." These community counsellors are the salesmen and public relations men who try to convince parents to send their child to one school or another. They are the educational hucksters in the OEO plan who are on the federal payroll to assure "grass roots" support.

Item 10 deals with a "representative committee" to advise the board relating to the demonstration, but no effort is made to define what a representative committee is and how such a committee is chosen.

Item 11 deals with the evaluation of the demonstration and makes clear that the OEO, which is pushing the voucher experiment, and the Board, which would endorse it, would be the ones making the evaluation. *In other words, those who have committed themselves to the voucher plan would evaluate their own judgment—a clear and obvious conflict of interest.*

Item 12 makes clear that parents really do *not* have the opportunity to pick their own schools except for "vacancies" because the school would be able to decide by a "lottery" which students would attend from those applying. *This is no more than "open enrollment" where vacancies are available!*

Operations

It is very clear that the objective of the voucher plan is to keep costs down rather than raise the quality of education. If research proved that a program could be developed which would have tremendous success in raising reading scores, it could not be put into effect if the costs were above the amount of money allotted to the vouchers, which would be no more than the costs "in the previous school year at the elementary level with an additional amount to reflect rises in the cost of living." *Ironically, in an effort to innovate cheaply, the federal government will put in approximately $5 million to duplicate certain services:*

"On the other hand, central functions such as psychological services, curriculum coordination and audio-visual materials, should and would be purchased at the discretion of the individual schools. In the event that the central office personnel associated with providing these services were not utilized adequately by the schools, the District would lose the funds to pay their salaries. Since we are obligated to protect central office personnel during the demonstration, we can 'voucherize' these central services only if OEO guarantees reimbursement for any losses incurred through this aspect of the program."

Of course, when the federal government fails to renew the funds, the school system would be left with duplicate personnel in many categories and the choice of firings or a tremendous tax rise.

It is noted in this section that ". . . only public schools . . . will be eligible to participate in the demonstration."

However, in the section *New Schools,* it is pointed out that new private schools could be established and used ("quasi-public schools" through legal agreements with the Board of Education). While new schools must be approved in accordance with "guidelines," no guidelines are offered in the report and federal money would be used to start up these new schools, including money to lease a school site. OEO, it is pointed out, is expected to pay reasonable rent and renovation costs for outside facilities, *but what happens when the federal money is withdrawn after the experimental period, in two or four years, and there are 12 or 14 additional schools with the rent and other expenses that each of them entail?*

Transportation

In this section, the report says that the federal government would pay the additional transportation for the time of the experiment—a highly expensive proposition because in a school of 500, suppose 150 students decided to go to different schools. 15 of them might want to go to one school, and another 15 to another school. Ten vehicles would be required on a daily basis just to move 150 students from one school to ten different schools. Multiply that by all of the schools in the Rochester school district! *After these students have attended their new schools for a year, or two or three or four, and the experiment is ended, the school district would be forced to move everybody back to their original school or take on this staggering transportation cost.*

By the way, think of the job each year of figuring *who goes in what bus* when students have a chance to change their schools every year. And think of the instability which can result from shuttling students back and forth among schools.

Counselling and Information Dissemination

This section was designed to insure community support for this program by giving local people jobs in the program. Again, the federal government would pay for these jobs in the beginning for the experiment (as federal funds are granted only for a period of one to two years). After that the school district would have scores of "information specialists," on the payroll—unless they abandon the program.

Admissions

This section points out that if a good school is "over-applied," steps will be taken to try to increase its size through "mobile classrooms, classes in other buildings, etc."

This does not sound like bold innovative education, but rather patchwork education. Again, through such a program, many buildings would be half empty, while others would have to add mobile classrooms.

The section on *Integration* receives scant treatment. It merely states that the Board would take "corrective action" if the schools become further segregated. No amplification is given as to what "corrective action" is.

In the section on *Transfers,* the makers of this proposal make the unbelievable statement that "it is probable that school population would be more stable under a voucher system." Such a statement is patently ridiculous. How could stability of student population exist when scores of people on the public payroll are running all over town explaining the virtues of one school against another?

Administration

In this section an Advisory Committee would be created which would put tremendous public pressure on the board to become a rubber stamp by making policy recommendations to the Rochester School Board regarding the administration of the voucher plan. The proposal on staff structure in this section would create a large additional administrative bureaucracy for the school district.

Teacher Rights

This section states that teachers would have their rights under state law and Rochester Board of Education policy, but then goes on to talk about displaced certified employees and teacher contract buy-up, and then discusses the "extreme case that there is no position available" for a teacher who is displaced.

The proposal mentions the existing teacher contracts, but the federal guidelines that are created by an OEO-School District Plan may very well make a fair and equitable teacher contract most difficult to negotiate for next fall—provoking needless conflict and possible serious confrontation.

WHERE WE STAND: ROCHESTER'S FIGHT IS OUR FIGHT*

BY THOMAS HOBART†

The City of Rochester may become the second city in the nation and the first in this state to approve a voucher plan. Rochester's Board of Education is currently carrying out a feasibility study funded by the Office of Economic Opportunity, and will decide in January whether to go the voucher-system route for 10,000 of the city's children.

Approval would give the City of Rochester the dubious distinction of joining with Alum Rock, California, in a grandiose experiment in which children, parents, and teachers become pawns and in which the foundations of public school education are undermined, perhaps permanently and irreparably.

The teachers of Rochester have wisely and courageously voted to conduct an all-out fight against the voucher plan, and they are being backed in their efforts by the New York State United Teachers and our national organizations.

* Reprinted from the New York *Teacher,* Nov. 26, 1972.
† Thomas Hobart is President of N.Y.S. United Teachers.

It is the favorite pastime of some anti-education critics to label teacher opposition to anything as "reactionary," based on the presumption that teachers are only concerned with preserving the status quo or with protecting their own interests.

These critics should look carefully at the Rochester situation before they make such a judgment.

First, Rochester teachers are urging *expansion* of "successful special education programs, open enrollment programs, and other innovative programs" that have existed in Rochester but that are on the way out due to fiscal retrenchment in that city (Rochester's three unique and innovative alternative schools will not survive beyond this year because of budget cuts enacted by the city).

Second, Rochester teachers are concerned with the polarization of racial and ethnic groups in the city. Rochester's current program is designed to bring children *together;* the voucher plan would drive them *apart,* since the plan calls for schools that could be created and designed by any group of parents and would thus open the door to all-black schools, all-white schools, or all-anything schools desired by a particular group. The voucher plan, in short, panders to the separatist sentiments now prevailing among some groups in the city.

Third, Rochester teachers realistically appraise the voucher plan as an open door to aid to private schools. Once implemented, parents could carry their vouchers to quasi-public schools and dilute already thinning funds for public education. The eventual result would be direct vouchers to private schools.

In combatting the voucher plan in Rochester, teachers are not operating on preconceptions or misconceptions about what the voucher plan is all about. Evidence has been mounting that the OEO's pet project poses distinct and major threats to integrated education, to adequate funding of public schools, to the proper education of children, to the professional freedom and contractual rights of teachers, and to the rights of parents to strong, central elected boards of education.

The voucher plan being developed in Rochester also clearly opens the door to such gimmicks as performance contracting. The Draft Proposal for the project contains the following language: "Ideally, each principal should have discretionary authority over the expenditure of all administrative costs for the children in his school. Each principal and his staff then would determine which services were needed and whether or not to purchase them through the central administration or directly from some outside supplier." This language obviously allows "services" to be construed in any manner, and would permit an individual school—controlled by parents—to contract for services presently performed by qualified professional staff.

Another aspect of the voucher plan is that the Office of Economic Opportunity, trying to maintain its function under an Administration that has already promised a "Spartan era" for education in the next four years, desperately needs approval from at least one other district somewhere in the United States as a companion project to Alum Rock.

Turned down by Gary, Indiana, and most recently stalled in New Rochelle, the OEO needs a "success," and they have targeted in on Rochester—regardless of consequences to children, parents, and teachers in that city.

The voucher plan is admittedly an "experiment" designed to test assumptions about managing education for the urban disadvantaged. To be based on five- to eight-year tryouts in several districts around the nation, the OEO hopes to gain success and swing to full implementation in schools across the country.

Totally missing in that experiment is a sense of reality about public school education as it exists today, for the experiment derives from the notion that public school education is failing.

On the contrary, public school education is *working* where adequate funds are provided and where equality of educational opportunity exists. We need full and sound commitment to public school education—the kind of commitment that is noticeably lacking today at the state and national level—instead of experiments that make pawns out of children, parents, and teachers.

We stand solidly behind our Rochester teachers in their fight, which is a fight for all of us.

VOUCHER PROPOSAL DEFEATED IN ROCHESTER*

The Rochester Teachers Association has won its ten-week-long, uphill battle against the Office of Economic Opportunity, turning back a voucher plan the OEO had hoped to implement in Rochester.

The Rochester Board of Education, citing community opposition to the voucher proposal, voted down the plan at its meeting on Thursday evening, Feb. 1, 1973.

The Board's vote represented a smashing victory for the RTA, which had mounted an intensive city-wide campaign to expose the racial polarization and the buttressing of non-public schools with public funds that would have grown out of implementation of vouchers.

Board members Lewis Bianchi, Dorothy B. Phillips and Joseph Farbo said killing the possibility of the voucher program ended only one threat to change in the school system. The city still faces the possibility of large spending cutbacks which could change schools. Rochester also faces the possibility that federal courts will rule the school board must racially balance schools.

"People in this city have such terrible war nerves right now," said Mrs. Phillips. "You can't forget that the U.S. Supreme Court and Judge Henderson are still deciding the school desegregation issue," she told the *Rochester Democrat Chronicle.*

The Board back on Jan. 22 informally rejected a watered-down voucher study proposal that Superintendent John M. Franco said he prepared after it became "obvious" the Board would not support his earlier recommendation.

The earlier recommendation had been for a year-long federally funded study and planning period.

Franco's alternative recommendation would have allowed central office administrators to explore ways of adapting the voucher idea to an "expansion of the school district's city wide open enrollment program."

* Reprinted from the New York *Teacher,* Feb. 11, 1973.

RTA President Dave Glossner, in a statement on Feb. 2, said that "the voucher issue was one of the most significant ever faced by the Association."

"It had serious implications for public education not only in Rochester but throughout the country," he noted. "Its defeat is important to the future of public education in America."

Glossner praised NYSUT for the state organization's assistance to his local during the campaign against the voucher plan.

He noted that NYSUT Vice Presidents Dan Sanders and Toni Cortese had been instrumental in launching the RTA campaign by participation at an RTA Delegate Assembly meeting in November that voted to oppose the voucher plan. Glossner said, "NYSUT's help from that starting point was continuous and extensive."

Aid to the RTA included public relations assistance provided by UTNY PR specialists Dave Ford and Fred Lambert. NYSUT Vice President Dan Sanders also accompanied RTA leaders to Alum Rock, California, for a first-hand look at the only other voucher plan in operation in the nation.

Sanders' analysis of the Alum Rock plan proved valuable in the RTA's community campaign.

Also assisting the RTA were NEA research and public relations staff members.

Another major factor in the RTA victory was the support of AFL-CIO unions in Rochester and Monroe County.

At a meeting on Jan. 11, the Rochester, New York, and Vicinity Labor Council, AFL-CIO, representing more than 55,000 members of more than 100 AFL-CIO unions in and around Rochester, adopted a motion supporting Rochester teachers in the voucher plan controversy. The Council communicated that motion to the Board of Education.

In addition to gaining support from the AFL-CIO area labor council, the RTA also solicited and gained support from the Monroe County Presidents Council, from Monroe County PEARL (Public Education and Religious Liberty Coalition), and from the Rochester Chapter of Americans United for Separation of Church and State.

The RTA also met with Congressman Frank Horton in January to seek support in their fight against the OEO project, which would have affected 8,000 children in 14 of the City's schools.

Glossner told the Rochester Board of Education at its Feb. 1 meeting that because of the "opposition and the sentiment of large numbers of parents and teachers throughout the district, it behooves the Board to reject completely any further consideration of such a plan."

NYSUT Co-presidents Tom Hobart and Al Shanker congratulated the RTA this week on its victory. Hobart said, "The RTA has won a victory for all teachers and all students. The fight in Rochester was a fight for public education everywhere."

FEW USING VOUCHERS TO PAY FOR SCHOOL*

BY ROBERT REINHOLD†

Five years after education vouchers were widely proposed and debated as a device to broaden educational choice and to give parents more control over their children's schooling, the notion is still having difficulty taking root.

Some persons say the idea was flawed; others say that it was sabotaged by organized teachers who found it threatening. Whatever the reason, few school districts have nibbled at the millions of dollars in Federal money that was held out to test the concept, under which a family could shop for school services with a voucher worth what the local district spends to educate each child.

Nevertheless, one voucher system—albeit a highly compromised and limited one that involves only public schools— is operating with 9,300 pupils here in the Alum Rock Union Elementary School District on the east side of San Jose.

Teachers Are Gaining

Having spent about $7-million in Federal money, the Alum Rock experiment is reaching the end of its third year of opera-

---

* © 1975 by The New York Times Company. Reprinted by permission from *The New York Times* (May 25, 1975).

† Robert Reinhold is a writer for the New York *Times*.

tion with results that are still inconclusive. Ironically, given the bitter hostility that the voucher concept has evoked from national teacher groups, it is the Alum Rock teachers, not the parents, who seem to have acquired the most influence and authority under the new scheme.

Two more far-reaching tests of vouchers, in which both private and public schools will be allowed to compete for parent vouchers, are expected to begin in September of next year. One is a highly regulated plan in East Hartford, Conn., and the other a more free-wheeling one in a consortium of five small districts in southern New Hampshire.

The New Hampshire plan will allow parents to redeem their vouchers at any school in the United States as long as the school meets certain minimum standards.

Despite many setbacks and potent political opposition, some proponents of vouchers remain mildly optimistic. "There seems to be a growing public acceptance of the idea," said Denis P. Doyle, an official of the National Institute of Education in Washington, which supervises the Federal demonstration grants for voucher projects.

The voucher idea has been offered as a device to create more educational variety and to remedy a number of ills besetting the public schools.

More Responsiveness Seen

Various models have been proposed, but the basic theory is that if each family were given a public voucher worth the local cost of educating a child in the public schools, parents would be able to seek school services in a competitive free market system much the way they buy automobiles or groceries. The result, it was said, would be schools that were more diverse, and more responsive to pupil needs, particularly for the offspring of the poor.

In an odd convergence of interest, the idea drew support from both the political left and right, although for different reasons. Left-leaning scholars like the sociologist Christopher Jencks, argued that vouchers would give the poor the range of choice and personal control that the wealthy have long enjoyed in purchasing schooling and would vary the monotonous and often ineffectually bland educational diet offered by the public schools.

More conservative thinkers, like the economist Milton Friedman, saw vouchers as a means of reducing government involvement in education and subjecting it to the presumed benefits of the competitive free market system, in which only the best survive.

And Roman Catholic parents and educators saw vouchers as a means of saving the faltering parochial vouchers money that can constitutionally be redeemed by such schools.

Opponents of vouchers—mainly organized teacher groups like the National Education Association and the American Federation of Teachers—have said they would serve mainly to foster racial and economic segregation, lead to unseemly hucksterism and decimate the Americana public schools, which they argued would become "schools of last resort."

Grants for Experiment

To test the validity of these conflicting claims, the United States Office of Economic Opportunity (whose role in this area was later transferred to the N.I.E.) provided grants to several school districts: Gary, Ind., Seattle, San Francisco, New Rochelle and Rochester, N.Y. and Alum Rock. Only one, Alum Rock, eventually pushed ahead.

At the time Alum Rock began its program, it was prohibited from channeling public money into private schools. So the district decided to break up its once-traditional schools into a series of competing "minischools" offering different types of programs to satisfy different parent demands.

The district, mainly Mexican-American and black in ethnic make-up, is one of California's poorest. It spreads over a large and growing suburban area.

It has little industrial tax base and the voucher scheme, with all the new Federal money it brought, has allowed the district's superintendent, William J. Jefferds, to accelerate the process of administrative decentralization that he had already started.

Because only public schools are involved, some critics maintain that Alum Rock is not so much a free market voucher system as an elaborate open enrollment scheme. In addition, severe compromises had to be made at the outset to make the plan politically acceptable. Teachers were given guarantees against dismissal and enrollment limits were imposed on the most popular minischools.

Still a considerable measure of parent choice is available. Under this "transition model," as the compromise plan is called, 50 minischools have sprung up in 14 of the district's elementary and middle schools, each run by a group of teachers who share a particular pedagogical philosophy. They range from strict basic skills approaches to permissive open classroom settings.

There are minischools that stress fine arts, individualized instruction, bilingual education and other concepts. They go by such alluring names as "the learning odyssey," "self expression," "little red schoolhouse" and "great beginnings." Each is allowed to "advertise" for students in a 72-page tabloid publication now being distributed to parents for next year's enrollment. An accompanying document compares the 50 schools in terms of test scores, student attitudes and budgets.

Each student brings a "basic voucher" worth $904. Those from deprived backgrounds who qualify under the Federal free lunch program bring the minischool an additional "compensatory" voucher worth $275 and this money provides the school with most of "discretionary" funds that can be used to give the minischools their special character.

Some have used the money to buy special reading programs, others to buy field trips or to hire teaching aides or to purchase special audio-visual equipment.

Money to Hire a Poet

What are the results?

Despite some disagreements over budgeting authority and parent involvement, teachers and principals seem to be the most pleased by the experiment.

"The best thing was the money," said William Jones, a vice principal at the Pala Middle School. "We got $13,000 the first year and went crazy buying books and things."

Penny Bowen, a teacher in the "World of Fine Arts" minischool at the Dorsa School, says she "feels like the whole school belongs to us." She and her colleagues have used the new money to hire a poet, an artist and a dancer to add to their program, which has attracted 333 pupils.

Ironically, considering that vouchers were meant to give

more power to parents, the Alum Rock community has been unexpectedly passive. Only a small, though increasing, number of parents are sending their children to schools other than the nearest one to home, suggesting that they have not understood the range of choices available.

The assumption of voucher advocates was that, given meaningful choices, parents would take an active role and make intelligent decisions for their children. The Alum Rock experience has not yet borne out these hopes.

"Voucher advocates seem to have overlooked the simple fact that it costs parents time and anxiety to become informed about schools and to make troubling decisions about the education of their children" wrote David Stern, a Yale economist, who added that parental resistance to decision-making at Alum Rock "raises fundamental questions about the theory of vouchers."

Achievement test scores as analyzed by the Rand Corporation, which is evaluating the project for the N.I.E., have been contradictory. In some tests the voucher students did better than similar students in nonvoucher schools, on others worse. Rand concluded in its first-year report that "voucher students have not been exposed to a relatively normal learning routine for long enough to warrant even tentative conclusions about the effects of a limited voucher model on achievement."

Segregation Fears Ended

The Alum Rock experiment, so far, has dispelled fears that vouchers would lead to racial segregation. The ethnic distribution in the voucher schools differs little from the over-all ethnic make-up of the district, although the area was well integrated to begin with.

There is much debate over whether Alum Rock is really a voucher system. "I don't think it is fair to call what is happening in Alum Rock a voucher demonstration," said Daniel Weiler, head of the Rand study. "This is an example of a multiple-option system in that there are real alternatives and parent choice. In that light, it is a terribly interesting experiment."

However, Mr. Levin maintains that "we have a market system" even if "the variety of offerings is constrained by social values about what is okay to offer." He points out that a couple of minischools have folded for lack of interest and others have expanded to their limits.

California legislation was passed recently to allow vouchers to be redeemed by private schools as long as they operate within the district and adhere to its standards. Last year a group of young teachers tried to organize such an alternative private school, called Greater Resources Organized with Kids. The effort failed for lack of "business," however.

Whether vouchers can progress beyond these rudimentary beginnings is uncertain. Teacher leaders oppose it passionately. In an interview, Albert Shanker, American Federation president, said his group would fight any scheme to funnel public funds into non-public schools because "to destroy the public school system is the height of irresponsibility."

Many persons familiar with the voucher situation are not overly optimistic about the future.

"I am making the personal political prediction that vouchers are not in the cards," said Mr. Weiler of Rand. "But I do see a number of attempts within the public schools to build in parent alternatives."

TEACHER PREPARATION
FOR ALTERNATIVE SCHOOLS

EDITOR'S COMMENTS

Invariably the question arises: Do we need a different type of teacher to staff alternative schools? What are the implications for teacher education both at the pre- and in-service levels? Do we need a new kind of teacher? It should be clear that at this stage of our development of alternative schools we rely a great deal on the teacher, the teacher's competence, and the teacher's style. Teacher training institutions have an integral role to play in the process of developing alternative education. After all, the next generation of teachers will have to be not only knowledgeable about alternative schools, but must be able to function within them. At this early stage, we do have some beginning experience with the question of teacher education. These articles reflect the beginning interest in this field. As with some of the other areas that have been dealt with in this book, the question of teacher education is dealt with both at the formal and informal levels—in both the undergraduate and graduate areas. The reader may be struck by some of the imaginative ways in which certain alternative schools themselves and teacher education agencies have begun to deal with this problem. It seems apparent that the development of educational alternatives will depend on the competence of the educational personnel working for it. The vehicles for staff development, whether on the job, in teacher training institutions, or a combination of both, will no doubt become a crucial part of alternative education. No person interested in the movement toward options can ignore the importance of staff development and can afford not to be knowledgeable in this area.

This section deals with the following questions:

What is it like for the teacher inside an alternative school?

Why are teachers confronting new situations?

How can these situations be overcome through cooperation?

How can in-school training help and what should it be based on?

How can universities better prepare teachers for alternative schools?

What types of special college curriculums have been established?

What problems do these programs attempt to overcome?

INTERN SURVIVAL HANDBOOK FROM SHANTI SCHOOL, HARTFORD, CONNECTICUT*

Visiting Shanti: What to Look For

It has been suggested by core staff and the intern group that any prospective intern plan at least a three-day visit to Shanti before making any formal commitment. Since Shanti is different from traditional schools in many ways, such a visit seems necessary for gaining a feel for the school and how the school and intern can meet each other's needs.

When you visit Shanti, you can expect to stay with one of the members of the Shanti community, probably another intern. If you bring a car, you may have problems parking. Shanti rents only a few parking spaces, located behind the school under the railroad tracks; other than these, most spaces are short-term and quite expensive.

Okay. Most things, classes and such, are happening between 9 am and 3 pm, Monday through Friday, so plan to be present at the school between these hours. While you are at school, you should attempt to sit in on classes, a home group meeting, a task force meeting and/or a community meeting (generally held Wednesday afternoons), all this while talking with students, core staff and, especially, interns. Some things to prepare yourself for would be noise, confusion, chaos, and an occasional lack of toilet paper. Try to be tolerant of these things and eventually the ambiguity may begin to fall into place and feel more comfortable. Throughout all of this visitation and conversation, try to be open to the implications of the multiracial, multicultural aspects of Shanti. Of course, it will also be advantageous to read the school literature and to

* Reprinted from the *Intern Survival Handbook* with permission of Shanti School, "Visiting Shanti" by Kimen Yoder, "Planning Your Internship" by Steve Ruth, "Organizing Classes" by David Dowley, "What Shanti Kids Are Like" by Arnie Wolfson, "What Not to Do" by Diane Shucard, "How to Teach at Shanti" by Bill Halikias, "Home Groups, Task Forces" by Martha Beauchamp and Paul Donohoe and "Where to Find What You Need" by Martha Beauchamp and Paul Donohoe. Feb. 1975.

check out its resources, both within the school building and within the Greater Hartford community.

At the end of all this comes the most important part of the preliminary visit: taking stock of what the school can offer you and you the school, and evaluating how your personal disposition will fit into the personality of the school.

Have a good visit!

What Shanti Kids Are Like

Shanti kids come from all sorts of backgrounds. Some come from upper middle class places like Glastonbury and Simsbury; others come from areas of Hartford that are urban, to say the very least. Kids have many different reasons for coming to Shanti. Some are here because they couldn't make it in their old schools. Others could easily make it anywhere but choose Shanti because of the freedom they can have and the wide variety of resources they can have access to here. Everyone probably has one thing in common: a dissatisfaction, of one sort or another, with traditional high school. Freedom seems to be the one big advantage that kids see, although it is structured.

Shanti is a multiracial, multicultural community. It is not always one happy family, but people do try to recognize tensions, racial or otherwise, when they exist. Communication between staff and students is usually very good. Expect personal and group problems to arise. You'll be expected to take responsibility for dealing with them as openly and honestly as possible. It's a challenge, to say the least.

There are special interest groups at the school. Kids get together to develop photographs, play music, go camping, just do about anything they want to do. Shanti isn't always full of activity: sometimes you can sit around for long periods of time and just watch people float around the place. Don't let this inbetween time mislead you. A lot of pretty important things go on out in the central area by the staff desks. This is the best way to get to know the kids that you'll be working with. Relax and enjoy the chaos and informality of the school. Take your time to get a feel for what's going on. Kids are usually pretty talkative and are quick to get involved in a good rap.

There are "lost souls" at Shanti, people you rarely see or

hear from. Some just find it hard to adjust to all the relative freedom and responsibility with which they are suddenly faced. It sometimes takes new students a cycle or two to really get into some serious work. Others chose Shanti as a lesser of two evils. They don't really want to be in school but, since the law or their parents say they must be, here they are. To them freedom is even more difficult to deal with.

The kinds of problems kids at Shanti have are pretty similar to the problems of many other high school kids in traditional situations. They vary from academic to social to family and so on. Staff and interns do a lot of informal counseling. *Home groups* serve as support groups for students and when they work kids hopefully feel comfortable enough to deal with what might be bothering them. I would strongly recommend involvement in a home group for all interns teaching at Shanti. Home groups spend two hours each week together and take trips and plan various things together. It gives you the chance to shed your teacher role for a while and be just a human being. Not to say that teachers aren't human, but sometimes I have wondered.

Don't hesitate to talk over any problems you are encountering with core staff people. They will always be glad to help you out when they can. They're usually well informed about what's happening with specific kids and their home situations. *Intern meetings* are probably your best opportunity to learn about kids from core staff and other interns. I would strongly advise you to participate in these meetings as much as possible. They are informal, very enjoyable, and instructive.

Shanti is a place to experience, not read about. There is no substitute for first hand contact with Shanti people!

Planning Your Internship/Getting Your Goals Together

Perhaps one of the most difficult problems a new intern faces is that of expectations. The initial visit to the school may help to resolve some of those unsure expectations as to the functioning of the school, but there is always the question, "Just how do I fit into the school, and just what can I do?"

The important thing here is to get a handle on what it is that you feel most comfortable teaching. *Know your interest areas.* At Shanti, it is important that you are doing what it is that you do best. You may want to preplan a course that you could possibly teach. At least, you should have an idea of what you want to do.

Next, you should check into any specific needs of the school. It just may be that what you feel most comfortable with is already being taught. Or, there just may be no need or desire among the students to have a class on your subject. Speak to students. Feel them out. You may find that you can easily spark an interest in them. Or perhaps you can pick something up from them and turn it into a class. There may be some courses that staff feel need to be taught (especially in basic skills). Home group leaders and the Curriculum Task Force may also be helpful.

Although the possibility for support among interns is great, you will also find a great amount of personal responsibility for your own courses. Unless you ask for supervision, you probably won't get much. So be prepared to take on the task of setting up your own courses and seeing that they are going well. One hint here is about the usual success of team teaching. If this is your first time teaching, you may find some comfort in pairing up with one or more interns or staff for a course. Besides being a comfort, there are some learning benefits of teaching with someone else.

Some interns have had nobody sign up for their courses. This is a real possibility. Just be prepared to do something else. Don't take it personally. Independent study contracts can be worked out; you may ask another intern or staff person if he or she could use some help in his or her courses. Don't panic, or at least try not to. Oftentimes students will hesitate to sign up with a teacher they don't know.

All of the interns have gone through various experiences in planning their internships. They are your best source of moral and practical consolation. If it seems that all your plans are falling out from under you and you're beginning to doubt your abilities as a teacher and you're getting the last minute shits, don't be afraid to ask for help. You may not get it, but most probably somebody will at least listen and offer ideas.

Organizing Classes

It is good to have something specific in mind that you want to share with other members of the Shanti community. Talk to other staff to be sure that another intern isn't planning to do the same thing. If you find that your course is being offered by another, either change your approach so that your course looks different or, better, arrange to team teach and combine your resources. Check out the list of community resources and be prepared to integrate them during and outside of class time. Be aware of happenings in town, conferences, concerts, exhibits, etcetera, that might in some way enhance what you're trying to do. Don't be turned off by price tags and entrance fees. You can usually get money from task forces. If, after all that resource hustling, you still think you need books, order your books. It may well take half a cycle to get them if they are not available in local stores (Huntington's, Brentano's, colleges). You will need a Purchase Order to buy things where Shanti has no charge account.

The next big issue is getting a good time slot. Find out when the master chart goes up so you can get first pick. Morning classes seem to be best for academic kinds of subjects. Conflicts with other classes are often a problem. After the master chart come course descriptions. On Wednesday of the last week of the cycle, people begin posting their course offerings for the succeeding cycle on cards or posters you may design. Fill out a card with a flashy description and see what happens. If you get no takers, change your description real fast or go the team teaching route. Whatever you decide to do, *have something prepared and planned for each class.*

Now it is Monday and you're ready for your first class at Shanti. The first thing to think about is *where* it's going to happen. Hopefully, class locations will have been prearranged. People will be milling around the front desks, but don't be surprised if by 9:15 members of your 9:00 class still haven't shown up. Your first task when you get everybody together is to establish what your limits are regarding attendance and starting time. If attendance is important to you, *be very clear at the outset.* Remember that you, not the students, are running the class. Be sensitive to their needs and suggestions, but *be firm with whatever is decided upon.* Be prepared for students who will try to negotiate a different time for your class to meet. If it's a reasonable request and doesn't conflict with other schedules, you might consider it, but don't let yourself be negotiated out of existence: don't put up with bullshit.

What Not to Do

Don't panic! *Don't* overextend yourself but, at the same time, *don't* be afraid to try teaching something you may not have wanted to. *Don't* expect people to come or participate in classes out of their motivation; you may have to drag, remind, or at least encourage students to come to class. *Don't* be afraid to present your expectations for a course and where you are with it; without being inflexible, *don't* surrender these requirements *too* easily. *Don't* put up with bullshit: in the end it doesn't help anyone. *Don't* expect kids to give you the course (the famous "What do you want to do?" approach): you have to do *some serious work*. *Don't* assume social and academic maturity can be taken for granted. *Don't* buy kids' friendship—for every dime, you lose a dollar. Be *consistent* in meeting classes; how can you expect them to be there if you aren't? *Don't* bring or leave valuables around. *Don't* get set up; your rise to popularity will quickly fade. Above all, AVOID GUILT: it has no survival value!

How to Teach at Shanti

One important objective toward which a Shanti teacher should strive is a balance between factual material and class discussion. To lean significantly toward one or the other may cause difficulties in terms of class interest. To be overly directive in one's approach toward a subject area, as in a traditional school, does not work too well at Shanti. But one must also have some objectives and direction or class discussion will have no basis and, more often than not, it will be non-existent.

It is a good idea to lay your expectations out to a class the first day (see checklist enclosed). This may well save you much confusion and conflict at the end of the cycle when evaluations are written up. As the teacher, you should make clear to the student what is expected if he or she is to receive full credit. The first part of the evaluation form should be filled out at the beginning of each cycle.

In organizing your course and carrying it out, you should have a fair idea of your objectives. This includes not only expectations, but the material to be covered, resources you may use (books, people and events outside the school, other interns, etcetera), what you hope to inspire in the students, and what you personally want to gain from the course. Don't just depend on a text and readings, but use other resources as well.

It should be noted that, unless you are an outstanding scholar and speaker, class preparation is essential. To enter a class with a solid notion of the direction it will take often works better than constant improvisation resulting in a stream of free association which may have nothing whatever to do with your subject area. At the same time try to stay loose about what you hope to cover in a particular day (and even in a cycle). It is, once again, a question of balance, of being able to direct itself when the situation arises. You must be the judge of this.

In dealing with students try to be as open and sensitive to their needs as possible. This is important. But please remember that *you* as an individual have needs also. It could be bad judgment to allow yourself to be taken advantage of. In other words, don't take bullshit. If you've been clear about your objectives and expectations right from the start, it could well be a disservice, not only to yourself but to the student and school as well, if you allow an individual to take advantage of the fair and flexible credit system of Shanti. This applies directly to evaluations. At the end of each Shanti cycle, a period of seven weeks, the student evaluates the course in terms of self-achievement and satisfaction. The instructor then evaluates the student.

Now if, at the end of the cycle, you are aware that a particular student has done none of the work you assigned, attended few or no classes, and seemed as interested in your subject as he or she is in memorizing the speeches of Spiro Agnew, then it certainly would be unfair to give that individual credit.

The Shanti evaluation and point system is a relatively flexible and very humanistic method of recognizing an individual's achievements. It is harmful to both student and school to allow an individual recognition for non-achievement. Unfortunately this does happen, but not very often. The evaluation form is part of a student's permanent record and deserves thoughtful consideration from you. (Courses that meet 4 hours per week are generally worth 4 points per cycle. Points are not used as "grades".)

These words of explanation and warning do not symbolize well what will actually happen to you as a teacher here. For teaching is an art and, like any artistic expression, the style varies depending on personality, material, and subject matter. Obviously the greatest understanding of the Shanti experience will come when you encounter the school itself and share your art.

Home Groups, Task Forces, and Decision Making

Most decisions within the Shanti community are made by task forces which are composed of students and staff. These were instituted to save endless hours in the regular community meetings spent in deciding how each penny should be spent and what art supplies were needed. The task forces at the present time are:

ADMINISTRATION AND BUDGET
ARTS
COMMUNICATIONS
CURRICULUM AND RESOURCES
EVALUATION
INTERNAL ENVIRONMENT

When a decision affects the whole school, such as the philosophy and goals statement or a major policy, the appropriate task force presents its recommendations to the community who will then decide the final policy. All interns are welcome to join a task force as well as to participate in the dynamics of community meetings.

Also integral to the Shanti structure are the home groups. These meet two hours once a week, and each student must belong to a group (one of the few requirements of the school). From our experiences during the past year, we'd recommend that all interns join a home group.

Every home group is as unique as its individual members. It's hard to convey the sense of what your home group would be like, but these are some activities that groups have done during the past year: camping, encounter group exercises, self-awareness exercises, picnics, discussions about school, talking about problems in the family, and relationships to other students. You might even want to explore the possibilities of shared or co-leadership of a group.

Home groups basically function as an information source and a support group. Visit the home groups and decide which would most fit your needs.

Where to Find What You Need

As a member of the Shanti community and the larger Hartford community you will have numerous resources available to you. These existing community resources will often meet many of your needs. Those needs that require additional assistance should be made known to the Shanti community, for the community has a responsibility to be responsive to your needs.

Within the Shanti community you will have many of your needs met by the personal support of its individual members. Students, parents, interns, and core staff each have something to offer.

The basic support group of Shanti is the home group. It is one place to help you get what you need. The other support group that exists for you consists of your fellow interns and co-staff persons. This group meets bi-weekly as the "interns' meeting" to discuss problems, to offer support, to just get together. These meetings have been said to be among the best meetings an intern will experience at Shanti. The Home Group Leaders meet once a week for 2 hours, usually during the day.

There is a variety of places in Hartford to find what you need. Ask someone for the booklet, "Where to Get Help in Greater Hartford" published by the Hartford Courant.

Checklist for Shanti Instructors

Before classes start:

Write outline of course giving major assignments expected. Question each student or their home group leader to find if they have had a similar class before. If they have, it is important to be sure that the class you are teaching is not a duplication.

First day of class: (use your own good judgment if the following are appropriate)

Clarify expectations concerning student's attendance. Ask that students contact you if they are to miss a class.
Ask students to have a notebook and pen at each class meeting.
Fill in evaluation sheets with each student (first section).
Put name of student's home group leader on the evaluation sheets.
Indicate that there will be periodic tests.
Indicate that there will be at least four writing assignments during the course.
Develop a method of keeping attendance.
Develop a method of informing students if you cancel a class.

After class is started:

Submit blue sheet with course outline. Put in Curriculum Task Force box in office.
Contact students each time they are absent.
Contact home group leader of all students who are signed up but have not attended class.
Contact home group leader of all students who have been absent two times or if this looks like this will be a chronic problem!

¡TENGA BUENA SUERTE!

TEACHER ADAPTATION TO AN INFORMAL SCHOOL*

BY AASE ERIKSEN AND
FREDERICK M. FISKE†

The environment and program of an informal school provide for new kinds of relationships between teachers and

* Reprinted with permission of the authors and the *National Association of Secondary School Principals Bulletin.*
† Frederick M. Fiske is a journalist at *Bucks County-Courier Times*, Levittown, Pa., and a former assistant with Dr. Eriksen.

students, and hold great potential for exciting and meaningful study. At the same time, however, the program creates new kinds of demands on students and teachers. When it is located in a large urban area, the adjustment is slow and difficult for students used to overcrowded conditions. They must overcome many bad habits and accept responsibility for their social interaction as well as learning. Teachers have to adjust. In respecting their students as individuals they must encourage them to take the initiative for learning. Their patience will be taxed by initial failures and often unforeseen problems.

Mutual Trust Between Teachers Necessary

To withstand the strains and pressures of a new informal school program, teachers must bridge their separateness and learn to rely on one another, developing methods of interacting in and out of class.

This article describes one group of teachers and their efforts to work together during the first three semesters of the West Philadelphia Community Free School. The information, observations, and conclusions included are drawn from analysis of teachers' field notes, interviews conducted at the end of each semester, informal discussions, notes from planning meetings, school records and observations of teachers at work.

The West Philadelphia Community Free School was designed as an alternative within public high school education in one of Philadelphia's predominantly black school districts. The innovative aspects of the school are outlined in the PASS Model (Public Alternative School System),[1] and extend from its physical structure to its educational program. The school consists of "Houses" scattered throughout the community. The first House opened in February 1970 with 200 students; two more Houses opened in September, bringing the total number of students to 500. Within the Houses, each teacher is responsible for a "Family Group" of no more than 15 students. The focus of the educational program is on the mastery of basic skills through individual and small group instruction. Grade levels are eliminated, and marks are replaced by detailed evaluations. The educational program is also carried outside the school. Students spend at least 20 percent of their time working and studying with volunteer instructors in community businesses and institutions.

Students Gain More Control

The goals of the PASS Model are directly concerned with students in an informal environment. The educational program is meant to give students a chance to control what happens to them and encourages them to take part in the development of the school. The model stresses the importance of the Family Group unit as the key to the House structure. The Family Group is defined as the starting point for all other relationships in the House. The teacher's role, according to the Model, is to "view learning from the learner's perspective"; of the 10 teaching criteria listed, nine deal specifically with the teacher's ability to help students assume responsibility for learning.

Fifteen teachers were selected to work full-time in the Community Free School's first House. Eight of these teachers were certified, and paid by the board of education; the remaining seven were graduate students from an experimental program at the University of Pennsylvania's Graduate School of Education. All of the teachers were young. The eight certified teachers had taught previously at West Philadelphia High School; the graduate interns had little or no teaching experience. In their applications and preliminary statements, all of the teachers revealed their primary concern with the student in the new environment; specifically, teachers most frequently expressed a desire to overcome the negative effects of traditional education on students, improve student-teacher relationships, and make education relevant to the student.

Teachers were faced with an enormous challenge in implementing the educational program. They would be working with 200 students, drawn by random sample from the rolls of West Philadelphia High School. They would have to help these students adapt from a traditional atmosphere of structured learning to an informal one permitting and encouraging self-exploration. In addition, they were responsible for developing curriculum which would interest students, for encouraging them to work in this new environment, and for responding to their widely varying academic needs.

Disorientation Marks Start of Program

During the first month of school, students and teachers separated into Family Group units. Each teacher spent the entire school day working with a small group of students on individual projects. The break with tradition was sharp for both students and teachers. Students were being asked to participate in activities for which they had no precedent, in an environment which disoriented them. As might be expected, many responded with bewilderment. For teachers, too, the experience was disconcerting; their students' disorientation only added to the confusion. Teachers were dismayed with students' inability to analyze material, to distinguish between goals and means, and to make choices between simple alternatives.

Many teachers blamed themselves for this initial confusion, attributing student failures to their own failure as teachers. Faced with bewildered and disoriented students, some teachers found themselves responding in traditional ways, providing structure and direction they had hoped students would develop on their own. Teachers chastised themselves for this tendency. After all, one of the reasons they had chosen to work at this school was to move away from "directive" teaching. In their confusion, teachers naturally turned to each other as the most logical and accessible source of help.

The most immediate function of teacher interaction at the school, then, was to provide assurance and support to those who needed it. Once a teacher realized that his problems were not unique, the personal anguish and self-doubts were somewhat relieved. Teacher interaction was critically important during the first month. It allowed teachers to share their initial experiences and deal with their frustrations as a group. During subsequent months, interaction became the primary process for decision-making and the basic operating principle of the school.

Team Teaching—Success and Problems

During the first term, over 75 percent of combined teaching hours were spent in teams composed of both regular teachers and graduate interns. The teacher-student ratio was small.

While class size and teacher teams varied, a typical team-taught class would consist of one regular teacher, two graduate interns, and 35 students. The class was often separated into small groups, with one teacher responsible for each group. In this kind of classroom, teachers noted, it was possible to plan and evaluate the class as a team, and to work effectively with individuals in small groups. The size of the team-taught class allowed teachers to work both in large and small groups, and to experiment with various approaches to the same subject, geared to the different needs and academic levels of the students.

Small-group work in teams represents the first step away from the traditional classroom. By removing the walls between smaller classes, teachers and students were able to communicate freely with one another, while maintaining the familiar link of one teacher with a small group of students.

Teachers experienced some problems in team-taught classrooms. When several teachers led a class together, the result was sometimes erratic. One teacher, after describing a successful lesson in which two teachers role-played, went on to say that she and her colleagues frequently contradicted each other in class, confusing the students. The problem of delegating responsibility among teachers for team-taught classes was diagnosed early in the year. The solution, teachers felt, lay in adjusting the teacher teams and increasing the amount of planning time.

During the second year of the program, the school expanded to three Houses and 500 students, with 20 certified teachers and 12 graduate interns. In the three Houses, teachers worked in a variety of team-teaching situations. They planned shorter classes, four- to six-week "mini-courses", and often worked in teams which crossed disciplines. By the end of the year, teachers in one House had developed an integrated curriculum, a series of team-taught and individually-taught classes that combined disciplines. One of the teachers in the House taught her first class alone during the last six weeks of the school year. She noted that teachers in her House had developed processes for interaction that enabled them to work simultaneously in groups and by themselves, within and between disciplines. They felt confident in all of these situations, she wrote, and continued to plan and evaluate the overall program together.

The flexibility of the educational program always allowed for a certain amount of natural selection to take place among teachers. During the first term, several teachers continued to teach alone, while the majority taught in teams. Several adjustments were made early in the semester within the teams. One group of teachers who had difficulty working as a large team was divided into two smaller teams after a month. Other teachers started working in two teams simultaneously. Teaching schedules varied and teachers spent at least a quarter of their time outside the classroom, in conference with individual students. Family groups continued to meet regularly, at the discretion of students and teachers involved. The flexible program and varied teaching schedules also permitted teachers to visit other classrooms and participate in other team situations.

Planning and Evaluating Openly

Planning and evaluation meetings were frequent. House teacher meetings were held each week, and teachers met in small groups during the day, in the evening, and on weekends when necessary. After class in the afternoon, several teachers would usually remain to exchange ideas and constructive criticism. Some teachers were hesitant to express themselves freely in front of the students who often sat in on these meetings, especially when discussion turned to problems with the educational program. It was hard enough to talk about uncertainties and failures with other teachers, without students listening. The result of such a discussion, it was feared, might be to convey to students an unfairly pessimistic impression of the school, its teachers, and students. On one occasion, a teacher related, a student came up to her after listening to a particularly problem-laden discussion and asked if teachers did any planning outside of class.

While some teachers expressed their misgivings about open meetings, all of them recognized the potential of this process; free and open discussion could be a means for improving teacher-student relationships, clearing up misunderstandings, and encouraging the same kind of interaction to develop among students. Teachers who cannot cooperate, communicate, and deal with problems openly among themselves shouldn't expect their students to be any more successful, one teacher wrote. On the other hand, when the teachers do attempt to interact, the result can be a learning experience both for participating teachers and students. Teachers recognized this, and the open meetings continued throughout all three semesters. Students continued to sit in on these meetings, asking questions and offering suggestions.

Teachers were very vocal in criticizing their own work in teams, principally their lack of cooperative planning. They had begun the year without clearly defined plans for the curriculum, partly because they had expected students to participate in planning the program. During the first semester, when teachers realized that they had to assume most of the responsibility, they needed to spend a great deal of time with each other as well as with their students. This time was not always available. Besides teaching classes and meeting with students in conferences and Family Groups, they had to plan and adjust student rosters, deal with student attendance problems, and attend to many other administrative procedures and emergencies during the year. As a result, it was hard for teachers to stay ahead of their classes—and this they considered the most serious obstacle to successful team-teaching.

At the end of the first semester, some teachers felt they had been able to work well together, especially in planning the curriculum, and were enthusiastic about student progress. Others, however, were self-critical. They felt an urgent need to communicate more effectively, to devise processes for planning more efficiently, and to have more time to work together.

Both Teachers and Students Affirmative

The importance of the teaching unit was established beyond question at the end of the first term. Seven of the eight certified teachers chose to remain at the school. All of the graduate interns applied for full-time positions. In their applications, they stressed the importance of teacher interaction as a primary condition for the success of the program. Unlike traditional high schools, one teacher wrote, the Community Free School has provided an environment in which three new kinds of teacher interaction take place: in planning curriculum, in evaluating the strengths and weaknesses of the program, and in coordinating and implementing daily activities. Despite problems encountered within each of these processes, teachers felt that progress had been made, and were unanimous in requesting that the original faculty group be retained in order to build on the experiences of the first semester.

Students were also vocal in their demand that the teaching staff remain intact. They submitted a petition signed by 60 percent of the student body, requesting that the graduate interns be appointed. One of the teachers noted how insistent students were that all the teachers stay with the school next year. She emphasized that this concern was not based only on loyalty to particular teachers; neither did it develop in ignorance of the problems teachers had working together. Instead, she wrote, students felt they belonged to a fairly cohesive and integrated family in which teachers, despite internal quarrels, understood and supported them.

While teachers' reactions to their own attempts at teamwork were just as often critical as favorable, their growing concern with the teaching staff as a whole demonstrates an important shift in teacher priorities. From an initial focus on the student-teacher relationship, teachers began to place more and more emphasis on relations between each other. Analysis of data pertaining to teachers' experiences at the West Philadelphia Community Free School reveals that teachers as well as students needed time to adapt to the informal environment. Their experiences in Family Group meetings at the beginning of the year had a profound impact on teachers. They realized that the task of helping students adjust to the school environment, while meeting the educational needs of students with widely differing academic backgrounds, was too great for teachers to accomplish as individuals.

Naturally, teachers turned to one another for support and assistance. They shared their initial doubts and frustrations; they planned, taught, and evaluated their classes together, recognizing that cooperation and communication among teachers must precede student interaction and that a meaningful educational program must be flexible enough to withstand continual adjustment and change.

Teachers never reached a point where they were satisfied with the effectiveness of their interaction; neither did they ever assert that the school's objectives had been achieved. However, by the end of the first three semesters of the West Philadelphia Community Free School, they were enthusiastic about the potential of the program and anxious to continue developing and improving their work as a group. One teacher had summarized this enthusiasm earlier in the year:

> I have worked very hard with other teachers in trying to arrive at a curriculum that is important and exciting. Perhaps we have not always achieved these things, but there have been many rewarding moments, both in classrooms and conferences. I think students can benefit most from teachers who have had this experience.

The process of developing effective methods of teacher interaction proved to be a difficult one; however, teachers recognized that their own need to adapt to the informal environment was a prerequisite to the school's success, and that increasing the extent and variety of interaction among teachers provided the means for that adaptation.

FOOTNOTE

1. Aase Eriksen, *Model for a Public Alternative School System* (PASS), Graduate School of Education, The University of Pennsylvania (unpublished), 1970.

INDIANA UNIVERSITY ALTERNATIVE SCHOOL TEACHER EDUCATION PROGRAM*

BY ROBERT D. BARR†

Background:

During recent years, public school systems throughout the country have begun diversifying their educational programs by developing a wide variety of alternative learning options. Today over 500 alternative public schools in over thirty states are now in operation; Mario Fantini has called this development the "only major movement in American education today." The concept of developing alternative public schools has gained impressive support; it has been recommended by the

* Reprinted with permission of the author.

† Robert D. Barr is Director of the Alternative School Teacher Education Program, School of Education, Indiana University.

1970 White House Conference on Children, the 1972 President's Commission on School Finance, and by a number of prominent educational leaders: James Coleman, Dwight Allen, John Bremer, Kenneth Clark, and John Gardner. Alternative public schools have also been the focus on special issues of most of the major educational periodicals—*Harvard Educational Review, Phi Delta Kappan, Education U.S.A., Nation's Schools, NASSP Bulletin,* and *The Elementary School Principal.* They have also drawn the attention of *Time* and *Newsweek.* So established has the idea become that the North Central Association is now developing guidelines for evaluating alternative schools.

The types of alternative public schools that have been developed represent a complete spectrum of learning environments. The following outline suggests the variety:

Open Schools
with learning activities individualized and organized around interest centers within the classroom or building
Schools Without Walls
with learning activities throughout the community and with much interaction between school and community
Learning Centers, Educational Parks, Magnet Schools
with a concentration of learning resources in one center available to all of the students in the community
Multicultural Schools, Bilingual Schools, Ethnic Schools
with emphasis on cultural pluralism and ethnic and racial awareness
Behavior Modification Schools
using programmed learning, external rewards and individualized study
Street Academies, Dropout Centers, Pregnancy-Maternity Centers
with emphasis on learning programs for students in targeted populations
Schools-Within-a-School
could be any of the above organized as a unit within a conventional school
Integration Models
could be any of the above with a voluntary population that is representative in racial, ethnic, and socioeconomic class makeup of the total population of the community

Free Schools

with emphasis on greater freedom for students and teachers. This term is usually applied to non-public alternatives, but a very few are operating with public school systems today

New Teachers for New Schools:

As public schools have begun to diversify educational environments through the creation of alternative Free Schools, Open Schools, Schools-Without-Walls, Street Academies, Drop-out Centers . . . and the wide variety of new optional educational experiences listed above, the one most common concern of local educators is where to find trained and experienced teachers to staff these schools and programs. They have been quick to discover that there are very few teachers available who have experience in non-conventional education, and even fewer universities that have training programs to prepare teachers for these new positions. Administrators have also found that "good" teachers in conventional schools do not necessarily make an effective transition into new educational environments, and that teachers without some kind of re-training tend to "burn out" at a rather high rate. Far more disturbing, educators have begun to realize that an entirely "new" conception of "teacher" is often needed to operationalize many of these new schools and programs. When alternative public school administrators met in 1972 at the Wingspread Conference on Alternative Schools, they discovered few college and university training programs that related to their staffing needs. They concluded their meeting by calling for the creation of a completely new kind of teacher training program for both new and experienced teachers who desire careers in alternative public schools. Since that time, school officials in a number of public school systems throughout the country have worked closely with Indiana University in developing an alternative school training program.

Indiana University and Alternative Schools

A number of unique situations have made Indiana University the nation's primary center for the study of alternative public schools. The National Consortium on Options in Public Education was founded and is housed at Indiana University. The Consortium newsletter, *Changing Schools* is likewise published here. A continuing series of meetings, workshops, and conferences on alternative schools are hosted annually by Indiana University.

Of equal importance is the Consortium resource file on alternative public schools, which includes program descriptions, evaluations, and research reports. All of these components combine to make Indiana University an attractive site for a training program in the area of alternative schools.

Teacher Education as Self-Actualization:

The Indiana University Alternative School Program was cooperatively developed by university and public school administrators and teachers. It is a completely individualized, field-based program of teacher self-actualization. The program consists of a small faculty team, flexible courses, maximum independent study, and extensive field teaching experiences. As such it represents a sharp distinction from conventional teacher training programs.

The Alternative School Program is designed for people interested in a career in alternative public schools. The program is designed to help participants develop a theoretical and conceptual background in alternative schools, survey a wide variety of different learning styles and learning environments, and attempt to prepare themselves for a particular role in alternative public schools.

Students who enter the Alternative School Program at Indiana University are encouraged to clarify their own values and career goals, articulate their personal philosophies of education, and diagnose their own capabilities and liabilities as teachers. This means that students conduct an intimate self-examination and self-exploration of their personalities, skills, interests, and problems. Simultaneously, the students survey a wide variety of different teacher-roles and learning environments through intensive readings, on-site visits to alternative schools, and continuing discussions with alternative school personnel. This survey involves comparative analysis of the various kinds of curricula and teacher roles found in alternative schools. Throughout this process, students try to match their own unique capabilities and philosophies to teaching roles in specific types of alternative school learning environments. In this sense, students are continuously encouraged to identify what kinds of teachers they want to become. As such, this movement toward self-actualization is as much a process, as it is a program. Once a student has identified the kind of teaching role he or she wishes to pursue, the student is assisted in organizing an individualized program of self-development designed to actualize and maximize personal potentials for obtaining the desired teaching role. Students are helped to identify competencies, skills, and experiences which they feel they "need" and to select learning activities that are compatible with their personal teaching goal.

NATIONAL ALTERNATIVE SCHOOLS PROGRAM*

BY PHIL DETURK AND RAY IVEY†

The School of Education at the University of Massachusetts is joining in a partnership with two or three public school districts in the United States to create, implement and sustain Alternative Public Schools to serve students in those communities.

Each school will be unique in that from the very beginning it will be commissioned to plan for the implementation of an educational undertaking whose intent and practices will be totally fresh and new. Rather than introducing one or two innovative components, the school will be innovative in every aspect of its being so that it will truly exist as an institution representing a viable alternative approach to the education of young people.

Further, the Alternative School planning staff as well as those students, staff and interested citizens who later join with the school to help foster and nurture this program are to be relieved of many traditional restraints usually imposed upon

* Reprinted with permission of the National Alternative Schools Program, School of Education, University of Massachusetts, Amherst, Mass.

† Phil DeTurk and Ray Ivey have been active in pursuing the goals of NASP.

innovators by less change-oriented members of the school community. This will be accomplished by insisting that only those students, staff members and others who *volunteer* to be associated with the Alternative School Project are to participate.

There can be no definition for an "alternative school." To be a true alternative, the concept must be left open-ended and creative. The idea of an alternative school is an evolutionary phenomenon in the history of attempted educational change. It exists, but the shape and dimensions of its definition will be subject to constant alteration. An alternative school offers the choice of a different kind of schooling for clientele in the public sector.

Examples of such schools are the Parkway Program and the Pennsylvania Advancement School in Philadelphia, Harlem Prep and the John Dewey School in New York, John Adams High School in Portland, the Metro School in Chicago and the Focus and Impact Schools in Louisville. Although there may be considerable gap between potential and reality, the basic intent of these programs presents a genuine alternative to the existing system.

The involvement of the School of Education is intended

1) to provide resources and expertise to persons involved in the design and implementation of *alternative school processes,* and

2) to build into the alternative school a lasting and meaningful interaction between school, community and university.

By "alternative school process" is meant the means with which educational participants have addressed the great issues of schooling; issues such as

racism
setting educational priorities
financial allocation and control
curriculum
educational decision-making
identification and utilization of learning resources
the reward system
the nature of learning
student grouping
compulsory attendance
the school structure
the role of the teacher
community involvement
teacher training

The School of Education

The School of Education has had three major priorities since its reincarnation four years ago.

1. Projecting an *alternative educational leadership model* which will train personnel to study, plan and implement institutional change.
2. *Combat institutional racism* by both exhortation and practice.
3. Address the plight of *deteriorating urban schools* head on.

Structure. To effect its goals the School of Education has made radical structural departures from the normal perception of the School of Education.

1. The elimination of departments and the installation of interest *Centers*. The 1971–1972 Centers will be—Aesthetics, Occupational Education, Media, Research, Foundations, Humanistic, Human Relations, International, Leadership and Administration, Urban, Human Potential, Teacher Education and Innovation.
2. The introduction this year of a diverse undergraduate and graduate teacher education program which includes fifteen program options for students ranging from the integrated day school to an opportunity to operate an alternative school.
3. The development of special programs, in and out of state, across school and campus lines, both at the undergraduate and graduate levels within the University of Massachusetts system.

Projects. To put teeth into its commitments to devise a new teacher education model, to combat racism particularly in schools, and to provide resources to urban schools, the School of Education receives over 50% of its operating budget from non-state resources.

A list of a few of the many project activities will give an indication of the depth and breadth of the School's involvement in action research and development.

1. A New England and New York Head Start Program with 150 trainees.

2. Teacher and administrator intern programs in many locations including the Parkway School, Philadelphia, Pennsylvania; Harlem Prep, New York City and Temple City, California.

3. A Career Opportunities program in Brooklyn, New York, and Worcester, Massachusetts, for 300 paraprofessionals—all degree candidates from the University of Massachusetts. The program in Brooklyn has 235 students, 35 faculty and 50 doctoral students from the School of Education, and faculty and students from the English Department, Geology Department and Government Department. The students earn approximately 6,750 credits for an academic year. The faculty make 3 trips to Brooklyn per week.

4. Operation of the Tororo Girls School in Uganda.

5. A comprehensive elementary teacher education program based on performance criteria.

6. A three-year Ford Foundation grant in humanistic education.

7. A program in Comprehensive Achievement Monitoring jointly sponsored with the New York State Education Department.

8. Cooperation with the Clearinghouse for Student Initiated Change; the Union for Experimenting Colleges and Universities; Contemporary University, a "university without walls" in conjunction with sixteen other universities; and the White House Conference on Children and Youth.

9. Research project in early childhood education for releasing human potential.

10. Differentiated Staffing Institute.

11. Teacher Corps projects in Providence, Rhode Island, and Worcester, Massachusetts.

12. School Personnel Utilization Leadership Training Institute.

13. Project to have 20,000 youngsters spend the summer on military installations throughout the country.

14. Title I Evaluation Program.

15. Project designed to prepare non-white college graduates without courses in teaching for teaching positions in the Boston Public School System.

School of Education Support to Alternative Schools

The School of Education has a remarkable opportunity through a grant from the Office of Education to work with a few communities anywhere in the United States which have evidenced their share of commitment to radical change. Possible types of School of Education involvement in planning and operation of an Alternative School at University expense:

1. Personnel available to meet with planning task forces of the school.
2. Use of nationally known resource people.
3. Identification and dissemination of resource materials to school participants.
4. Designing problem-solving and management techniques.
5. Developing an action research and evaluation potential for the school system.
6. Helping to select and train community teaching assistants.
7. Designing programs with help of appropriate centers from the School of Education.
8. Developing and maintaining new systems of governance.
9. Supplying staff and support resources for workshops for credit or no credit.
10. Designing and implementing staff and community planning and training programs.
11. Assisting in the exploration of major innovative procedures such as flexible scheduling, differentiated staffing, micro-teaching, achievement monitoring, computerized resource bank and modular credit.
12. Documentation and evaluation of the evolution of joint projects in the school development.
¹13. Developing a community resource bank for the community.
14. Design of cross-disciplinary curriculum programs.
15. Design of cross-generational community education.
16. Development of teacher intern programs in which interns are community residents for a semester or more.
17. Presenting a variety of alternative school models such

as "the school without walls," the feeder or cone system, a prep school for drop-outs, the community school, the university school, the social service school.
18. Develop project and funding sources jointly.
19. Spread resources supplied by the alternative school to other schools in the area.
20. Negotiate for removal of external restraints.
21. Establish an off-campus center for staff training with University credit.
22. Negotiate appointment of school personnel as adjunct professor, or appointment of school personnel to master or doctoral program.

Bases for Co-operative Development of Alternative Schools

The Alternative Schools are to be thought of as subsystems of the larger existing public schools. Though maintaining interdependence in many ways, it is through the avenues of freedom from restraints that new ways of dealing with racism, governance, community involvement, student participation, curriculum, staffing and training, financing, and innovations can be cooperatively developed, implemented and evaluated for potential replication in the larger world of public education.

Voluntarism. Voluntarism refers to the way in which *all* parties will become involved in the process of developing an alternative school model. Parents, students, staff (professional and non-professional) and the school district itself must wish to participate. Conversely, those who do not wish to be involved in an Alternative School have that freedom.

Financial Relationship to Larger Districts. In general, the financial relationship will take the form of a "performance contract" with the Alternative Schools receiving the current cost per pupil found elsewhere within the same districts.

Programmatic Relationship to Larger Districts. The Alternative Schools will be providing new sources of training, curriculum development, mechanisms for governance and decision-making, as well as numerous other contributions to the knowledge base of the teaching-learning process from which the total district will be able to draw.

Enrollment. Affluent families excepted, the mass of children, particularly the urban low-income, have had no choice other than "dropping out." Racial imbalance has created another set of educational concerns. In an attempt to discover ways of dealing with social problems, the Alternative School will use "open-enrollment" mechanisms to *build a voluntary student enrollment while attempting to create a racial balance which will provide exposure and experiential appreciation of diversity.*

Staffing. The staffing pattern would reflect differentiation of interest and responsibility. Extensive use would be made of community paraprofessionals, community professionals and volunteers. The notion of the "Teacher and His Staff" would prevail. A "career ladder" program would be established with the University of Massachusetts. The emphasis in staffing will stress the "process" of developing a differentiated staff.

Training. Community and students can be expected to play a large part in the development and implementation of training programs.

Humanistic methodology within a democratic-participative, inquiry-oriented learning environment will be a main thrust of training.

A model of individualized in-service will be developed, making use of community, university, consultant and peer support.

A continuous product of all training will be the development of packageable and exportable in-service training materials.

A "multiplier mechanism" will be developed which can open the training program to other teachers within the district, state, etc.; the purpose of the multiplier being the propagation of behaviors, skills, knowledge gained from the operation of the Alternative School. The mechanism would allow the school to have impact on participants beyond the staff of the Alternative School, as well as provide a means of feedback from new trainees.

Governance and Decision-Making. Mechanisms will be developed to bring the community, staff and students into meaningful roles of school governance.

Students will be formally involved in the determination and evaluation of their individual programs. The major role of staff might well be the development and management of alternatives from which students make choices.

Curriculum. The nature of human relationships, the value of self, appreciation of diversity, cooperation and self-discipline provide the basis for a "process" of participatory curriculum development. The "curriculum" may occur within or without school walls, with others or independently, with or without formal instruction, short term or long term.

Procedure. The planning staff will consist of faculty and student personnel from the School of Education and members of the staff, student body, and citizens within the school district for which the Alternative School is being planned.

It will be a Project Director's responsibility to coordinate the activities of the initial planning period, which will include designing the composition of the school as well as the creation of the procedures for implementing the program (staffing, student admission, resource allocation, etc.). Throughout the planning stages, every effort will be made to assure that all plans reflect commitment to the establishment of a truly unique, alternative approach to the educational experiences for young people. Changes will not be piecemeal, superficial, or half-hearted.

Innovative practices which will have penetrating effects on the student learning processes will be incorporated. Accent will be put on the daring, unorthodox, but promising, educational procedures. The fact that all project participants will have volunteered for such an experience will imply that they are willing to join in a program that will involve radical departures from traditionally oriented programs. And the fact that the School Committee wishes to participate in such a project of experimentation in the first place will assure that those charged with the design and implementation of Alternative Schools have public support for their creative efforts.

Hopefully this kind of joint commitment by a school district and a school of education to a program designed to foster bold, sweeping change in the form of an Alternative School is an unusual and promising concept. It will provide a unique opportunity to discover what really might be accomplished in behalf of the school child when an arsenal of resources can be marshaled to function in a setting free of customary educational expectations, methods and standards.

Site Selection

CRITERIA:

1. Established relationship or favorable base for relationship with the School of Education

2. Innovative personnel

3. Expressed commitment to alternative schooling as per the elements described in paper *National Alternative Schools Program*

4. Agreement by district school committee to the following contractual terms:
   a. Complete autonomy for Alternative Schools in decision-making and control regarding curriculum, staffing, staff ratio, scheduling, governance, financing, student participation, community involvement and credential requirements
   b. Equal per pupil expenditures
   c. Controlled voluntarism of student enrollment and staff assignment
   d. Students and staff selected to combat bigotry
   e. Workshops on combating institutional racism for staff and students
   f. Minimum of 200 students
   g. Mechanisms other than curriculum requirements for college entrance consideration
   h. Involvement of all children of school age

   Optional Elements:

   minimum two-year charter for joint participation by the school district and the School of Education

   governance which involves representatives from all areas of the school community

   twenty-five per cent of the district staff rotated in and out of the alternative school each year

DESIGNATION:

Sites will be designated on the basis of:

1) Their willingness to meet stated criteria
2) Their uniqueness in terms of program
3) Their willingness to combat bigotry
4) The magnitude of their commitment
5) The potential of interfacing other funded programs

EVIDENCE OF COMMITMENT:

A contract will be negotiated with each school board spelling out the specific terms of school district and School of Education commitment to the development of an Alternative School.

National Alternative Schools Program—Secondary Sites

What. The establishment of a secondary system of alternative schools is considered a major thrust of the total National Alternative Schools Program. "Secondary" in this context refers to its relationship to "primary" as in order of importance, not as descriptive of grade levels in the school system.

Secondary, in the sense that the primary thrust involves heavy commitment of all possible resources, University of Massachusetts, N.A.S.P., District, to developing and implementing three major alternative school sites. The "secondary sites" would not be in the heavily committed category, but rather would serve other functions:

a. could involve alternative schools already in operation as well as in planning stages
b. would represent a more diverse segment of geographical, socio-economic areas than the primary sites
c. would allow a comparison of developmental and organizational processes
d. would serve as models of funding in contrast to N.A.S.P. primary sites
e. might serve as potential primary replacement sites
f. might possibly be alternative schools not within the local school district

Relationship of Resources. As already mentioned, the secondary alternative schools will be financially solvent due to district or other agency funding.

The University of Massachusetts can, on the basis of a limited budget, provide resources and services of this type:

- recognition and national visibility of your effort
- linkage with other alternative schools
- incorporation of secondary site staff in conferences, workshops, etc., run for and by primary sites
- duplicating and dissemination of training or resource materials that are developed on sites or at the University
- access to resource center on innovation and alternative school materials
- groups of student teachers or interns (to be negotiated)
- N.A.S.P. will help finance teacher exchanges from one site to another for the purpose of visitation, consulting, training, etc., as long as the exchanges involve teachers
- potentiality of regional workshop for secondary sites
- documentation by University of developmental process
- help in securing outside funding to continue or expand your project
- a sharing of process, training models, governance models, curriculum, etc., as occurs in all sites

The secondary sites component of N.A.S.P. will not include more than five to eight sites. This is necessitated by the scope of services to be offered and the concern for being able effectively to provide delivery of those services.

FOOTNOTE

[1] The identification and use of people (nurses, lawyers, law enforcers, gardeners, sales personnel, volunteer action groups, etc.) and places in the community that can strengthen the curriculum.

BIBLIOGRAPHY

Needless to say, we have not exhausted the topic of alternative education. Rather, in the preceding pages we have tried to provide elements that could trigger further interest in the reader. In the process of reviewing the foregoing pages, the reader may have been struck with the different resources, human and material, which are available to deal with the growing interest in alternative education. Consequently, we felt that it might be appropriate to provide a bibliography which provides additional information concerning these resources. Again, these are not exhaustive, but as one begins to probe a particular reference, one will inevitably be led to other sources which may be useful. In this way the interested party can keep his or her own ongoing file on sources that can be tapped to further the particular set of educational objectives with which one is concerned at any particular time.

Books on Alternative Education

BREMER, JOHN and MICHAEL VON MOSCHZISKER. *The School Without Walls: Philadelphia's Parkway Program.* New York: Holt, Rinehart and Winston, Inc., 1971.

    Bremer, Parkway's first director, describes the planning and development of Parkway, a prototype of the school-without-walls.

FANTINI, MARIO D. *What's Best for the Children? Resolving the Power Struggle Between Parents and Teachers.* Garden City, New York: Anchor Press-Doubleday, 1974.

    Offers an approach for avoiding a collision between parents and teachers, suggesting instead a sensible mobilization of the cooperative energies of both groups in the constructive reform of our public system of education.

FANTINI, MARIO D. *Public Schools of Choice: A Plan for the Reform of American Education.* New York: Simon and Schuster, Inc., 1974.

    Shows how public education in the United States can be saved without dismantling the existing structure or alienating any of those who are part of it.

GLATTHORN, ALLAN A. *Alternatives in Education*. New York: Dodd, Mead and Co., 1975.

    Offers practical suggestions for implementing alternative approaches to curriculum, staffing, facilities, counseling, community involvement, and student evaluation.

GRAUBARD, ALLEN. *Free the Children: Radical Reform and the Free School Movement*. New York: Pantheon Books, a Division of Random House, 1972.

    The author presents a critical but sympathetic look at both the theory and practice of this new wave of radical school reform. In combining his own experience with that of other teachers and organizers, the author probes deeply into the successes and failures of these new schools, which stress the freedom and spontaneity of the child.

SMITH, VERNON H. *Alternative Schools: The Development of Alternatives in Public Education*. Lincoln, Nebraska: Professional Educators Publications, Inc., 1974.

    Presents a brief picture of the development of optional alternative public schools, their status today, and their potential for tomorrow.

Periodicals, Monographs, and Booklets on Alternative Education

Alternative Programs in the Philadelphia Public Schools, 1975. Division of Alternative Programs, the School District of Philadelphia, Philadelphia, Pa. Center for the Study of Evaluation. "Evaluation of the Los Angeles Alternative School: A Report to the Board of Education of the Los Angeles Unified School District." UCLA Graduate School of Education, Los Angeles, California, August 1973.

Educational Leadership, November 1974. "Alternative Educational Programs: Promise or Problems?" Washington, D.C.

Harvard Educational Review, Vol. 42, No. 3, August 1972. "Alternative Schools."

Harvard Graduate School of Education Association *Bulletin,* Vol. XIX, No. 1, Fall, 1974. Cambridge, Massachusetts. "Alternative Schools."

Matters of Choice: A Ford Foundation Report on Alternative Schools. Ford Foundation, Office of Reports, New York, N.Y. September 1974.

National Education Association, Instruction and Professional Development, Washington, D.C., August 1974. "Alternatives in Education; Infopac No. 8."

The National Elementary *Principal,* Vol. LII, No. 6, April 1973, Arlington, Va. "The Great Alternatives Hassle."

Phi Delta Kappan, March 1973, Bloomington, Indiana. "Alternative Schools."

Providing Optional Learning Environments in New York State Schools. Albany, N.Y.: The State Education Department, October 1973.

The Public Schools of New York City, Staff Bulletin, May 1972. New York, N.Y. "Design for Change."

RIORDAN, ROBERT C. *Alternative Schools in Action,* Phi Delta Kappa Educational Foundation, Bloomington, Indiana, 1972.

SMITH, VERNON, DANIEL J. BURKE, and ROBERT D. BARR. *Optional Alternative Public Schools,* Phi Delta Kappa Educational Foundation, Bloomington, Indiana, 1974.

Social Education. National Council for the Social Studies, Vol. 38, No. 3, Washington, D.C., March 1974. "Social Studies in Alternative Schools."

WALKER, PENELOPE, ed. *Public Alternative Schools: A Look at the Options.* Amherst, Massachusetts. National Alternative Schools Program, 1973.

Organizations Promoting Alternative Schools

Center for New Schools, 59 East Van Buren, Suite 1800, Chicago, Illinois 60605.

Center for Options in Public Education, Indiana University, in cooperation with the International Consortium for Options in Public Education, School of Education, Indiana University, Bloomington, Indiana.

National Institute of Education, Department of Health, Education and Welfare, Washington, D.C. (Voucher Project, Alum Rock Union Elementary School District, San Jose, California).

The Ontario Institute for Studies in Education, Toronto 5, Ontario, Canada. Publication: "Education for Diversity: Readings in Educational Pluralism."

Reports on Alternative Schools

Alternative High Schools: Some Pioneer Programs. Educational Research Service Circular, No. 4, 1972. Washington, D.C.: American Association of School Administrators and National Education Association Research Division.

Alternative Schools: Pioneering Districts Create Options for Students.

Education U.S.A. Special Report. Arlington, Virginia: National School Public Relations Association, 1972.

More Options: Alternatives to Conventional Schools. Curriculum Report 3:2, March 1973. Washington, D.C.: National Association of Secondary School Principals.

Directories and Bibliographies on Alternative Education

Changing Schools: Options in Public Education. Selected Bibliography on Optional Alternative Public Schools, 1972–1974, No. 011, 3:3, 1974. School of Education, University of Indiana, Bloomington, Indiana.

A National Directory of Public Alternative Schools, 1974. National Alternative Schools Program, School of Education, University of Massachusetts, Amherst, Mass.

Resource Centers

International Consortium for Options in Public Education, School of Education, Indiana University, Bloomington, Indiana.

National Alternative Schools Program. School of Education, University of Mass., Amherst, Massachusetts.

North Central Association of Colleges and Schools, Commission of Schools, 5454 South Shore Drive, Chicago, Illinois 60615.

Slides and Films

Slides:

Education by Choice, the Story of Quincy II High's *Schools Within Schools.*

Choice Not Chance, the Story of Seattle's *Jefferson High School Within a School Program.*

Films:

Parkway: The story of the first school without walls, Philadelphia
Dr. John Robertson
Produced by Films, Inc., Wilmette, Illinois

More Than a School, Merrick, Long Island, Alternative High School
Dr. John Robertson
Produced by Films, Inc., Wilmette, Illinois

The Meaning of Our Experience, Alternative College of New Rochelle, Inside the College of New Rochelle
Dr. John Robertson
Produced by Films, Inc., Wilmette, Illinois

Approaches to High School Discipline and Learning, a series of films on the Quincy II High School Program, Education by Choice
Produced by Dave Bell Associates, Inc., Los Angeles, California

INDEX

Academy of Mathematics & Science (Cincinnati school system), 181–82

Accreditation (North Central Association of Colleges and Schools), 308–12; non-discriminatory selection of students, 309; period of, 309–10; review of annual reports, 310; school effectiveness and, 311; school evaluation, 311–12; schools qualifying for, 308–9; of special function schools, 309

Addams, Jane, 59, 62

Alcohol, 159

Allen, Dwight, 471

Allen, Hilary, 297–98

Allen, Jeffrey, 298

Allen, Richard F., 296–98

Aller, Dwight, 102

Alternate College of the State University College (Brockport, N.Y.), 186–99; curriculum, 189–91; evaluation, 192–93; faculty, 188–89; future and, 193–96; instructional pattern, 191–92; profile of student at, 196–99; student body, 187–88

Alternative education: background of, 3–16; CBE viewpoints, 48–55; deschooling the culture, 34–48; evaluation of, 299–347; finances, 349–93; implementation of, 203–69; outside the system, 57–104; politics, 395–449; problem of differing needs, 22–26; programs, 26–33; progressive reform, 8–16; radical reform, 6–8; Southeast Alternatives (Minneapolis), 271–98; teacher preparation, 451–84; traditional school as, 16–22; within the system, 105–201. *See also* Free school movement; names of schools

Alternative High School Program (Needham, Mass.), 256–67; criteria for evaluation, 262–64; guidelines, 257–59; implications for the future, 264–66; planning and implementation, 260–62; rationale, 256–57; statistical analysis, 266–67

Alternative Junior High College Preparatory Program (Cincinnati school system), 180–81

Alum Rock voucher experiment, 6, 444–49

American Federation of Labor-Congress of Industrial Organizations (AFL-CIO), 443

American Federation of Teachers (AFT), 6, 15, 414, 446

Americans United for Separation of Church and State, 443

Association for Alternative Public Schools, 255

Atterbury, Thelma, 380

Bakalis, Michael, 221–52

Baker, Don, 124

Barnett, Dick, 127

Baron, Paula, 127

Barr, Robert D., 470–74

Baylor Medical College, 23

Bayside High School (New York City), 16–22

Beauchamp, Martha, 453

Beckman, Ronald, 158

Berg, Ivar, 36

Berkeley Alternate Schools Proposal, 11, 364–66

Berkeley Unified Public Schools, 419–20

Bianchi, Lewis, 442

Bilingual program (Cincinnati school system), 177–78

Blackman, Nathaniel, Jr., 421

Blacks, 50, 53, 61, 67–68, 72, 82–84, 402, 446
Black Studies programs, 80
Board organization, 219
Bode, Boyd, 62
Borea, Marilyn, 297
Boundaries, school, 218–19
Bowen, Penny, 447
Boyce, Joseph, 328
Brautigan, Richard, 398
Bremer, John, 15, 471
British infant schools, 5, 77, 120
British primary schools, 29, 50
Brodsky, Alan, 18
Bronfenbrenner, Urie, 65
Bronx High School of Science, 17
Brookings Urban Policy Conference, 429, 432
Brown School (Louisville), 11
Brunnetti, Jerry, 273
Burke, Armand, 186–99

CAM Academy (Chicago), 61, 86
California Assembly Bill No. 1052, 389–93
Cambridge School Committee, 85
Cameron, Gary, 200–1
Campbell, Burt, 87–88
Campbell, Joan, 126
Career school (Education by Choice program), 146–49; attendance and discipline, 149; curriculum, 148; introduction, 146–47; method of instruction, 148–49; non-class time, 149; philosophy, 147–48; student evaluation, 149; time schedule, 149
Carnegie Corporation, 386
Carpenter, Ed, 385–86
Case studies, implementing alternatives and, 221–52; communicating with the community, 230–31; decision making within school, 243–45; decisions about learning program, 238–42; decisions about students, 231–34; decisions about teachers, 235–38; evaluation, 247–50; getting started, 223–31; goals and objectives, 227–28; governance issues, 242–45; impact, 250–51; introduction to, 221–23; leadership, 224–25; money issues, 245–47; planning group, 225–27; resources outside planning group, 228–30; school district relationship, 243

Catalogue of Assistance (Department of Health, Education, and Welfare), 362
Catcher in the Rye (Salinger), 17
CCED School (Boston), 80
Center for New Schools (Chicago), 303
Changing Schools (publication), 301, 304
Children's Community Workshop School (New York City), 73–74, 85, 96
Children's Television Workshop, 63
Chou En-lai, 402
Cigarette smoking, 159
Cincinnati Public Schools, 171–86; Academy of Mathematics & Science, 181–82; Alternative Junior High College Preparatory, 180–81; bilingual program, 177–78; City-Wide Learning Community, 183–84; College Preparatory Alternative, 179–80; Creative and Performing Arts, 179; decision for (question and answers), 184–85; fundamental program, 173–74; IGE program, 176–77; Isip program, 171–72; Montessori education, 171–72; Multi-Age Non-Graded Magnet School, 174–75; Reading Centers, 175–76; SCPP program, 182–83; vocational education, 184
City High School (Minneapolis), 74
City-Wide Learning Community (Cincinnati school system), 183–84
Civil rights movement of 1960s, 4, 27, 61, 68
Clark, Kenneth, 53, 128, 471
"Classical" free school, 76
Classroom alternatives, progressive reform and, 9–10

Clockwork Orange, A (motion picture), 64
Cole, Larry, 7
Coleman, James, 64, 471
College Bound, 113
College Preparatory Alternative (Cincinnati school system), 179–80
Comenius, John Amos, 36–37
Commerce Business Daily, 362
Committee for an Alternative Public School, 85
Committees, importance of, 216–17
Community-at-large, communicating with, 230–31
Community board, functions of, 213–14
Community Development Act, 363
Community elementary schools, 79–80
Community resources, use of, 241–42
Community schools, 68, 420; progressive reform and, 12
Community Schools Council, 429
Comprehensive Employment Training Act (CETA), 363
Contemporary School program (Southeast Alternatives), 279–80; mathematics, 280; parents' role, 281; philosophy, 279; reading, 279–80
Continuous Progress School program (Southeast Alternatives), 281–82; changes for 1972–73, 282; elective courses, 281; intermediate curriculum, 281; philosophy, 281; primary curriculum, 281; teacher's role, 282
Cook, Constance E., 96
Coons, John, 370
Cornog, William H., 49–50
Cortese, Toni, 433
Council for Basic Education (CBE), 48–55
Counterculture movement, 4–5
Counts, George, 62
Creative & Performing Arts (Cincinnati school system), 179
Cremin, Lawrence A., 59–65
Crisis in the Classroom (Silberman), 5, 55, 63, 84

Crocker, Brandt G., 132–53, 333–47
Curtis-Smith Associates, 158

Daitch, Jonathan, 406–9
Davis, John B., 273, 274, 296–97
Decision-making process, 212–21; board organization, 219; committees, 216–17; criteria for, 221; director's role, 214–15; functions of the board, 213–14; group (family, or tribe), 215; and human values, 212–13; problem solving, 219–20; processes and boundaries, 218–19; staff meetings, 217–18; town meeting, 216; within the school, 243–44
Denig, Nancy, 128
Dennison, George, 5, 61, 67
Deschooling the culture, 34–48, 62; assumptions of education and, 39; curriculum, 35–38; hidden structures in, 35–42; knowledge and educational market, 39–42; meaning of, 42–43; self-chosen "poverty," 46–48; use of technology for, 43–46
Designing process, implementing and, 205–11; de-bureaucratizing education, 211; developing a master schedule, 209–10; emerging needs of students, 205–6; evaluating effectiveness, 210; identifying quantitative standards, 208–9; importance of interest, 206–7; interest in, 206–7; master schedule, 209–10; needs of students, 205–6; organization, 207–8; quantitative standards, 208–9; summary of, 210–11
Detroit Free Press, 65
Deturk, Phil, 474–84
Dewey, John, 5, 59, 60, 62, 65, 282
Director, role of, 214–15
Dixon, Assemblyman, 389
Dolphin, Jud, 88
Domingo, Ruth, 380
Doyle, Denis P., 445
Drop-outs: high schools for, 78–79; mini-schools for, 112–15
Drugs, 159, 400

Dunlap, Assemblyman, 389
Dykstra, Robert, 273

East End Cooperative Ministry (EECM), 87–89
East Harlem Block Schools, 86, 384
Educational Leadership, 26
Education and Jobs: The Great Training Robbery (Berg), 36
Education by Choice program, 132–53; career school, 146–49; evaluation of, 333–47; fine arts school, 142–46; flexible school, 136–39; P.I.E. program, 139–42; project parents, 344–46; project students, 333–41; project teachers, 341–44; special education school, 151–53; traditional school, 134–36; work-study school, 150–51
Egan, Susan S., 93–100
Elementary and Secondary Education Act of 1965, 363, 367, 421
Encyclopaedia Britannica, 63
Eriksen, Aase, 153–60, 462–70
Evaluating alternatives, 247–50, 299–347; Education by Choice program, 333–47; High School in the Community (New Haven), 313–27; NCA accreditation, 308–12; program, 247–48; Shanti School, 301–4; student, 248–50, 304–7; of teacher performance, 248; transcripts, 328–32
Everett, John S., 124
Experimental Programs Promising Practices (Southeast Alternatives movement), 293–95; environmental studies, 294; industrial arts, 294; K-12 language arts, 294; teacher cadre, 295; teacher center, 295; TV media studio, 294–95
Exploring Family School (San Diego), 82
Exxon Education Foundation, 386

Fact Sheet in Sources of Federal Funding, 361–62

Faithorn, Walter E., 126
Fantini, Mario D., 1, 3–16, 22–33, 107–11, 115–24, 367–77, 414–21, 470
Farbo, Joseph, 442
Farrell, Greg, 166
Fayerweather Street School (Cambridge), 77
Featherstone, Joseph, 77
Fersch, Ellsworth, 169
Finances, 245–47, 349–93; aspects of, 351–54; California Assembly Bill No. 1052, 389–93; finding funds, 245–46; Ford Foundation report on, 383–88; housing and transportation, 353–54; money spending, 246–47; no opposition on basis of cost, 354; per pupil costs, 353; proposals, 355–66; staffing cost situations, 351–53; voucher system, 367–83
Financial proposals, how to write, 355–66; Berkeley Alternative Schools program, 364–66; budget, 359; evaluation, 358; Federal information, 361–64; future funding, 361; introduction, 355–56; methods, 357–58; non-personnel, 360; personnel, 359–60; problem statement (assessment of need), 356–57; program objectives, 357; summary, 355
Fine Arts School (Education by Choice program), 142–46; attendance and discipline, 144; curriculum, 143–44; method of instruction, 144; philosophy, 142–43; significant points, 144–46; student evaluation, 144
First Amendment, 40
Fiske, Frederick M., 462–70
Flask v. Gardner, 373
Flexible School (Education by Choice program), 136–39; attendance and discipline, 139; curriculum, 136; introduction to, 136; method of instruction, 136–37; non-class time, 138; student evaluation, 139; time schedule, 137–38
Focus Schools (Louisville), 475
Ford, David, 433, 443

Ford Foundation, 74, 383–88
Ford Foundation Report, 3, 383–88; on going public, 384–86; prospects, 388; on quid pro quo, 386–87
Foster, Richard L., 364–66
Foundation Goes to School, A (Ford Foundation), 3
Fourteenth Amendment, 372
Franco, John M., 442
Freedman, Henry, 126, 129
Freedom House (Madison, Wisc.), 74
Freedom schools, 4, 27, 67
Free Gymnasium (Copenhagen), 156, 157
Free school movement, 59–104; basic theoretical concept of, 67; compared to progressive education movement, 59–63; conditions to be free, 38; data and typology, 69–80; distribution by state, 71; enrollment, 6–7; future and, 85–86; ideological sources for, 67–69; independent public schools, 93–100; number of schools, 6, 70; perspectives, 59–65; philosophy of, 7; politics, free choice and, 397–406; radical reform and, 6–8; size and finances, 72–76; social change and, 80–85; staff characteristics, 71–72; tuition costs, 73–74; types of schools, 76–80. *See also* names of schools
Free School program (Southeast Alternatives), 285–88; first year, 286; Glendale Street Academy, 286–87; governing board, 287; philosophy, 285–86; second year, 287
Free Schools (Kozol), 62, 69, 214
Free the Children: Radical Reform and the Free School Movement (Graubard), 7, 16, 57, 61, 66
French, Sally, 273–95
Frey-McConahay, Shirley, 313–27
Friedenberg, Edgar Z., 67
Friedman, Milton, 6, 378
Friedman model (voucher plan), 377–83; augmented resources, 382; evaluations, 381; extra

funds for food, 379–80; fears of, 378–79; harmony among leaders, 381–82; parents and, 380
Fundamental program (Cincinnati school system), 173–74

Ganeless, Larry, 19, 22
Gardner, John, 471
Gardner, William, 273
Garnett, Preston, 124, 128
Gehrhardt, Ed, 382
Genesis II (Springfield, Mass.), 74
Genius of American Education, The (Cremin), 60, 61
Glatthorn, Allan, 212–21
Glendale Street Academy, 286–87
Glines, Donald, 133
Glossner, Dave, 432, 433, 443
GNE (gross national education), 47
Goals, setting, 227–28
Gompers, Samuel, 59
Goodman, Paul, 5, 67
Goslin, David, 65
Grantsmanship Center (Los Angeles), 355–64
Graubard, Allen, 7, 16, 57, 61, 66–87
Gresham's law (in education), 55
Group organizational structure, 215
Group School (Cambridge), 78
Gruber, Judith E., 313–27
Guidelines proposal, for alternative schools (Los Angeles Board of Education), 252–56

Haaren High School (New York City), 10; mini-school programs, 114–15
Hahn, Dr. Kurt, 165
Hale, Phale, 429–32
Hall, Edward T., 160
Harambee Prep (New York City), 113
Harlem Prep (New York City), 6, 61, 74, 79, 84, 86, 96, 384–86, 475
Hart, Philip, 388
Haugh, Richard F., 132–53, 333–47

Hawley, Willis D., 313–27
Hawthorne School (Washington, D.C.), 386–87
Herman Miller Associates, 158
Herndon, James, 61
Hesse, Hermann, 398
Highland Park Free School, 74
High School for Health Professions (Houston), 23
High School in the Community (New Haven) evaluation, 313–27; classroom, 318; classroom environment, 324–25; implementation of job descriptions, 319; in-service (math and English), 317; math performance, 316–17; methodology, 324–27; overview of the report, 314; parents' attitudes, 317–18; post high school plans, 319; reading and writing performance, 316; recommendations, 320–23; revised job descriptions, 318–19; sampling of classes, 325–26; student acceptance of others, 320; student attitudes, 317; student interest, 319–20; student performance, 326–27; summary of findings, 315–16; teacher attitudes, 317
Hoagland, Melvin, 274
Hobart, Thomas, 439–41, 444
Hollister, Joan, 101
Holt, John, 5, 27, 61, 67, 76–77
Home Base School (Watertown, Mass.), 328–32
Horton, Frank, 443–44
Houston school system, 23
Howell, Bruce, 205–11
Hughes High School (New York City), 113
Human values, decisions and, 212–13
Human Zoo (Morris), 127
Hutchinson, Paul, 380

IGE (Individually Guided Education) Magnet School, 176–77
Illich, Ivan, 1, 5, 27, 34–48, 62, 63
Illinois Network for School Development (INSD), 222
Impact Schools (Louisville), 475

Implementation, public school alternatives, 203–69; Alternative High School Program (Needham, Mass.), 256–67; case studies, 221–52; decision making 212–21; designing and, 205–11; guidelines (Los Angeles schools), 252–56; mini-schools 267–69; politics of, 409–13
Indehar, Vernon, 274
Independence High School (Newark), 74
Independent Learning Center (Milwaukee), 74
Independent public schools, 93–100; hypotheses, 98–100; legal definitions of, 95–100
Indiana University, 15, 303; teacher education program, 470–74
Informal school, teacher adaptation, 462–70; disorientation 465; planning and evaluation meetings, 467–68; students and control, 464; teacher interaction 468–70; team teaching, 465–67 trust between teachers, 463
Interest, importance of, 206–7
IPSIP (Impact of a Primary School and Interracial Program), 171–72
IQ, 88; ability grouping by, 32
Ivey, Ray, 474–84

Jackson, Fred, 127
Jacobsen, Bonnie, 380
Jacobson, Vivian, 128
Jefferds, Bill, 382
Jefferson Elementary School (Berkeley, Calif.), 10
Jencks, Christopher, 6, 53, 64, 379 445
Jenkins, Evan, 377–83
Jennings, Wayne, 160–64
John Adams High School (Portland), 475
John Dewey School (New York), 475
Johnson, Dr., 48
Johnston, William J., 252–56
Jones, William, 447
Joy, Daniel F., III, 381

Junior High School program (Southeast Alternatives), 290–91

Kaner, Marsh, 273
Kidd, Hazel, 21
Kilpatrick, William Heard, 52
Knowledge, defined, 42
Knowledge-capitalism, 36, 44, 48
Kohl, Herbert, 5, 7, 27, 61, 67
Kozol, Jonathan, 7, 51–52, 57, 61, 62, 67, 69, 214, 397–406
K-12 support staff (Southeast Alternatives program), 291–93; business advisor, 292–93; community education, 292; community liaisons, 292; director, 291–92; evaluation team, 293; public information, 293; staff development, 292; student support services, 293

Lakoduk, Art, 273
Lambert, Fred, 443
Lamburt, Ron, 273
Laverne, Thomas, 96
Lawrence, Bessie F., 421, 422
Lawton, Rudy, 433
Leadership, 224–25
Learning program, decision about, 238–42; selecting and creating materials, 240; teacher's role, 239–40; time scheduling, 240–41; using community resources, 241–42; what students learn, 239
Lee, Dr. Robert E., 167
Leonard, George, 67
Le Traunik, Ken, 128
Levers, B. Luke, 381
Levin, Joel M., 381
Lewis, Darrell, 273
Lewis, Debbie, 21
Lewis-Wadhams, 68
Liberles, Mike, 127
Life (magazine), 402
Lincoln-Sudbury Regional High School (Mass.), 169–70

McConahay, John D., 313–27
McLuhan, Marshall, 38

Maeroff, Gene I., 1, 16–22
Magna Didactica (Comenius), 36–37
Making New Schools (Turner), 62
Mao Tse-tung, 402
Marcus Welby, M.D. (TV show), 64
Marcy School (Minneapolis), 13
Margaret Sibley School for Educational Research and Demonstration (Plattsburgh, N.Y.), 87
Marihuana, 159
Marin, Peter, 50
Markles Flats (Ithaca City School District Public School System), 406–9
Marshall-University High School, 273, 275, 276; created, 288; discipline and interdiscipline at, 288–89; guide groups, 290; individual direct study, 289; modes of study, 288; Off Campus Learning Experience, 289; philosophy program, 288; program, 288–90; senior high program, 288; student body, 288
Marx, Karl, 36
Master schedule, developing, 209–10
Materials, selecting and creating, 240
Maynard, Larry O., 429–32
Merwin, Jack, 273
Metropolitan Achievement Tests (New York City), 95–96
Metro School (Chicago), 125–31, 475; academic program, 125–30; evaluation of, 131; main building, 130; politics at, 421–23; selection of students and staff, 130–31
Michael Community School (Milwaukee), 86
Mini-schools, 112–15; change and, 112; children's needs (and your own), 268–69; choosing, 267–69; curricular freedom, 112–13; Haaren programs, 113–15; location of, 113; meaning of, 112; streetworkers, 112; student body, 112; types of programs, 267, 268–69

Minneapolis Public School System. *See* Southeast Alternatives Program

Minneapolis Tribune, 296

Miquon School (Philadelphia), 70

Miquon Upper School, 70–71

Money. *See* Finances; Financial proposals, how to write

Montessori, Maria, 171

Montessori education, 6, 10, 27, 29, 94, 120; Cincinnati Public School system, 171–72

Morgan Community School (Washington, D.C.), 80

Morris, Desmond, 127

Motley School (Minneapolis), 13

Mulcahy, Gene, 301–4

Multi-Age Non-Graded Magnet School (Cincinnati school system), 174–75

Multiculture schools, 11–12, 24, 27, 420

Murray Road Alternative School (Newton, Mass.), 11

Nairobi Community School (East Palo Alto), 61, 82–83

National Alternative School Program (University of Massachusetts), 303, 474–84; bases for co-operative development, 479; curriculum, 481; enrollment, 480; financial relationship, 479; governance and decision-making, 481; procedure, 481–82; programmatic relationship, 479–80; projects, 476–77; relationship of resources, 484; School of Education, 476, 478–79; secondary sites, 483–84; site selection, 482–83; staffing, 480; structure, 476; support to alternative schools, 478–79; training, 480; voluntarism, 479

National Association of Elementary School Principals, 3

National Consortium on Options in Public Education, 15, 472–73

National Education Association (NEA), 6, 15, 414, 446

National Institute of Education, 275–77

Natural learning space, 155

Neill, A. S., 5, 7, 27, 57, 61, 67, 83

New Community School (Oakland), 80

New School for Children, 74, 86

New Schools Directory Project, 69

Newsweek (magazine), 402

New Trier High School, 49–50

New York Times, 22, 85

New York Times Guide to Suburban Public Schools, The, 17

Nike School (New York), 11

19th Ward Community Association, 429

Nixon, Richard, 3, 367, 377, 416

Nold, Joseph J., 164–71

North Central Association accreditation, 308–12; non-discriminatory selection of students and, 309; period of, 309–10; review of annual reports, 310; school effectiveness and, 311; school evaluation, 311–12; schools qualifying for, 308–9; special function schools and, 309

Northeast Area Development Association, 429

Northside Street Academy (Minneapolis), 74

Ober, Nathaniel, 273

Objectives, setting, 227–28

O'Connell, Tom, 285

O'Connor, Daniel, 328

Off Campus Learning Experience (O.C.L.E.), 289

Office of Economic Opportunity, 6, 377

Olson, Philip A., 297

Open classrooms, 5

Open School program (Southeast Alternatives), 282–85; goals, 283; model I, 283; model II, 283; 1972–73 changes, 285; parent involvement, 284; philosophy, 282; staff involvement, 284; teacher's role, 283–84; University of Minnesota involvement, 284–85

Organization, importance of, 207–8

Orr, Alexander, 387

Oswald, Ken, 211

O'Toole, Kathy, 432

"Outside the system" schools, 57–104; data and typology, 69–80; future and, 85–87; independent public schools, 93–100; perspective of, 59–63; social change, 80–85. *See also* names of schools

Outward Bound schools, 164–71; aim of, 165; alternate semester, 170–71; as alternative to traditional physical education, 167–69; concepts and methods, 165–71; curriculum enrichment, 169–70; motivational programs, 165–66; program requirements, 164–65

Parents, politics between teachers and, 414–21; ground rules, 417–19; options within the framework, 419–21; retaliation, 415–16

Parent-teacher cooperative elementary schools, 76–77

Parent-Teachers Association (PTA), 212

Park East High School (New York City), 100

Parker, Francis W., 62

Parkhurst, Helen, 62

Parkway Program (Philadelphia), 125, 376, 419, 475

Parsons, Cynthia, 275, 277

Peck, Eleanor, 429–32

Peninsula School (California), 72

Penn Circle Community High School, 87–93; founded, 88–89; student learning at, 89–93

Pennsylvania Advancement School, 475

Peppercorn, Ira, 21

Phillips, Dorothy B., 442

Piaget, Jean, 282

P.I.E. School program, 139–42; attendance and discipline, 141; curriculum, 140; introduction to, 139–40; method of instruction, 140; non-class time, 141; significant points, 141–42; student evaluation, 141; time schedule, 140–41

Pilot School (Cambridge, Mass.), 24

Pioneer II School (Ann Arbor), 305

Pittsburgh Board of Public Education, 88

Pittsburgh Theological Seminary, 87

Planning for a Change (resource catalogue), 230

Planning groups, 225–27; using outside resources, 228–30

Plato, 64

Politics, 395–449; between parents and teachers, 414–21; Free Schools, free choice and, 397–406; of implementation, 409–13; at Markles Flats (Ithaca, N.Y.), 406–9; Metro program, 421–23; Seattle Public Schools, 423–28; vouchers to pay for school, 429–49

Postman, Neil, 67

Pratt, Caroline, 62

Pratt School (Minneapolis), 13

Price, Donald A., 132–53, 333–47

Private learning space, 155

Problem-solving, 219–20

Programs, 26–33; in the mainstream, 27–28; in the movement, 29–30; options, 30–33; schools within schools, 22–26. *See also* names of schools

Progressive education movement, 5, 32, 59–60, 62, 86; progressive reform and, 8–16

Project AWARE (A Wilderness Air Research Experience), 289

Providence Free School, 74

Public Education and Religious Liberty Coalition (PEARL), 443

Public funding. *See* Finances; Financial proposals, how to write

P.S. 184 (New York City), 20

Public schools: alternatives within, 30–31; attendance, 8; progressive reform and, 8–16

Public Schools of Choice (Fantini), 107

Public Schools of Choice system, 115–24; basis of, 115–16; educational options under, 118–21; framework of alternatives, 121–24; ground rules for, 116–18

Quantitative standards, identifying, 208–9

Quincy All-Choice Continuum (test), 333–39

Quincy Area Vocational Technical Center, 146

Quincy Public Schools, Education by Choice program, 132–53

Quincy II High School (Illinois), 23; evaluation of, 333–47

Rand Corporation, 448

Reading Centers (Cincinnati school system), 175–76

Redmond, James F., 421

Reimer, Everett, 5, 27

Reinhold, Robert, 444–49

Research and Design Institute, 158

Rochester, N.Y., voucher plan, 429–44; administration, 438; admissions, 438; counselling and information dissemination, 438; defeat of, 442–44; general objectives of, 435; main features of, 435–36; objections to, 431; operations, 436–37; overview of, 433–34; teacher rights, 439; transportation and, 437

Rochester *Democrat-Chronicle*, 432, 442

Rochester Teachers Association (RTA), 429–44

Rodman, Karl, 100–4

Roman Catholic Orphan Asylum v. Board of Education, 95, 100

Roosevelt, Theodore, 59

Roxbury Community School, 68, 74

Roxbury Federation of Community Free Schools, 74

Rustad, Ken, 273

Safe Streets Act of 1968, 366

St. Paul Open School, 11, 14, 160–64; cost of education, 163–64; how it works, 161–62; learning approach, 162; teachers and teaching, 162–63

Sakala, John, 328

Sanders, Dan, 433–39, 443

Saturday Review of Education, 34

School administrator, role of, 13–14

School and Society, The (Dewey 60

School district relationship, 243

Schooling, alternative to. Se Deschooling the culture

School Sentiment Index, 333–39

Schools within schools, 10–1' choosing a program, 25–2(problem of differing needs an(22–26; program selection, 2 reaction to old system, 24–2 selection of, 23

Schools without walls, 9, 12, 41' 420; idea for, 125; Metro pr(gram (Chicago), 125–31; ph losophy of, 124–25; progressiv(reform and, 12

School Without Walls (Philade phia), 6, 14, 25, 376

Schrag, Peter, 39

Seattle Public Schools, plannin process for, 423–28; alternativ(school proposal criteria, 425 26; budget, 425; evaluation, 42: general proposal format, 423 24; goals and objectives, 424; th plan, 424–25; review checklis 427

Seeden, Jim, 273

Seiden, Don, 128–29

Separate alternative schools, 11

Serrano v. Priest, 97, 372

Shady Hill School (Cambridge 70

Shady Lane School (Pittsburgh' 72, 77

Shanker, Albert, 85, 444

Shanti School (Hartford, Conn. 23; background of student 454–55; checklist, 303–4; chec(list for instructors, 461–62; d(cision making, 460–61; evalu(tion, 301–4; finding what yc need, 461; how to teach, 458 60; organizing classes, 456–5' teacher preparation, 453–6: what not to do, 458; what (look for, 453–54

Silberman, Charles E., 5, 50, 5 63, 84

Sizer, Theodore, 369

Skinner, B. F., 39

Smith, Gene M., 159

Smith, Mortimer, 48–55

Social change, free schools and, 80–85

Social Frontier (journal), 62

Socializing space, 155

Solet, Irene, 377

Southeast Alternatives Program, 12–13, 271–98; approval for, 296–98; basic direction, 376; Board of Education decisions, 273–74; budget, 277; contract, 275–77; individual uniqueness, 277–78; K-12 support staff, 291–93; preparation, 278–79; programs, 277–95; staff quality, 277

Space for learning, 153–60; circle, 154; conceptualization of, 154–55; developing teacher skill in using, 158–59; disobedience and poor grades, 159; examples of, 156–58; movable walls, 153; natural learning, 155; private learning, 155; socializing and, 155; ways of seeing, 155–56

Special College Preparatory Program (Cincinnati school system), 180, 182–83

Special Education School (Education by Choice program), 151–53; attendance and discipline, 153; curriculum, 152; introduction to, 151; method of instruction, 152; non-class time, 152; student evaluation, 153; time schedule, 152

Special Programs (Southeast Alternatives movement), 291

Speicher, Howard, 21

Speiser, Lester, 18, 20

Staff meetings, 217–18

Starr, Jane, 273

State Planning Agencies (SPA), 366

Street Academy (New York City), 6

Structured Skills-Training Schools, 12, 420

Student evaluations, 304–7

Student Instructional Report (SIR), 192

Students: emerging needs of, 205–6; evaluation of progress, 248–50; grouping, 232–34; initiative and responsibility, 234; key decisions about, 231–34; selection of, 231–32

Sugarman, Alan, 409–13

Summerhill (Neill), 61, 67

Summerhill Ranch School (Mendocino, Calif.), 76

Summerhill schools, 27, 61, 68, 70, 76, 94, 120

Sunset High School (Las Vegas), 200–1

Taylor, James B., 253

Taylor, Shelby, 124

Teacher education program (Indiana University), 470–74; and Alternative Schools, 472–73; background, 470–72; "new" conception of teacher, 472; as self-actualization, 473–74; types of schools, 471–72

Teacher preparation, 451–84; Indiana University program, 470–74; to an informal school, 462–70; Shanti School, 453–62; University of Massachusetts program, 474–84

Teachers: decisions for, 235–38; in-service education, 237–38; orientation of staff, 236–37; performance evaluation of, 248; politics between parents and, 414–21; role, learning program and, 239–40; selection of, 235–36; team teaching, success and problems of, 465–67

Teaching-learning styles, matching, 107–11; approaches to, 108–9; characteristics of (open versus traditional), 110–11; personality and, 110

Television, 24, 64, 127, 400

Thoreau School (New York), 100–4

Time scheduling, 240–41

Town meetings, 216

Traditional School (Education by Choice program), 134–36; attendance and discipline, 135; basic concept of, 136; curriculum, 134–35; introduction to,

134; method of instruction, 135; non-class time, 135; philosophy, 134; student evaluation, 136; time schedule, 135

Traditional schools, as alternative education, 16–22

Training schools, progressive reform and, 12

Transcripts, evaluating, 328–32; college reactions to, 328–29; final evaluation, 331; implications of, 331–32; key to, 329–30; monthly interpersonal memo, 330–31; process and procedure, 320; statement of transcript, 331

Transformation of the School, The (Cremin), 59, 61

Trickett, Edison J., 313–27

Troup, Alice, 91

Turner, Joseph, 62

Tyler, Ralph, 62

U. S. Department of Health, Education, and Welfare (HEW), 361–62

U. S. Office of Education, 52

Urban League, 79

Vakos, Harry, 273, 274

Vasconellos, Assemblyman, 389

Village School (Great Neck, N.Y.), 11

Vocational Education Program (Cincinnati school system), 184

Voucher system, 6, 34, 367–83; 429–49; budgeting authority, 447–48; external and internal, 367–77; feasibility of, 368; Friedman model, 377–83; grants for experiments, 446–48; politics of, 429–49; responsiveness to, 445–46; segregation fears, 448–49; teachers and, 444–45; various plans for, 369–77. *See also* Rochester, N.Y., voucher plan

Waldrip, Donald R., 171–86

Waldron, Vince, 127

Wallace, Vera, 126

Wallkill Board of Education, 100, 103–4

Walt Whitman High School (Maryland), 10

Washington, Booker T., 59

Washington Senior High School, 206

Webster College School (St. Louis), 87

Weingartner, Charles, 67

Weitzman, Sharon, 128

Welk, Lawrence, 64

West Philadelphia Community Free School, 156–58, 159, 463, 464, 469

White, William, 351–54

Whitten, Phillip, 369

Williams, G. Howard, 273

Wingate High School (New York City), 113

Wingate Prep (New York City), 113

Wisconsin Research and Development Center for Cognitive Learning, 177

"Within the system" schools, 105–201; Education by Choice program, 132–53; matching teaching-learning styles, 107–11; mini-schools, 112–15; Public Schools of Choice system, 115–24; schools without walls, 124–31; space for learning, 153–60. *See also* types of programs; names of schools

Wood, Frank, 273

Working-class schools, 78–79

Work-study school (Education by Choice programs), 150–51; attendance and discipline, 150–51; curriculum, 150; method of instruction, 150; non-class time, 150; philosophy, 150; significant points, 151; student evaluation, 151; time schedule, 150

World War II, 5, 45

Wyman, Rosalind, 380

Yohalem, Mark, 19

Zabinsiki, Geri, 128

Zarembka, David, 87–93